CERAMICS, CHRONOLOGY, AND COMMUNITY PATTERNS

An Archaeological Study at Moundville

This is a volume in

Studies in Archaeology

A complete list of titles in this series appears at the end of this volume.

CERAMICS, CHRONOLOGY, AND COMMUNITY PATTERNS

An Archaeological Study at Moundville

VINCAS P. STEPONAITIS

Department of Anthropology
State University of New York at Binghamton
Binghamton, New York

1983

ACADEMIC PRESS

A Subsidiary of Harcourt Brace Jovanovich, Publishers
New York   London
Paris   San Diego   San Francisco   São Paulo   Sydney   Tokyo   Toronto

ACADEMIC PRESS, INC.
111 Fifth Avenue, New York, New York 10003

United Kingdom Edition published by
ACADEMIC PRESS, INC. (LONDON) LTD.
24/28 Oval Road, London NW1 7DX

Library of Congress Cataloging in Publication Data

Steponaitis, Vincas P.
  Ceramics, chronology, and community patterns.

  (Studies in archaeology)
  Includes index.
  1. Mound State Monument (Ala.) 2. Mississippian
culture. 3. Indians of North America--Alabama--Pottery.
4. Land settlement patterns, Prehistoric--Alabama.
I. Title. II. Series.
E99.M6815S73   976.1'43   81-17672
ISBN 0-12-666280-0   AACR2

PRINTED IN THE UNITED STATES OF AMERICA

83 84 85 86   9 8 7 6 5 4 3 2 1

For Laurie

Aerial view of the Moundville site, looking northwest. The Black Warrior River is visible in the background. Photograph was taken in July 1979.

Contents

Illustrations

Tables

Preface

Moundville, located on the Black Warrior River in west-central Alabama, is one of the best known and most intensively studied prehistoric sites in North America. It first gained wide recognition just after the turn of the century, when it was visited, excavated, and reported on by C. B. Moore. Later, during the Great Depression, large-scale excavations at Moundville produced a wealth of information on the lifeways and material culture of the Mississippian people who lived there. Later still, in the 1960s and 1970s, the site gained further importance as the locus of investigations into the social and political structure of one of the most complex indigenous societies north of Mexico (e.g., Peebles 1971, 1978a, 1978b).

Yet despite all this work, even as late as 1978, many aspects of the site's internal chronology remained obscure. Prior to this time, all artifacts and features at the site were assigned to a single "Moundville phase," which, in effect, compressed five centuries of cultural development into a single undifferentiated mass. The excessive length of this phase had many undesirable consequences, not the least of which was that it prevented anyone from clearly delineating the pathways and mechanisms by which this complex site and its regional system evolved.

The research discussed in the following chapters was mainly designed to rectify this problem. It was evident from the start that the most practical way to improve the chronology was through a detailed study of Moundville ceramics, large samples of which were available in museum collections. We visited the museums, photographed the ceramics, and with these and other data in

hand, gradually hammered out the new chronology. Using this refined sequence, it was possible to trace changes in community patterns, which in turn
shed light on Moundville's development.

This book should prove useful to scholars in a variety of ways, for it deals
with culture-historical, methodological, and evolutionary issues. In addressing
matters of culture history, the study presents a detailed and well-documented
Mississippian chronology—one of the very few in existence. It systematizes
and describes the late prehistoric ceramics from an important site, providing a
benchmark that can be used in future studies of trade and stylistic interaction.
And, perhaps even more importantly, it synthesizes the available information
on Moundville's development, taking into account settlement, subsistence, and
mortuary evidence.

The methodological contributions of this book are twofold: First, the
chapter on ceramic technology introduces a variety of approaches, borrowed
from materials science, that heretofore have not been applied to archaeological
materials. Second, the methods used to define the ceramic chronology are in
certain ways novel and provide one of the few existing illustrations of how to
seriate grave assemblages using modern numerical techniques.

Finally, with regard to the subject of cultural evolution, the changes in
complexity that occurred in the Moundville region during late prehistoric
times are reconstructed, and some possible causes are suggested. The cultural
evolutionary and methodological aspects of this book should prove interesting
to archaeologists regardless of their geographical specialty.

Chapter 1 provides the general background for the study, describing the
Moundville site and its setting, the history of archaeological research there,
and describing the nature of the ceramic sample on which the various analyses
were carried out. Chapter 2 deals with the materials and techniques of pottery
manufacture at Moundville and would profit any reader with a general interest
in ceramic technology. Chapter 3 presents a new classification of Moundville
ceramics, intended primarily for the regional specialist. Chapter 4 sets forth the
refined ceramic chronology, along with the evidence that led to its formulation; this chapter should be of use not only to the regional specialist, but also
to anyone interested in the application of numerical seriation techniques.
Chapter 5 examines changes in community patterns at Moundville as revealed
by this chronology, and Chapter 6 discusses the significance of these and
related changes in the context of the region as a whole. For anyone concerned
with the evolution of chiefdom-level societies, these two concluding chapters
are especially relevant.

Acknowledgments

The present endeavor is actually part of a larger project that was organized by Christopher Peebles in 1977. The overall aim of the project was to attain a better understanding of the Moundville phase, particularly with regard to questions concerning the development and decline of the complex Mississippian society that the phase appeared to represent. At its inception, the project was planned as a cooperative venture among four researchers: Margaret Scarry was to reconstruct subsistence using excavated food remains; Margaret Schoeninger was to be concerned with the biocultural aspects of nutrition, using osteological data from human burials; Peebles was to conduct a surface reconnaissance in order to gather detailed information on settlement patterns; and I was to construct a ceramic chronology so that fine-grained temporal control in all areas of investigation could be achieved. Although each of these lines of inquiry was to be pursued somewhat independently, the hope was that ultimately the various lines would converge to attain the project's overall aims. The project was funded by a National Science Foundation grant to the University of Michigan (BNS78–07133). Fieldwork began in June 1978, and was carried on intermittently until August 1979. A tremendous amount of information was gathered during this interval by all the investigators, and much of this information is, at this writing, still in the process of being analyzed.

For my own part of the project, "fieldwork" was mostly carried out indoors, recording data on whole vessels from Moundville in extant museum collections. I was assisted in this task by Laurie Cameron Steponaitis, who photographed all the vessels, developed and printed the film, and helped the fieldwork along in innumerable other ways. It is safe to say that without her talents, we would never have accomplished as much on this project as we did. Other people who, at various times, helped us sift through these collections are John Blitz, Gail Cameron, Mary Meyer, Masao Nishimura, Jeffrey Parsons, John Scarry, Margaret Scarry, Letitia Shapiro, Deborah Walker, and Paul Welch. Their willingness to put up with the tedium and dust while looking through countless boxes is gratefully acknowledged.

Our obsessive search for Moundville collections eventually took us to five museums in four different states. Although not all of the collections were found to contain whole vessels, the work was invariably made more comfortable and productive by the staffs of the institutions we visited. Among those to be thanked are Joseph Vogel, John Hall, and Dorothy Beckham of the Alabama Museum of Natural History; Richard Krause, Kenneth Turner, and Amelia Mitchell of the Department of Anthropology, University of Alabama; Carey Oakley, Eugene Futato, and Tim Mistovic of the Office of Archaeological Research, University of Alabama; David Fawcett, James Smith, and Anna Roosevelt of the Museum of the American Indian, Heye Foundation; Vincent Wilcox, Joseph Brown, and Marguerite Brigida of the Department of Anthropology, National Museum of Natural History, Smithsonian Institution; Barbara Conklin of the American Museum of Natural History; and Richard MacNeish of the R. S. Peabody Foundation, Andover.

Once the data had been collected, the bulk of the analysis was carried out at the Smithsonian Institution, where I was appointed a predoctoral fellow. Bruce Smith, my advisor while on fellowship, was truly a stimulating colleague with whom to work. He not only shared freely his ideas on Mississippian culture, but also provided logistic, bureaucratic, and moral support in more ways than I can possibly enumerate. A number of other people at the Smithsonian contributed substantially to the effort as well. David Bridge was instrumental in helping me grasp the complexities of SELGEM, the data-banking program with which I managed to keep track of all the vessels. Jane Norman helped by reconstructing beautifully a vessel which seemed to be fragmented beyond hope. Also to be acknowledged is Florence Jones, who, as a Smithsonian Institution volunteer, ably drew most of the rim profiles that appear in this report.

The technological studies of ceramics were all done at the National Bureau of Standards in Gaithersburg, Maryland. I arrived at the bureau as a complete novice in materials science, mindful of issues that needed to be studied, but with no inkling of how to actually go about doing it. I was most fortunate, therefore, to fall in with a group of experienced colleagues who never seemed to tire of my endless questions. Carl Robbins, for one, spent countless hours showing me how to use a petrographic microscope, and helping me with mineralogical identifications. He also produced all of the x-ray diffraction patterns on which many of my conclusions are based. When it came to matters concerning physical properties (or, as the division title quaintly put it, "Fracture and Deformation"), Alan Franklin, C. K. Chiang, Ed Fuller, and Steve Freiman were the experts. Together, they introduced me to some rather unaccustomed definitions of "stress" and "strain," and showed me how to make the measurements that were critical to the successful outcome of my research. All of this work was made possible by my appointment as a guest worker at the bureau, under the sponsorship of Carl Robbins. I am also particularly grateful to Alan Franklin and Jacqueline Olin (Conservation Analytical Laboratory, Smithsonian Institution), who were both instrumental in bringing about this arrangement. Ceramic thin sections were obtained through the courtesy of Daniel Appleman, chairman of the Department of Geology, Smithsonian Institution.

Most of the actual writing was done while I was on the faculty at the State University of New York at Binghamton. Several people at this institution helped a great deal in edging the (sometimes reluctant) manuscript toward its completion. Sherd photographs were taken by David Tuttle, who also did some supplementary darkroom work. The vast majority of figures were capably prepared for publication by Laurie Cameron Steponaitis, and the rest by Stan Kauffman. Robert Stuckart of the Computer Center helped by showing me how to get SUNY—Binghamton's overgrown (and accident-prone) calculator —to do what it was supposed to do.

As noted earlier, the project was, from the very start, a multifaceted affair, designed to make the most out of a collaboration between researchers working on different aspects of a common goal. To my colleagues on this project— Christopher Peebles, Margaret Scarry, Paul Welch, Tandy Bozeman, Margaret Hardin, and Margaret Schoeninger—I owe a great deal for their stimulating thoughts, for their willingness to share information, and, in general, for making our collaboration such a pleasant one.

Other people who offered valuable help and suggestions are William Autry, Jeffrey Brain, Ian Brown, Ben Coblentz, David DeJarnette, Richard Ford, James B. Griffin, Ned Jenkins, David Kelley, Keith Kintigh, William Macdonald, Dan Morse, J. Mills Thornton, Sander van der Leeuw, Stephen Williams, and Henry Wright. It was van der Leeuw who first opened my eyes to the need for a detailed understanding of ceramic technology. Brain, Brown, Ford, Griffin, Kintigh, and Williams were particularly generous with their comments on the manuscript, all of which were appreciated, although not all were accepted. Autry, Coblentz, Kelley, and especially Jenkins shared their knowledge of southeastern pottery, and helped identify nonlocal vessels in the collections. Finally, it was Morse who spared me untold embarrassment by gently pointing out that the weirdest "Mississippian" jar I had ever seen was actually a Formative period Mexican type that had been mistakenly catalogued as coming from Moundville.

With all the help that I have received from these people and others, it should be clear that any and all faults that remain in the book are entirely my own responsibility.

1

Introduction

In the tenth and eleventh centuries A.D., there developed along the interior river valleys of southeastern North America a number of societies that are now called Mississippian. It is well known that the Mississippian people were sedentary farmers who grew maize and other crops. It is also generally accepted that these people possessed a relatively complex social organization, with evidence of internal social ranking and political hierarchies that extended beyond the range of the local community. Societies of this type are often categorized in general evolutionary terms as "chiefdoms," and questions relating to the organization of such societies and how they developed continue to be matters of wide interest and considerable debate.

This study deals with the Moundville culture of west-central Alabama, a Mississippian society that existed from about A.D. 1050 to 1550. Sites of this culture are located in the valley of the Black Warrior River, south of the fall line at Tuscaloosa. By far the largest of these sites is Moundville, after which the culture was named. In its time, Moundville was a political and religious center of major proportions. Indeed, it was the second largest Mississippian community in all of eastern North America, second only to the great Cahokia site in the American Bottoms near present-day St. Louis.

During the past decade, a tremendous amount of research has been devoted to reconstructing the social, political, and economic organization of Moundville's former inhabitants. Mortuary data have been analyzed for evidence of social differentiation (Peebles 1971, 1974), settlement patterns have been examined for evidence of political organization (Peebles 1978, Steponaitis 1978), and environmental data have been brought to bear in explaining certain aspects of community size and location (Peebles 1978). Although these studies have contributed greatly to our understanding of Moundville, considerably more remains to be learned. One limitation of prior studies is that they were all essentially synchronic in outlook. A number of social, political, and economic patterns were identified, yet questions relating to how these patterns developed through time were never adequately addressed. This shortcoming was not at all due to lack of interest, but rather was imposed by the state of knowledge at the time. The Moundville phase, as it was then defined, encompassed a 500-year span within which no temporal distinctions could be perceived. As long as this block of time remained undivided, evolutionary studies could not proceed.

This, then, was the context in which the present study was conceived. Long years of excavation at Moundville had produced large collections of ceramics, including many whole vessels from grave contexts, that had never been analyzed but were still being curated at various museums. These collections were an ideal source of data with which a ceramic chronology could be constructed, a chronology which could then be used to partition the archaeological record into finer temporal units, thereby revealing the trajectory by which the sociopolitical complexity at Moundville developed, and later declined.

The chapters that follow will not answer all the questions related to the processes of development at Moundville, nor will they attempt to. The goal instead is to provide a sound diachronic framework that will allow certain previous interpretations to be refined, and that will also provide the first glimpse of how the size and configuration of the Moundville site changed through time. Achieving these goals requires a detailed understanding of the formal variation in Moundville ceramics, a subject to which the greater part of this volume is devoted.

The present study addresses itself to five major areas of concern. First, the materials and technology of pottery manufacture at Moundville are examined. This discussion not only lays the groundwork for describing the ceramic assemblage, but also demonstrates how certain pottery attributes, often thought to be purely conventional, are directly related to vessel function.

Second, a new classification of Moundville ceramics is presented. This classification consists of six analytically separate dimensions of design, ware and shape, which together constitute the formal categories on which the chronology is based.

Third is a presentation of the chronology itself. This chronology was formulated using two kinds of evidence: (*a*) a seriation based on whole vessels excavated in the years between 1905 and 1941, and (*b*) stratigraphic analysis of sherds obtained from test excavations conducted at Moundville in 1978 and 1979. These lines of evidence have allowed the 500-year block of time, formerly known as a single "Moundville phase," to be broken up into three shorter phases—Moundville I, Moundville II, and Moundville III. Adding these three new units to the two previously defined phases that come before and after, the entire late prehistoric sequence now consists of five phases spanning the period from A.D. 900 to 1700.

Fourth, the spatial distribution of burials and ceramic vessels, dated according to this chronology, is examined at Moundville for each phase in turn. In so doing, the site's evolution from a small village, to a minor center, to a large regional center is traced, and certain implications of this sequence are discussed.

Fifth and finally, the Moundville data are considered from a regional perspective. The late prehistory of the Black Warrior drainage is sketched, outlining the major trends in subsistence, settlement, and organization. The study then concludes with a consideration of factors that may have helped cause some of the cultural changes observed.

As a prelude to these chapters, let us begin by describing the Moundville site and its setting in more detail, reviewing the history of investigations there, and describing the particulars of the ceramic sample on which the study depends.

THE SITE AND ITS SETTING

> I do not think in the Southern States there is a group of Mounds to compare to Moundville, in the arrangement and state of preservation of the mounds [Moore, quoted in Owen 1910:44].

The Moundville site, so highly acclaimed by Moore, is located in west-central Alabama astride the Hale–Tuscaloosa county line, about 25 km south of the city of Tuscaloosa (Figure 1). It sits on a low terrace overlooking the east bank of the Black Warrior River, nestled in an alluvial valley that cuts through the gently rolling Fall Line Hills.

During the prehistoric occupation, this region was characterized by a high diversity of physiographic zones and forest biomes. As Peebles has aptly described:

> The forests that were above the floodplain of the Black Warrior River were a mixture of oak–hickory and pine facies that mirrored the physiographic complexity of the area. As [Figure 1] illustrates, four major physiographic provinces lie within 20 miles of Moundville. To the north of the fall line, in the Ridge and Valley Province and the Cumberland Plateau, the oak–hickory forest is the climax biome. South of the Black Belt, the pine barrens of the Coastal Plain was the dominant forest type. Between these two forests, in the Fall Line Hills, the interfingering of these two forests plus the floodplain vegetation produced a broad ecotone forest. Both the oak–hickory and the forest edges of the ecotone forest supported high densities of deer and turkey, the faunal mainstays of the Southeastern Indians [Peebles 1978b:43, see also 1978a:388–393].

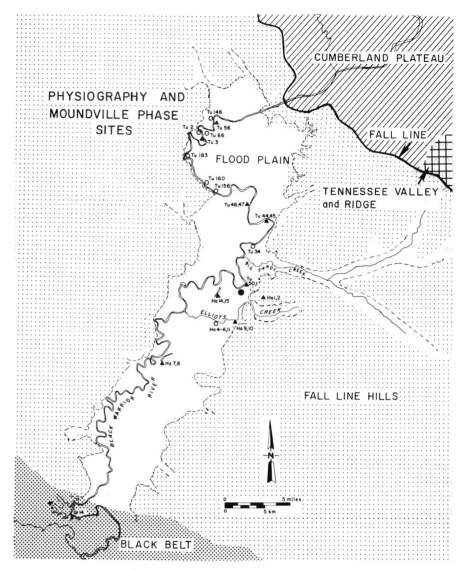

FIGURE 1.   Location of Moundville and other Moundville phase sites in the Black Warrior River Valley (after Peebles 1978a:Figure 13.10). (Key: ●, major center [moundville]; ▲, minor center; ○, settlement without mounds.)

Within the valley proper, the floodplain soils constituted another resource of great importance to the prehistoric inhabitants, for these soils are known to have had a high fertility and were eminently suited to the growing of maize, the principal Mississippian crop (Peebles 1978:400–412).

The site itself contains at least 20 artifical mounds, neatly arranged around a rectangular plaza (Figure 2). The largest of these mounds, Mound B,

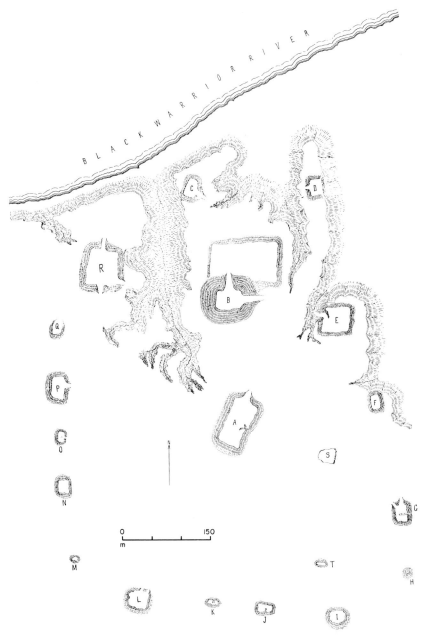

FIGURE 2. The Moundville site as it appeared in 1905 (after Moore 1905:129).

is about 17 m high, and about 100 m² at the base; the other mounds range from about 8 m to 1 m in height (McKenzie 1966:Table 5; Moore 1905:128). Many, if not all, of these mounds were used as platforms for structures, either for public buildings ("temples") or for the dwellings of important individuals. The plaza alone covers some 32 ha, and if one includes the various areas that were occupied around the periphery of the plaza, the total extent of the site comes to about 100 ha. At one time, the three sides of the site away from the river were surrounded by a bastioned palisade, traces of which show up in air photographs, and the existence of which has been confirmed by archaeological excavation (Peebles 1979:Figure I-1, passim). In terms of both its size and architectural complexity, Moundville is certainly one of the most impressive late prehistoric sites north of Mexico.

INVESTIGATIONS AT MOUNDVILLE PRIOR TO 1978

> Near Carthage... there are many mounds of various sizes, some of which are large [Pickett 1851/1900:168].

No doubt because of its tremendous size, Moundville has attracted the attention of antiquarians for quite some time. The site was mentioned in print as early as 1851 (in the passage just quoted), and additional references continued to crop up in the literature throughout the second half of the nineteenth century (e.g., Brewer 1872:271; Thomas 1891:13; Thruston 1890:Figure 84). Variously called the "Carthage group" (after a nearby town) or the "Prince mounds" (after the landowner), these earthworks owed at least some of their recognition to the work of the fledgling Smithsonian Institution, which twice sent its agents to investigate. The first of these recorded visits was made in 1869 by N. T. Lupton, a local scholar of some repute, who mapped the site, briefly described it, and placed an excavation in Mound O (Lupton 1869). Some years later, in 1882, a second visit was made by James D. Middleton, who brought back a modest surface collection and another description (Middleton 1882). Although neither investigator's observations were ever published in full, many of the unusual artifacts they found were illustrated in works by Rau (1879:Figures 49, 150, 151) and Holmes (1883:Plate 56 [Figures 1-4], Plate 66 [Figure 6], 1903:Plate 58f).

It was not until the early years of the twentieth century that Moundville saw its first large-scale excavations, undertaken by the indefatigable Clarence Bloomfield Moore. Moore and his crew came to Moundville on two occasions: once in 1905 and again in 1906, staying about a month each time. During these two forays, they managed to put "trial holes" into practically every one of the mounds, and into many off-mound areas as well. All in all, they turned up over 800 graves, many accompanied by pottery vessels and other artifacts of shell, copper, and stone. Moore's excavation techniques were crude by today's standards, but, fortunately for us, he was much more competent than a good many of his contemporaries. He consistently maintained an accurate set of field notes, in which he recorded individual gravelots and their contents, and kept track of the general localities in which his various finds were made. Even more importantly, much of this information soon found its way into two profusely illustrated volumes (Moore, 1905, 1907). These volumes contained the first accurate map and extensive description of the site to appear in print, and, to this day, they remain virtually the only source of information on what was inside the mounds.

The second major episode of excavation at Moundville began in 1929, and lasted until 1941. This work was begun by the Alabama Museum of Natural History, but, with the onset of the Great Depression, it soon came under the sponsorship of various federally funded relief agencies—the Works Progress Administration (WPA), the Civilian Conservation Corps (CCC), and the Tennessee Valley Authority (TVA). At first, the excavation techniques were no better than those of Moore: graves were the only class of feature recognized, and the field records kept were rather spotty. As time went on, however, the techniques greatly improved, so that by the mid-1930s, the excavators had learned to record with consistency postholes, wall trenches, hearths, and other structural features that had previously been ignored. Paralleling these improvements in feature recognition was a greater effectiveness in artifact recovery; sherds and other small artifacts began to be retained, and their proveniences were recorded with greater horizontal and vertical control. Most of the improvements were brought about by David L. DeJarnette, who had been trained at the University of Chicago field school in Fulton County, Illinois, and who effectively directed most of the work at Moundville from 1932 on. By the time the depression-era excavations ended, some 4.5 ha of the site's surface had been opened, yielding over 2000 burials, about 75 structure patterns, and innumerable other finds (Peebles 1979; 1978b:10–13).

The mass of data produced by the 1905–1941 excavations obviously required synthesis and interpretation, and these concerns were not lost on the investigators at the time. Archaeologists in the 1930s had developed an overriding concern with space–time systematics—the process of defining cultural units and their relationships to other units in space and time—and this was the issue that dominated interpretive statements on Moundville until well into the 1960s. Reference to the existence of a "Moundville culture," characterized by a distinctive set of material traits, appeared in print as early as 1932 (Jones 1932). This concept then underwent a gradual process of elaboration and descriptive refinement (Jones and DeJarnette n.d.; DeJarnette and Wimberly 1941; DeJarnette 1952; Wimberly 1956), a process which eventually culminated in McKenzie's (1966) synthesis of what he called the "Moundville phase." The principal hallmarks of this phase included pyramidal platform mounds, square or rectangular wall-trench dwellings, extended burials with grave goods, corn agriculture, and a number of distinctive shell-tempered pottery types, many of which had a "black filmed" surface and were sometimes engraved with elaborate zoomorphic motifs. Geographically, the phase included sites in the Warrior drainage, and some as far north as the Pickwick Basin on the middle Tennessee River. Based on stylistic crossties with other regions, McKenzie estimated that the phase lasted from A.D. 1200 to 1500—a range which, as we now know, did not begin sufficiently early, but was otherwise nearly correct.

Thus, by the late 1960s the broad outlines of a culture–historical unit called the Moundville phase had been delineated. And with this accomplished, the focus of research on Moundville began to change. Issues of unit definition were emphasized less, as archaeologists became more and more interested in understanding the sociological meaning of variability within the unit itself. It was with such concerns that Christopher Peebles began working with the Moundville material, and the studies he eventually carried out underlie most of our present notions of how the prehistoric society at Moundville was organized.

Using the data on burials recovered in the 1905–1941 excavations, Peebles performed a set of numerical analyses, by means of which he isolated several distinct segments within the burial population (Peebles 1974, see also 1971; Peebles and Kus 1977). He argued that one segment, representing the "superordinate dimension," consisted of individuals who belonged to the social and political elite. These individuals were always buried in or near mounds, with an elaborate mortuary ritual, and were consistently accompanied by certain distinctive artifacts that probably served as symbols of their political office or social rank. The remaining segments of the burial population, constituting the "subordinate dimension," apparently contained individuals of lower standing, as evidenced by both mortuary ritual and the poorer nature of their grave offerings. A consideration of the age–sex composition within each segment further suggested that access to elite statuses was principally determined by birth, rather than by life history or achievement. Thus, Peebles's evidence indicated the existence of a marked social hierarchy, in which nobility was largely based on descent.

Not only could ranking be seen in the burials, but a hierarchy could also be discerned among the Moundville phase sites themselves (Peebles 1978). Moundville, with its 20 mounds and its vast extent, was by far the largest and most complex site in the Warrior Valley. Nearby were 10 smaller centers, each with only one mound, as well as numerous villages and hamlets with no mounds at all. Comparision between the sizes of these sites and the agricultural potential of the surrounding soils suggested that the outlying settlements were self-sufficient in their food supply, but that the inhabitants of Moundville were at least partly provisioned by tribute brought in from other sites (Peebles 1978:400–410). Thus, the settlement data indicated a political hierarchy of three levels—major center, smaller center, and village–hamlet—with Moundville clearly at the apex.

Further analysis showed that the spatial distribution of Moundville phase settlements corresponded closely to an ideal configuration, which tended to minimize the costs of moving tribute and administrative information between centers and the populations they controlled (Steponaitis 1978:417–444). In comparing the relative sizes of mounds at minor centers, evidence was also found to suggest that Moundville exacted more tribute labor from the centers in its immediate vicinity than it did from those slightly farther away (1978:444–448).

Such, briefly recounted, was the state of our knowledge in 1978, the year in which this study began. A great many analyses had been carried out, and a great many conclusions had been reached, but all this work shared the one affliction mentioned earlier—the lack of fine chronological control. Data gathered in the years after McKenzie's (1966) first chronological estimates had exacerbated the problem even further, by showing these estimates to be too short. Preceding Moundville, the West Jefferson phase had been isolated with a good terminal date of A.D. 1050 (Jenkins and Nielsen 1974); following Moundville, the Alabama River phase had been defined as beginning no later than 1550 (Sheldon 1974). Thus, by 1978 it was clear that the Moundville phase itself spanned some 500 years—quite a long time, even by archaeological standards. A great deal of cultural change could well have taken place during that amount of time, yet there was never any choice but to regard all burials and sites that dated anywhere within this span as being contemporary. Neither the prior West Jefferson phase nor the sequent Alabama River phase showed any evidence of moundbuilding or hierarchical organization. Thus, Moundville's social and political complexity must have evolved and declined entirely within that undivided 500 year span. Obviously, there was no way this process of development could be studied until a finer chronology was achieved—and achieving that chronology became this study's first concern.

ASPECTS OF THE CERAMIC SAMPLE

The ceramic sample on which this study is based consists of two parts. One part, in many ways the most important, subsumes the complete or nearly complete vessels excavated by Moore and the depression-era archaeologists prior to 1941. These specimens were mostly found with burials, and they will be referred to collectively as "whole vessels," despite the fact that not all of them are entirely whole. The second part consists of pottery fragments found during the recent University of Michigan test excavations north of Mound R. These ceramics were mostly associated with house floors and refuse deposits, and collectively will be called our "sherd" sample.

The Whole Vessel Sample

The whole vessels included in the sample belong to three museums: the Alabama Museum of Natural History (AMNH) in Tuscaloosa, the National

Museum of Natural History (NMNH) in Washington, D.C., and the Museum of the American Indian (MAI) in New York. The AMNH houses most of the artifactual materials from the depression-era excavations, along with all of the surviving field notes. The NMNH has in its collections a small number of vessels also from the depression-era excavations, given to it by the AMNH in the 1930s. The MAI maintains most of Moore's excavated material, and also his fieldnotes. Although there are small numbers of Moundville pots in other museums (e.g., R. S. Peabody Foundation in Andover, Florida State Museum, Alabama Department of Archives and History), the three collections that were examined together contain the vast majority of all the extant material.

Dimensions of the Sample   It was known at the outset of this project that the number of vessels excavated at Moundville was large; but it was not known exactly how many of these vessels could still be located and studied. As the museum work progressed, each collection posed its own peculiar problems, and these problems sometimes imposed constraints that allowed only certain vessels to be studied at the expense of others. The resulting selectivity may well have introduced some biases to the sample, and it is important that these be made clear.

The major problem we encountered at the AMNH was lack of time. During the early stages of the work, every vessel that was located was recorded in detail, and thereby included in the sample. Gradually, however, it became apparent that the collection was so large that there was no hope of recording it all in the amount of time available. From this point on, only vessels with secure burial provenience were recorded, and the rest were left out. It should also be noted that a number of vessels were left out because they could not be located in the first place. Most of the Moundville material, though well-curated, was boxed in storage with no key to finding individual cataloged specimens. Thus, securing our sample involved searching through hundreds of boxes one by one, looking for vessels packed in among many other kinds of artifacts, including sherds. Whole vessels that were unbroken, or broken and reconstructed, were easy to pick out. Whole vessels that were stored in fragmentary condition, on the other hand, could easily be mistaken for sherds, and undoubtedly in some instances were missed. Museum files indicate that the depression-era excavations produced about 1400 vessels, most of which were at one time in the AMNH collection. During our 3 months with this collection, we managed to locate about 1100 of these vessels, the rest having been dispersed to other museums or inadvertently missed. Of the vessels that were located, 935 were included in the sample—713 with secure burial provenience and 222 without.

The second major collection was that of Moore at the Museum of the American Indian, and here the factors governing selectivity were different. The problem was not that the collection was too large, but rather that it was, in a sense, too small. All the vessels in the collection were located and recorded, but this number represented less than half the total Moore had originally excavated. Although a few of the missing vessels may yet turn up at other museums, I strongly suspect that most of them are no longer available for study. The vessels now in the MAI are conspicuously the nicer ones that Moore found; the missing vessels, on the other hand, tend to be those which Moore described in his notes as being "roughly made," "crude," or otherwise unsavory. In other words, it seems most likely that Moore's collection was deliberately high-graded between the time of excavation and the time of accession at MAI—whether by Moore himself or by someone else is unknown. Of the 342 pots that Moore unearthed, we recorded 160 (including 9 not in the MAI, but illustrated in Moore's reports). Of these 160 vessels, 110 could be assigned to burials or other closed features.

Finally, the small collection of Moundville vessels at the National Museum of Natural History was recorded in its entirety: 22 specimens in all, 10 from gravelots.

Adding all these figures together, we find that our whole vessel sample totals 1117, or about 70% of the estimated 1600 vessels excavated at Moundville between 1905 and 1941. Within this sample, 833 vessels (ca. 75%) can be assigned to specific gravelots or features.

Methods of Recording Data   Each vessel included in the sample was photographed from at least one side, and a set of descriptive characteristics were recorded on a standard form (this form, incidentally, was revised and simplified as the project wore on). The kinds of characteristics noted were generally qualitative in nature, such as the presence or absence of secondary shape features, features of design, and obvious indications of wear on the base or on the lip. Early in the fieldwork, each vessel was measured in detail with calipers, and surface colors were recorded with a Munsell chart, but these practices were eventually dropped for lack of time. In a number of instances, vessels that could not be found in the collections were recorded on the basis of photographs in the AMNH files and in Moore's published reports.

For the purposes of reconstructing burial proveniences, I relied as much as possible on the original depression-era burial forms on file at the AMNH, and on Moore's original field notes kept at the MAI. Considerable use was also made of the three Moundville site reports (Moore 1905, 1907; Peebles 1979), not only as sources of supplementary information, but also as keys to decipher-ing the original field records.

Vessel Numbers   Each vessel in the sample has a catalog number, which may consist of three parts: an alphabetic prefix, a serial number, and (some-times) a suffix. The prefix and serial number are usually equivalent to the orig-inal field specimen designation assigned by the excavator. The suffix serves to define the particular episode of fieldwork during which a vessel was recovered—a necessary piece of information, since the same field-specimen designations were often reused by excavators working at different times.

The prefix generally refers to the locality within the site where the vessel was found. Often such a prefix consists of a compass direction combined with a lettered mound designation. Thus, for example, the prefix SD represents south of mound D, and SWM represents southwest of mound M. If the compass direction is left off, the locality referred to is the mound itself. There are also some locality prefixes that do not follow these conventions, but are simply *ad hoc* abbreviations for particular named areas of excavation. Examples of such prefixes are Rho for the Rhodes excavation, and Rw for the Roadway excavation. Finally, there is also a prefix that does not refer to a specific locality at all: Mi stands for miscellaneous, a designation that was sometimes used by the AMNH for vessels whose within-site provenience was unknown. The various prefixes are summarized in Table 1, arranged in the conventional order of precedence used when vessels are listed by catalog number (as they are in Appendix A).

TABLE 1

Locality Prefixes and Special Symbols, Listed in the Conventional Order of Precedence. [1]

Prefix	Locality	Prefix	Locality
AdB	Administration building	H	Mound H
MPA	Museum parking area	EH	East of Mound H
Rho	Rhodes site	SEH	Southeast of Mound H
RPB	Picnic building west of Mound R	EI	East of Mound I
		K	Mound K
Rw	Roadway excavation	L	Mound L
B	Mound B	SL	South of Mound L [2]
NB	North of Mound B	SM	South of Mound M
WB	West of Mound B	SWM	Southwest of Mound M
C	Mound C	NN'	North of Mound N (prime)
NC	North of Mound C	WN	West of Mound N
NEC	Northeast of Mound C	O	Mound O
D	Mound D	EO	East of Mound O
ND	North of Mound D	WP	West of Mound P
NED	Northeast of Mound D	WP'	West of Mound P (prime)
ED	East of Mound D	NQ	North of Mound Q
SED	Southeast of Mound D	NR	North of Mound R
SD	South of Mound D	WR	West of Mound R
NE	North of Mound E	W	Mound W [3]
EE	East of Mound E	NW	North of Mound W
SE	South of Mound E	SW	South of Mound W
F	Mound F	NWW	Northwest of Mound W
EF	East of Mound F	Mi	Miscellaneous
NG	North of Mound G	<I>	Incorrect provenience
SG	South of Mound G	<M>	Provenience missing
SWG	Southwest of Mound G		

[1] For further information on the location of these areas, see Peebles (1979).

[2] All the artifacts from this excavation were originally cataloged with the prefix SK.

[3] This refers to an elevated area west of Mounds O and P, which was not actually an artifically constructed mound.

Following the prefix is usually a serial number. Excavators assigned these serial numbers sequentially to the vessels from each locality; however, the numbers were not always consecutive from year to year. An independent numbering sequence was used, and therefore the same serial numbers were reused, in each of three periods of excavation: (*a*) Moore's 1905 season, (*b*) Moore's 1906 season, and (*c*) the depression-era work between 1929 and 1941. Thus, although the original field-specimen designations for vessels are unique within these periods, they are not necessarily unique across all periods. The most practical way for me to deal with this problem was to add suffixes to the original numbers assigned by Moore. Vessels excavated in 1905 and published in Moore's first report (1905) are suffixed 2/M5. Vessels excavated in 1906 and published in Moore's second report (1907) are suffixed /M7. Numbers pertaining to vessels excavated after 1929 are left unsuffixed. For example, there are three vessels in our sample that were originally designated SD1; the one excavated in 1905 is here cataloged as SD1/M5, the one excavated in 1906 is cataloged as SD1/M7, and the one found after 1929 is simply cataloged SD1.

As inevitably happens when dealing with large museum collections, occasionally there were vessels for which the original field-specimen designations were either incorrectly marked or missing entirely. When the proper designations could be reconstructed from photographs or other museum records, the vessels are here cataloged as described above. Otherwise, the vessels are listed with one of two special symbols. The symbol <I>, followed by a field-specimen designation, indicates that the latter number is written on the vessel but is incorrect. The symbol <M>, followed by an arbitrary number or a museum catalog number, indicates that no field-specimen designation appears on the vessel at all. Whichever of these symbols is used, their practical import is the same: the within-site provenience on such vessels has been lost.

Burial Numbers   Burial proveniences are here usually designated by the burial or skeleton numbers assigned by the excavator, except that, as with vessel catalog numbers, it was sometimes necessary to add suffixes to avoid redundancy.

Moore numbered his burials sequentially within each locality, starting a new sequence each time he visited the site. Thus, it is necessary to suffix all of Moore's burial numbers with the locality and season in which they were found, using the same abbreviations as in the vessel catalog numbers just described. For example, 1/SD/M5 refers to the first burial found south of Mound D in 1905, and 2/WR/M7 refers to the second burial found west of Mound R in 1906.

Moore also described in his notes finding features that contained whole vessels but no visible skeletal remains. It is possible that these features were indeed burials in which the skeletal material had decayed away, or they may have been former graves from which the buried individual had been removed as part of an extended mortuary ritual. In some respects the question is academic, since these features are "closed-finds," which for chronological purposes can be treated just the same as actual gravelots. Moore did not number these features, but I have done so: they are designated here by the symbol F., followed by an arbitrary numeral and a suffix analogous to those appended to burial numbers—for example, F.2/O/M5.

The depression-era excavators used two slightly different systems for numbering burials, changing from one to the other in 1932. The earlier excavators, like Moore, maintained a separate sequence of skeleton numbers for each locality within the site. The later excavators, however, instituted a master numbering system that applied a single sequence to the site as a whole. Thus, for present purposes, skeleton numbers below 800 are always suffixed by the locality in which they were found—for example, 42/EI (note that the absence of /M5 or /M7 in the suffix implies that the burial was excavated after 1929). Skeleton numbers above 800 are unique within the master numbering system, but for the sake of consistency these have been given locality suffixes as well.

Finally, it should be noted that multiple burials—that is, burial features that contain more than one individual—are for chronological purposes treated as single gravelots. In other words, all the vessels found in such a feature are regarded as being contemporary, even if they are listed in the notes as being associated with different individuals. Multiple burials are denoted by concatenating a series of individual skeleton numbers, separated either by commas (when the numbers are not consecutive) or by hyphens (when the numbers are consecutive), and followed by the usual suffix. Thus, 1181–83/EE denotes a multiple burial found east of Mound E, containing individual skeletons 1181, 1182, and 1183.

The Sherd Sample

The excavations that produced our sherd sample were carried out in the summers of 1978 and 1979, under the capable direction of Margaret Scarry (University of Michigan Museum of Anthropology). Two 2 × 2-m squares, designated 6N2W and 8N2E respectively, were opened in the locality north of Mound R. These squares were positioned about 2 m apart, and were excavated to subsoil through cultural deposits more than 2 m thick. The units were taken down with extreme care, using trowels only; features were meticulously isolated, and the deposits were taken out in natural levels whenever possible (Scarry 1981a). These efforts resulted in very fine control, especially in the lower levels where stratigraphic mixture was virtually nonexistent. Complete description of the excavations will have to await a future report; for present purposes, a synopsis of the stratigraphic levels is presented in Appendix C.

Dimensions of the Sample   Virtually all the pottery from these excavations was studied, except for the few sherds that might still be hiding in the unprocessed flotation samples from 1979. If and when these sherds do appear, some of the counts given here may change a bit, but it is unlikely that any conclusions based on present evidence will have to be altered. All told, the excavations yielded 8212 sherds that could be used in the stratigraphic analysis (see Chapter 4). This total excludes the pottery found in post molds, pits, and other features that intruded into earlier midden and thus were stratigraphically mixed.

Methods of Recording Data   When brought into the laboratory, all sherds were tested with a 1.2-cm mesh screen. Those small enough to pass through were bagged by provenience and placed in storage with nothing more than a cursory glance. Sherds in the larger fraction, which did not pass through, were weighed by provenience and counted according to the classification presented in Chapter 3. The resulting sherd counts and weights by level are tabulated in Appendix D.

Level and Feature Designations   Throughout the text, stratigraphic levels will be indicated by the abbreviation L., followed by number, and suffixed with the designation of the excavated unit. Thus, for example, L.6/8N2E refers to Level 6 in unit 8N2E. Feature proveniences are similarly indicated by the abbreviation F., followed by the feature number and the excavation unit.

2

Ceramic Technology

Despite the many obligatory references to Anna Shepard in the literature, detailed technological studies of Mississippian pottery have been few and far between. Two people have been mainly responsible for what little recent work on this subject there is. Porter, for one, has published a number of thin-section descriptions of Mississippian pottery from southern Illinois and elsewhere (Bareis and Porter 1965; Porter 1964a, 1964b, 1966, 1971, 1974; Porter and Szuter 1978). Also, Million has been quite active in doing replication experiments and mineralogical studies, particularly with reference to Mississippian pottery from northeast Arkansas (Million 1975a, 1975b, 1976, 1978).

What follows is by no means a comprehensive treatment of the Mississippian ceramic technology at Moundville. More coverage has been given to some aspects than others, usually reflecting the relative abundance (or lack) of systematic work that has been done. At the very least, the information presented is intended to clarify some of the observed variability in the Moundville assemblage, and also to serve as the basis for future technological comparisons with culturally related assemblages, both across space and through time. Ultimately, such comparisons will not only be fruitful in elucidating patterns of interregional exchange, but also, I suspect, will reveal that a good many of the ceramic changes and distinctions that we have long taken for granted as being stylistic are fundamentally technological in nature.

CLAYS

Numerous clay outcrops exist in the vicinity of Moundville. Geologically, most of these outcrops belong to the Tuscaloosa group, an extensive sedimentary deposit of late Cretaceous age (Clarke 1964, 1966, 1970).

In order to see what sorts of clays would have been most readily available to the Moundville potters, 10 samples were collected from various outcrops within a kilometer of the site (Table 2). The mineralogical composition of these samples was determined by means of x-ray diffraction; the results of this analysis are summarized in Table 3. Despite evident differences in color and sometimes in texture, the clays are remarkably uniform in the minerals they

TABLE 2
Clay Samples from Outcrops in the Vicinity of Moundville

Sample number	Unfired color	Fired color[1]	Location of outcrop[2]
C-1	Grey (N5.5)	Pinkish white (7.5YR8/2)	NW1/4, SE1/4, Section 36, T24N, R4E
C-2	Light grey (N5.5)	Light red (7.5YR8/2)	NW1/4, SE1/4, Section 36, T24N, R4E
C-3	Grey (5Y6/1)	Reddish white (2.5YR8/2)	NW1/4, SE1/4, Section 36, T24N, R4E
C-4	Red (10R5/6)	Red (10R5/6)	NW1/4, SE1/4, Section 36, T24N, R4E
C-5	Grey (N4.5)	Pinkish white (7.5YR8/2)	NW1/4, SE1/4, Section 36, T24N, R4E
C-6	Light brownish grey (2.5Y6/2)	Pinkish white (7.5YR8/2)	NW1/4, SE1/4, Section 36, T24N, R4E
C-7	White (2.5Y8/1)	Pinkish white (7.5YR8/2)	NW1/4, SE1/4, Section 36, T24N, R4E
C-8	Weak red mottled with yellow (7.5R5/2-2.5Y6/4)	Pale red (7.5R6/4)	SE1/4, NE1/4, Section 36, T24N, R4E
C-9	Red (10R4/6)	Red (10R4/8)	SE1/4, NE1/4, Section 36, T24N, R4E
C-10	Greyish brown (2.5Y5/1)	Light reddish brown (5YR6/4)	NW1/4, NW1/4, Section 31, T24N, R5E

[1] The samples were fired in air at 650°C for 45 minutes.
[2] All samples were collected from the east bank of the Black Warrior River, no more than 2 m above water level (August 23, 1978). Geologically, these deposits belong to the upper portion of the Tuscaloosa Group (see Clarke 1970:10-11).

TABLE 3
Mineralogical Composition of Clay Samples[1]

Mineral phase	Sample number									
	C-1	C-2	C-3	C-4	C-5	C-6	C-7	C-8	C-9	C-10
Quartz	X	X	X	X	X	X	X	X	X	X
Muscovite/Illite	X	X	X	X	X	X	X	X	X	X
Feldspar[2]	X	X	X	X	X	X	X	X	—	X
Kaolinite	X	X	X	X	X	X	X	X	X	X
Hematite	X	X	X	X	X	?	?	X	X	?
Maghemite	—	—	—	X	—	—	—	X	X	—
Zircon	—	?	—	—	?	—	—	?	—	—
Garnet[3]	—	X	—	—	—	—	—	—	—	—
Unknown (6.6 Å)[4]	X	X	X	—	—	X	X	X	X	X

[1] Key: X, definitely present; ?, probably present; -, absent or not detected.
[2] Mostly Microcline.
[3] Grossularite.
[4] This phase is represented by a low, very broad peak at about 6.6 Angstroms. Our best (tenuous) guess is that it may be a clay mineral of the attapulgite-palygorskite group (Grim 1968:Table 5-16).

contain. Consistently present are the clay minerals kaolinite and illite, along with the nonclay minerals quartz, muscovite, feldspar, and hematite. Maghemite, a form of iron oxide closely related to hematite, is detectable only in the iron-rich red clays, but not in the grey. The heavy minerals zircon and garnet, when observed at all, are present in very small concentrations, and so their apparent absence in many of the samples could simply be due to insufficient sensitivity in the detection technique. All in all, the range of minerals corresponds closely to what one finds in Moundville sherds (which will be discussed in a subsequent section), indicating that clays of this sort were indeed used by the Moundville potters.

Apart from these kaolinite–illite clays, deposits of montmorillonite clay also occur in the Black Warrior River valley. Geologically, these clays come from the lower portions of the Tuscaloosa group, and they tend to outcrop most frequently to the north and east of Moundville (Clarke 1966, 1970). The closest reported outcrop is in the vicinity of Snows Bend, about 36 km upstream along the Warrior (Clarke 1966:75). Although these outcorps could conceivably have been exploited, we have no evidence from our mineralogical studies of sherds that they were. In fact, this apparent lack of exploitation makes perfect sense from a potter's viewpoint, since montmorillonite-rich clays typically have very high shrinkage rates and are usually considered inferior as raw materials for making pottery (Shepard 1956:376–377).

It should also be noted that various geologically recent alluvial clays would presumably have been available in the floodplain of the Warrior River.

However, none of these clays was sampled in the field, and, to my knowledge, no published descriptions of their mineralogical composition exist.

TEMPERING MATERIALS

The vast majority of Moundville pottery is tempered with crushed shell. This shell was probably obtained from locally available mussels, a presumption which is strengthened by the fact that temper particles, when viewed microscopically in thin sections, commonly exhibit the kinds of internal shell structures that are typical of the family Unionacea—a taxon that includes a large portion of the bivalves native to the interior rivers of the Southeast (see Taylor *et al.* 1969:109–115).

Although direct archaeological evidence of the practice is still lacking in our region, it is quite likely that shells were deliberately heated before being added to the paste as temper (Million 1975a:218–219; Porter 1964a:3–4). Such heating would have offered the potter two practical advantages. The first and most obvious benefit is that heating whole shells makes them extremely friable, and greatly reduces the effort required to crush them to the appropriate size. The second benefit has to do with certain changes in shell mineralogy that take place at elevated temperatures. Unionid shells in their natural state consist mainly of the mineral aragonite (Porter 1964a:2; Taylor *et al.* 1969:109), which, when heated to about 500° C, alters irreversibly to calcite (Hutchinson 1974:454). Although both these minerals are crystalline forms of calcium carbonate, the shift from one to the other entails an expansion in volume that could cause some damage if it were to occur inside the vessel wall during firing. Preheating the shell reduces the risk of such damage by allowing the expansion to take place before the shell is even added to the paste. Million (1975a:219, 1975b:202) has found conclusive evidence that Mississippian potters in northeast Arkansas used burned shell as temper, and, given the cultural similarities between the two regions, there is no reason to believe that the Moundville potters would have done otherwise.

Estimates derived from examining thin sections of Moundville pottery indicate that shell temper comprises from 20 to as much as 50% of the fired ware by volume (see Table 7 on p. 32). One should realize that these percentages are probably underestimates, because our microscopic technique was capable of counting only the particles large enough to be resolved at 125 magnifications, leaving out the fine silt- and clay-sized carbonate "dust," which is reportedly produced when burned shell is crushed (Million 1975a:219).

Another tempering material that sometimes appears in Moundville pottery is grog, which consists of crushed sherds. Grog occurs as the sole tempering agent only in the very early and (possibly) in the very latest part of the occupation at Moundville; during most of the "Middle Mississippi" occupation (Moundville I–Moundville III), grog was used only in combination with crushed shell, never by itself. The one grog- and shell-tempered sherd examined in thin section was estimated by point counting to contain about 23% grog by volume (S-2 in Table 5 on p. 30).

It should also be noted that a small, but consistent proportion of the pottery found in Mississippian contexts at Moundville appears to be untempered. I say "appears to be" because I have not looked at any of those specimens in thin section, and the slim possibility exists that they once contained very fine shell, now leached out. These vessels tend to be relatively small, and usually are made in rather simple shapes. They also consistently exhibit a distinctive grey color, both in surface and in core, which is unlike the reddish tones seen in most tempered pottery, but is very similar to the color of certain local, unfired clays (e.g., C-1, C-2, and C-3 in Table 2). This may well indicate that such vessels were fired neither at a high enough temperature nor for a long enough time to oxidize the clay of which they were made—perhaps a technological necessity in the absence of temper.

VESSEL FORMING, FINISHING, AND DECORATION

No complete or very detailed study has yet been undertaken of the forming techniques used by Moundville potters. We are fortunate, however, in that van der Leeuw and Hardin—both ceramic technologists with much more experience in such matters than I—have had the opportunity to spend some time looking at a sample of whole vessels, and have arrived at some preliminary conclusions in regard to how these vessels were constructed. The descriptions to be presented here rest largely on their reports (van der Leeuw 1979, 1981; Hardin 1979, 1981), supplemented to some extent by my own observations.

At least four generalized vessel building methods or "traditions" can be recognized in the Moundville assemblage. Two of these methods make use of the technique usually referred to as coiling, in which the vessel wall is built up by successively adding horizontal strips or rings of clay, one above the other (Shepard 1956:57–59). The other two methods make use of slab construction and hand modeling, respectively.

Coiling with a Support   This method was frequently employed in making bottles, cylindrical bowls, pedestaled bowls, and simple bowls. Its distinguishing feature was the use of a flat or basin-shaped support on which the vessel's base could rest. Minimally, the support acted as a pivot on which the vessel could be turned as coils were added to the walls; in some cases the support also served as a mold in which the base was formed by squeezing out of a lump of clay (van der Leeuw 1979:2–5). It is difficult to say exactly what the support itself consisted of, but a large sherd or shallow bowl would have served the purpose well.

Also worthy of note are two building procedures that appear less frequently than the "standard" method described above, but are probably just extreme variants within the same technological tradition. The first is simple coiling without the use of a support; a minority of bottles and bowls seem to have been constructed in this way. The second is a highly efficient technique whereby the base and shoulder of a bottle were molded separately in hemispherical supports, and the two halves were joined to form a subglobular body, in which an orifice was subsequently cut out and a neck added. Noting that the latter variant only seems to occur relatively late in the ceramic sequence (i.e., Moundville III), Hardin (1979:2–3) has suggested that the function of the support in vessel building may have undergone a gradual development through time: Early on, the support may only have been used to rotate the pot; later it began being used to mold the shape of the vessel's base, and later still to mold the shape of the entire body—an intriguing hypothesis that deserves further attention.

Coiling with Paddle-and-Anvil Finishing   This method was employed in building most unburnished jars, as well as some flaring rim bowls. Van der Leeuw reconstructs the procedure as follows:

> All through the period covered by the Moundville materials these vessels seem to have been made in one and the same basic manner, i.e., by coiling without the use of any support or rest. After thus shaping the pot roughly, the potter would "iron out" most irregularities by beating it with a paddle, supporting the inside with an anvil. The paddle was flat and smooth, not covered with string or any other substance [1979:5].

Evidence that the paddle-and-anvil technique was used "comes basically from the surface treatment of all the vessels concerned: faceted surfaces which, after smoothing or polishing, have a 'hammered' appearance [van der Leeuw 1979:5]." One might add that the pottery "trowels" (Figure 3a) that are found on the site probably served as the anvils in such a procedure, an interpretation first proposed by Thruston (1890:161–162) and Holmes (1903:35–36) a good many years ago.

Slab Building   This rather distinctive method was used in making rectanguloid vessels, including some of the terraced bowls, which, though generally rare, seem to turn up more often at Moundville than anywhere else. As inferred by van der Leeuw,

> The technique is one of rolling out slabs of paste, cutting those into the desired shape, and joining them at the edges, then assembling the whole vessel. In some cases, more than one surface may be constructed out of one and the same slab by bending at right angles, if and only if the clay is coherent enough to support such an action [1979:5].

Hand Modeling   This method simply involved starting with a lump of clay, and manipulating this lump by hand directly into the desired vessel shape. Vessels made in this way were usually simple bowls and miniatures of various

FIGURE 3   Ceramic artifacts from Moundville: (a) pottery "trowels" (MAI-17/2795) and (b) an unburnished jar showing evidence of scraping on exterior (WR69).

forms. Apparently, the simple nature of the technique precluded its use in the building of large and or intricate pieces.

After a vessel was completely built up by one of the methods just described (but especially the coiling methods), the vessel's walls were often scraped to thin them and make them lighter. Of course, the striations left by the scraping tool only remain visible in those places where they were not obliterated by subsequent finishing. Thus, the marks are seen most frequently on the relatively inconspicuous interior surfaces of constricted-orifice vessels such as bottles; they do, however, occasionally turn up on exterior surfaces as well (Figure 3b).

The two most common surface finishing techniques used by Moundville potters can be referred to as smoothing and burnishing. The former involved evening out the surface of the vessel while the clay was still fairly wet, probably by wiping the surface with something relatively soft and pliant (Shepard 1956:187–191). The finish that results from this treatment is fairly smooth, but not compacted or lustrous. Burnishing, on the other hand, was accomplished while the clay was in a somewhat drier state by rubbing the previously smoothed surface with a hard, blunt instrument—possibly a waterworn pebble (Shepard 1956:191). This treatment produces a compacted surface that is often lustrous or "polished" in appearance. Our sample contains numerous instances in which the potter was perhaps not meticulous enough in rubbing, and the striations left by the burnishing tool are still plainly visible. A burnished finish is usually found on bowls and bottles; a smooth unburnished finish is usually found on jars.

A number of Moundville vessels show clear evidence of having been slipped. Often a slip was used in cases where the temper in the paste was fairly coarse but the potter wished to produce a burnished finish. Since it is difficult to satisfactorily burnish a coarsely tempered vessel—the larger temper particles tend to drag in the clay as the tool is moved across the surface—a slip of untempered clay was applied over the coarse paste and the slip itself was burnished. Slips also were employed to achieve particular surface colors in firing. For example, a white color could be produced by firing under oxidizing conditions a clay containing little or no hematite. Moundville potters sometimes used such white-firing slips on vessels otherwise constructed of pink-firing clays. A case in point is provided by one of the thin-sectioned sherds (Table 4): Mineralogically, the slip in this sherd is quite different from the vessel wall, in that the slip contains relatively abundant quartz, mica, and feldspar, but completely lacks hematite.

A number of red-filmed vessels also occur in the Moundville assemblage. It is clear that the bright red color was achieved by applying hematite to the surface and firing under oxidizing conditions. In many cases, the hematite seems to have been applied in the form of an iron-rich clay slip, but I am not sure that this method was the only one used.

TABLE 4
Mineralogical Composition of Slip and Vessel Wall in Specimen S-1[1]

Mineral phase	Slip[2]	Wall[3]
Calcite (shell)	—	49.7
Quartz	21.3	4.0
Hematite	—	1.8
Muscovite (mica)	5.3	—
Feldspar	2.1	—
Zircon	1.1	—
Undifferentiated matrix	69.1	39.6
Void	1.1	4.8

[1] Relative abundances are here expressed as percentages of total volume. These estimates were derived by point counting under a polarizing microscope at a magnification of 125x; only grains larger than approximately 10 microns in diameter were sufficiently well resolved to be counted. The number of points sampled was 94 for the slip, and 767 for the wall.
[2] The fired color of the slip is white (7.5YR6/3).
[3] The fired color of the vessel wall is pale yellow-red (7.5YR7/4).

This brings us to a consideration of the "black film" so common on the Moundville bowls and bottles, and the evidence for how this color was produced. It has traditionally been maintained that the black film results from an organic paint applied directly to the surface by the potter. This idea was first proposed by Moore more than seventy years ago, based on both visual and chemical evidence.

> The Moundville ware, except in the case of cooking vessels, is almost invariably covered with a coating of black, more or less highly polished on the outer surface. This coating was not produced by the heat in firing the clay, but was a mixture intentionally put on by the potters. Scrapings from the surface of a number of vessels were furnished by us to Harry F. Keller, Ph.D., who, by analysis, arrived at the conclusion that the black coating on the earthenware is carbonaceous matter.... From its appearance and chemical behavior, Dr. Keller concludes that it must have been applied in the form of a tarry or bituminous matter, which upon heating out of contact with air, was converted into a dense variety of carbon. Doctor Keller is of the opinion that a mixture of soot and fat or oil might produce the effect, though the numerous lustrous particles resembling graphite rather suggest the carbonization of a tar-like substance [1905:140].

Considerably later, Matson did a series of experiments on black-filmed sherds from Guntersville Basin that led him to a similar conclusion.

> An examination of a group of Moundville Black Filmed sherds showed that several of them had an oxidized core buff to salmon in color, while other pieces with gray cores had an oxidized area at one or both surfaces. Upon the surfaces themselves, covering the light area, appeared the black film. That this film could not have been produced while the vessels were being fired was indicated by the oxidized region just beneath it....
>   It would be possible to obtain such a black surfacing either by using a slip containing iron which when fired under reducing conditions would produce a black iron oxide coating, or by applying an organic paint that a reducing atmosphere would carbonize [quoted in Heimlich 1952:29].

Matson's experiments adequately demonstrated that the dark surface color was not the result of an iron oxide paint or slip; therefore, by process of elimination, he concluded that the color had to be due to an organic paint (Heimlich 1952:30–31). Furthermore, he argued that the paint had to be applied with a second firing, because the initial firing that produced the oxidized core in these sherds would at the same time have oxidized (i.e., burned off) any organic paint on the surface.

Although these arguments have gained some acceptance over the years, they are not as convincing as they would appear to be at first glance. The conclusions of both Keller and Matson rested on the dubious premise that the carbonaceous matter on the surface could only have been the residue of an organic paint applied before firing. Only by taking this premise for granted could Matson have argued reasonably for the necessity of a second firing in order to obtain a dark surface over an oxidized core.

It should be noted that there does exist a simple method of producing a black film apart from direct painting. This process is referred to as "smudging," which is described by Shepard as a "means of blackening pottery by causing carbon and tarry products of combustion to be deposited on it [1956:88]." A vessel can be smudged after firing, or smudging can take place during the process of firing itself. All it requires is a smoldering fire that burns with a sooty smoke, and a certain amount of care to ensure that the soot deposited on the vessel's surface is not burned away by direct contact with the flames.

A key point that Matson did not consider is that the firing atmosphere need not remain constant during the course of a single firing. The burning of charcoal in an open firing tends to produce a neutral or oxidizing atmosphere; the burning of fresh fuel tends to produce a reducing atmosphere (Shepard 1956:217). Thus, it is quite possible to vary the atmosphere during open firing by manipulating the fuel supply and to some extent by controlling the draft.

These considerations raise the possibility that the black-filmed wares owe their surface color not to an organic paint, but rather to a process of deliberate smudging and reduction in firing. The observed characteristics of these wares could well have been produced in a single firing and without the use of paint, if the following procedure were used: First the vessels could have been placed in a "clean" fire, which would oxidize both the surface and the core. Then, in the very last stages of firing, fresh fuel that burned with a sooty smoke could have been added; this fuel would have produced a reducing atmosphere and inevitably have brought about some degree of smudging. Both the reduction and the smudging would contribute to blackening the vessel, because reduction darkens the color of iron oxides in the clay, and smudging deposits carbon. As long as the reduction and smudging were of relatively short duration, their effects would be confined to the surface, and the core of the vessel wall would still remain oxidized. Exactly this kind of technique for producing blackwares has been documented among traditional Catawba potters (Fewkes 1944:91).

It is difficult to demonstrate conclusively that this procedure was actually the one used in making the black-filmed wares at Moundville. We can, however, show that it was indeed possible to produce the dark color in this way using locally available clays. As noted previously, a number of apparently local vessels at Moundville exhibit zones of red paint on a whitish surface, colors that could only have been achieved by deliberate firing under oxidizing conditions. Such vessels invariably have a few irregular patches on their surface where the whitish color has turned black (Figure 4b, left). These patches of black are obviously not the result of painting; rather they can only be interpreted as places where the surface was accidentally reduced and/or smudged in firing. Conversely, black-filmed vessels sometimes exhibit patches of whitish color that have resulted from accidental oxidation (Figure 4b, right). These observations clearly suggest that differences in surface color—from white to

FIGURE 4   Fire clouding on white- and black-surfaced vessels: (a) the vessels in upright position and (b) the vessels turned to reveal fire clouding (Scale is in centimeters). Note that the accidentally reduced areas on the white-surfaced vessel (left, Rho302) are black, and oxidized areas on the black-surfaced vessel (right, Rho304) are white.

black—can be produced simply by varying the conditions under which the clay is fired. Additional confirming evidence has come from a series of replication experiments conducted by Robert Lafferty and Ned Jenkins of the University of Alabama (personal communication). Using clay from a single local source, they were able to produce both white- and black-surfaced wares without paint just by changing the nature of the firing atmosphere.

Moundville potters usually applied no more than one surface color to any given vessel, yet there are cases in which two or even three colors were combined. Among the combinations used were red and white, red and black, black on white, and (in one case only) both red and black on white.

The red and white effect usually was achieved by first slipping the vessel with a white-firing (iron-deficient) clay, and then covering certain areas of the slip with red-firing (iron-rich) clay. Sometimes the two kinds of clay were applied to separate parts of the vessel, rather than one over the other. With either method, simply firing the vessel under oxidizing conditions would bring out the desired colors.

Considerably trickier was the red-and-black effect, since black can only be produced by reduction in firing, and red can only be produced by oxidation. Judging from the evidence on the vessels themselves, this technological dilemma was circumvented as follows: After the vessel had been built and burnished, the areas to be colored red were covered with a noticeably thick layer of hematite-rich clay. The vessel was then fired in the usual way to produce a black film—initially oxidized, then smudged-reduced at the very end to leave a thin layer of black on the surface. As long as the smudging did not penetrate too deeply, the desired color contrast could be achieved by mechanically abrading away the darkened surface only in those places where the hematite-rich clay had been applied, exposing the oxidized, bright red color below. Supporting this reconstruction of the technique are two observations: (*a*) the red areas often have a matte, slightly rough texture, which contrasts with the burnished appearance of the surrounding black areas; and (*b*) in some patches where it was not fully abraded off, the original darkened surface can still be seen covering the red.

The black-on-white effect was apparently produced by means of a negative painting technique. First, the vessel was white slipped and fired under oxidizing conditions. Next, after the vessel had cooled, the design was executed on the surface with a "resist" material, and the surface was coated with carbon black—perhaps by exposure to sooty smoke, or possibly by applying an organic paint and briefly reheating (see Shepard 1956:210). When the resist material was removed, the areas that had been covered would still retain their original color, and stand out as white against a dark background. The red-and-black-on-white effect was produced in essentially the same way, except that the additional step was taken of applying hematite-rich clays over portions of the white slip before firing. The nature of the resist material used by Mississippian potters is still unknown, and it is not likely to be known until replication experiments are undertaken.

Turning now to a different subject, let us briefly consider the two predominant forms of tooled decoration used on Moundville pottery: incising and engraving. The basic difference between these two techniques lies in the state of dryness of the paste at the time the decoration is applied. Although I find it convenient to discuss these terms in dichotomous fashion, it should be apparent that they refer to two halves of a continuum in decorative execution, and a precise boundary between them is often difficult to find in practice.

Incising refers to lines that were cut into the vessel when the paste was either plastic (i.e., very wet) or leather-hard (i.e., partially dry). Plastic incisions typically have burred margins and pushed-up heels at the ends of lines—evidence that the paste was able to "flow" readily as it was being displaced by the tool. Leather-hard incisions, on the other hand, tend to have a compact trough and clean edges—indicating that the paste was somewhat firmer when the tool was applied (Shepard 1956:198). The Moundville potters used plastic incisions mostly in decorating unburnished jars, and leather-hard incisions mostly in decorating burnished bowls and bottles.

The lines I conventionally refer to as engraved were cut when the paste was considerably less moist, either when it was very dry prior to firing or sometimes even after firing. Such lines tend to be relatively narrow, and often exhibit chipping along the margins and in the trough. Contrary to certain widely accepted assertions (cf. McKenzie 1966:7), most, if not all, engraving on Moundville pottery was done before firing, not after. Evidence of this fact can be found in the lines themselves: When examined with a hand lens or even with the naked eye, usually some areas of the trough are found to be smooth and compact, a texture that could only have been formed while the clay was still somewhat plastic. On vessels that have been black-filmed or smudged in firing, it is also noteworthy that the trough of the engraved line usually exhibits the same dark color as the rest of the surface—contrary to what one would expect of postfired engraving, in which the line would necessarily cut through the dark surface exposing the lighter color below (Shepard 1956:198). Although it is not uncommon to find vessels on which the engraving at first glance does appear to be lighter than the rest of the surface, closer examination almost always reveals that the lighter color is an illusion caused by the presence of very fine soil particles caught in the line. Moundville potters used engraving to decorate burnished bowls and bottles, but never jars.

Some engraved vessels also exhibit the technique of excising, whereby relief is added to certain areas of the design by removing the surface to a shallow depth. Excising at Moundville was apparently not done with a gouge, but rather seems to consist of multiple engraved incisions, as though entire areas were "scribbled in" with the same narrow, pointed tool used in executing the rest of the design.

Punctation as a decorative technique is relatively uncommon at Moundville. It was occasionally used to decorate unburnished jars, and was always done when the paste was still in a wet, highly plastic state. In most cases, the punctating implement had a blunt and narrow (3- to 4-mm) tip, which was applied perpendicularly to the vessel's surface. Sometimes the punctations exhibit raised centers, indicating that the implement was hollow, perhaps a reed.

Apart from tooled decoration, many kinds of modeled and appliqué decorations occur in the Moundville assemblage as well. Under this rubric fall appliqué nodes, notched appliqué bands, indentations, lugs, handles, appliqué neck fillets, and various effigy features, to name a few of the more common. However, since I have little to say about these features that is technological rather than purely descriptive, I will not take them up in detail here. What little technological information has been gathered will be presented in the appropriate descriptive sections.

CERAMIC MINERALOGY AND FIRING TEMPERATURE

Mineralogical studies were carried out on a sample of 10 sherds from Moundville (Table 5). The sherds were selected so as to make the small sample as representative as possible of the paste types and major shape categories present in the Moundville assemblage. Another important criterion was that the sherds be consistent with what I perceived to be the local style; in other words, obvious imports were avoided. The 10 sherds were examined by means of x-ray diffraction in order to identify the mineral phases present in relatively large amounts. In addition, the specimens were thin sectioned and examined under a polarizing microscope, not only to gather some quantitative and qualitative information on their microstructure, but also to see which, if any, minerals were present in amounts too small to be detected with the x-ray technique.

The major constituents of all the sherds were found to be quartz, muscovite–illite, feldspar, hematite, and calcite (Table 6). Present in minor

TABLE 5
Sherds From Moundville Used in Mineralogical Studies

Sample number	Type, variety	Additional description
S-1	Bell Pl., *Hale*	Restricted bowl, rim fragment, white slipped
S-2	Moundville Eng., *unspecified*	Subglobular bottle, slab base fragment
S-3	Mississippi Pl., *Warrior*	Standard jar, rim fragment
S-4	Mississippi Pl., *Warrior*	Flaring-rim bowl, rim fragment
S-5	Mississippi Pl., *Warrior*	Standard jar, shoulder fragment
S-6	Mississippi Pl., *Warrior*	Standard jar, folded rim fragment
S-7	Moundville Eng., *unspecified*	Cylindrical bottle or bowl, body fragment
S-8	Mississippi Pl., *Warrior*	Standard jar, rim fragment
S-9	Bell Pl., *Hale*	Subglobular bottle, shoulder fragment
S-10	Bell Pl., *Hale*	Flaring-rim bowl, rim fragment

TABLE 6
Mineralogical Composition of Sherds from Moundville[1]

Mineral phase	Sample number									
	S-1	S-2	S-3	S-4	S-5	S-6	S-7	S-8	S-9	S-10
Quartz[2]	X	X	X	X	X	X	X	X	X	X
Muscovite/Illite[3]	X	X	X	X	X	X	X	X	X	X
Feldspar[4]	X	?	?	X	X	X	X	X	X	X
Hematite[5]	X	X	X	X	X	X	X	X	X	X
Calcite (shell)	X	X	X	X	X	X	X	X	X	X
Zircon	?	X	X	X	?	X	X	X	X	X
Tourmaline[6]	?	X	—	—	—	X	X	?	X	X
Garnet	—	?	—	—	?	—	?	—	—	—
Unknown (6.6Å)[7]	—	—	—	X	—	X	X	—	—	X

[1] Key: X, definitely present; ?, possibly present; —, absent or not detected.
[2] Most grains consist of single crystals. Microcrystalline and cryptocrystalline grains were observed in a few instances, but these forms are rare.
[3] These two minerals are treated together because they are very similar in their crystalline structure, and hence are difficult to tell apart by means of x-ray diffraction. Fortunately, when dealing with clays, identifying them separately is not critical, because muscovite mica is one parent material from which illite, a clay mineral is formed. Flakes of muscovite can be seen in all the thin sections, and so the presence of illite is strongly implied, even though the latter mineral is too fine grained to be identified optically.
[4] The predominant variety of this mineral seen in our thin sections is microcline. Only one possible grain of plagioclase was observed in S-4.
[5] In thin section, the hematite usually appears in anhedral, rounded masses of varying size, often containing quartz and/or muscovite inclusions.
[6] Most of the crystals observed were yellowish brown in ordinary light, suggesting that the specific variety may be dravite. A few olive-green crystals were also noted, which may be schorlite.
[7] This phase is represented by a low, very broad peak at 6.6 Angstroms. Our best (tenuous) guess is that it may be a clay mineral of the attapulgite-palygorskite group (Grim 1968:Table 5-16).

amounts were the heavy minerals zircon, tourmaline, and possibly garnet—none of which were sufficiently plentiful to be picked up by x-ray diffraction. The quantitative data on relative abundance for the coarse fraction of the mineral assemblage are summarized in Table 7. These data were obtained by point counting the thin sections under a polarizing microscope. Since mineral grains smaller than about 10 μm in size were not resolved at the magnification used, they could only be regarded as "undifferentiated matrix."

TABLE 7

Relative Abundances of Coarse Mineral Grains in Sherds, Estimated as a Percentage of Total Volume[1]

Mineral phase	Sample number									
	S-1	S-2	S-3	S-4	S-5	S-6	S-7	S-8	S-9	S-10
Quartz	4.1	4.1	3.3	4.8	2.1	7.8	8.3	5.9	8.5	9.2
Muscovite (mica)	—	0.6	0.2	—	—	0.2	0.8	—	0.3	0.2
Feldspar	—	—	—	—	—	0.2	—	0.2	0.2	—
Hematite	1.8	2.2	0.6	4.6	2.9	4.7	3.0	1.7	0.9	1.6
Calcite (shell)	49.7	14.2	33.4	31.6	37.2	35.7	17.9	23.5	23.9	20.0
Zircon	—	—	—	0.4	—	—	—	—	—	0.2
Tourmaline	—	—	—	—	—	—	—	—	0.2	—
Matrix	39.5	75.4	59.6	53.2	53.2	48.0	67.3	64.9	60.8	63.3
Void	4.8	3.5	2.9	5.4	4.7	3.5	2.8	3.8	5.2	5.1

[1] Estimates were derived by point counting under a polarizing microscope at a magnification of 125x; only grains larger than approximately 10 microns in diameter were sufficently well resolved to be counted. The number of points sampled was 767 for S-1, 492 for S-2, 488 for S-3, 541 for S-4, 487 for S-5, 513 for S-6, 532 for S-7, 527 for S-8, 636 for S-9, and 564 for S-10.

Not surprisingly, most of the minerals in the sherds correspond to those in the Moundville clays (see pp. 18–20), with only a few interesting and rather important exceptions. Kaolinite, which occurs in all the clays, is consistently absent in the sherds; and calcite, absent in the clays, is always present in the sherds, having been added by the potters as temper.

By comparing the mineral phases present in the sherds with those in the unfired clay, we can arrive at an estimate of firing temperature, since the temperatures at which various phases decompose are known. In this case, the two critical phases for temperature determination are kaolinite and calcite. Kaolinite is known to decompose at temperatures between 550 and 625° C (Grim 1968:Figure 9–8; Hutchinson 1974:228; Isphording 1974:Figure 1; Searle and Grimshaw 1959:657). Therefore, since kaolinite is absent in the sherds, we can infer that they were fired at least as high as 550° C. This inference rests of course on the presumption that kaolinite was originally contained in the paste of which the sherds were made. Such a presumption is justified not only by the circumstantial evidence seen in the composition of Moundville clays, but also by the mineralogy of the sherds themselves. Kaolinite is a weathering product of alkali feldspars (Shepard 1956:12), and the presence of the latter in our sherds strongly suggests that the former was once present as well.

Incidentally, a firing temperature this high may also explain why maghemite, a mineral found in some of the reddish local clays (Table 3), does not appear in any of the sherds, since maghemite alters to hematite at between 200 and 700° C (Deer *et al.* 1962:73–74).

The upper boundary for firing temperature is implied by the presence of calcite. At high temperatures, calcite will decompose to calcium oxide, giving off carbon dioxide in the process. If the calcium oxide is exposed to air, it will gradually hydrate to form calcium hydroxide—a transformation that entails a large increase in volume. If this reaction takes place within the vessel wall, it will at the very least cause surface spalling and cracking, and at worst cause the vessel to completely fall apart (Rye 1976:120–121). Neither of these results is desirable, and so it is very much in the potter's interest to prevent the calcite from decomposing in the first place. Most published sources place the rapid decomposition of calcite somewhere in the range between 860 and 910° C (Hutchinson 1974:453; Searle and Grimshaw 1959:657; Shepard 1956:22). I have found experimentally, however, that firing a sherd to as low as 800° C for 45 minutes is sufficient to calcine most of the shell near the surface, resulting in considerable damage to the sherd. Since evidence of such damage is lacking on most Moundville pottery, it is unlikely that firing temperatures reached 800° C for any length of time.

Thus, 550–750° C appears to be the most likely range in which Moundville pots were fired, with 650° C being a good median estimate. This corresponds quite closely to Million's estimate of 600° C for Mississippian pottery in northeast Arkansas (1975a:600–601) and Matson's estimate of 500–750° C for Late Woodland pottery in Michigan (1939), both values derived from replication experiments rather than mineralogy. Such temperatures are well within the range that can be achieved in open firing (Shepard 1956:74–91), indicating that kiln devices were not required in manufacturing these late prehistoric wares.

THE EFFECT OF PASTE COMPOSITION ON PHYSICAL PROPERTIES

Moundville pottery can be divided into two broad groups, which differ from each other in both function and paste composition. One group consists mostly of bowls and bottles that were used as eating and storage vessels, but were not used for cooking. Typically, these noncooking vessels are tempered with finely ground shell, and have a dark surface finish produced by deliberate smudging and reduction during firing. Indeed, the fact that most of them are "black-filmed" implies that they were not used for cooking, because contact with a cooking fire would have oxidized the surface and made it lighter.

The second group, the cooking ware, consists of unburnished jars. These vessels, in contrast to the noncooking wares, are usually tempered with coarse shell, and tend to have an oxidized, reddish brown surface color consistent with what one would expect on a vessel used over a fire.

One can see the difference in the way these two functional groups are tempered by looking at the histograms shown in Figure 5. These histograms illustrate the frequency distribution of the third largest temper particle visible

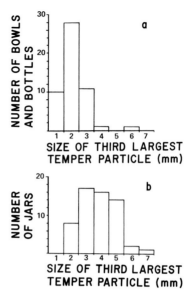

FIGURE 5 Frequency distributions for the size of the third largest temper particle in Moundville vessels: (a) bowls and bottles (noncooking vessels) (51 observations, mean particle size = 2.1 mm) and (b) unburnished jars (cooking vessels) (58 observations, mean particle size = 3.8 mm).

in the vessel's surface, based on a sample of about 50 vessels in each group. (The third largest particle tends to be more representative of the size of the coarse fraction in the paste, since even a finely tempered vessel is likely to have one or two anomalously large shell particles visible on the surface). Although the two distributions overlap somewhat, the unburnished jars clearly tend to have larger shell inclusions than the bowls and bottles. The mean size of the coarse particles is about 4 mm for jars (the cooking vessels) as compared to only 2 mm for bowls and bottles (the noncooking vessels).

Not only do the two groups sort out according to the size of the shell inclusions, but they also tend to differ in amount of visible shell they contain. The histogram in Figure 6 illustrates the volume percentage of visible shell found in the small, but fairly representative sample of 10 sherds that were examined in thin section. One can see that the distribution is bimodal, with most of the cooking vessels having relatively abundant shell, and most of the noncooking vessels having relatively sparse shell.

Quite clearly, Moundville potters tended to use different paste compositions in making vessels designed for different uses. Cooking vessels were usually made with large particles and abundant visible shell, whereas noncooking vessels were usually made with finer particles and not as much visible shell. Why should this have been so? Many archaeologists, I suspect, have tended to view this distinction as being purely a matter of aesthetics or cultural conven-

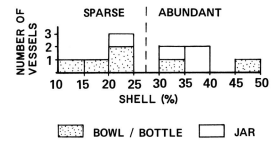

FIGURE 6 Frequency distribution for the abundance of visible shell temper, expressed as a percentage of total volume (data from Table 7).

tion. That is, the fine paste vessels are often thought of as being the "ceremonial" or "nice" ware, whereas the coarse paste vessels are regarded as the common "utilitarian" ware. The difference in composition is thus implicitly seen as the result of effort minimization: The utilitarian ware did not need to look as nice, and so the Indians did not take the trouble to grind up the shell as finely.

There is good reason, however, to question such an interpretation, at least insofar as the Moundville materials are concerned. Given that the shell was heated before being crushed, very little extra effort would have been required to make the shell particles fine. Moreover, ethnographers have documented a number of cases in which traditional potters make a conscious distinction between cooking and noncooking vessels, and use different paste compositions for each (e.g., Arnold 1971; DeBoer and Lathrap 1979; Rye and Evans 1976:28; Thompson 1958). A number of people have suggested that such customs may well be based on practical considerations, stemming from different physical characteristics required of vessels used for different purposes (Hulthén 1977; Rye 1976; Rye and Evans 1976:8; van der Leeuw 1977).

It therefore seemed reasonable to investigate the possibility that Moundville potters deliberately manipulated paste composition in order to make some vessels more suited for cooking and other vessels more suited for noncooking tasks. If this explanation for the paste distinctions observed was indeed correct, then logically one would expect to find evidence of two things: first, that the fine paste favored for noncooking wares would impart a high resistance to breakage from mechanical stress—the kind of stress that might result from a vessel being accidentally dropped or kicked; and second, that the coarse paste favored for cooking wares would impart a high resistance to failure from thermal stress—the kind of stress that results from a vessel being subjected to rapid changes in temperature.

The various measurements designed to test these hypotheses were carried out on the 10 sherds for which composition had already been determined (Table 5), along with a few additional sherds for which there was no mineralogical information. In order to lessen the possibility of error resulting from postdepositional effects, only specimens which were not significantly leached or eroded were included in the sample.

The one major difficulty encountered in this work arose from the fact that all the available sherds were of limited size. Many of the necessary measurements were destructive, and had to be made on a relatively large piece of the specimen. Thus, even on the larger sherds, not very many measurements could be made before a specimen was entirely used up. The fact that certain kinds of measurements were intrinsically susceptible to statistical error further compounded the dilemma, because in such cases the same measurement had to be repeated more than once. This problem explains why the number of replications per measurement was kept to a minimum, and also explains why some kinds of measurements, lower in priority, could not be made at all.

Despite these and other minor disadvantages encountered along the way, some consistent and rather intriguing results were obtained. The exposition in the following sections will present the substantive findings, but, out of compassion for the reader, will avoid discussing the intricacies of the measurement techniques employed. An adequate treatment of the latter subject appears in Appendix E.

Resistance to Mechanical Stress

Testing the first part of the hypothesis was relatively straightforward: slabs were cut from each of the 10 sherds that had already been thin sectioned and x-rayed, and their modulus of rupture was measured by means of a three-point bending test (Table 8). The modulus of rupture is a measure of tensile strength (S), the higher the modulus, the more resistant the material to fracture from mechanical stress. When the modulus was plotted against the volume

TABLE 8
Physical Properties Measurements[1]

Sample number	Tensile strength (kg/cm^2)	Apparent porosity (% volume)	Diffusivity (cm^2/sec)	Elasticity (kg/cm^2)
S-1	126.0	29.2	20.0	12240
S-2	174.4	28.0	16.4	18882
S-3	119.2	28.0	14.9	6936
S-4	126.9	27.7	19.0	11904
S-5	117.9	26.7	18.5	13200
S-6	83.5	31.6	18.6	6978
S-7	163.9	30.2	21.0	19092
S-8	116.6	27.2	16.2	7626
S-9	147.5	27.4	21.0	12984
S-10	148.6	30.0	16.0	11646

[1] Values shown are the medians of two or three measurements on each sherd.

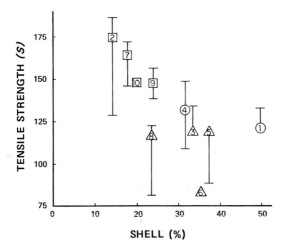

FIGURE 7 Tensile strength (*S*) plotted against the percentage of visible shell temper. The median value of *S* is plotted for each specimen, the error bars indicating the range of values obtained. The squares denote the finely tempered bowls and bottles, the triangles the coarsely tempered jars, and the circles the coarsely tempered bowls. Numbers within the symbols correspond to the sample numbers in Tables 5–8.

percentage of shell temper, the expected relationship was found to hold true (Figure 7): the less shell present in the paste, the higher the tensile strength ($r = -.68$). Thus, the finely tempered bowls and bottles indeed appear to be stronger and more resistant to breakage from mechanical stress than the coarsely tempered jars.

Of course, one might legitimately wonder to what extent the strengths measured in the laboratory might have been affected by the kinds of stresses to which the vessels had been subjected when in use. Could it be, for example, that the coarsely tempered jar sherds have lower strengths because they were subjected to thermal shock and weakened in day-to-day cooking, whereas the bowls and bottles were not? Perhaps, but note that the two coarsely tempered bowls, neither of which was likely to have been used for cooking, also have low strengths compared to their more finely tempered counterparts. It therefore seems likely that the relationship between strength and paste composition is intrinsic to the material, and is not simply a spurious outcome of different thermal histories while in use.

Resistance to Thermal Stress

The first problem one encounters when dealing with thermal stress resistance is in deciding exactly what property one needs to measure. Unlike many other physical properties, thermal stress resistance is not defined in absolute terms; rather, it can best be thought of as a set of related properties, each of which is relevant to a different set of practical situations. In order to see what sorts of measurements may be relevant to the question at hand, it is useful to consider the theory of thermal fracture in ceramics that has been worked out by Hasselman (1969).

The diagram shown in Figure 8 illustrates what happens to the strength of a ceramic material when it is subjected to thermal shock. The vertical axis represents strength, and the horizontal axis denotes the severity of thermal shock. Thermal shock occurs when a body is suddenly quenched from one temperature to another; the greater the temperature difference (ΔT), the steeper the thermal gradient within the material, and the more severe the thermal shock. The diagram shows that as the severity of thermal shock increases, there is no change in strength until a certain critical temperature difference (ΔT_c) is reached. At that point the material will crack (usually microscopically), and the strength will instantaneously decrease to a lower level. Strength will remain stable at this lower level, until a second critical point ($\Delta T'_c$) is reached, after which the strength will decline gradually as ΔT increases.

For present purposes, it is of interest to compare the ware groups at Moundville in terms of two properties, each of which can be taken as a measure of thermal shock resistance. One is the severity of shock necessary to initiate cracking (i.e., the value of ΔT_c). The second is the amount of loss of strength that occurs when ΔT_c is reached. A material with high thermal shock resistance either will have a high value of ΔT_c, or it will exhibit a minimal degradation in strength when ΔT_c is reached.

The ideal approach in measuring these properties would be to determine the shape of such a curve empirically. This would require having many slabs of

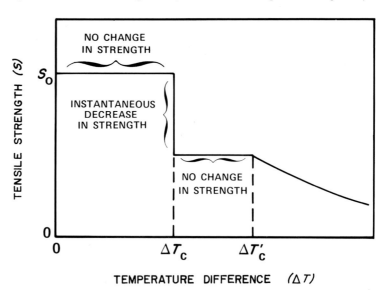

FIGURE 8   Tensile strength (S) of a ceramic material as a function of thermal history (after Hasselman 1969:Figure 2).

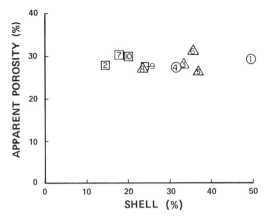

FIGURE 9 Apparent porosity (percentage of volume) plotted against the percentage of visible shell temper. In every case, the range of values obtained was smaller than the vertical height of the symbol. (See Figure 7 legend for key to geometric shapes used here).

each material, subjecting these slabs to varying degrees of thermal shock, and then measuring their remaining strength. The problem with doing this, however, was, again, the limited specimen size. Each sherd could only be cut into a few slabs, and the strength of each slab could be measured only once. This limitation virtually assured that there would not be enough points to accurately determine the shape of the curve, and so a different approach had to be taken.

The alternative chosen was to measure a number of physical properties that affect thermal shock resistance, and then to use these measurements in calculating a set of thermal shock resistance parameters, by means of which the different paste compositions could be compared. The significant properties examined were apparent porosity, thermal diffusivity (D), elasticity (E), and tensile strength (S) (Table 8).

Porosity, defined as the fractional volume of pore space, can have an effect on thermal shock resistance, but the precise nature of the effect is somewhat ambiguous. Although Shepard (1956:126) and others (e.g., Hulthén 1977) have argued that high porosity increases thermal shock resistance, Coble (1958:223) has published evidence to the contrary. One reason for this ambiguity may be that porosity per se is often less important in predicting thermal shock resistance than several other closely related factors—pore shape, density, and the frequency distribution of pore sizes (Hasselman 1969; Kennedy 1977; cf. Rye 1976). For present purposes, none of these factors had to be assessed directly, since their effect is felt through their influence on other measurable properties that enter into our calculated parameters (e.g., tensile strength, elasticity, diffusivity). Nevertheless, porosity was measured in our specimens to see if there are any consistent differences between the ware groups. As shown in Figure 9, the apparent porosity of Moundville pottery stays remarkably constant at about 30%, regardless of how much shell is added as temper.

Thermal diffusivity (D) measures the ease with which heat is dissipated through a material. The higher the diffusivity, the faster the heat is dissipated. High diffusivity contributes to thermal shock resistance in that it tends to reduce thermal gradients within the material, hence reducing internal stress. The data obtained on our specimens (Figure 10) show much more scatter than the porosity measurements, but once again no clear pattern is detected in relation to the percentage of shell present.

Elasticity (E), measured in terms of Young's modulus, corresponds roughly to what we think of colloquially as the "stiffness" of a material. More precisely, it expresses the amount of stress (pressure) produced in a material per unit of tensile strain (deformation). The effect of elasticity on thermal shock resistance varies, and depends on the kind of resistance being measured. In regard to increasing the severity of thermal shock required to initiate cracking (ΔT_c), a low value of elasticity is desirable, because such a material will experience less internal stress for a given amount of thermally induced strain. Once ΔT_c has been reached, however, a high value of elasticity is desirable, because a "stiffer" material tends to inhibit crack propagation, thereby decreasing the material's degradation in strength. The elasticity measurements obtained on our specimens (Figure 11) reveal a weak, but definite negative correlation with the percentage of shell temper ($r = -.47$): the less shell, the higher tends to be the value of the elastic modulus. Thus, the finely tempered bowls and bottles tend to be made of stiffer material than the coarsely tempered jars.

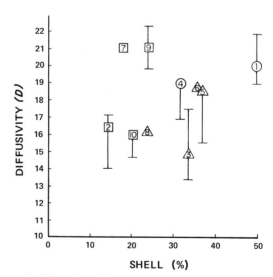

FIGURE 10 Thermal diffusivity (D) plotted against the percentage of visible shell temper. The median value of D is plotted for each specimen, the error bars indicating the range of values obtained. (See Figure 7 legend for key to geometric shapes used here.)

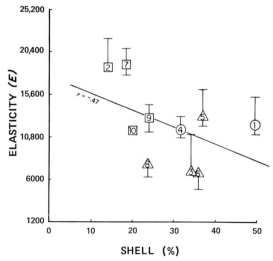

FIGURE 11   Elasticity (E) plotted against the percentage of visible shell temper. The median value of E is plotted for each specimen, the error bars indicating the range of values obtained. (See Figure 7 legend for key to geometric shapes used here.)

Finally, tensile strength (S) is related to thermal shock resistance, and again the nature of the relationship varies with the circumstances. High tensile strength tends to increase the severity of thermal shock that can be withstood before cracking begins, but (for reasons fully understood only by physicists) also tends to increase the degradation in strength that takes place once cracking has begun (Hasselman 1969). As shown previously, tensile strength is negatively correlated with the percentage of shell in Moundville pottery, the fine wares generally being stronger than the coarse wares (Figure 7).

How then are these properties combined to estimate thermal shock resistance? In the present case, the resistance to initial cracking from thermal stress can be compared by means of the theoretically derived parameter:

$$ R = \frac{S(1 - \nu)D}{\alpha E} . $$

Given the mineralogical similarity of our specimens, and the fact that calcite temper has about the same thermal expansion characteristics as low-fired clay (Rye 1976:117), it is reasonable to assume that Poisson's ratio (ν) and the thermal expansion coefficient (α) are constant for our wares (for a definition of the variables ν and α, see Nash 1972:6–7). Such being the case, this parameter reduces to

$$ R = \frac{SD}{E} . $$

The greater the value of this parameter, the higher is the temperature difference that can be endured before any degradation in strength occurs (at least in theory) (Hasselman 1970).

Once cracking has occurred, on the other hand, the resistance to loss in strength should be proportional to

$$R' = \frac{GE}{S^2 (1 - \nu)} .$$

Unfortunately, limitations on the size of our specimens precluded measurement of the surface fracture energy (G)—which may or may not be affected as the percentage of shell changes. The only thing we can do for now is to treat G as a constant, in which case the parameter reduces to

$$R' = \frac{E}{S^2} .$$

The greater the value of this parameter, *ceteris paribus*, the less strength should be lost when ΔT_c is reached (Hasselman 1970).

If we plot the values of these parameters against the volume percentage of shell, we can begin to assess the relative effects of paste composition on thermal shock resistance in Moundville pottery. The parameter R, which pertains to fracture initiation, does show a very weak positive correlation with the percentage of shell (Figure 12), but the relationship is so weak that it probably has little significance $(r = .21; p = .56)$. Thus, the data suggest that there is probably no substantial difference between coarse and fine wares in the level of thermal shock required to bring on a degradation in strength.

The parameter R', on the other hand, shows a much stronger positive correlation with the percentage of shell (Figure 13). Although the correlation is not strong enough to inspire absolute confidence $(r = .51; p = .13)$ the relationship is definite enough to suggest that the coarse wares would tend to lose proportionally less strength once cracking had begun.

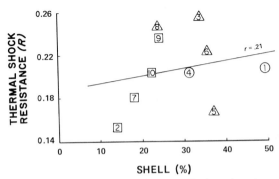

FIGURE 12   The thermal shock resistance parameter R plotted against the percentage of visible shell temper. (See Figure 7 legend for key to geometric shapes used here.)

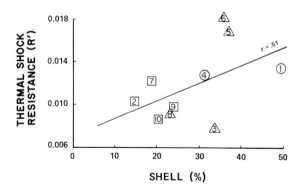

FIGURE 13   The thermal shock resistance parameter R' plotted against the percentage of visible shell temper. (See Figure 7 legend for key to geometric shapes used here.)

One can also look at the same relationship in somewhat different terms: It has been shown that the loss in strength after thermal shock should be inversely related to the percentage of shell temper. It has also been demonstrated that the percentage of shell temper is inversely related to initial strength. Therefore, the drop in strength after quenching should be positively related to initial strength.

Such a relationship can be seen in Figure 14, which shows strength as a function of quenching temperature for three different sherds. Although there are no accurate data on the composition of these specimens, one can see that the amount of drop does seem to be related to initial strength. In looking at these graphs, it is useful to keep in mind that the measured initial strength of the sherds in our overall sample usually falls in the range between 80 and 180 kg/cm². Notice that the sherds with a moderate initial strength (i.e., the uppermost two) lose only about 10–20% of that strength after quenching, and still retain enough strength to remain in the middle of the usual range of values. The sherd that started out with a very high initial strength, on the other hand, lost more than 50% of its strength after quenching, and ended up at the very bottom of the usual range of values.

Figure 15 shows a plot of the fraction of strength retained versus initial strength for a sample of seven sherds that were quenched over a temperature difference of 400° C. Although the number of points is small, and the scatter is relatively large, the data do seem to show the expected trend. The higher the initial strength, the more strength is lost after thermal shock (for an interesting parallel case, see Gupta 1972).

All in all, our data suggest that the Moundville potters may have been faced with a trade-off in choosing which paste composition to use. A finely tempered vessel would have a high initial strength, but would lose a very large proportion of that strength if subjected to thermal shock. A coarsely tempered vessel, on the other hand, would have less initial strength, but would retain

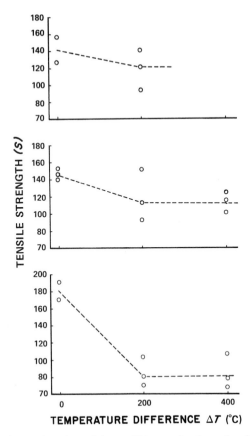

FIGURE 14   Strength as a function of thermal history for three sherds from Moundville.

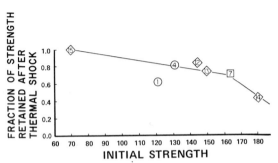

FIGURE 15   The fraction of initial strength retained after thermal shock plotted against initial strength. (See Figure 7 legend for key to geometric shapes used here.)

most of that strength even after a severe thermal shock. This being the case, a coarsely tempered pot would probably have been more resilient and longer lasting as a cooking vessel.

DISCUSSION

Our physical properties findings thus tend to support the interpretation that Moundville potters maintained the distinction between coarse and fine wares for reasons that were fundamentally technological, rather than purely aesthetic. Of course, the differences between the two paste compositions would not have been perceived by the Mississippian potters in the same technical terms used here. Instead, the practical advantages of each paste composition would have been discovered through a gradual process of trial and error, informed by experience and cultural tradition. The potters themselves could have observed that certain compositions resulted in better pots, ones that could be used for a longer period of time before they broke.

In closing, it perhaps should be stressed again that the argument in favor of the technological hypothesis still rests on rather limited evidence. The thermal shock parameters indeed have been suggestive, but they do not in themselves constitute the strongest kind of empirical proof. Moreover, the number of samples we were actually able to test is rather small. Unassailable proof can only be attained by testing a large sample of each material, and the only practical way to produce such a sample is to replicate the material in large quantities. Our mineralogical work has now given us a basis for sound replication, and further work with larger and better-controlled samples will be required to confirm these preliminary results.

3

Classification of Moundville Ceramics

The purpose of this chapter is to define the morass of classificatory terms that are applied to Moundville pottery. The categories to which these terms refer not only form the basic units of description, but are also the principal analytic units with which the chronology will be formulated and presented.

The classificatory units we are concerned with fall into six crosscutting dimensions, each of which can be treated independently of the others:

1. types and varieties
2. representational motifs
3. painted decoration
4. basic shapes
5. secondary shape features
6. effigy features

Dimensions 1 and 4, though formulated with reference to different sorts of criteria, are classifications of whole artifacts, whether vessels or sherds. Dimensions 2, 3, 5, and 6, on the other hand, subsume categories that operate at a different level. These categories refer not to whole artifacts as such, but rather to features or aspects of whole artifacts that may or may not be present on any given specimen. Such classificatory devices would correspond to what archaeologists have sometimes called "modes" (e.g., Phillips 1970:28–29). Each of these dimensions is briefly characterized below.

1. Types and varieties are classes of sherds and whole vessels defined on the basis of paste composition, surface finish, and tooled decoration. These are the kinds of units traditionally used for pottery analysis in the eastern United States; by convention, such units are given proper names and constitute what is generally called the "ceramic typology."
2. Representational motifs are special categories of design that are found on engraved and incised vessels, but do not uniquely correspond to varieties in dimension 1, and must therefore be treated separately.
3. Painted decoration includes categories defined on the basis of deliberate manipulation of the surface color, whether by slipping, smudging, rubbing in pigment, or painting in the strict sense.
4. Basic shapes are the generalized categories of vessel form that take into account the profile of the entire vessel.
5. Secondary shape features, on the other hand, refer to various simple kinds of modeled or appliqué elaborations added onto a basic shape.
6. Effigy features, last in our list, refer to certain more complex modeled or appliqué elaborations of basic shape, which generally are intended to make the vessel resemble a life form of some sort.

In applying the various classificatory terms to Moundville ceramics, I have consistently tried to take into account the distinction between local and nonlocal wares. Making this distinction is important for at least two reasons. The first reason has to do with chronology: Ceramic styles in different regions do not always change exactly in step, and this may confuse any attempt at seriation or chronological ordering unless the distinction between local and nonlocal wares is recognized. The second reason has to do with description: Southeastern ceramic classifications, especially the traditional typologies, are notoriously region specific, and this one is no exception. Although in part this regional specificity is a historical phenomenon—archaeologists working in different regions have used different names for the same sorts of artifacts—I suspect that it also has something to do with certain properties inherent in the kinds of classification that archaeologists generally find most useful. Most stylistic classifications devised by archaeologists, including the ones used here, tend to be polythetic in nature. A polythetic class is one that cannot be strictly defined by specifying a set of necessary and sufficient conditions for membership; rather, it is generally conceptualized as consisting of a set of artifacts that are perceived (by whatever combination of criteria) to be more similar to each other than they are to members of other classes. Because the analytical utility of such a class depends on its internal coherence and distinctiveness vis-à-vis other classes, a polythetic classification can only be meaningfully employed with reference to some bounded universe of possible members. For the archaeologist, the universe usually consists of artifacts manufactured in the context of a regional stylistic tradition. All this is what lies behind the common-sense observation often made by archaeologists, that artifact classifications "do not work" or "do not make sense" if applied to material from outside the region for which they were originally formulated.

The upshot for present purposes is that vessels (and sherds) that appear to have been made in the Moundville region are described in terms of our local classificatory framework. Vessels that appear to be nonlocal, on the other hand, are generally described according to the typologies appropriate to the regions from which these vessels were presumably brought in. This chapter presents only those terms that pertain to local vessels; nonlocal vessels are described separately in Appendix F.

One might wonder, of course, how local and nonlocal vessels can be distinguished in the first place. I have had no choice but to do this on the basis of visual criteria, realizing full well that in the absence of good chemical provenance studies any attributions as to place of manufacture are bound to be suspect. Vessels designated local are generally those having nuances of shape, decoration, and paste that occur commonly in the Black Warrior region. Vessels called nonlocal, on the other hand, generally exhibit many unusual and distinctive features, especially features known to occur commonly in other regions. Whenever possible, style comparisons have been used to identify likely source areas for the imported wares. Obviously, all the attributions made in this way, whether local or nonlocal, depend a great deal on subjective judgement, coupled with a detailed knowledge of the variability in Mississippian ceramics at Moundville and elsewhere. Undoubtedly, some of the assignments I have made are incorrect, and will have to be revised when (and if) additional data become available. To the extent that one can tell in such matters, I suspect that my overall tendency has been to err on the side of calling vessels local that really are not. The reader should also realize that "local" is a relative term; it refers not strictly to Moundville itself, but to a much wider area within which ceramic styles are visually indistinguishable from those at Moundville. Although it is impossible at this stage to pin precise boundaries on this wider area, it probably includes the Black Warrior drainage, the central Tombigbee drainage, and perhaps extends as far north as the Pickwick Basin in the middle Tennessee Valley.

Of the 1121 whole vessels in our sample 954 (85%) are considered local, and 176 (15%) are considered nonlocal. Of the 8212 excavated sherds, 8191 (99.7%) are classed as local, and only 21 (0.3%) seem to be nonlocal. Without a doubt, the relative paucity of imports among sherds as compared to vessels stems at least in part from problems in recognition, since fragments tend to exhibit fewer distinctive features than do complete artifacts. Yet it is also possible that the differences may reflect behavioral factors as well, in that imports may have been preferentially guarded from breakage and/or preferentially included in the burial contexts from which most of our whole vessels come.

Returning now to the principal issue at hand, the sections that follow present the classificatory terms falling into the six dimensions discussed earlier. The emphasis will be on concise definition of terms, rather than on a description of the ceramics to which these terms refer. The major effort at describing the pottery, by type and variety, is deferred until Appendix F.

Quantitative information on the number of sherds that fall into the categories described below appears in Appendix D. Counts of whole vessels by category can be reconstructed from the indexes in Appendixes G and H.

TYPES AND VARIETIES

As its name implies, the type–variety classification makes use of a hierarchical nomenclature, which refers to categories defined at two levels of inclusiveness: types are the broader categories, and each type may subsume any number of more specifically defined varieties. My adoption of this sort of nomenclature was partly conditioned by the fact that the ceramic types defined by earlier workers in the area (e.g., DeJarnette and Wimberly 1941; McKenzie 1964, 1966) were too broad to be useful in making the fine-grained temporal distinctions I desired. The hierarchical nomenclature permitted the recognition of finer categories—varieties—without having to discard the overall structure of types analogous to those used previously. The adoption of type–variety nomenclature also had the advantage of making the local typology much more consistent with those that have recently been introduced in neighboring regions (e.g., Coblentz 1978; Jenkins 1981; Schnell *et al.* 1981).

In applying the type–variety system to Moundville pottery, I have for the most part adhered to the methodological and nomenclatural conventions set forth by Phillips (1970:24–28). Types are generally defined on the basis of fairly gross characteristics of paste, surface finish, and decorative technique. Varieties, on the other hand, tend to be defined on the basis of minor variation in paste composition, or on the basis of specific characteristics of design. Both types and varieties, once defined, are given proper names; variety names are italicized to prevent confusion.

Specimens that can be assigned to a type, but not to a specific variety of that type, are described by the type name followed by the designation *variety unspecified*. The unspecified category is a catchall that may subsume both (*a*) specimens of which the characteristics are known but do not fit the criteria for any of the established varieties, and (*b*) specimens that may in fact belong to one of the established varieties but are too fragmentary for positive identification. Specimens that cannot be identified even as to type are simply listed as unclassified.

The relationships among the local types can be parsimoniously illustrated by means of a dendritic key such as the one in Figure 16. Thus, the local typology is logically a tree-type classification (Whallon 1972) in which (*a*) there is a hierarchy of importance among attributes that determines the order in which attributes are considered when assigning specimens to types, and (*b*) the criteria for definition shift, depending on which "branch" of the tree is being followed in the process of assignment. Here the primary attribute in the hierarchy is temper; shell-tempered types all stem from one branch, grog-tempered types from another. Once the appropriate branch has been determined, another set of attributes may then be considered. To differentiate among the shell-tempered types, one takes into account surface finish (burnished–unburnished) and decorative technique, in that order. To differentiate among grog-tempered types, one need only consider decorative technique. Once a specimen has been assigned to a type, a similar process of branching (omitted from the diagram for lack of space) may be followed in determining the variety to which the specimen belongs.

The local types and their varieties are defined in abbreviated fashion in the following sections. More complete descriptions—including complete lists of references to illustrated specimens—are presented in Appendix F.

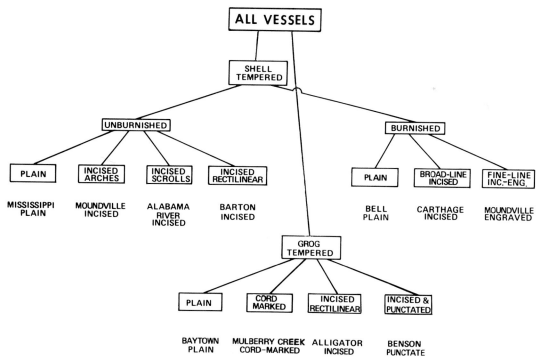

FIGURE 16   Dendritic key for local types.

Alabama River Incised

This type includes unburnished, shell-tempered vessels that are decorated with incised scrolls (not arches), executed in a fairly wet paste. Most vessels of this type are jars (e.g., Figure 62r[1]). Alabama River Incised is rare at Moundville, and in the absence of a good comparative sample, no specific varieties have yet been defined.

Alligator Incised

This type includes ceramics decorated with rectilinear designs, executed with relatively sloppy, wet-paste incisions. The paste, by definition, is tempered predominantly with grog. Only one variety has been recognized in our sample.

Variety Geiger   This can be recognized by a design consisting of oblique parallel lines in a band that encircles the vessel just below the lip (Figure 67a).

Barton Incised

Barton Incised subsumes unburnished, shell-tempered vessels that are decorated with rectilinear designs, consisting of multiple parallel lines incised in a wet paste. This is another rare type at Moundville, with only one local variety defined.

Variety Demopolis   The variety's distinguishing characteristic is a band of vertical or oblique parallel lines on the neck of a jar (Figure 56i).

Baytown Plain

By definition, this type includes undecorated vessels that are tempered predominantly with grog, and sometimes with a little sand as well. Only one variety occurs in the Moundville sample.

Variety Roper   This is a plain ware tempered with grog alone, lacking deliberate sand inclusions (Figure 67c–h).

Bell Plain

This type includes shell-tempered ceramics that lack tooled decoration but have a burnished surface. The shell temper particles have a tendency to be finer than those in Mississippi Plain, but this in itself is not considered a defining criterion. Grog may also be present as an additional tempering agent.

[1]Figures 39–67 are collected in the vessel and sherd illustration section on pp. 175–225.

Variety Hale This variety subsumes all local vessels of Bell Plain. Such vessels are usually bottles and bowls, and commonly (but not always) have a darkened or "black-filmed" surface (e.g., Figures 39a and 41c–j).

Carthage Incised

Carthage Incised is defined to include shell-tempered vessels with a burnished surface that are decorated with broad, "trailed" incisions. Typically, these incisions are from 1.5- to 2-mm wide and are U-shaped in cross section, having been executed when the vessel was in a leather-hard state of dryness. The most common vessel forms in Carthage Incised are bottles and bowls, many of which are black filmed. Six local varieties of this type have been defined, based on variations in design.

Variety Akron This includes vessels on which the major design is a horizontal band of two or more lines running parallel to and just below the lip (Figure 17a). The band of lines is commonly embellished with loops and/or folds. This variety is known to occur only on bowls.

Variety Carthage Vessels in this category are decorated with two- to four- line running scrolls (Figure 17b). Common vessel forms include the subglobular bottle with simple base, the short-neck bowl, and the flaring-rim bowl.

Variety Fosters This is characterized by free-standing representational motifs, usually depicting hands and forearms bones (Figure 17c). (These repre-

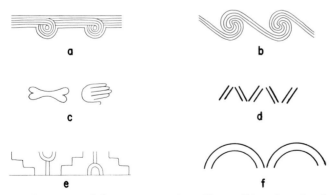

FIGURE 17 Carthage Incised designs: (a) variety *Akron,* (b) variety *Carthage,* (c) variety *Fosters,* (d) variety *Moon Lake,* (e) variety *Poole,* and (f) variety *Summerville.* (Freehand drawings reproduced with permission from *Sun Circles and Human Hands, Southeastern Indians, Art and Industry,* Plates 36–38, pp. 73–75, edited by Emma Lila Fundaburk and Mary Douglass Foreman, Luverne, Alabama, Box 231, Fundaburk Publisher, © 1957.)

sentational motifs are discussed in more detail in a subsequent section of this chapter.) Vessels of this variety are usually flaring-rim bowls or short-neck bowls.

Variety Moon Lake   These vessels are decorated with zones of parallel (usually oblique) line segments, arranged in chevronlike patterns (Figure 17d). Such designs are placed on the interior of flaring-rim bowls, or on the exterior shoulder of short-neck bowls.

Variety Poole   This variety is defined by a design that consists of step motifs enclosing (or alternating with) concentric rayed semicircles (Figure 17e). It is only known to occur on short neck bowls.

Variety Summerville   This is characterized by the presence of incised arches arranged end to end around the circumference of the vessel (Figure 17f). At Moundville, this variety usually occurs on restricted bowls.

Mississippi Plain

The following characteristics define the type Mississippi Plain: (*a*) a paste tempered predominantly with shell, (*b*) a lack of tooled decoration, and (*c*) a surface that, though it may be smoothed, is not burnished. The shell-temper particles in Mississippi Plain tend to be coarser than those in Bell Plain. Predominant vessel forms are jars and bowls. Two local varieties of this type are recognized on the basis of differences in paste composition.

Variety Hull Lake   This has a paste that contains grog in addition to the shell temper (e.g., Figure 41p–q).

Variety Warrior   By far the most common in the sample, this variety has a paste that is tempered with shell alone (e.g., Figures 39l and 41k–o).

Moundville Engraved

In this type are shell-tempered vessels with burnished surfaces decorated with fine, dry-paste incisions or engraving. The lines that make up the design are always less than 1.5 mm wide, and are usually no more than 1 mm wide. The type most commonly occurs on bowls and bottles, which often exhibit a black-filmed surface. Twelve local varieties have been recognized, each characterized in terms of a particular decorative motif or set of motifs.

Variety Cypress   The characteristic design consists of scrolls contained within rectangular panels. The horizontal and vertical bands that border the panels are often filled in with lines, concentric semicircles, punctations, and other elements that sometimes occur in the representational designs of variety *Hemphill* (Figure 18a). The variety usually occurs on subglobular bottles with simple bases.

    Variety Elliots Creek   This is marked by engraved designs that are embellished with areas of excision (Figure 18b). The designs themselves may consist of either curvilinear scrolls, or rectilinear patterns made up of numerous closely spaced lines. This variety occurs on bowls and slender ovoid bottles.

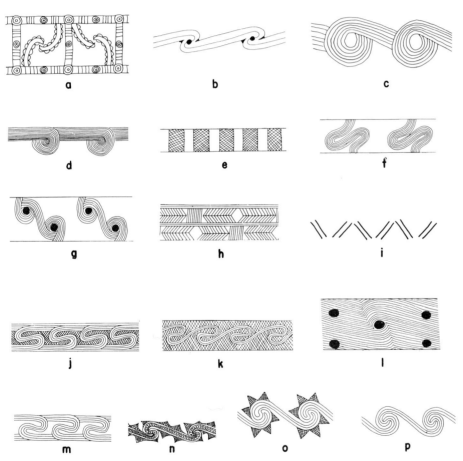

FIGURE 18 Moundville Engraved designs: (a) variety *Cypress*, (b) variety *Elliots Creek*, (c) variety *Englewood*, (d) variety *Havana*, (e) variety *Maxwells Crossing*, (f and g) variety *Northport*, (h) variety *Prince Plantation*, (i) variety *Stewart*, (j and k) variety *Taylorville*, (l) variety *Tuscaloosa*, and (m–p) variety *Wiggins*. (Freehand drawings reproduced with permission from *Sun Circles and Human Hands, Southeastern Indians, Art and Industry*, Plates 36–38, pp. 73–75, edited by Emma Lila Fundaburk and Mary Douglass Foreman, Luverne, Alabama, Box 231, Fundaburk Publisher, © 1957.)

Variety Englewood   This category is defined by a 6- to 10-line curvilinear scroll that runs entirely around the circumference of the vessel (Figure 18c). The most common vessel shape is the subglobular bottle with a simple base.

Variety Havana   This variety includes vessels on which the major design consists of a horizontal band of two or more lines running parallel to and just below the lip (Figure 18d). The bands of lines are usually embellished with loops and/or folds. Common vessel shapes are the cylindrical and the simple bowl.

Variety Hemphill   These vessels are decorated with free-standing or representational motifs, most of which have at one time or another been considered part of the iconography of the Southeastern Ceremonial Complex. A wide range of specific motifs is included in this variety, and these are discussed individually in a later section of this chapter (see pp. 58–63, and especially Figure 20 on p. 60). Among the more common vessel shapes found in this variety are cylindrical bowls and subglobular bottles with simple, slab, and pedestal bases.

Variety Maxwells Crossing   This is characterized by designs that consist mainly of crosshatched vertical bands, spaced at intervals around the circumference of the vessel (Figure 18e). Occasional variations can occur in this basic theme, such as the presence of additional crosshatched elements in the spaces between the bands, or the presence of bands with an irregular boundary on one side. The variety is found on subglobular bottles with pedestal, slab, or simple bases.

Variety Northport   The characteristic design consists of 4- to 10-line vertical scrolls, that is, scrolls that begin at the upper boundary of the design field and end at the lower (Figure 18f and g). The variety is known to include only subglobular bottles with pedestal or slab bases.

Variety Prince Plantation   Under this rubric fall vessels that are engraved with a herringbone design, in which horizontal bands are filled with zones of vertical and oblique parallel lines. The boundaries between adjacent bands are made up of one or several closely spaced horizontal lines (Figure 18h). The design is known to occur only on subglobular bottles with pedestal or slab bases.

Variety Stewart   These vessels are decorated with zones of oblique parallel lines, forming either chevrons or line-filled triangles (Figure 18i). This variety has been found only on flaring-rim bowls, with the design placed on the interior of the rim.

Variety Taylorville   The characteristic design is made up of a three- or four-line running scroll superimposed on a crosshatched background (Figure 18j and k). Vessels of this variety include subglobular bottles with simpel, slab or pedestal bases, cylindrical bowls, and pedestaled bowls.

Variety Tuscaloosa   This includes vessels decorated with a curvilinear scroll made up of 15 to 40 closely spaced lines (Figure 18l). The scroll encircles the vessel and is wide enough to take up almost the entire design field. Vessels of this variety are always subglobular bottles with pedestal, slab, or simple bases, and are almost always embellished with indentations in the wall.

Variety Wiggins   This variety is characterized by a design consisting of a two- to five-line scroll encircling the vessel's circumference (Figure 18m–p). Occasionally, the scroll is embellished with fill-in cross-hatching or with cross-hatched triangular projections. The vessel form most commonly found in this variety is the subglobular bottle with simple base.

Moundville Incised

The designs that mark this type consist of incised arches arranged end to end around the upper portions of the vessel. The surface of these vessels is smoothed but not burnished, and the paste is tempered predominantly with shell. The incision is typically done in a wet paste. Only jars are known to occur in this type. Three local varieties have been defined on the basis of variations in the way the arch is executed.

Variety Carrollton   This has a design in which one or more parallel arches occur alone (i.e., the arches are not embellished with radiating incisions or punctations [Figure 19a]).

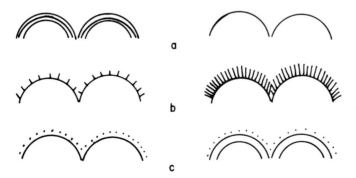

FIGURE 19   Moundville Incised designs: (a) variety *Carrollton*, (b) variety *Moundville,* and (c) variety *Snows Bend.*

Variety Moundville   This is marked by a design in which numerous short incisions radiate upward from (and normal to) the arch (Figure 19b).

Variety Snows Bend   This has a design embellished with punctations above the arch (Figure 19c).

Mulberry Creek Cord Marked

This type includes ceramics with an overall surface treatment of cord-marking. The paste is tempered predominantly with grog, equivalent in composition to that of Baytown Plain. One local variety appears in the Moundville sherd sample.

Variety Aliceville   The cord-marked ceramics of this variety are tempered exclusively with grog, and have no significant sand inclusions (Figure 67b).

REPRESENTATIONAL MOTIFS

Let us begin with some definitions. I use the term *design* to refer to the entire content of the decorated portion of a vessel's surface. The decorated portion itself is termed the *design field*. A design is made up of one or more *motifs;* motifs, in turn, may be made up of several *elements*. Though the whole scheme may sound disarmingly precise, the fact is that deciding where to draw the line between individual motifs, and at what level of specificity to define them, can be a tricky and sometimes arbitrary business. The categories I have isolated as motifs tend to be fairly complex stylistic units that constitute the major portion of any given design—units that are more or less equivalent to what Phillips has called "themes" (Phillips and Brown 1978). I would not defend these motifs as being necessarily real, in the sense that they need not, and in many cases probably do not, reflect categories that had meaning to the artisans who produced the designs. Rather, I present them simply as useful categories for description and chronological analysis.

The motifs I loosely refer to as representational are found on vessels of two local varieties-Moundville Engraved, *variety Hemphill,* and Carthage Incised, *variety Fosters.* Most of these motifs depict recognizable (but often not realistic) creatures and objects, and have at one time or another been considered part of the Southeastern Ceremonial Complex or "Southern Cult" (e.g., Waring and Holder 1945). I have also tentatively assigned to this group a few of the more complex abstract motifs, which do not depict anything immediately recognizable, but do seem to have certain things in common with the more obviously representational ones. The commonality is evident because they tend to co-occur in the same designs, and/or because they tend to be used in designs in the same way (i.e., as free-standing depictions, not embedded in any sort of directly interlocking or continuous pattern).

Bilobed Arrow   This well known motif consists of an arrow with two semicircular lobes, one on each side (Figure 20a and b) (Moundville Engraved, *variety Hemphill*).

Bird with Serpent Head   This motif depicts a creature with an avian body and a serpentine head, complete with avian wings, tail, and feet. It occurs only on one vessel in the entire sample, and unfortunately, the only photograph I have of this vessel does not show the motif in its entirety (Figure 52h). (Moundville Engraved, *variety Hemphill*).

Crested Bird   This bird, commonly referred to in the literature as the Moundville "woodpecker," is characterized by an even (not jagged) crest, and a head marking that surrounds the eye and runs down the neck (Figure 20c). Another distinctive feature of this bird is that it often has something resembling a ribbon or a string of beads (yet undoubtedly neither) held in its beak. Although in one case the head appears alone, in most cases the bird is depicted in the round, with the head shown on the front of the vessel, the tail in the back, and the wings on the two sides. In contrast to other creatures depicted in this manner, the crested bird is always shown inverted, with the head, wings and tail hanging from the upper boundary of the design field. Crested bird heads may also occur as an integral part of the paired tails motif, and when they do they are counted under that rubric (Moundville Engraved, *variety Hemphill*).

Feather   This distinctive motif may represent a feather or the feathered end of an arrow (Figure 20d). It consists of a central line segment, with a series of oblique parallel line segments attached on either side. The central line segment may be either straight or gently curved (Moundville Engraved, *variety Hemphill*).

Feathered Arrow   Rare as a motif at Moundville (Figure 20e), it only occurs on one vessel in a design that also exhibits the bilobed arrow and the Greek cross (Moore 1907:Figures 39 and 40) (Moundville Engraved, *variety Hemphill*).

Forearm Bones   This motif depicts a conventionalized radius and ulna, with a bilobate epiphysis at each end of the combined shafts (Figures 17c and 20f and g). It is almost always accompanied on local vessels by the hand and eye; only once in the sample is it not (Figure 62h) (Moundville Engraved, *variety Hemphill*, and Carthage Incised, *variety Fosters*).

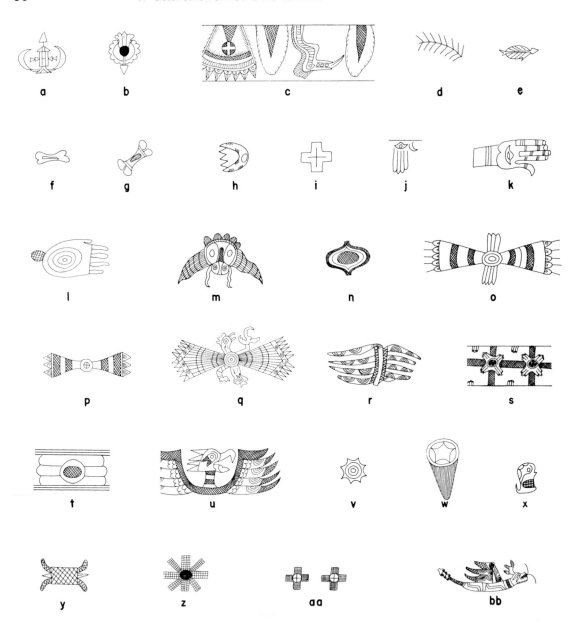

FIGURE 20   Representational motifs: (a and b) bilobed arrow, (c) crested bird (in the round), (d) feather, (e) feathered arrow, (f and g) forearm bones, (h) forked eye surround, (i) Greek cross, (j–l) hand and eye, (m) insect, (n) ogee, (o–q) paired tails, (r) paired wings, (s and t) radial fingers, (u) raptor, (v) rayed circle, (w) scalp, (x) skull, (y) turtle, (z and aa) windmill, and (bb) winged serpent. (Freehand drawings reproduced with permission from *Sun Circles and Human Hands, Southeastern Indians, Art and Industry*, Plates 36–38, pp. 73–75, edited by Emma Lila Fundaburk and Mary Douglass Foreman, Luverne, Alabama, Box 231, Fundaburk Publisher, © 1957.)

Forked Eye Surround   Very common as an element in depictions of the raptor and winged serpent, this well known representation occurs as a free-standing motif in only one case (Figure 20h; Moore 1905:Figure 74) (Mound-ville Engraved, *variety Hemphill*).

Greek Cross   This is the equal-armed cross, not filled in with cross-hatching (Figure 20i). It is rare on Moundville vessels, occurring only twice. The possibility should be kept in mind that it and the windmill motif are two variant expressions of the same idea (Moundville Engraved, *variety Hemphill*).

Hand and Eye   This motif is a depiction of a human hand, on which one finds either a somewhat naturalistic or fully conventionalized eye (Figures 17c, 20j–l); in one deviant case, the eye appears beside the hand instead of directly on it (Moore 1905:Figure 123). This is one of the most common representional motifs on Moundville pottery, and shows quite a bit of stylistic variation (Moundville Engraved, *variety Hemphill*, and Carthage Incised, *variety Fosters*).

Human Head   The one occurrence of this motif is on a vessel illustrated by Moore (1905:Figure 93). This vessel was not in any of the museum collections I studied and is known only from the published photograph. Without having had a chance to examine it closely, I would not discount the possibility that it may be nonlocal (Moundville Engraved, *variety Hemphill*).

Insect   This is a depiction of a beetlelike insect (Figure 20m) that occurs on only one vessel (Moundville Engraved, *variety Hemphill*).

Ogee   This motif was nicely described by Phillips and Brown (1978:Plate 16) as "a circular or oval outline (usually double) with two opposite ogival points and a smaller circular or oval nucleus inside [Figure 20n]." It is found as a free-standing motif on three whole vessels in the sample, and also on a sherd illustrated by Moore (1905:Figure 142) (Moundville Engraved, *variety Hemphill*).

Paired Tails   This is a very common motif at Moundville, what Phillips calls "birds in court-card symmetry" (Phillips and Brown 1978). It minimally consists of two avian tail elements arranged on either side of a circular central element (Figure 20o and p). Sometimes two bird heads are also appended to the central element; in such cases the heads lie along an axis at right angles to that of the tails (Figure 20q). The heads appended can be of the crested bird, the raptor, or one of each (Moundville Engraved, *variety Hemphill*).

Paired Wings   This motif consists of two conventionalized wings, of the sort that are often attached to raptors and winged serpents. The wings are arrayed side by side, but with the featherlike projections pointing in opposite directions (Figure 20r). The symmetry is thus bilateral around a vertical axis, not the twofold rotational symmetry ("court-card symmetry") usually found with paired tails. The paired wings motif occurs on only two vessels (Moundville Engraved, *variety Hemphill*).

Radial Fingers   This is a complex motif in which groups of three or more closely spaced fingers are arranged radially around a circular central element. In some cases four such groups radiate from the central element (Figure 20s), in other cases only two (Figure 20t) (Moundville Engraved, *variety Hemphill*).

Raptor   This bird characteristically has a forked eye surround, a hooked beak, and a jagged crest. One common variant shows the bird in the round, head in front, tail in back, and wings on the vessel's sides (Figure 20u). When so depicted, the bird is usually right side up; only in one case is the bird inverted, with the body parts hanging from the top of the design field (Figure 52n). An alternative variant shows the raptor's head alone, without the other body parts (Moore 1907:Figures 7–9). Mention should also be made of the peculiar composite illustrated by Moore (1905:Figures 114 and 115), which has a raptor's head connected to an ophidian neck that turns into a wing. The raptor's head may also occur as an element in the paired tails motif (Moundville Engraved, *variety Hemphill*).

Rayed Circle   This consists of concentric circles with triangular elements projecting from the outer circumference (Figure 20v). The motif occurs twice on local Moundville vessels. In one case, the innermost circle contains a Greek cross (Moore 1907:Figures 39 and 40) (Moundville Engraved, *variety Hemphill*).

Scalp   This motif basically consists of a circular element from which depends a line-filled triangular element (Figure 20w). It probably represents a scalp stretched in a hoop (Hudson 1976:251) (Moundville Engraved, *variety Hemphill*).

Skull   This motif appears to be a conventionalized death's head (Figure 20x). In designs, it is usually accompanied by the hand and eye, and/or forearm bones (Moundville Engraved, *variety Hemphill*).

Turtle   The motif depicts what appears to be a turtle as viewed from above (Figure 20y). It occurs on only one vessel (Moundville Engraved, *variety Hemphill*).

Windmill   This motif consists of a circular central element, with at least four crosshatched bars radiating from it horizontally and vertically (Figure 20z and aa). The crosshatch lines within each bar virtually always parallel the dimensions of the bar itself. The windmill could well be semantically a variant of the Greek cross. It also may bear some relationship to the radial fingers motif, since the latter is sometimes drawn superimposed on an element similar to the windmill (Moundville Engraved, *variety Hemphill*).

Winged Serpent   This is one of the most common representational motifs in the Moundville sample, depicting a rattlesnakelike creature with wings (Figure 20bb). Optional features include antlers and a forked eye surround. The tail usually terminates in ophidian rattles, although in rare cases, it is replaced with the tail of a bird. The typical pose shows the creature from the side. Examples also exist presenting the winged serpent in the round, with the head on the front of the vessel, the tail on the back, and the wings on the sides. In such cases, the creature is positioned as if the thorax, which may or may not be actually depicted, passes under the vessel along the base (Moore 1905:Figures 160 and 161, 1907:Figure 56) (Moundville Engraved, *variety Hemphill*).

PAINTED DECORATION

Painted decoration here refers to any kind of deliberate manipulation of surface color, whether by smudging, adding a clay slip, rubbing on pigment, or painting in the strict sense. Exactly how painted decoration enters into the classificatory framework depends a great deal on the apparent origin of the vessel being classified. For local vessels, painted decoration never enters into the definition of types and varieties; rather, painted decorative treatments are counted independently as modes which crosscut types and varieties. The same, however, does not necessarily hold true for nonlocal vessels, which are here generally described with reference to the nomenclature used by archaeologists working in the area where the vessels originate. It is not uncommon for nonlocal types to be defined with painted decoration as a key criterion, and I have made use of such typological designations when appropriate.

The various painted surface treatments found on local vessels are enumerated and briefly defined in the following. A consideration of the technological means by which these colored effects were produced was presented in Chapter 2.

Black Film   This is a black or very dark brown coloring that covers the entire exterior and/or interior surface. The term is limited here to refer to such coloring only when it occurs on a burnished surface (e.g., Figure 4, right).

Red Film   This is a bright red coloring that covers the entire exterior and/or interior of the vessel. The surface may be either burnished or unburnished (Figures 41j and k, 49h, and 56m–p).

White Film   This is white coloring that covers the entire exterior and/or interior of the vessel. The surface is usually burnished (Figures 4, left; 41j and k, 49i and j, and 56j and k).

Red and Black   In this treatment, zones of red coloring occur on a surface that is black filmed everywhere else (Figures 49k and 56l).

Red and White   This treatment consist of zones of red coloring on a surface that is otherwise white. Usually the red pigment is applied directly over the white, but in some cases the red and white colorants are applied separately to different parts of the surface. In most cases, the red pigment is confined to the area of the rim (Figures 51g and o and 62p and q).

Black on White   This term refers to zones of black color appearing on a white-filmed background. In most cases, the black seems to be applied by means of negative painting (Figure 41i).

Red and Black on White   This is a treatment in which a white-surfaced vessel was first painted with zones of red, then later was negative painted in black (Figure 63d).

Red Engraved   This term describes a treatment in which engraved lines are filled with red pigment (Figures 40c, h, i, l, o, and p and 63a and b).

White Engraved   This treatment is like the one just described, except that the engraved lines are filled with white pigment (Figure 40n).

BASIC SHAPES

Most vessel shapes at Moundville are variants of three overarching categories: bottles, bowls, and jars. Also present in the collection are a number of composite and double vessels, whose profiles are, in effect, combinations of two simpler shapes.

In discussing shapes, it is convenient to refer to a set of "characteristic points" that can be recognized in a vessel's profile. These characteristic points are of four kinds: (*a*) end points of the profile, occurring at the base and at the lip; (*b*) points of vertical tangency, which correspond to points of maximum diameter where the profile is concave, and to points of minimum diameter where the profile is convex; (*c*) inflection points where the curvature changes from concave to convex, or vice versa; and (*d*) corner points where there is a sharp change in the profile's contour (Shepard 1956:226). Examples of such points as they occur on bottles, bowls, and jars are shown in Figure 21.

It is also handy to assign names to certain portions of the vessel that can be

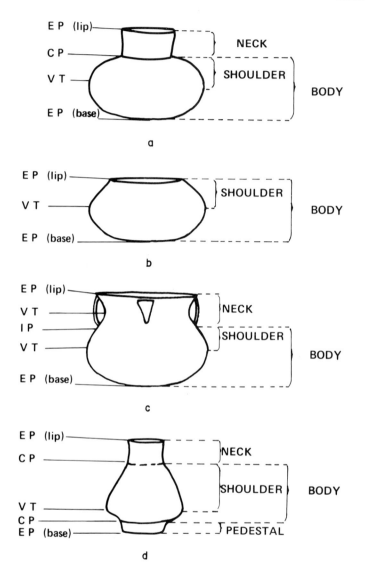

FIGURE 21   Critical points in a vessel profile: (a) bottle, (b) bowl, (c) jar, and (d) bottle with pedestal base. Key: EP, end point; CP, corner point; VT, vertical tangency; and IP, inflection point.)

defined in terms of such points. Generally speaking, the *body* of a vessel is that portion between the base and the highest inflection or corner point; if no such inflection or corner point exists (as is the case with most bowls), then the top of the body is simply defined by the lip. The *neck*, if present, is situated directly above the body and is defined as that portion of the vessel between the highest inflection or corner point and the lip. The *shoulder* is a subdivision of the body, the portion above the point of (convex) vertical tangency. These rules are modified slightly when applied to vessels with a pedestal at the base, in that the lower bound of the body is considered to be the corner or inflection point that defines the top of the pedestal (Figure 21d).

Brief definitions of all the recognized basic shapes in the local complex are now presented under the four general headings mentioned earlier—bottles, bowls, jars, and composite–double shapes.

Throughout the report, individual vessels that do not fit any of the more specific shape categories are described by a more inclusive term, such as "bowl" or "jar."

Bottles

In the most general sense, I take bottles to be vessels that have a distinct body and a more or less vertical neck. Characteristically, the neck is at least a third as high as the body, and the diameter at the rim is less than three fourths of the maximum diameter of the body. The specific kinds that appear are defined as follows.

Cylindrical Bottle   This form has an approximately cylindrical body and a relatively wide neck (Figure 22a).

Narrow-neck Bottle   This is a bottle with a moderately tall, narrow neck, a subglobular body, and an unmodified, rounded base. The neck usually has a gracefully curving biconcave profile, like the so-called "carafe" form (Figure 22b).

Slender Ovoid Bottle   This form has an ovoid "teardrop" body, a pedestal base, and a relatively wide neck of medium height. The maximum diameter of the body is small relative to the total height (Figure 22c).

(Subglobular Bottle)   This term is enclosed in parentheses because I hardly ever use it as a category in itself, without a modifier describing the base. It is listed here separately only for convenience's sake so that I can define it once and thereby avoid repetition. A subglobular bottle is characterized by a globular, ellipsoidal, or wide ovoid body, with the point of vertical tangency situated no higher than midway up the body's height. This sort of bottle always has a wide neck of medium height.

Subglobular Bottle, Pedestal Base   This is a subglobular bottle (see previous definition) whose body rests atop a distinct pedestal. The pedestal base is hollow and is an integral part of the vessel as a container, rather than merely a stand on which the container rests (Figure 22d).

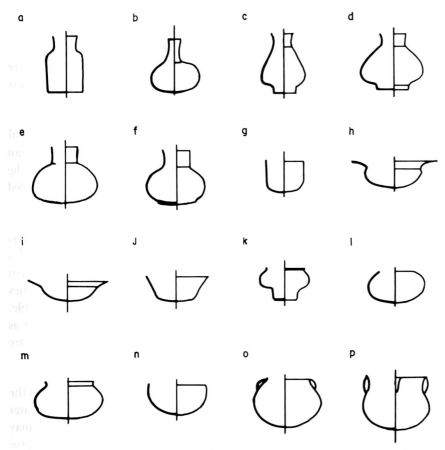

FIGURE 22   Basic shapes: (a) cylindrical bottle, (b) narrow-neck bottle, (c) slender ovoid bottle, (d) subglobular bottle with pedestal base, (e) subglobular bottle with simple base, (f) subglobular bottle with slab base, (g) cylindrical bowl, (h) flaring-rim bowl (deep), (i) flaring-rim bowl (shallow), (j) outslanting bowl, (k) pedestaled bowl, (l) restricted bowl, (m) short-neck bowl, (n) simple bowl, (o) neckless jar, and (p) standard jar.

Subglobular Bottle, Simple Base   The base of this subglobular bottle (see previous definition) is neither visibly thickened on the exterior, nor separated from the rest of the body by a distinct corner or inflection point. Such a base is commonly rounded; sometimes it is flattened, but not sharply enough to create a distinct corner point (Figure 22l).

Subglobular Bottle, Slab Base   This kind of subglobular bottle (see previous definition) has a base that is visibly thickened, but not hollow as is a pedestal base. The slab base always has a distinct edge in profile along the exterior surface. This sort of base is intermediate, morphologically and chronologically, to the pedestal and simple forms, and it grades into both (Figure 22f).

Bowls

Vessels of this category either have no neck at all, or at most a relatively short vertical neck, everted lip, or diagonally flaring rim. The height of bowls typically does not exceed twice their maximum diameter.

Cylindrical Bowl   This is a bowl that has straight, approximately vertical sides in the upper half to two thirds of its profile. By "approximately," I mean that the straight sides do not diverge from the vertical by more than 20°. The lower portion of the body may be cylindrical as well, but usually it is rounded (Figure 22g).

Flaring-Rim Bowl   Bowls in this category have a more or less hemispherical lower portion and a sharply outflaring rim (the latter could be called a "neck" in the strictest sense of our definition, but I prefer not to use the term in this case because of its somewhat misleading connotations). Two subcategories of flaring-rim bowls are recognized, depending on the shape of the profile. Bowls that have a point of vertical tangency on the body are referred to as "deep" (Figure 22h), and those that lack a point of vertical tangency are referred to as "shallow" (Figure 22i).

Outslanting Bowl   This form is marked by relatively straight walls in the upper half to two thirds of its profile, which slant outward at an angle greater than 20° from the vertical. The "relatively straight" portion of the wall may sometimes contain an inflection point, but the degree of curvature is not pronounced. The base of such vessels is generally rounded (Figure 22j).

Pedestaled Bowl   In bowls of this category, the body rests atop a distinct pedestal. The pedestal is hollow and forms an integral part of the vessel as container. Usually, the lip on such vessels is sharply everted, and is either scalloped or notched (Figure 22k).

Restricted Bowl   This kind of bowl has a smoothly curving subglobular profile, whose diameter at the lip is less than three fourths of the maximum diameter of the body (Figure 22l).

Short-Neck Bowl   This form exhibits a subglobular body, a restricted orifice, and a short, vertical neck (Figure 22m).

Simple Bowl   This category includes vessels that have an approximately hemispherical profile, without inflection or corner points. The lip diameter must be greater than three fourths of the maximum diameter; on simple bowls that lack a point of vertical tangency, the lip diameter is equivalent to the maximum diameter (Figure 22n).

Terraced Rectanguloid Bowl These are perhaps the most unusual forms at Moundville; Moore was so unsure of how to categorize one he found that he chose to call it an "object of earthenware" rather than a vessel (1907:357). As the name implies, these bowls are rectangular, and have a terraced or castellated rim (Figure 63c–e; Moore 1907:Figures 22 and 23). Usually, the rim on one side of the vessel is lower than it is on the other three sides. A total of six such bowls have turned up at Moundville, and only two are known from sites elsewhere: one example was found at Smith Plantation on the Big Black River in Mississippi (Ford 1936:121–122), and another was quite recently excavated at the Lubbub site on the central Tombigbee (C. S. Peebles, personal communication).

Jars

These are vessels that have a more or less globular body, and a wide neck that is constricted in profile. The neck is typically less than one third of the height of the body, and the minimum diameter of the neck is no less than three fourths of the maximum diameter of the body. Jars in the present sample almost always exhibit two or more handles in the area of the neck.

(Burnished Jar) This is not strictly speaking a basic shape category, but I often use it as though it were, and so it seems reasonable to define it here. The label refers to any jar that has a burnished surface finish, as distinct from a jar in which the surface is smoothed but not burnished (Figures 46f and 54m). Making this distinction is useful in several respects, prime among them being the fact that burnished jars tend to exhibit strongly contrasting stylistic features as compared to unburnished ones. For example, burnished jars are usually black filmed, never have more than two handles, and often exhibit beaded rims or frog effigy features. Unburnished jars, in contrast, are usually not filmed, often have four or more handles, and generally lack effigy features. There is also a major functional difference, in that black-filmed burnished jars were certainly not designed for cooking, whereas unburnished jars probably were (see p. 33 ff.). Leaving aside the attribute of surface finish, most burnished jars have the basic shape of a standard jar (see subsequent definition).

Neckless Jar The name of this category may be a bit misleading, because such jars do indeed have a neck as defined by an inflection point below the lip. What sets these jars apart from other categories is that the neck never reaches a point of vertical tangency; in other words, the tangent to the profile slants inward at the lip (Figure 20o). Although all the neckless jars in the Moundville sample are too fragmentary to show positively the number of handles, it seems unlikely that they generally had more than two, given their chronological position within the sequence (see Chapter 4).

Standard Jar   The distinguishing characteristic of this jar form is that the neck slants outward at the lip. Thus, either the neck is concave in profile and has a point of vertical tangency, or else the neck is approximately straight and leans outward from a corner point at the top of the body (Figure 22p). Unburnished standard jars can have two, four, eight, or even more handles, depending largely on the chronological phase during which they were made.

Composite and Double Shapes

Under this heading fall vessels which are made by compounding a pair of simpler basic shapes. Composite vessels are those in which one shape is portrayed resting on or partly inserted in another. Double vessels consist of two shapes joined side by side.

Composite Bowl   This vessel in profile appears to consist of one bowl set on top of another (Figures 46g and 62k). There are three such whole vessels in the collection.

Composite Bowl–Jar   This shape is built to look as though a bowl had been set on top of a jar (Figure 46c). In the sample of whole vessels, this form occurs only once.

Composite Jar–Bowl   This vessel in profile appears to be a jar set on top of a bowl. Only one occurs in the collection.

Double Bowl   This vessel consists of two bowls connected to each other side by side. There are five double bowls in the collection: one consisting of attached simple bowls (Figure 51k), one of cylindrical bowls (WP71), one of rectanguloid bowls (SW21), and two effigies in which each half resembles a mussel shell (EE82, SWG67).

SECONDARY SHAPE FEATURES

Under this heading are described some simple elaborations of form that appear on Moundville vessels. Obviously, it is not possible to list every feature of this kind, since the number of idiosyncratic variations in form that one could seize upon and describe is endless. The secondary shape features enumerated below were selected either because they seem to show significant time-dependence, or because they are distinctive enough to be useful in drawing comparisons with assemblages elsewhere.

Appliqué Neck Fillets This is a form of modeled decoration in which strips of clay are applied to the neck area of a standard jar. The strips are placed vertically or obliquely, and are closely spaced around the neck's circumference (Figures 59t and 62r).

Band of Nodes This feature consists of a series of closely-spaced nodes arranged in a horizontal band around a vessel's circumference. It appears on the shoulder of one burnished jar (Figure 62j), four restricted bowls, and just below the lip of one simple bowl.

Beaded Rim This term refers to a notched appliqué band, positioned horizontally on the rim just below the lip (Figures 44g, j, and k; 46c, f, and g; 49d and e; 51f–k; 54m; and 58f–j). Usually, the band completely encircles the circumference; the only consistent exception is found on fish effigy bowls, where the notched appliqué band depicts the dorsal fin and therefore continues only partway around the vessel. The beaded rim is a very common feature on simple bowls and burnished jars.

Beaded Shoulder This refers to a notched appliqué band placed horizontally well below the lip, usually at the point of maximum diameter on a restricted bowl (Figures 41c, 46h and i, 51c, and 62m). The feature may occur independently (<M>13), or it may be found as an integral part of most alligator and turtle effigies, and even of a few fish effigies in which the dorsal fin has been placed farther than usual below the lip. There is one bottle in the collection that has a beaded shoulder, but it is so unusual in shape that it could well be an import (<M>4).

Cutout Rim This feature is found on certain pedestaled bowls where the lip is not horizontal, but is broken up by a series of cutouts in the rim. The cutouts may be terrace-shaped, V-shaped, or keyhole-shaped. This feature is invariably accompanied by a lowered lip (see subsequent definition) on one side of the bowl. Two examples are known from Moundville (Figure 63f; Moore 1905:Figure 76), and one from Bessemer (DeJarnette and Wimberly 1941: Figure 67).

Downturned Lugs These are lugs placed at the lip of a standard jar that are tilted downward at the same angle as the tops of the handles and are also the same width as the tops of the handles. Such lugs alternate with handles around the circumference of the rim. The feature occurs twice on jars with two handles (Figure 54j) and twice on jars with four handles (Figure 54c and h).

Folded Rim This is a jar rim that is folded over to the exterior, and thereby thickened. The lip on such a rim is rounded (Figures 39m; 41o; 42h and m; 43m–p, and u; and 60a). Although this feature is quite common in sherd collections from Moundville, it occurs only twice on our whole vessels. The reason for this discrepancy is mainly chronological: the feature is diagnostic of the Moundville I phase, a time from which we have very few gravelots at the site.

Folded-Flattened Rim   This sort of rim not only is thickened by folding or adding a coil to the exterior, but also is distinctly flattened at the lip. The flat lip may be either horizontal or beveled to the interior (Figure 43v and w). In the Moundville sherd collections, this feature is found on unburnished standard jars and neckless jars. It also commonly occurs on sherds at Bessemer (DeJarnette and Wimberly 1941:Figure 66, top). None of the jars in our whole vessel sample have a folded-flattened rim, but again this lack is probably due to the fact that we have very few gravelots dating to the time during which this feature was popular (Moundville I phase).

Gadrooning   This is a form of modeled decoration in which the body of the vessel is vertically fluted at regular intervals around the circumference. There is one gadrooned bottle from a gravelot at Moundville (Figure 44m), and another from Bessemer (DeJarnette and Wimberly 1941:Figure 65), but it is difficult to be sure whether they are in fact local. The only other place where gadrooning occurs with any frequency is in and around the Cairo Lowland of southeast Missouri. However, our Alabama specimens differ radically in shape from the typical Cairo Lowland bottles, thereby depriving us of the only known alternative source.

Grouped Nodes   These Nodes are placed in a horizontal band around the vessel, but are not uniformly spaced; rather, the nodes are clustered in groups, the groups themselves (usually four in all) being widely spaced from each other. At Moundville, this feature occurs on the shoulder of one burnished jar (Rw480, see Figure 41b), one restricted bowl, and on the rims of five simple bowls. Grouped nodes also occur on the shoulder of a pedestaled subglobular bottle from the Lubbub site (Jenkins 1981:Figure 63).

Handles   Handles are common appendages on the necks of jars; the top of the handle is typically attached at or just below the lip, and the bottom is attached to the shoulder (Figures 39l and m, 43q–s, 46a–e, 48h–k, 50h and i, 54a–o, 57a–d, 59p–r, 60c, and 63i and k). Handles tend to be equidistantly spaced around the circumference, and the total number on any given jar is almost invariably a multiple of 2. The numbers of handles, as well as their shape, are both good chronological indicators, but discussion of this must be deferred to Chapter 4. Among the burnished jars at Moundville, 21 have 2 handles and 4 have no handles. Among the unburnished jars, 60 have 2 handles, 56 have 4 handles, 1 has 5 handles, 12 have 8 handles, and 4 have more than 8 handles, the actual number ranging from 12 to 24.

Indentations   These are round shallow indentations, about 1–3 cm in diameter, placed in the vessel wall. Thirty-six local bottles in the whole vessel sample have indentations on the body; any given bottle can exhibit as few as 4, spaced equidistantly around the plane of maximum diameter, or as many as 27, arranged around the body in several tiers (Figures 45e, f, h, and j; 52e and o; 63g and h). Bowls sometimes have indentations as well. One cylindrical bowl has a simple indentation on the base (Figure 44f), and one simple bowl exhibits 4 indentations on its sides (NE38).

Lowered Lip   This is a feature of certain bowls on which a portion of the lip dips downward forming a kind of window in one side of the vessel. The inventory of lowered lips at Moundville is as follows: four terraced rectanguloid bowls (Figure 63c–e, Moore 1907:Figure 22), and four pedestaled bowls (Figure 63f; Moore 1905:Figures 76 and 135). This feature is also found on a pedestaled bowl from Bessemer (DeJarnette and Wimberly 1941:Figure 67). Interestingly, on all these vessels, the lip not in the lowered portion is always somehow elaborated by means of terraces, cutouts, notches, or nodes.

Notched Everted Lip   This term describes a bowl lip that is turned abruptly upward and/or outward and is notched along the top (Figure 53f; Moore 1907:Figure 15). The feature occurs on six pedestaled bowls, two restricted bowls, two simple bowls, and one miniature cylindrical bowl.

Notched lip   This is a lip that is notched, but not necessarily everted (see the description of the notched everted lip). Among the whole vessels that appear to be local, a notched lip is found on two flaring-rim bowls (Figure 53j) and three simple bowls. The feature turns up in our sherd tallies as well (Table 21 and Figures 47f and 58l). All in all, notched lips occur on imported vessels much more often then they do on local ones at Moundville.

Opposing Lugs   This feature consists of two lugs placed on opposite sides of a bowl, projecting horizontally outward from the lip. Two possibly local vessels at Moundville have this feature, an outslanting bowl and a simple bowl. The lugs on the latter vessel (NE54) are elaborated with vertical ridges, and the vessel itself may have been intended as an effigy of some sort.

Scalloped Rim   This is a feature of flaring-rim bowls, on which the rim is elaborated by a continuous series of round projections. A scalloped rim occurs only once among our whole vessels (NE89), but turns up with greater frequency in the sherd collections (Table 21 and Figures 41d and e and 58n).

Single Lug   This term describes a broad horizontal lug that projects outward from the lip of a bowl with no other appendages (Figures 44a–c, and 53m, n, and p). A single lug is most commonly associated with cylindrical bowls (28 occurrences), and less often with simple bowls (13 occurrences).

Spouts This term refers to the presence of two spoutlike appendages added to the rim of a bowl, projecting outward on opposite sides of the vessel. Thus, when viewed from above, the lip is roughly ogival in outline. The four occurrences at Moundville are all on simple bowls (Figure 44j).

Vertical Lugs This feature consists of vertically oriented and elongated lugs that are applied to the exterior of a bowl, widely spaced, and positioned a short distance below the lip. The sole occurrence at Moundville is on a fragment from a bowl (NE461), which, judging from its decoration, was probably made in late Moundville III times.

Widely Spaced Nodes This is a treatment in which appliqué nodes are placed individually at wide equidistant intervals around the circumference of a bowl or jar. Usually there are four such nodes on any given vessel, but one can find examples with as few as two or as many as six. On jars and restricted bowls, the nodes are placed on the shoulder, at or just above the point of maximum diameter; on simple bowls, the nodes are generally a short distance below the lip. The tally of whole vessels in the Moundville sample is as follows: nine simple bowls (Figures 44h–j and 46k), one restricted bowl (Moore 1905: Figure 150), one pedestaled bowl, seven burnished jars (Figure 54m; Moore 1905:Figure 155), and three unburnished standard jars (Figure 63i–k). All the unburnished jars with the feature are decorated with incised arches (Moundville Incised), the nodes being positioned at the points where adjacent arches meet.

EFFIGY FEATURES

Effigy features are, in a sense, secondary shape features too. The only excuse for treating them separately is that effigies in many cases are made up of several different kinds of secondary shape features, appearing together on a single vessel. A fish effigy bowl, for example, may have appropriately modeled adornos to depict the head and tail, simple nodes to depict the ventral fins, and a beaded rim for its dorsal fin. Thus, we are here concerned just as much with how particular features are combined, as we are with what those features consist of.

Speaking in general terms, there are two sorts of effigy vessels at Moundville. One sort is the lug-and-rim-effigy bowl, made by adding two complementary appendages to the rim of a bowl, usually a simple bowl. On one side of such vessels is an adorno depicting a head, which projects upward from the lip; on the opposite side is a horizontal lug, which projects outward from the lip. Apart from these appendages, the basic shape of the bowl remains unaltered. The second sort of effigy vessel can be called, for lack of a better term, the structural type. Rather than having the appendages stuck to the rim, such effigies consist of various features applied to and modeled in the vessel wall. In certain cases the degree of modeling is extensive enough to fundamentally alter the vessel's basic shape.

Some effigies represent their subjects with enough detail to make them easily recognizable, and these are easy to name. Others, however, are so conventionalized (or incompetently done) that identification of their subject matter is considerably less reliable. Of course, such trifling impediments have never deterred archaeologists from attaching labels anyway. I have long suspected that the "identification" of the more obscure Mississippian effigy forms generally tells us more about the archaeologists' imagination than it does about the Native Americans'. The upshot is that none of the names with which I refer to effigy forms should be taken too literally, since many are just convenient guesses. Where there is considerable doubt about the validity of the guess, the effigy label is followed parenthetically with a question mark.

Alligator(?)   This effigy form is constructed by placing two conical protrusions of similar dimensions on opposite sides of the vessel. One protrusion represents the head and is endowed with eyes and sometimes a mouth. The second protrusion is presumably the tail. A notched appliqué band runs completely around the vessel's shoulder and onto the protrusions; perhaps this is meant to convey the impression of the jagged scales around the edge of the alligator's back. A notched appliqué strip is also added to the top of the tail and (usually) to the head, running from the vessel wall to the tip of the protrusion. This effigy type occurs three times at Moundville—once each on a simple bowl, a restricted bowl (Figure 62m), and a burnished jar without handles (Moore 1905:Figure 69).

Beaver   This effigy is constructed by adding adornos representing the head, legs, and tail to the sides of a bowl. The beaver is depicted gnawing on a stick that is being held in its front two paws. This sort of effigy is found once on a simple bowl (Figure 51d) and once on a restricted bowl.

Bird   This is by far the most common representative at Moundville of the lug-and-rim-effigy bowl, the modeled head being that of a bird. In most cases, there is good reason to believe that the bird is a duck, but the level of detail in the depiction is seldom enough to warrant certainty. Two variant forms of the head adorno occur on these bowls: One is a "flat" variant, which is highly conventionalized, rarely has a distinct neck, and exhibits a two-dimensional quality that can be described as a "cookie-cutter" appearance (13 occurrences) (Figures 39e and f and 63l; McKenzie 1966:Figure 11c; Moore 1905:Figure 51). The second variant is the "gracile" form, which tends to be a bit more naturalistic in execution, usually has a distinct neck, and shows its modeled features in three dimensions (six occurrences) (Figures 51a and 62l; McKenzie 1966:Figure 11a). These two variants of the bird effigy adorno also tend to

TABLE 9
Cross-tabulation of Head Form versus Orientation on Effigy Bowls

	Form		
Orientation	Flat	Gracile	Total
Inward	10	0	10
Outward	3	6	9
Total	13	6	19

differ in how they are oriented on the rim. Most of the flat heads face inward, whereas all of the gracile heads face outward (Table 9). As will be discussed in Chapter 4, this variation is mostly related to time, the flat, inward-facing heads being early, and the gracile, outward-facing heads being late. It is worthwhile noting that most of the lug-and-rim-effigy bowls with the head adorno now missing were probably bird effigies to start with; in at least two cases we can be certain of it, since the bowls have incised wings depicted on the sides (WP153, WP218) (Figure 39i).

Conch Shell   This is a structural effigy, characteristically a modified bowl. A circular or semicircular arrangement of nodes is placed on one side to represent the spire, and a spoutlike projection is modeled in or applied to the opposite side to represent the "beak" or tip of the shell (Figure 39h; Moore 1905:Figure 94). There are five such bowls in our sample of whole vessels, and one fragment from the excavations north of Mound R (Figure 41g).

Feline(?)   This is a lug-and-rim-effigy form that occurs only once in our sample (Figure 62q). The outward-facing head has a slightly upturned snout and what may be a snarling mouth, highly conventionalized; the lug is made to look like a tail that curls upward into a spiral. A sherd from Moundville that depicts a similar head has been illustrated by Holmes (1903:Plate 58f).

Fish   Fish effigies are built by adding a modeled head to one side of the vessel, and a modeled tail to the other. The two remaining sides are taken up by fins: the dorsal fin is represented by an appliqué band, usually notched, and the ventral fins are usually depicted with appliqué nodes. When the vessel is standing upright, the fish appears to be lying on its side. Among local vessels, such features are found on 10 simple bowls, 7 restricted bowls, (Figure 51c), 1 composite bowl (Figure 62k), one burnished jar, and two bottles (Moore 1907: Figure 26).

Frog   Unmistakable effigies of this creature are among the most common at Moundville. The head is modeled or applied on one side of the vessel, and often a small node or dimple on the opposite side suggests the derrière. The legs are depicted on the remaining sides of the vessel by applying strips of clay. Local frog effigies were usually made from burnished jars (11 occurrences) (Figure 51b; McKenzie 1966:Figure 14, and Moore 1905:Figure 78), and occur less commonly on restricted or simple bowls (2 occurrences), and bottles (3 occurrences) (Moore 1907:Figure 30).

Frog Heads   This effigy form occurs twice on bowls, and consists of four frog heads applied to or modeled in the vessel wall at equal intervals around the circumference.

Human-Head Medallions   This term refers to medallions of clay modeled in the form of human heads, which are then applied to the vessel wall. Among the vessels that have this feature, those which may be locally made are all simple bowls with a beaded rim (six occurrences) (Figure 51g). Each bowl has four medallions at or just below the lip, spaced at equal intervals around the circumference. Given the great frequency with which beaded rim bowls occur in our sample, it is reasonable for now to regard those with human-head medallions as local. However, one should also note that virtually identical "medallion" bowls are a common item in Tennessee (Lewis and Kneberg 1946:Plate 54; Myer 1928:Plate 115a; Thruston 1890:Figure 58, Plate VIII), raising the possibility that some, if not all, of the Moundville specimens may be imports.

Mammal, Unidentified   This designation is applied to bowls of the lug-and-rim-effigy type, when the identity of the mammalian creature whose head is depicted is unclear. Effigies of this sort have at times been called "bat" and "bear", to which list one could add squirrel and beaver as equally good possibilities. The features are simply not distinctive enough to be sure. In two cases, the heads are inward-facing (SWM95 [McKenzie 1966:Figure 13b], WP160), and in one case, it is outward-facing (SED7). The last vessel is highly unusual in that it has a modeled, apronlike collar that extends from the lug to the effigy head along each side of the rim (Figure 62n). The collar seems to be part of the effigy, but what it was meant to represent is unclear.

Mussel Shell   This effigy consists of a bowl modeled into the shape of a mussel shell (Figure 46j). In five cases, only a single valve is represented; in two cases, a pair of valves are joined at the hinge, forming a double bowl (McKenzie 1966:Figure 13).

Shell Spoon   This is a bowl that has a notched lug on one side and is modeled into the shape of a shell spoon. It occurs only once in the sample. The real shell spoons, of which this is a ceramic imitation, were typically made from the shell of a freshwater bivalve (see Peebles 1979:Figure IV-25; Thruston 1890:Figure 219).

Turtle   This effigy is made from a bowl, to the shoulder of which have been added a modeled head, a tail, and a notched appliqué band (Figure 46h and i). The notched appliqué band is positioned horizontally at the level of the head and tail, and probably is intended to represent the edge of the carapace. When the bowl is upright, so is the turtle. There are five such vessels in the sample—four restricted bowls and one simple bowl, the latter unusual in that it lacks the notched appliqué band (SD855).

Turtle(?), inverted   Here is a form so conventionalized that calling it an effigy may just be wishful thinking. It is made by adding six horizontally projecting lugs to the rim of a single bowl. The lugs are not equidistantly spaced, but arranged in such a way that they could conceivably represent the head, tail, and legs of a turtle. When the bowl is inverted, the alleged turtle is upright, with the bottom of the bowl as the carapace. The lugs on our one vessel (NE451) hardly look turtlelike in any way. The only reason to suspect that they are, in fact, effigy features lies in their uneven, but bilaterally symmetrical spacing, which is analogous to that of the more realistic adornos that are found on inverted turtle effigies in Tennessee (Thruston 1890:Figure 57).

Also present in the Moundville sample are a number of (presumably) local effigy vessels that cannot be categorized by any of the terms described here. Some are simply too fragmentary for identification, as is the case with 17 lug-and-rim-effigy bowls and 1 restricted bowl that was originally a structural effigy of some sort (SEH88). A few others defy pigeonholing despite the fact that they are complete: one is a miniature bird effigy bowl with a head attached to the vessel wall below the level of the lip (SED3); three more are unique effigy forms whose subjects are too conventionalized for easy recognition (Moore 1905:Figures 12, 79, and 108).

4

Ceramic Chronology

The late prehistoric chronology in the Black Warrior drainage is schematically set forth in Figure 23. Here we are concerned only with the span of time between A.D. 900 and 1700, beginning with the terminal phase in the Late Woodland period, and lasting through the Mississippi period up until the onset of European colonization. The period names on the left side of the diagram correspond to those advocated more than thirty years ago by Griffin (1946), which have by now become entrenched (with minor variations) in the archaeological vernacular throughout the eastern United States. On the right side of the diagram are the five phases that can currently be recognized within this span. The first and last of these phases—West Jefferson and Alabama River, respectively—were already defined as culture–historical units at the time the present study began; therefore, we will here only briefly review the content of their known ceramic complexes. It is the definition and chronological placement of the middle three phases—Moundville I–III—to which the greater part of this chapter is devoted.

Before moving to a discussion of the gravelot seriation and the stratigraphic evidence on which the middle portion of the sequence is based, let us briefly characterize the ceramics that were manufactured during the two phases previously defined.

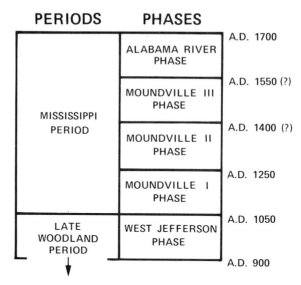

FIGURE 23   Late prehistoric chronology in the Black Warrior drainage.

West Jefferson Phase   This phase was first recognized by Jenkins, on the basis of material excavated from three small sites on the Locust Fork of the Black Warrior River, west of Birmingham (Jenkins and Nielsen 1974). Later reanalysis of the same material (O'Hear 1975), along with the excavation of another component in the upper reaches of the Cahaba drainage (Ensor 1979), has also helped refine our understanding of this phase.

The ceramic complex consists almost entirely of undecorated grog-tempered pottery, classified as Baytown Plain, *variety Roper* (Figure 67c–h[1]). The very few decorated grog-tempered sherds (usually less than 1%) most often fall into the types Mulberry Creek Cord-Marked, *variety Aliceville* (Figure 67b), Alligator Incised, *variety Geiger* (Figure 67a), and Benson Punctate, *variety unspecified* (see Jenkins 1981 for a discussion of these ceramic types vis-à-vis the temporally equivalent Gainesville phase on the central Tombigbee). Recognizable vessel shapes include bowls and jars, but not bottles. Many of the jars were made in the standard form with two handles—virtually identical in shape to the shell-tempered Moundville I phase examples. The handles themselves tend to be parallel-sided and relatively thick.

Traces of shell-tempered pottery sometimes turn up in West Jefferson phase contexts as well. Among the types found are Mississippi Plain, *variety Warrior,* and Moundville Incised, *variety Carrollton.* As might be expected, the appearance of shell-tempered sherds in otherwise Woodland contexts has engendered a debate between those who would see in them evidence for the

[1]Figures 39–67 are collected in the vessel and sherd illustration section on pp. 175–225.

in-migration of Mississippian peoples (e.g., Jenkins 1976a), and those who would regard them simply as evidence that local potters were beginning to experiment with new techniques (e.g., Peebles 1978b). For present purposes only two things need to be stressed. First, the kinds of West Jefferson contexts in which shell-tempered sherds have been found strongly imply that these sherds are indeed in situ, and are not there simply as a result of stratigraphic mixture whether aboriginal or recent. Second, it appears that in the Warrior drainage the wholesale adoption of shell tempering by the local potters was an extremely abrupt process. In West Jefferson contexts, however late, rarely more than 2% of the sherds contain shell temper, but in the immediately following Moundville I phase, virtually 100% of the sherds contain shell.

Ten good radiocarbon determinations have been obtained on the West Jefferson contexts found at four different sites, and these dates are summarized in Table 10. The dates range from A.D. 875 to 1065, suggesting a span for the phase of about A.D. 900–1050.

By statistically analyzing the radiocarbon dates from 1Je31, 1Je32, and 1Je33, O'Hear (1975:26–27) was able to identify certain changes in the ceramic assemblage through time. He calculated a weighted average of A.D. 1014±30 (corrected) for those contexts that contained shell-tempered pottery, versus A.D. 928±43 (corrected) for those that did not, suggesting that pottery tempered solely with shell did not appear in the complex until after about A.D. 1000. The one pit at 1Je34 that yielded a date of A.D. 900±60 did, however, contain a single shell-and-grog-tempered sherd, indicating that such mixed paste compositions may have come into use somewhat earlier (Ensor 1979:8, Figure 13d).

Alabama River Phase   The Alabama River phase, which comes after Moundville III, was first named and formally defined by Cottier (1970), and

TABLE 10
West Jefferson Phase Radiocarbon Dates

Site	Laboratory number	Date[1]	Reference
1Je32	UGa-625	A.D. 1060±60	Jenkins and Nielsen 1974:156
1Je31	UGa-649	A.D. 1060±75	Jenkins and Nielsen 1974:155
1Je33	UGa-611	A.D. 1005±70	Jenkins and Nielsen 1974:158
1Je33	UGa-612	A.D. 1005±70	Jenkins and Nielsen 1974:158
1Je32	UGa-624	A.D. 965±65	Jenkins and Nielsen 1974:156
1Je33	UGa-610	A.D. 995±65	Jenkins and Nielsen 1974:157
1Je33	UGa-609	A.D. 945±60	Jenkins and Nielsen 1974:157
1Je32	UGa-633	A.D. 900±60	Jenkins and Nielsen 1974:157
1Je34	—	A.D. 900±60	Ensor 1979:8
1Je31	UGa-652	A.D. 875±70	Jenkins and Nielsen 1974:156

[1] Dates (uncorrected) are based on a 5568-year half-life.

later described in more detail by Sheldon (1974). Curren's very recent fieldwork in the Black Warrior Valley, much of it still unpublished, has also contributed a great deal to our understanding of the phase (Curren and Little n.d.). Though its formally defined status is relatively new, the phase has been recognized informally since the turn of the century, when it was simply referred to as the "burial urn culture" of central and southern Alabama (e.g., Moore 1899).

In terms of the present typology, the Alabama River phase ceramic complex includes Mississippi Plain, *variety Warrior* and Bell Plain, *variety Hale* as its principal undecorated wares; among the decorated wares are Carthage Incised, *varieties Carthage, Poole,* and *Fosters,* Barton Incised, *variety Demopolis* (Figure 56i), along with a number of distinctive variants of Alabama River Incised (Figures 56h and 62r), Carthage Incised, and Moundville Engraved (Figure 62o), to which formal variety names have not yet been assigned. Common vessel forms include simple bowls, flaring-rim bowls (both shallow and deep), short-neck bowls, and subglobular bottles with simple bases. Standard jars are common, generally with at least 4 handles, and often more than 10. Jars that lack apparently functional handles are often embellished with stylized handles, consisting of appliqué fillets or pinched-up ridges of clay, closely spaced and positioned vertically or obliquely on the rim. Black filming is present but decidedly less common than in the preceding phases. Vessels painted red and white are found in the complex as well.

The only radiocarbon dates for this phase are a few mid-sixteenth and seventeenth century determinations recently obtained by Curren on his sites in the Warrior Valley (Curren and Little n.d.:Table 11, passim). In round numbers, a reasonable span for this phase would seem to be A.D. 1550–1700. At present, our absolute dating is not refined enough to say for sure whether the DeSoto dateline of 1540 fell within the late Moundville III or the early Alabama River phase; suffice it to say that it must have fallen very close to the transition between the two.

GRAVELOT SERIATION

Gravelots are ideal archaeological units with which to construct a temporal seriation. For one thing, gravelots represent events in time of short, and approximately equivalent duration, and so it is eminently reasonable to try to order them serially, without worrying a great deal about problems of overlap and differing spans through time. Second, inasmuch as the artifactual associations within graves are relatively free from the ambiguities inherent in stratigraphically mixed deposits, a sequence of such "closed finds" usually provides a reliable framework on which a detailed ceramic chronology can be based.

With regard to the data from Moundville, three procedural questions had to be resolved before the analysis could proceed: (*a*) which gravelots should be selected for the analysis? (*b*) on which ceramic attributes within the gravelots should the seriation be based? and (*c*) by what method should the sequencing of the gravelots be accomplished? Our solutions to these questions are described in the following sections.

Choice of Gravelots and Ceramic Attributes

It is best to discuss the procedures used in selecting gravelots and attributes under the same heading, since, as will soon become apparent, the two kinds of choices were somewhat interdependent. In each case, selectivity was dictated not only by the requirements of the method, but also by a desire for efficiency in the analysis.

To begin with, I decided to consider only those gravelots that contained at least two vessels on which we had recorded data. Such gravelots tended to exhibit much more stylistic information than gravelots with only a single vessel; adding single-vessel gravelots to the seriated sample would have greatly increased the trouble involved in the analysis, without materially improving the result.

The prime criterion in choosing attributes on which to base the sequencing was that they be chronologically sensitive (i.e., that they exhibit a consistent pattern of change through time within the period encompassed by our sample). Such attributes were initially identified by doing a "quick-and-dirty" seriation by hand. Photographs of all the vessels found in each gravelot were placed in a separate row, and the rows were arranged and rearranged on a (very, very large) tabletop until some consistent patterns of stylistic change were discerned. It was on the basis of this initial attempt that a preliminary article on the Moundville chronology was written (Steponaitis 1980).

In looking for chronologically sensitive attributes, and indeed in all aspects of producing the final seriation, obvious nonlocal vessels were excluded from consideration. This strategy was adopted as a precaution against violating the assumption of smooth stylistic change on which the validity of seriation depends. Since there was no guarantee that stylistic developments in neighboring regions proceeded in step with those at Moundville, the inclusion of foreign vessels had the potential of introducing serious errors in sequencing.

Once a preliminary list of chronologically sensitive attributes was formalized, each of the selected gravelots was examined in turn, and the attributes were recorded as being either present or absent. Any gravelot that did not have at least two of these attributes present was discarded, since such a gravelot would have contributed little chronological information in the final analysis. For the most part, attributes present in fewer than five gravelots were also eliminated, again for the sake of computational efficiency. The process of discarding gravelots and eliminating attributes was repeated several times in succession, until a "stable" configuration was reached in which no gravelot had fewer than two attributes present, and no attribute (with some exceptions) was present in fewer than five gravelots. Exception to the latter rule of thumb was made in the case of three attributes that seemed to appear only in the very earliest or the very latest gravelots, since without these attributes, the two extreme ends of the sequence would not have been represented in the seriation at all.

The resulting data set contained 87 gravelots of vessels (Figure 25, left column), characterized by 24 chronologically sensitive attributes of shape,

TABLE 11
Chronologically Sensitive Attributes Used in Seriation[1]

Types and varieties
    (17) Carthage Incised, *Summerville*
    (18) Moundville Engraved, *Havana*
    (15) Moundville Engraved, *Northport*
    (14) Moundville Engraved, *Taylorville*
    (16) Moundville Engraved, *Tuscaloosa*
    (13) Moundville Engraved, *Wiggins* or
        Carthage Incised, *Carthage*[2]

Representational motifs
    (22) Hand and eye
    (21) Paired tails
    (20) Winged serpent

Painted decoration
    (19) Red and white

Basic shapes
    (1) Cylindrical bowl
    (2) Short-neck bowl
    (3) Flaring-rim bowl (deep)
    (4) Slender ovoid bottle
    (5) Subglobular bottle, pedestal base
    (6) Subglobular bottle, slab base
    (7) Subglobular bottle, simple base
    (8) Burnished jar
    (23) Standard jar (unburnished, 8 or more handles)

Secondary shape features
    (9) Beaded rim
    (10) Widely spaced nodes (bowl, burnished jar)
    (11) Indentations

Effigy features
    (12) Lug-and-rim-effigy (inward facing)
    (24) Fish effigy

  [1] Numbers in parentheses correspond to the attribute designations used in the seriation diagrams (Figures 24, 25, and 26).
  [2] These two varieties were combined for the purposes of seriation because they exhibit exactly the same design motif, differing only in the width of the line with which the motif is executed.

design, and painted decoration (Table 11). It was this data set to which the numerical seriation method was applied.

Numerical Seriation

The numerical seriation of gravelots was accomplished using an elegant method devised by Cowgill (1972), which is especially suited for presence–absence data sets in which the number of attributes is considerably less than the number of gravelots to be sequenced. The method involves three steps:

1. A symmetric matrix of distance coefficients between attributes is computed using a coefficient that estimates the relative separation of these attributes in time, based on their degree of cooccurrence in gravelots.
2. Based on the distance coefficients calculated in step 1, the attributes are scaled (nonmetrically) in a two-dimensional space, and the dimension that corresponds to the passage of time is isolated. The relative positions of the attributes along this temporal dimension can then be measured.
3. With reference to the relative temporal positions of the attributes estimated in step 2, a "best-fit" or most probable position for each gravelot is computed based on the attributes present within it. When the gravelots are ordered according to this "best-fit" criterion, the sequencing has been achieved.

The procedures involved in each of these three steps will now be described, as will the results of their application to the data at hand. I will deliberately keep discussion of the mathematical end of things short, going into only as much detail as is necessary for the reader to get a basic understanding of the results. Anyone interested in the fine points of, and the justification for, the mathematical techniques employed is strongly urged to read Cowgill's own lucid exposition (1972).

The distance coefficient computed in the first step of the process is based on a model that conceives of each attribute as having a chronological range, which range can be characterized in terms of a midpoint and an overall span. If we have an ideal set of gravelots, attributes of which could be seriated perfectly into vertical columns without gaps (as they are in Figure 26 on p. 91), the span of an attribute could be thought of as the number of gravelots in which it occurs, and the degree of overlap between the spans of any two attributes could be thought of as the number of gravelots in which both attributes occur together. By means of a rather lengthy logical argument, Cowgill (1972:399–406) has shown that one can calculate a useful index of "distance" between the midpoints of any two attributes, by taking into account their total span and their degree of overlap—both of which can be estimated prior to actually seriating the gravelots. One begins by determining four simple quantities: A_{ij} is the number of gravelots in which attributes i and j occur together; B_{ij} is the number of gravelots in which i occurs but not j; C_{ij} is the number of gravelots in which j occurs but not i; and G is the total number of gravelots. One can then calculate the distance between the midpoints of the two attributes (W_{ij}) as follows:

$$\begin{aligned} W_{ij} &= 0 \quad \text{if either } B_{ij} = 0 \text{ or } C_{ij} = 0 \\ W_{ij} &= 1 \quad \text{if } A_{ij} = 0; \\ W_{ij} &= (B_{ij} + C_{ij})/G \text{ otherwise.} \end{aligned} \quad (1)$$

If the two attributes do not overlap (i.e., cooccur) at all, then the distance coefficient takes on a value of 1. If the overlap is complete (i.e., the presence of one attribute is always accompanied by the presence of the other), then the distance coefficient becomes 0. And if the overlap is partial (i.e., each attribute occurs sometimes, but not always, without the other), then the coefficient takes on values that are intermediate between 0 and 1.

After the distance coefficients are calculated, the next step in the procedure is to arrange the attributes (or their midpoints in time) into a plausible relative sequence. To accomplish this, Cowgill's method relies on a well-established mathematical technique called nonmetric multidimensional scaling, which, though computationally intricate, can be accomplished easily with the aid of a computer (Guttman 1968; Kruskal 1964a, 1964b; Lingoes and Roskam 1971; R. Shepard 1962; R. Shepard et al. 1972). Briefly put, multidimensional scaling is a way of seeking configurations of points, each point representing an entity, such that the rank order of the distances between the points corresponds as closely as possible to the rank order of a set of distance coefficients specified between the entities at the outset. For example, if one were to begin with a table of mileages between cities, nonmetric scaling could be used to reconstruct, at least approximately, the positions of these cities relative to one another in space. Applied to the problem of chronological ordering, the technique works in essentially the same manner: We begin with a set of chronological "distances" between pairs of attributes, and, based on these distances, nonmetric scaling produces the best possible "map" to fit these distances, showing the approximate relative positions of the attribute midpoints in time.

As its name implies, the technique is capable of producing configurations of points in any number of dimensions (limited only by the number of entities being compared), and the choice of an appropriate dimensionality depends to a large extent on the circumstances of the particular application. Since the distance coefficient should reflect the separation between attribute midpoints, principally with respect to time, one might logically expect in this case to find an adequate configuration of points in one dimension only. But as Cowgill (1972:397) and others (Kendall 1971:223; Kruskal 1971) have emphasized, it is usually desirable to work with a configuration in two dimensions, for several reasons. One advantage in doing so is strictly computational: the computer algorithm, when working in only one dimension, has a much greater chance of stopping at a suboptimal configuration, even when a better solution exists. Another reason, more a matter of interpretive importance, is that the two-dimensional scaling of points provides a built-in test of the assumptions on which the seriation's validity depends. As Cowgill put it,

> multidimensional scaling in two or more dimensions . . . amounts to a test of the "one-axis" hypothesis. The data may or may not fit into an essentially one-dimensional pattern. If they do, and if chronological data from other sources are consistent with this one axis being a time axis, then it makes sense to go ahead with a pure seriation technique [1972:384].

Otherwise, if a one-dimensional configuration fails to appear, the investigator is forced to reconsider the appropriateness of the analysis in terms of at least two possibilities. Either the gravelots do not vary significantly with respect to time and the entire analysis is misconceived, or the attributes being measured are poor chronological indicators and should be replaced with better ones.

Practical experience with multidimensional scaling applied to archaeological seriation has shown that acceptable one-dimensional configurations found in two-dimensional space need not always be linear. In fact, linearity seems to be the exception rather than the rule; it is much more common for the points to end up in an arcuate or sinuous configuration, what Kendall (1971) refers to as a "twisted one-dimensional object" (also see Drennan 1976a:293–294, 1976b:52–53; LeBlanc 1975:35).

With this background in mind, let us now return to a consideration of the data from Moundville. Using the distance coefficients calculated by means of Equation (1) as input, our attributes were scaled in two dimensions by means of the Guttman–Lingoes program MINISSA-I (Lingoes 1973:39–79). The resulting configuration of points is shown in Figure 24. Not surprisingly, the

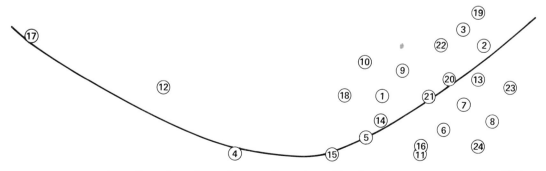

FIGURE 24 Nonmetric scaling of attributes in two dimensions. The fitted curve represents time (Guttman–Lingoes's coefficient of alienation = 0.155; Kruskal's stress = 0.123).

configuration is an elongated, essentially one-dimensional arc; the coefficient of alienation, a statistic that measures departure from a perfect rank correspondence between the input and the achieved distances, takes on a value of 0.155, indicating a reasonably good fit (see Drennan 1976b:50–52). (Kruskal's stress, an analogous statistic, also has a low value of 0.123).

In order to scale more precisely the relative positions of the points along this (presumably) temporal dimension, a curve was fitted to the configuration by eye (Figure 24), and the positions of the points were projected perpendicularly onto the curve. Each point's location along this curve, measured from left to right in millimeters, could then be regarded as the predicted midpoint, in an arbitrary timescale, of the corresponding stylistic attribute.

Finally, once the attribute midpoints have been scaled in this manner, the third step in Cowgill's method involves actually seriating the gravelots themselves. This sequencing is accomplished by calculating a probable or "best-fit" position for each gravelot, taking into account the stylistic attributes it contains. The equation Cowgill proposes for doing this can be written in its most general form as:

$$L_U = \frac{\Sigma \dfrac{M_i}{G_i^k}}{\Sigma \dfrac{1}{G_i^k}} \, , \tag{2}$$

summed over the attributes present in gravelot U, where L_u is its best-fit position, M_i is the estimated midpoint (in our arbitrary timescale) of attribute i, G_i is the total number of gravelots that contain attribute i, and k is a parameter that can take on values of 0, 1, 2, and so on, depending on the result desired. Cowgill's equation is essentially a weighted mean of M_i for all the attributes that are present in gravelot U; the greater the value of k chosen, the more weight is given to rare attributes at the expense of common ones in assigning the gravelot's position. Having tried various values for this parameter in ordering the Moundville gravelots, I obtained the most satisfying result by setting $k = 0$, in which case Equation (2) reduces to

$$L_U = \frac{\Sigma M_i}{\Sigma 1} \, ,$$

which is simply the unweighted arithmetic mean of the attribute midpoints. The sequence of Moundville gravelots ordered by means of this expression is illustrated in Figure 25.

Chronological Interpretation

Abstracting a chronology from the seriation diagram in Figure 25 is fairly straightforward, provided that one caveat is kept in mind: the exact position of any particular gravelot in this sequence must not be taken too literally. Each gravelot is assigned a best-fit position on the basis of the attributes it contains,

ATTRIBUTES

GRAVELOT NUMBER	BEST-FIT POSITION	17	12	4	15	5	18	14	10	1	11	16	9	6	21	24	20	7	22	8	13	3	23	2	19
1261/EE	266.7																	ı					ı	ı	
2417/WP	265.0																	ı		ı	ı		ı	ı	
843/EI	261.0																	ı		ı	ı	ı			
1718/SWG	258.0																	ı		ı	ı				
1227/EE	257.0																	ı		ı	ı				
2733/Rw	254.3												ı					ı		ı	ı				
2068/Rho	252.8												ı											ı	
1007-08/NG	252.7										ı	ı								ı					
1185/EE	252.5											ı								ı					
18/NG	252.5											ı													
1423/SD	252.5											ı								ı					
1275/EE	250.0														ı						ı				
1515/SD	250.0										ı							ı			ı				
10/NR/M5	248.5																	ı		ı					
1089,94-96/NR	248.5										ı	ı													
1534/SD	248.0												ı							ı					
71/SD/M7	247.7											ı				ı	ı	ı							
1888/NN'	246.5										ı							ı		ı					
1065/WR	246.3										ı						ı	ı							
1563-64/SD	246.0										ı						ı	ı							
1234-37/EE	244.0										ı									ı					
1800/SWG	243.5															ı		ı							
1181-84/EE	242.0						ı				ı			ı			ı			ı			ı		
2136/NN'	241.5							ı			ı						ı	ı		ı					
2165-66/WP'	241.5										ı			ı					ı						
1717/SWG	240.5						ı															ı			
869/SEH	240.0													ı			ı								
20/NEC/M5	240.0													ı			ı								
1788-89/SWG	240.0													ı			ı								
1525/SD	240.0													ı			ı								
1751/SWG	240.0													ı			ı								
983/SWM	239.7										ı						ı	ı							
1225/EE	239.7										ı						ı	ı							
8,9/SD/M7	239.7										ı						ı	ı							
18/SEH	238.8								ı		ı							ı		ı	ı				
F.2/O/M5	238.0						ı				ı							ı	ı						
1277-78/EE	237.8					ı										ı		ı		ı					
1045/WR	237.5					ı										ı	ı			ı					
1539/SD	236.5										ı							ı							
1110/NR	236.5										ı							ı							
1088/NR	235.5						ı				ı							ı							
1,2,5/SD/M5	235.3							ı			ı	ı						ı		ı	ı				
1639/NE	234.7							ı			ı	ı		ı		ı		ı							
2137/WP'	234.0										ı			ı				ı		ı					
38/NR/M5	233.8						ı				ı							ı		ı					
1087,1100/NR	233.4							ı	ı		ı							ı		ı					
1281-82/EE	231.5						ı										ı	ı	ı						
3014/SL	231.0										ı	ı						ı	ı						
1284/EE	230.7							ı								ı		ı							
824/EI	230.5						ı											ı							
3001/SL	230.3						ı				ı	ı	ı					ı							
1651/NE	228.3						ı				ı							ı							
1394/EE	227.5								ı		ı							ı							
1262,65/EE	227.0							ı						ı				ı							
1407/EE	226.0							ı						ı				ı							
2496/WP	225.5							ı										ı							
150/SD/M7	224.8				ı						ı						ı	ı							
1638/NE	224.0				ı						ı		ı			ı		ı							
54/NE	222.0				ı						ı			ı					ı						
1496/SD	221.0				ı						ı							ı							
1587/NE	220.5				ı													ı							
1373-74/EE	219.5			ı														ı							
1620-21/NE	218.0							ı					ı					ı							
1542-44/SD	217.8				ı		ı	ı			ı							ı							
13/SD/M7	217.3			ı			ı													ı					
F.2/C/M5	216.3				ı						ı							ı							
2115/Rho	216.0			ı										ı		ı									
8/NG	214.8				ı						ı	ı	ı			ı									
F.1/O/M5	213.8				ı						ı	ı		ı											
2504/SW	212.3				ı						ı	ı	ı												
5,6/C/M5	210.5				ı	ı					ı	ı	ı		ı										
1968/Rho	210.3				ı						ı	ı			ı										
1735/SG	208.5				ı						ı														
1125-26/NR	208.3				ı						ı	ı													
39/O/M5	205.3				ı		ı	ı	ı		ı														
F.7/ND/M5	203.5				ı		ı				ı	ı													
965/SWM	200.0				ı		ı			ı															
961/SWM	196.3		ı		ı			ı			ı														
1104-05/NR	194.3				ı		ı				ı														
1977/Rho	194.3				ı		ı				ı														
2552-53/WP	194.0				ı		ı																		
9/SWM/M7	191.0			ı		ı		ı																	
2560/WP	162.3		ı	ı		ı																			
3/NG	133.0	ı					ı																		
2559/WP	95.0	ı	ı																						
2544/WP	95.0	ı	ı																						
839/EI	36.0	ı	ı																						

FIGURE 25   Seriated sequence of gravelots (attribute numbers correspond to those in Table 11 on p. 84).

but the best fit is by no means the only possible position, nor is it necessarily the "true" position in any strict sense—it is only the most likely position given the data at hand. Thus, all we can reasonably expect is that most gravelots have ended up in the right neighborhood, so to speak, without necessarily being at the correct address. This being the case, the overall chronological pattern among the attributes should be fairly accurate, despite the fact that some individual gravelots may be misplaced (for further discussion of the matter, see Cowgill 1972:414–417).

A convenient way to look at the results when building a chronology, then, is simply to divide the seriated sequence into segments, and to treat each segment as if it were a stratigraphic level of sorts. In this way, we can best characterize the trends through time, without being forced to put too much faith in the very fine details of where individual gravelots happen to be sequenced.

Actually deciding where boundaries between segments should be placed was a bit difficult at first, since no major discontinuities in the Moundville sequence exist. Based on the seriation diagram in Figure 25, another diagram was produced that depicted the total span of each attribute as an unbroken vertical bar (Figure 26). Horizontal boundaries were then positioned on this diagram so as to maximize the difference between adjacent segments, especially with reference to attributes that are relatively common in the collection and/or easily recognizable on sherds; although this kind of judgment was relied on as much as possible, the placement of each boundary was nevertheless somewhat arbitrary. All in all, it was useful to distinguish five segments within the sequence, which correspond to our ceramic phases as follows:

> Segment 3B—late Moundville III
> Segment 3A—early Moundville III
> Segment 2B—late Moundville II
> Segment 2A—early Moundville II
> Segment 1—Moundville I

To say that a segment "corresponds to" a phase does not imply that all the gravelots within the segment necessarily date to that phase; the problems with placing too much interpretive emphasis on the seriated positions of indiviudal gravelots have already been mentioned. Rather, the correspondence should be taken to mean only that the ceramic assemblage within a given segment is stylistically equivalent to the complex associated with a given phase. Assigning plausible dates to individual gravelots is a procedure analytically separate from the seriation itself, and is taken up in Chapter 5.

The data on types and varieties, shapes, motifs, and other features of the vessels falling within each segment are summarized in Tables 12–17. All local vessels from the pertinent gravelots are tabulated, whether or not they exhibit an attribute that was used in formulating the original seriation. Discussion of these data with reference to the ceramic chronology at Moundville must be

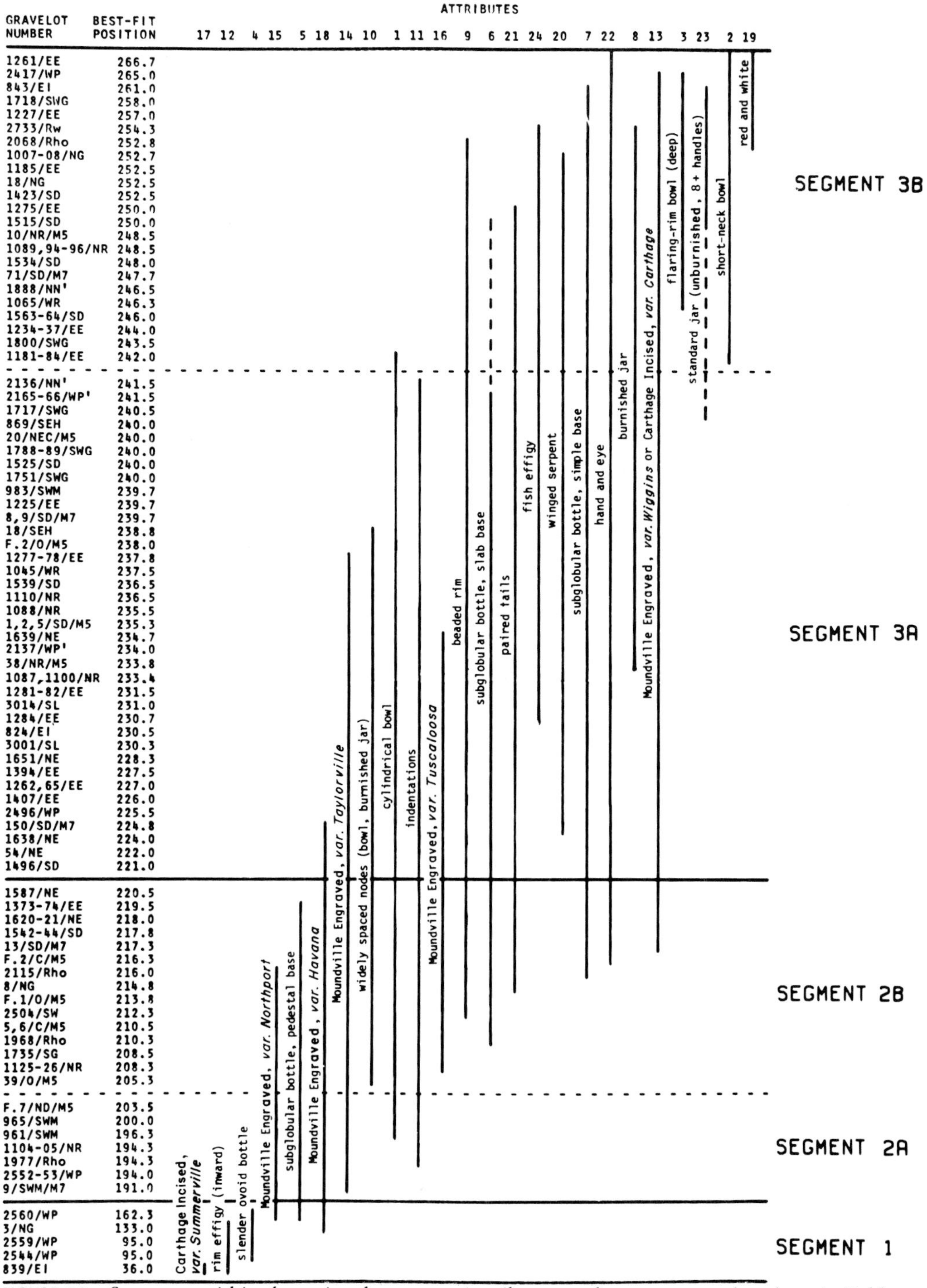

FIGURE 26 Segments within the seriated sequence (attribute numbers correspond to those in Table 11 on p. 84).

TABLE 12
Seriated Distribution of Types and Varieties

Type, variety	Segment				
	1	2a	2b	3a	3b
Bell Pl., *Hale*	6	3	17	32	18
Mississippi Pl., *Warrior*		1	5	13	20
Carthage Inc., *Akron*	3	1		1	
Carthage Inc., *Carthage*				1	6
Carthage Inc., *Fosters*					2
Carthage Inc., *Moon Lake*				1	
Carthage Inc., *Poole*					1
Carthage Inc., *Summerville*	1				
Moundville Eng., *Englewood*				2	1
Moundville Eng., *Havana*	1	4	7	1	
Moundville Eng., *Hemphill*		1	4	29	14
Moundville Eng., *Northport*	1	4	1		
Moundville Eng., *Taylorville*		2	4	8	
Moundville Eng., *Tuscaloosa*			5	3	
Moundville Eng., *Wiggins*			2	6	9
Unclassified			1	1	
Total	12	16	46	98	71

TABLE 13
Seriated Distribution of Representational Motifs

Representational motif	Segment				
	1	2a	2b	3a	3b
Bird with serpent head					1
Crested bird				3	
Forearm bones				1	2
Forked eye surround		1			
Hand and eye			1	3	6
Ogee			1		
Paired tails			1	6	2
Paired wings				1	
Radial fingers				2	1
Raptor				3	
Scalp				1	1
Skull				1	
Turtle					1
Windmill			1	1	
Winged serpent				5	4

TABLE 14

Seriated Distribution of Painted Decoration[1]

Painted decoration	Segment				
	1	2a	2b	3a	3b
Black film	*	*	*	*	*
Red film					1
Red and white					4

[1] Key: *, present on most burnished vessels, but precise count not available.

TABLE 15

Seriated Distribution of Basic Shapes

Basic shape	Segment				
	1	2a	2b	3a	3b
Cylindrical bottle		2		1	
Narrow-neck bottle					1
Slender ovoid bottle	3				
Subglobular bottle, pedestal base	1	6	8		
Subglobular bottle, slab base			4	8	2
Subglobular bottle, simple base			5	34	26
Bottle (miscellaneous)			1	4	1
Cylindrical bowl		3	8	9	1
Flaring-rim bowl:					
(deep)					7
(shallow)				2	1
Pedestaled bowl			1	2	
Restricted bowl	2		1	3	3
Short-neck bowl					4
Simple bowl	4	4	9	16	7
Terraced rectanguloid bowl		1			
Bowl (miscellaneous)			1		1
Burnished jar			1	5	1
Standard jar:					
(unburnished, 2 handles)			2	3	3
(unburnished, 4 handles)			3	8	9
(unburnished, 8 handles)				1	2
(unburnished, 10+ handles)					2
Jar (miscellaneous)					1
Composite bowl			1		
Composite bowl-jar			1		
Double bowl				1	
Unidentified (fragmentary vessel)	2			1	
Total	12	16	46	98	71

4. Ceramic Chronology

TABLE 16
Seriated Distribution of Secondary Shape Features

Secondary shape feature	Segment				
	1	2a	2b	3a	3b
Beaded rim			7	17[1]	7
Beaded shoulder	1		1[2]	1[3]	
Downturned lugs				1	2
Indentations		2	5	8	
Lowered lip		1			
Notched everted lip			1	2	
Notched lip				1	
Single lug		2	7	6	1
Spouts			1		
Widely spaced nodes: (bowl or burnished jar)			3	3	

[1] Three are dorsal fins on fish effigy bowls.
[2] The carapace edge on a turtle effigy.
[3] The dorsal fin on a fish effigy.

deferred for the time being, until after the complementary evidence from the stratigraphic excavation has been presented.

STRATIGRAPHY

All our stratigraphic data come from the 1978–1979 test excavations north of Mound R. These excavations consisted of two 2 × 2-m squares, designated 6N2W and 8N2E, which were troweled down to subsoil mostly by natural levels (see p. 14 and Appendix C). The cultural deposits within these

TABLE 17
Seriated Distribution of Effigy Features

Effigy features	Segment				
	1	2a	2b	3a	3b
Beaver				1	
Bird:					
(flat head, inward facing)	1				
(gracile head, outward facing)				1	
Fish				4	2
Frog				3	1
Human head medallions				2	1
Mammal, unidentified	1				
Mussel shell			1		
Turtle			1		
Turtle, inverted			1		

TABLE 18

Stratigraphic Distribution of Types and Varieties

	6N2W								8N2E					
Type, variety	AU.1 (no.)	AU.1 (%)	AU.2 (no.)	AU.2 (%)	AU.3a (no.)	AU.3a (%)	AU.3b (no.)	AU.3b (%)	AU.1 (no.)	AU.1 (%)	AU.2 (no.)	AU.2 (%)	AU.3 (no.)	AU.3 (%)
Bell Pl., *Hale*	626	40.5	185	28.2	469	28.9	241	26.7	347	27.3	228	28.9	364	25.4
Mississippi Pl., *Hull Lake*	5	0.3	1	0.2	3	0.2	2	0.2	3	0.2	5	0.6	5	0.3
Mississippi Pl., *Warrior*	796	51.6	428	65.1	983	60.6	599	66.3	821	64.7	494	62.6	980	68.4
Carthage Inc., *Akron*	3	0.2			1	0.1	1	0.1	2	0.2			1	0.1
Carthage Inc., *Carthage*			2	0.3	9	0.6	3	0.3			6	0.8	1	0.1
Carthage Inc., *Fosters*					1	0.1	2	0.2						
Carthage Inc., *Moon Lake*	1	0.1												
Carthage Inc., *Poole*							1	0.1	2	0.2			1	0.1
Carthage Inc., *Summerville*					1	0.1								
Carthage Inc., *unspecified*	7	0.5	6	0.9	16	1.0	14	1.5					16	1.1
Moundville Eng., *Cypress*	1	0.1			1	0.1			7	0.6			1	0.1
Moundville Eng., *Elliots Creek*														
Moundville Eng., *Havana*	3	0.2	2	0.3	1	0.1					2	0.3	2	0.1
Moundville Eng., *Hemphill*			2	0.3	11	0.7					1	0.1	5	0.3
Moundville Eng., *Maxwells Crossing*					1	0.1	6	0.6						
Moundville Eng., *Stewart*									1	0.1				
Moundville Eng., *Taylorville*					3	0.2	1	0.1					1	0.1
Moundville Eng., *Tuscaloosa*			1	0.2	2	0.1					3	0.4	1	0.1
Moundville Eng., *Wiggins*					5	0.3	1	0.1					1	0.1
Moundville Eng., *unspecified*	20	1.3	13	2.0	47	2.9	12	1.3	35	2.8	22	2.8	21	1.5
Moundville Inc., *Carrollton*	4	0.3	2	0.3	5	0.3	5	0.6	2	0.2	1	0.1	2	0.1
Moundville Inc., *Moundville*	49	3.2	9	1.4	6	0.4	4	0.4	27	2.1	7	0.9	10	0.7
Moundville Inc., *Snows Bend*	1	0.1			1	0.1			1	0.1	2	0.3		
Moundville Inc., *unspecified*	13	0.8	1	0.2	3	0.2	1	0.1	9	0.7	1	0.1	1	0.1
Alabama River Inc., *unspecified*					1	0.1								
Barton Inc., *Demopolis*					1	0.1								
Woodland period types	7	0.5	2	0.3	9	0.6	2	0.2	7	0.6	4	0.5	1	0.1
Nonlocal types	3	0.2			14	0.9	2	0.2			2	0.3	1	0.1
Unclassified	5	0.3	3	0.5	23	1.4	9	1.0	5	0.4	11	1.4	17	1.2
Total	1544	100	657	100	1616	100	905	100	1269	100	789	100	1432	100

squares basically took the following form: The uppermost 40 cm or so consisted of midden and/or fill, containing scattered pits and various hearthlike features, but exhibiting no definite floors, that is, no distinct horizontal lenses that could be interpreted as living surfaces. The next 30 cm or so was comprised of similar midden–fill, except that it was interspersed with occasional traces of sand floors; most of these floors were discontinuous, and could well have been aboriginally disturbed. Finally, the lowest 130 cm of deposit consisted of a series of closely superimposed sand floors, each usually no more than 5 cm thick, sometimes interspersed with thin lenses of midden. At the very bottom of 6N2W, a portion of a sunken house was encountered. This house apparently represents the initial episode of occupation in the deposit, since it was built intruding directly into sterile soil.

For the purpose of discussing the ceramic stratigraphy, I have found it convenient to group contiguous levels with similar ceramic assemblages into a set of analysis units (AU). Such analysis units were formulated for each excavation separately, since the stratification in the two profiles could not always be securely matched. Each analysis unit is listed below, along with the levels that comprise it and the chronological phase to which its assemblage mostly pertains,

6N2W:
    AU.3B L.1–L.2   late Moundville III (somewhat mixed)
    AU.3A L.3–L.5   early Moundville III (somewhat mixed)
    AU.2   L.6–L.7   Moundville II (somewhat mixed)
    AU.1   L.8–L.28 Moundville I
8N2E:
    AU.3   L.1–L.3   Moundville III (somewhat mixed)
    AU.2   L.4–L.6   Moundville II (somewhat mixed)
    AU.1   L.7–L.26 Moundville I

For the most part, levels assigned to comparable analysis units in the two excavations more or less correspond in terms of their position within the

TABLE 19
Stratigraphic Distribution of Painted Decoration

Painted decoration	6N2W				8N2E		
	AU.1	AU.2	AU.3a	AU.3b	AU.1	AU.2	AU.3
Black film	469	146	426	208	318	183	313
Red film	4	2	21	12	7	3	12
White film	15	6	11	8	4	2	5
Red and black			1		1	2	
Black on white					3		
Red engraved	3				10		
White engraved					1		

TABLE 20

Stratigraphic Distribution of Basic Shapes

Basic shape (rims and base fragments)	6N2W AU.1 (no.)	(%)	AU.2 (no.)	(%)	AU.3a (no.)	(%)	AU.3b (no.)	(%)	8N2E AU.1 (no.)	(%)	AU.2 (no.)	(%)	AU.3 (no.)	(%)
Bottle: (rims)	9	9.0	2	5.6	6	5.2	1	1.5	4	6.0	4	6.0	2	2.4
(pedestal base fragments)	3	—	2	—	1	—			3	—	3	—		—
(slab base fragments)											3	—		
Cylindrical bowl (rims)					1	0.8	1	1.5					1	1.2
Flaring-rim bowl (rims)	9	9.0	6	16.7	10	8.6	7	10.3	7	10.4	2	4.5	10	11.8
Outslanting bowl (rims)											1	2.3		
Restricted bowl (rims)	5	5.0	2	5.6	7	6.0	5	7.4	1	1.5	2	4.5	1	1.2
Short-neck bowl (rims)							5	7.4					2	2.4
Simple bowl (rims)	14	14.0	1	2.8	12	10.3	5	7.4	7	10.4	4	9.1	12	14.1
Burnished jar (rims)									2	3.0				
Neckless jar (unburnished, rims)	1	1.0	1	2.8					2	3.0				
Standard jar (unburnished, rims)	40	40.0	12	33.3	47	40.5	29	42.6	30	44.8	15	34.1	26	30.6
Miscellaneous rims	16	16.0	8	22.2	28	24.1	13	19.1	9	13.4	11	25.0	27	31.8
Total rims	100	100	36	100	117	100	68	100	67	100	44	100	85	100

overall depositional sequence. The only apparent exception to this state of affairs occurs in the case of L.5/6N2W and L.4/8N2E. According to the information supplied by the excavator (Appendix C), these two levels should correspond approximately to the same depositional stratum, yet I have assigned one to AU.3A/6N2W (early Moundville III) and the other to AU.2/8N2E (Moundville II). Given that both these levels stratigraphically adjoin the Moundville II–Moundville III transition, it may be more realistic to regard their assemblages as having elements from both phases. The disjunction in assignment comes about as a result of differences in the nature of the mix: L.5/6N2W contains considerably more Moundville III material than does L.4/8N2E; so for clarity of presentation, it makes sense to group the former assemblage with the levels above it, and the latter assemblage with the levels below.

Why L.5/6N2W should contain more Moundville III material is a question that may be difficult to resolve conclusively. However, it seems likely that there was an intrusion, undetected during excavation, that contaminated the deposit with artifacts from above. Note, for example, that sherds from a single vessel of Carthage Incised, *variety Carthage,* were found stratigraphically scattered through Levels 4, 5, and 6; similarly, pieces of a single vessel of Mound Place Incised, *variety Mobile* were spread vertically from level 2 to Level 6 (see Appendix D); one can also point to the fact that our only two Alabama River phase diagnostics turned up in Level 3, rather than at the very top where one would expect them. All this would bode ill for our attempts to refine the later end of the ceramic chronology were it not for the fact that our stratigraphic data are supplemented with a seriated sequence of closed finds.

The sherd and attribute frequencies for each analysis unit are presented in Tables 18–21. With these and the seriated data now before us, we now turn to a discussion of the three ceramic phases that have emerged.

TABLE 21
Stratigraphic Distribution of Secondary Shape Features

Secondary shape feature	6N2W				8N2E		
	AU.1	AU.2	AU.3a	AU.3b	AU.1	AU.2	AU.3
Beaded rim			6	3		2	5
Beaded shoulder					2		
Folded rim	20		2	5	20		2
Folded-flattened rim	2				1		
Indentations			2			1	1
Notched lip		1		1		2	3
Scalloped rim	4		1		5		1

MOUNDVILLE I PHASE

The Moundville I ceramic complex is most clearly exemplified by AU.1/ 8N2E and AU.1/6N2W, the lowest levels in the test excavations north of Mound R (Tables 18–21). Segment 1 of the seriation also pertains to this complex, but the number of whole vessels that can be securely dated to this phase at Moundville is rather small (Tables 12–17). Fortunately, this short-coming in our whole-vessel sample can be mitigated somewhat by refer-ring to the vessels excavated at two other sites of this phase, both of which contain ceramics virtually identical to those at Moundville. One of these sites is Bessemer, located in the upper Black Warrior drainage about 100 km to the northwest (DeJarnette and Wimberly 1941). The other site is Lubbub (1Pi33), located in the central Tombigbee Valley about 56 km to the west (Jenkins 1981).

Types and Varieties (Tables 12 and 18)

The most frequent categories in Moundville I sherd collections are the undecorated varieties Mississippi Plain, *variety Warrior* (Figure 41k–o) and Bell Plain, *variety Hale* (Figure 41c–j), which together make up some 90% of the assemblages in AU.1/8N2E and AU.1/6N2W. Also present in very small quantities is Mississippi Plain, *variety Hull Lake* (Figure 41p and q).

In regard to the decorated types, Carthage Incised is represented by va-rieties *Akron* (Figures 39e–h, and 40q), *Moon Lake* (Figures 39k and 40r), and *Summerville* (Figures 39j and 41a–b). *Moon Lake,* though it may occur on other vessel shapes in later phases, is found only on shallow flaring-rim bowls in Moundville I (Figure 39k; DeJarnette and Wimberly 1941:Figure 64—Vessel 8).

The varieties of Moundville Engraved that most commonly appear in this complex are *Elliots Creek* (Figures 39b, 40a–d, and 63a–b), *Havana* (Figure 40f and g), *Stewart* (Figure 40e), and *Northport* (Figure 39c). The last of these varieties seems to reach its greatest popularity during Moundville II, and I sus-pect that its appearance in Moundville I contexts is relatively late.

Decorated jars in this phase are usually Moundville Incised. The most common varieties of this type found in the Warrior drainage are *Moundville* (Figures 39m and 42a–h) and *Carrollton* (Figure 42i–l), while *Snows Bend* is quite rare (Figure 42o).

There is reason to believe that Barton Incised also forms a part of the local Moundville I complex despite the fact that none of it happened to be found in the early levels of our test excavations. A surface collection from 1Ha8, a small site only 13 km south of Moundville, contains a sherd of Barton Incised with a folded-flattened rim—a very distinctive local feature that dates to this phase. Also, small quantities of Barton Incised sporadically turn up in eleventh- and twelfth-century contexts on the central Tombigbee, just west of the Warrior basin (Jenkins 1981:61–63).

Painted Decoration (Tables 14 and 19)

The technique of black filming or smudging was frequently used during Moundville I to darken the surfaces of burnished vessels. Over 70% of the burnished sherds in AU.1/8N2E and AU.1/6N2W had been darkened in this way (e.g., Figures 40a–r and 41a–g).

A white film also sometimes occurs on Moundville I vessels; some 5% of the burnished sherds in the early levels exhibit this treatment (Figure 41h). It is interesting to note that almost all of the white-filmed rims in our excavation come from restricted bowls.

Three sherds from AU.1/8N2E exhibit black on white decoration, that is, a design formed by black negative painting over a white-filmed surface (Figure 41i). Although these sherds could well be imported examples of the Nashville Negative Painted type, the possibility that they were locally made should not be too rapidly dismissed. One of the terraced rectanguloid bowls found at Moundville exhibits black negative painting over a white-filmed and red-painted surface (Figure 63d). Admittedly, this vessel is unique in its decoration, but the fact that such bowl forms rarely occur outside the Moundville area suggests that the vessel is not an import, and that the local potters did indeed sometimes make use of the negative painting technique.

Red filming also turns up in the ceramic complex of this phase. Of the 11 red-filmed sherds in our Moundville I levels, six are painted on the exterior surface only, two on the interior only, and three on both the exterior and interior (Figure 41j–k). The only possible Moundville I vessel that shows this treatment is a Moundville Incised, *variety Carrollton* jar with a red-painted interior (Rho132).

The red and black treatment occurs on a singe rim sherd, probably from a bottle, found in good Moundville I context (AU.1/8N2E). The one whole vessel that exhibits this treatment is a pedestaled subglobular bottle (Moore 1907: Figure 21), which on the basis of its shape could be either Moundville I or Moundville II in date.

Finally, the addition of pigment to engraved lines appears to be an excellent Moundville I phase diagnostic. Some 20% of all the Moundville Engraved sherds in our early levels are red engraved (Figures 40h, i, l, o, and p and 63a–b), and a single example (1.5%) is white engraved (Figure 40n). It should also be noted that one red-engraved (or "hemagraved") vessel was excavated at Bessemer (DeJarnette and Wimberly 1941:90–91).

Basic Shapes (Tables 15 and 20)

The most characteristic Moundville I bottle form is the slender ovoid bottle, which always has a pedestal base (Figure 39a and b). Subglobular bottles with pedestal bases occur as well, probably with greater frequency in the later portions of the phase than in the earlier (Figure 39c). Occasionally, bottles with simple bases turn up in Moundville I contexts; such bottles tend to be small in size, and are generally quite rare (Figure 39d).

Common Moundville I bowl forms include the simple bowl (Figures 39e–g and i and 43f and g), the restricted bowl (Figures 39j and 43d and e), and the shallow flaring-rim bowl (Figures 39k and 43k and l). Considerably rarer is the pedestaled bowl; although no pedestaled bowls can be tied into a secure early context at Moundville itself, one such bowl (with a cutout lip and lowered rim) was found at Bessemer, where the Mississippian component is pure Moundville I (DeJarnette and Wimberly 1941:Figure 67).

Most unburnished jars in the Moundville I complex are of the so-called standard shape (Figures 39l and m and 43m–s). Neckless jars are less common, but nevertheless a good marker for the phase (Figure 43t–w). Judging from the eight whole specimens found in securely datable contexts at Moundville, Bessemer, and Lubbub, it appears that unburnished jars of this phase typically have only two handles (see Table 22 on p. 102).

Burnished jars occasionally turn up in Moundville I stratigraphic contexts (AU.1/8N2E) and gravelots (bu. 2884/Rw), but none of the specimens is complete enough to indicate whether or not such vessels had handles (Figures 41a, b and f and 43j).

Secondary Shape Features (Tables 16 and 21)

Grouped nodes were sometimes added to bowls, bottles, and burnished jars. It is not uncommon to find such nodes on vessels of Carthage Incised, *variety Summerville,* positioned at the points in the design where adjacent arches meet (Figure 41b; Jenkins 1981:Figure 63).

A feature much more tenuously assigned to this phase is the band of nodes. Nowhere is the feature found in good context. It does occur on a number of vessels that, judging from their overall shape and decoration, could conceivably date to Moundville I, but could just as easily be later. Among the vessels in question are two Moundville Engraved, *variety Havana* restricted bowls (Rho48, EI2) and a Bell Plain, *variety Hale* jar without handles (Figure 62i).

A scalloped rim is often found on flaring rim bowls dating to this phase (Figures 41d and e and 43l; DeJarnette and Wimberly 1941:Figure 63, upper right). About half the rims from such bowls in AU.1/6N2W and AU.1/8N2E exhibit this feature.

Beaded shoulders turn up in good Moundville I contexts (AU.1/8N2E; bu. 3/NG), but not with great frequency. The fragments in our sample come from either burnished jars or restricted bowls, but none are sufficiently complete for definite identification as to shape (Figure 41c).

The cutout rim and the lowered lip are definitely part of this complex, since both features are evident on the single (and rather unusual) pedestaled bowl from Bessemer (DeJarnette and Wimberly 1941:Figure 67).

Gadrooning is a rare feature that sometimes occurs on bottles. Although there are no known examples that date to this phase at Moundville, one gadrooned bottle was excavated at Bessemer (DeJarnette and Wimberly 1941: Figure 65).

Widely spaced nodes are found on several unburnished Moundville Incised jars, which could date to this phase or early Moundville II (Figure 63j–k). It is important to note, of course, that widely spaced nodes do not appear on burnished jars and bowls until late Moundville II.

There are two rim modes on unburnished jars that are excellent temporal diagnostics for Moundville I: the folded rim (Figures 39m, 41o, 42m, and 43m–p and u) and the folded-flattened rim (Figure 43v and w). Among the unburnished jar rims found in AU.1/6N2W and AU.1/8N2E, 53% are folded, 4% are folded-flattened, and the rest are unmodified.

Handles on Moundville I jars tend to be parallel sided rather than strongly tapered, and occur in a range of forms, including loop, strap, and intermediate types (Figure 41l and m). These generalizations can be put more precisely by making use of two descriptive ratios, each computed between a pair of measurements made on the handles themselves (Table 22). The first ratio, that of top width to bottom width, reflects the degree of taper; parallel-sided handles have values close to 1.0, and tapered handles have values somewhat higher. The present sample exhibits ratios ranging from 0.8 to 1.7, with a mean of 1.2 indicating relatively little taper. The second descriptive ratio, that of middle

TABLE 22
Handle Measurements of Moundville I Unburnished Jars

Site	Type, variety	Proven- ience	Handles (no.)
Bessemer[1]	Mississippi Pl., *Warrior*	Bu.1	2
Lubbub[2]	Mississippi Pl., *Warrior*	Bu.15	—
Lubbub[2]	Mississippi Pl., *Warrior*	Bu.16	2
Lubbub[2]	Moundville Inc., *Moundville*	Bu.20	2
Lubbub[2]	Mississippi Pl., *Warrior*	Bu.23	2
Lubbub[2]	Mississippi Pl., *Warrior*	Bu.28	2
Lubbub[2]	Moundville Inc., *unspecified*	Bu.31	2
Lubbub[2]	Moundville Inc., *Moundville*	Bu.31	2
Moundville	Moundville Inc., *Moundville*	Bu.1455	2
Moundville	Mississippi Pl., *Warrior*	L.22/GN2W	—
Moundville	Mississippi Pl., *Warrior*	L.12/8N2E	—

[1] Source: DeJarnette and Wimberly (1941:87, Figure 64).
[2] Source: Jenkins (1981:Figures 59–62, 64–66). The handles were measured by the present author.

width to thickness, is a convenient measure of "strapishness"; loop handles tend to have values around 1, and strap handles values of 2 or higher. Our Moundville I specimens range from 1.0 to 2.5 on this index, with the mean value being 1.8. Most handles are luted directly to the lip itself, and it is not uncommon to find the uppermost portion of the handle rising slightly above the level of the lip (Figure 43q–s). In at least a few cases, the bottom of the handle is attatched to the shoulder by riveting.

Jar handles are also sometimes decorated with appliqué nodes. Common arrangements include one, two, or three nodes aligned horizontally at the top; two nodes aligned vertically, one at the top and one in the middle; or three nodes in a triangular arrangement, with two at the top and one in the middle. Another decorative elaboration consists of a series of parallel notches along the top of the handle, transverse to the lip (Figure 41m).

Effigy Features (Table 17)

The most common Moundville I effigy form appears to be the simple bowl with a horizontally projecting lug on one side, and an inward-facing effigy head on the other. Usually, the effigy adorno is a stylized bird head, with a rather flat, "cookie-cutter" appearance (Figure 39e and f). Two rather distinctive rim effigy bowls have the additional feature of wings, depicted on the sides by means of modeling and incising (WP153 [Figure 39i], WP218); on both

TABLE 22 (Continued)

Top width (mm)	Middle width (mm)	Bottom width (mm)	Thickness (mm)	Vertical height (mm)	Clearance (mm)	TW:BW ratio[3]	MW:Th ratio[4]
—	16	—	—	25	—	—	—
28	20	24	8	60	16	1.2	2.5
10	10	13	6	36	8	0.8	1.7
32	20	19	12	65	17	1.7	1.7
16	16	18	10	39	11	0.9	1.6
15	13	12	9	37	9	1.2	1.4
7	4	5	4	18	3	1.4	1.0
9	6	9	3	20	7	1.0	1.0
10	9	10	5	25	6	1.0	1.8
28	22	22[5]	7	—	—	1.3	3.1
23	17	17[5]	10	—	—	1.4	1.7
						$\bar{x}=1.2$	$\bar{x}=1.8$

[3] This ratio is the top width divided by the bottom width.
[4] This ratio is the middle width divided by the thickness.
[5] This measurement is an estimation.

these vessels, however, the effigy heads are missing, leaving us totally in the dark as to the nature of the birds being represented. Only one rim effigy bowl found in good Moundville I context depicts a nonavian subject (WP150, bu. 2544/WP): Its inward-facing head appears to be that of a mammal, possibly a bear (Figure 39g).

Another distinctive effigy form is a bowl made to resemble a conch shell cup (Figures 39h and 41g), examples of which have been found in both gravelot and stratigraphic contexts dating to this phase (bu. 2562/WP, L.7A/ 8N2E).

Dating

Arriving at an absolute time range for the Moundville I phase is relatively straightforward compared to some of the other units in our sequence. Not only do we have radiocarbon dates from Moundville itself, but we can also make use of published dates on comparable material from Bessemer and various sites in the Tombigbee drainage to the west. The seven most pertinent absolute dates are listed in Table 23, and are discussed individually below.

In terms of association, the best radiocarbon date we have for this phase at Moundville is A.D. 1260±60 (DIC-1243). The charcoal sample was obtained in our test excavation from L.8B/8N2E, which consisted of debris from a wall that had burned and collapsed over a house floor. Stratigraphically this stratum occurs near the top of the Moundville I deposits, and the date should therefore correspond to the late end of the phase. A second charcoal sample from a different part of the same stratum (L.9/6N2W) was also processed, but it yielded an embarrassing date of A.D. 1830±60 (DIC-1241), quite obviously spurious.

The Bessemer date of A.D. 1070±55 was obtained on material excavated during the depression era, in this case charred cane associated with a square wall-trench structure (Walthall and Wimberly 1978). Although no tabulation of the artifacts from this particular structure is available, the architectural style of the house is distinctively Mississippian, and the entire Mississippian component at Bessemer is ceramically equivalent to Moundville I.

On the central Tombigbee, the Kellogg Village site (22Cl527) has yielded a relevant date of A.D. 1195±70 (UGa-910) (Blakeman 1975:95–98, 176–177). The post mold that contained the dated sample also contained a large sherd of Moundville Incised, *variety Moundville*, a good marker for this phase.

Two other absolute dates that probably pertain to Moundville I were recently obtained at the Lubbub site (1Pi61), also on the central Tombigbee (Jenkins 1981). The dates are A.D. 1240±80 (DIC-1003) and A.D. 1030±55 (DIC-1002), and they are associated with a pair of rectangular, partly subterranean houses, the cultural affiliation of which is a matter of some debate. Because more than 90% of the sherds in the fill of these sunken houses were grog-tempered, and less than 1% were shell-tempered, Jenkins assigned them

TABLE 23
Moundville I Phase Radiocarbon Dates

Site	Laboratory number	Date[1]	Sample composition	Context and associations	Reference
Moundville	DIC-1243	A.D. 1260±60	Wood charcoal	North of Mound R, Unit 8N2E, Level 8B; charcoal from fallen wall debris, stratigraphically within AU.1/8N2E and equivalent to L.9/6N2W	
Moundville	DIC-1241	A.D. 1830±60	Wood charcoal	North of Mound R, Unit 6N2W, Level 9; charcoal from fallen wall debris, stratigraphically within AU.1/8N2E, and equivalent to L.8B/8N2E	
Bessemer	UGa-1663	A.D. 1070±55	Charred cane	Structure 13; a square, wall-trench structure that almost certainly belongs to the Mississippian component at Bessemer (DeJarnette and Wimberly 1941:56, Figures 45 and 46)	Walthall and Wimberly 1978
Kellogg Village (22Cl527)	UGa-910	A.D. 1195±70	Charcoal	Feature 6; a post mold containing a large sherd of Moundville Incised, var. Moundville	Blakeman 1975:95-98, 176-177
Lubbub (1Pi61)	DIC-1003	A.D. 1240±80		Feature 17, Structure 1; a sunken, rectangular house with a sherd of Mississippi Plain, var. Warrior, in situ on the floor (Jenkins, personal communication)	Jenkins 1981: Table 1
Lubbub (1Pi61)	DIC-1002	A.D. 1030±55		Feature 92, Structure 4; a sunken, rectangular house adjacent to Feature 17, Structure 1 (Jenkins, personal communication)	Jenkins 1981: Table 1
Lyons Bluff (22Ok1)	UGa-1361	A.D. 1210±65	Wood charcoal	A post mold pertaining to the early occupation of the site, the Tibbe Creek phase	Marshall 1977

[1] Dates (uncorrected) are based on a 5568-year half-life.

to the Gainesville phase of the Terminal Woodland period (1981:29). One can just as reasonably argue, however, that these are in fact Mississippian houses that were built on an earlier Woodland midden and, after abandonment, were mostly filled in with that midden. Supporting this alternative interpretation are two major pieces of evidence: (*a*) the only sherd found definitely in situ on one of the floors was shell tempered, and (*b*) a formally similar sunken house was found in the lowest Moundville I phase levels of the test excavation at Moundville (L.28/6N2W) (Scarry 1980, 1981a).

Finally, at the Lyon's Bluff site (22Ok1) in east-central Mississippi, Marshall (1977) has reported a date of A.D. 1210±65 for the Tibbe Creek phase, the ceramic complex of which is very similar to that of Moundville I.

Considering this evidence and taking into account the terminal dates for the West Jefferson phase (p. 81), one can reasonably estimate that the Moundville I phase lasted from about A.D. 1050 to 1250.

MOUNDVILLE II PHASE

Moundville II is in many respects the least well defined of our phases. For one thing, the segments of the seriation that pertain to this phase, 2A (early) and 2B (late), contain only a rather modest number of whole vessels (Tables 12–17). And although material from this phase definitely appears in our stratigraphic tests, not much of it could be isolated in relatively pure context. Moundville II ceramics make their strongest showing in AU.2/6N2W and AU.2/8N2E, but in each case there could well be some mixture with earlier and/or later materials (Tables 18–21).

Types and Varieties (Tables 12 and 18)

The undecorated wares again make up the largest part of the assemblage. In AU.2/6N2W and AU.2/8N2E, Mississippi Plain, *variety Warrior* accounts for about 60% of the sherds (Figure 48f–n); Bell Plain, *variety Hale* makes up about 30% (Figure 49a–k); and Mississippi Plain, *variety Hull Lake* remains a small minority at 0.2% (Figure 48o).

The varieties of Moundville Engraved that occur in the complex include *Havana* (Figures 44a, b, and d; 46h and i; and 47e–g), *Northport* (Figure 45g and j), *Taylorville* (Figure 44c), and *Hemphill* (Figures 44e, h, k, l, and n; 45h and i; and 47c and d). Late in the phase, *Northport* seems to decline greatly in popularity, and two new varieties, *Tuscaloosa* (Figures 45e and f, 47a and b) and *Wiggins* (Figure 44m; Moore 1905:Figure 31, 1907:Figure 14), make their first appearance. The varieties *Maxwells Crossing* (Figure 45l) and *Prince Plantation* (Figure 45k) were also produced during this phase, since most examples occur on subglobular bottles with pedestal and slab bases— shapes that are good Moundville II markers (Figure 27). Some of the engraved

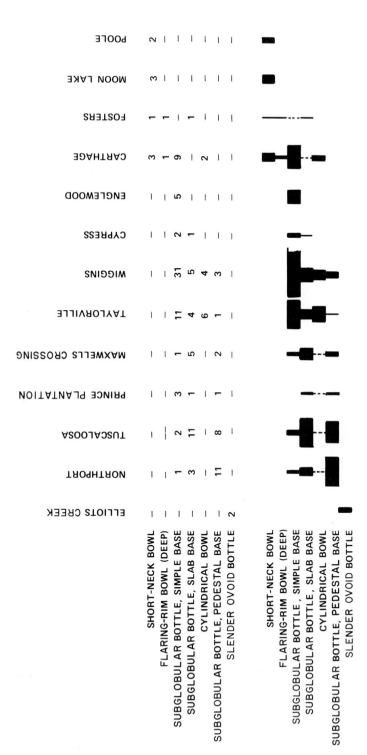

FIGURE 27 Distribution of varieties (top) by vessel shape (left) for Moundville Engraved (*Elliots Creek, Northport, Tuscaloosa, Prince Plantation, Maxwells Crossing, Taylorville, Wiggins, Cypress,* and *Englewood*) and Carthage Incised (*Carthage, Fosters, Moon Lake,* and *Poole*).

varieties just mentioned are not represented in the stratigraphic counts, but this is probably due to the fact that they tend to be difficult to recognize on small sherds and thus often get sorted as Moundville Engraved, *variety unspecified* (Figure 47h–l).

Carthage Incised is present during Moundville II as well, primarily in the form of *Akron. Variety Moon Lake,* since it is known to occur both in Moundville I and in Moundville III, may also be an element of this complex—but we have yet to find any in secure context. Two sherds of *variety Carthage* were found in AU.2/6N2W, but they are almost certainly intrusive from above, and not a part of the complex dating to this phase. Note that *Carthage* turns up only in Moundville III gravelots (Table 12), and that despite its abundance in the sample, it never occurs on pedestal or slab base bottles—the two forms most characteristic of Moundville II (Figure 27).

Moundville Incised also presents a bit of a problem. It is relatively abundant among decorated sherds in stratigraphic contexts, but it does not occur in the seriated gravelots at all. The question is, in which part of this conflicting evidence do we have more trust? Is the presence of the type in stratigraphic context the result of mixture, or is its absence in the gravelots the result of sampling error? In this case, I feel that the latter explanation is the more likely. Moundville Incised is restricted to unburnished jars, and only four such jars occur in the appropriate portion of the seriated sequence, all in Segment 2B. Thus, if this type was indeed produced during this time, as I believe it was, we would have little opportunity to find it in our gravelots. The varieties of Moundville Incised recognized in AU.2/6N2W and AU.2/8N2E are *Moundville* (13%) (Figure 48a and b), *Carrollton* (0.2%) (Figure 48e), and *Snows Bend* (0.1%) (Figures 48c and d and 63i). Given the type's popularity in Moundville I, and its virtual absence in Moundville III, I strongly suspect that most of the Moundville II examples date to the early part of the phase.

Representational Motifs (Table 13)

Representational motifs in the Moundville II ceramic complex occur only on vessels of Moundville Engraved, *variety Hemphill*. Motifs that appear in the seriated gravelots are: the forked eye surround (bu. 7/ND/M5) (Moore 1905:Figure 74), hand and eye (F.2/C/M5) (Moore 1905:Figure 21), ogee (bu. 13/SD/M7) (Moore 1907:Figure 41), paired tails (bu. 8/NG) (Figure 44e and f) and windmill (bu. 5,6/C/M5) (Moore 1905:Figure 30). Other motifs that do not occur on the seriated sample but can nevertheless be assigned to Moundville II on the basis of their association with pedestaled subglobular bottles are the bilobed arrow (e.g., Figure 45h; Moore 1905:Figures 87 and 148) and radial fingers (e.g., Moore 1905:Figure 143). The rayed circle, Greek cross, and feathered arrow can all be placed in this phase as well, since they are found in the same design with a bilobed arrow on at least one vessel (Moore 1907: Figure 39), and occur in gravelot association with other Moundville II markers

	BILOBED ARROW	OGEE	RADIAL FINGERS	WINDMILL	HAND AND EYE	FEATHER	SCALP	RAPTOR	PAIRED TAILS	CRESTED BIRD	WINGED SERPENT
SUBGLOBULAR BOTTLE, SIMPLE BASE	—	1	2	4	9	—	2	4	13	3	30
SUBGLOBULAR BOTTLE, SLAB BASE	—	—	1	2	3	2	2	4	4	—	—
CYLINDRICAL BOWL	—	—	2	—	4	—	1	2	3	1	—
SUBGLOBULAR BOTTLE, PEDESTAL BASE	2	2	1	2	3	—	—	—	—	—	—

SUBGLOBULAR BOTTLE, SIMPLE BASE
SUBGLOBULAR BOTTLE, SLAB BASE
CYLINDRICAL BOWL
SUBGLOBULAR BOTTLE, PEDESTAL BASE

FIGURE 28 Distribution of SCC motifs (top) by vessel shape (left) on Moundville Engraved, *variety Hemphill* (unique motifs are excluded).

(bu. 1437/SD, bu. 1520/SD). The feather motif adorns slab-base bottles (Figure 62a), which could date to late Moundville II, or equally well to early Moundville III (Figure 28).

Also worthy of note are three unusual vessels, classified as *Hemphill,* that on the basis of their shape and gravelot associations are assigned to Moundville II. In each case, the design is placed on one side of the vessel only, not at all the symmetrical or repetitive arrangement one usually finds on Moundville Engraved. Moreover, the designs tend to contain aberrant renditions of certain motifs that more commonly appear in later phases. The vessels in question are (*a*) an outslanting bowl with a Greek cross (?) and a scalp (Figure 44o), (*b*) a simple bowl with a rayed circle (Figure 44l), and (*c*) a pedestaled and gadrooned subglobular bottle decorated with the head of a raptor (Figure 44m). Assuming these vessels are of local manufacture—certainly a debatable proposition—they may represent an episode of experimentation with certain designs that were later to become much more abundant and standardized elements in the ceramic repertoire.

Painted Decoration (Tables 14 and 19)

Black filming is again the prevalent treatment on burnished wares, with 70% of the burnished sherds in our Moundville II levels exhibiting a smudged surface (e.g., Figures 47a, d, e, g–i, and l–q and 49a–d, g).

Red filming is present as well. Of the five sherds with this treatment found in Moundville II levels, two had red paint on the interior only, and three on the exterior only (Figure 49h).

The red-and-black decoration is evident on two sherds from AU.2/8N2E (Figure 49k). Both sherds come from a single vessel—a pedestaled bottle, not unlike the whole vessel exhibiting this treatment that was excavated by Moore (1907:Figure 21).

Some 2.3% of the burnished sherds in the Moundville II levels are white-filmed (Figure 49i and j), an abundance similar to that in the levels below.

Finally, the red-and-black-on-white treatment probably dates somewhere around the early part of Moundville II, since the only occurrence in our sample is on a terraced rectanguloid bowl (Figure 63d).

Basic Shapes (Tables 15 and 20)

The predominant bottle form throughout Moundville II is the subglobular bottle with a pedestal base (Figures 44m and n, 45a, b, e, and g–l, and 50n). Cylindrical bottles occur as well, but not with great frequency (Moore 1905: Figure 74, 1907:Figure 19). Subglobular bottles with slab and simple bases begin to appear mainly in the later portion of the phase (Figures 45c, d, and f, and 50o).

Moundville II bowls were made in simple (Figures 44g–l and 50b), cylindrical (Figures 44a–e and 50c–e), and restricted shapes (Figure 46h and j).

Flaring-rim bowls, which occur in our stratigraphic sample but not in our seriated gravelots, were probably of the same shallow form as one finds in Moundville I and early Moundville III (Figure 49a–c). Other distinctive but relatively uncommon shapes are the outslanting bowl (Figures 44o and 50f), the pedestaled bowl (Moore 1907:Figures 15 and 16), and the terraced rectanguloid bowl (Figure 63c–e).

Unburnished jars are most commonly of the standard form (Figure 46a, b, d, and e) and have an unmodified rim (Figure 50g–m). One rim sherd from a neckless jar was found in AU.2/6N2W (Figure 48l); significantly, it was neither folded nor folded-flattened, both of which modes seem to be associated predominantly with earlier vessels. Judging from our few whole specimens in good context (see Table 24 on p. 112), both two- and four-handled jars occur in this phase.

Burnished jars are found in Moundville II contexts, but in relatively small numbers. The one specimen from a seriated gravelot (Figure 46f) was made without handles.

The composite vessel is another relatively rare category that turns up late in the phase. We have two examples in seriated gravelots: a composite bowl–jar (Figure 46c) and a composite bowl (Figure 46g). It is reasonable to suppose that composite jar–bowls were made in late Moundville II as well, since they share many similarities with the other composite forms just mentioned. Also, it is worthwhile to note that a double bowl occurs in a gravelot (bu. 3001/SL) that happened to get seriated in Segment 3A, but based on the distinctive features the gravelot contains, it could just as easily date to late Moundville II.

Secondary Shape Features (Tables 16 and 21)

Indentations are a common feature of Moundville II bottles (Figure 45e, f, h, and j), and are sometimes found on cylindrical bowls as well (Figure 44f). Usually these indentations occur on engraved vessels, and serve as focal points around which the design is organized.

A single lug, projecting outward horizontally from the lip, is found on most cylindrical bowls and rarely on simple bowls (Figure 44a–c). Of the 11 cylindrical bowls in Segments 2A and 2B, 9 have such lugs.

A beaded shoulder is an integral part of the turtle effigy bowls that show up in late Moundville II (Figure 46h). Whether this secondary shape feature was used on vessels early in the phase is uncertain, but given that beaded shoulders were found in Moundville I contexts, it is a fairly good bet that this feature continues throughout Moundville II.

The beaded rim first appears late in the phase, and is found on both simple bowls and burnished jars (Figures 44g, j, and k, 46c, f, and g, and 49d and e).

Widely spaced nodes have differing chronological significance, depending on whether they are found on burnished or unburnished vessels. On burnished vessels, the feature seriates late in the phase, and is often associated with beaded rims (Figure 44h, i, and k, and 46k). On unburnished jars, the feature may well occur earlier, since the unburnished vessels on which it is found are invariably Moundville Incised (e.g., Figure 63i–k).

Grouped nodes are found on one bowl (NR106) in late Moundville II context, and probably persisted as a feature throughout the phase, given their earlier presence in Moundville I.

The band of nodes is a highly distinctive feature whose chronological distribution we know almost nothing about. Inasmuch as it occurs on vessels of Moundville Engraved, *variety Havana* (Rho48, EI2), it could date to Moundville II as easily as almost anywhere else.

Spouts are a late Moundville II feature, appearing on simple bowls. This mode may occur in combination with a beaded rim and widely spaced nodes (Figure 44j).

In general, lip notching is a rare embellishment on local vessels during this phase, sporadically turning up on bowls with and without a flaring rim (e.g., Figures 47f and 49c). Pedestaled bowls, infrequent as they are in the sample, almost invariably have a notched everted lip (Moore 1907:Figure 15).

Gadrooning occurs on a single pedestaled bottle found in Moundville II context (Figure 44m). This vessel is one of the unusual examples of Moundville Engraved, *variety Hemphill* discussed earlier; whether or not it was made locally is a matter of some doubt, as is the matter generally of whether to regard gadrooning as an element of the indigenous ceramic repertoire.

A lowered lip occurs on most terraced rectanguloid bowls (Figure 63c–e), including the one that seriated in Segment 2A (bu. 9/SWM/M7) (Moore 1907: Figure 22). Thus, it is safe to regard this feature as continuing at least into early Moundville II.

Previous mention was made that only four unburnished jars were found in secure Moundville II gravelots, all from the later end of the phase; the handle measurements from these jars are summarized in Table 24. Three of the jars

TABLE 24
Handle Measurements of Late Moundville II Unburnished Jars

Catalog number	Type. variety	Burial number	Handles (no.)
NE444	Mississippi Pl., *Warrior*	1620-21	4
NE452	Mississippi Pl., *Warrior*	1620-21/NE	4
SW40	Mississippi Pl., *Warrior*	2504/SW	2
SG15	Mississippi Pl., *Warrior*	1735/SG	4

have parallel-sided handles, whereas on the fourth (SG15), the handles are
strongly tapered near the bottom. Top-width to bottom-width ratios vary from
1.1 to 2.1, with the mean value being 1.4. Generally the late Moundville II
handles tend to be a bit more straplike than most Moundville I examples; their
middle-width to thickness ratio varies from 1.9 to 2.4, with a mean of 2.5.

As in the previous phase, unburnished jar handles are sometimes embellished with nodes (Figure 48j and k). Distinctive patterns within our small
sample include two or three nodes in a vertical arrangement, and four nodes in
a rectangular arrangement. Other handle embellishments that have been observed on probable Moundville II vessels are two nodes placed horizontally at
the top, and multiple parallel notches transverse to the lip.

Effigy Features (Table 17)

There are two lug-and-rim-effigy bowls in secure Moundville II gravelots.
Unfortunately, because the effigy head on each vessel is broken off, we cannot
be sure what sort of creatures were depicted or in what direction they faced.
For now, we can only guess by interpolating. Given that bird effigies appear in
abundance during Moundville I and Moundville III, it is reasonable to suppose
that they were also abundant during Moundville II. This being the case, it
seems likely that the rim effigies in early Moundville II were more like those in
Moundville I—flat "cookie-cutter" head facing inward; similarly, that the rim
effigies in late Moundville II were generally more like those in Moundville
III—gracile, less conventionalized head facing outward. In the absence of conflicting evidence (or any evidence at all), Moundville II also seems to be the
most likely time slot in which to place the three specimens having flat heads
facing outward (SED13, SEH82, NR43)—bird effigies stylistically intermediate between the two polar chronological types (Figure 63l). As to what
other sorts of lug-and-rim effigy bowls may have been present in this phase,
nothing can be said until more data become available.

TABLE 24 (Continued)

Top width (mm)	Middle width (mm)	Bottom width (mm)	Thick-ness (mm)	Vertical height (mm)	Clear-ance (mm)	TW:BW ratio[1]	MW:Th ratio[2]
19	16	18	6	44	10	1.1	2.7
17	13	15	7	35	9	1.1	1.9
20	16	17	6	31	6	1.2	2.7
34	15	16	6	34	8	2.1	2.5
						$\bar{x}=1.4$	$\bar{x}=2.5$

[1] This ratio is the top width divided by the bottom width.
[2] This ratio is the middle width divided by the thickness.

In regard to the structural effigies, one form definitely present in Moundville II is the mussel shell bowl (Figure 46j). Another form present may be the conch shell bowl, but here the evidence for assignment is weak: No conch shell bowls have been found in contexts that can be independently dated to Moundville II, but the modeled beak on some of these effigies (e.g., SE2) is very similar to the spouts that sometimes occur on late Moundville II simple bowls, suggesting that they may be contemporary.

One turtle effigy bowl found its way into Segment 2B of the seriation (Figure 46h and i). However, the vessel occurs in a borderline context (bu. 1587/NE) that could just as easily have been included in Segment 3A. It is therefore probably best to regard this form as dating to late Moundville II and early Moundville III, without confining it exclusively to one phase or the other.

The alligator effigy (Figure 62m) is in many ways morphologically similar to the turtle effigy, and on this basis, I suspect it also dates to late Moundville II and early Moundville III. One can further point to the formal similarity, both in basic shape and in the presence of a beaded rim, between the alligator effigy excavated by Moore (1905:Figure 69) and the burnished jar (lacking effigy features) that seriated in Segment 2B (Figure 46f).

Finally, based on its position in Segment 2B of the seriation (bu. 1620/NE), the inverted turtle effigy can also be assigned to late Moundville II.

Dating

Unfortunately, no direct radiocarbon dates are available from well-defined Moundville II contexts. By bracketing with respect to dates on earlier and later material, a reasonable guess would be that this phase lasted from about A.D. 1250 to about 1400.

MOUNDVILLE III PHASE

The Moundville III ceramic complex is most easily defined within the seriated sequence of gravelots. Segments 3A and 3B, corresponding respectively to the early and late portions of the phase (Tables 12–17), contain well over half of all the gravelots in the seriation, and so provide us with a very large sample of whole vessels in secure context. Moundville III material also appears in the uppermost levels of the stratigraphic tests, but the relevant deposits were somewhat mixed, and are not at all conducive to making fine chronological distinctions. Pottery of this phase predominates in AU.3 from 8N2E, also in AU.3A and AU.3B from 6N2W (Tables 18–21). At best, the distinction between AU.3A and AU.3B in 6N2W presents a rather fuzzy reflection of the early-to-late Moundville III trends, which stand out much more clearly in the seriation.

Types and Varieties (Tables 12 and 18)

Plainwares again make up more than 90% of the assemblage in stratigraphic context. The most abundant varieties are Mississippi Plain, *variety
Warrior* (65%) (Figures 56n–p and 57a–m), and Bell Plain, *variety Hale* (27%)
(Figures 56j–m and 58a–q). Mississippi Plain, *variety Hull Lake* is found in
trace amounts (0.2%) (Figure 57n–o).

Moundville Engraved, *varieties Havana* (Figures 53o and 55e and f),
Taylorville (Figures 52f and 39c), and *Tuscaloosa* (Figures 52e and 55a and b)
seriate to the early part of the phase only. Lasting throughout the phase are
varieties Hemphill (Figures 52c, d, g, and o, 53a–d, k–n, and p, and 55i–l),
Wiggins (Figures 52c, d, g, and o, 53f, and 55g; Moore 1905:Figure 124), and
Englewood (Figures 52b and 62f; Moore 1905:Figure 80). A single sherd of
Maxwells Crossing occurs in AU.3A/6N2W (Figure 55d); based on this slender
stratigraphic evidence, and judging from the bottle forms on which *Maxwells
Crossing* is found (Figure 27), it seems quite possible that this variety persists
into early Moundville III. Exactly the same argument can be made for *Cypress*
(Figures 55h and 62d), which is also probably best assigned to early
Moundville III (see Table 18 and Figure 27).

Within the type Carthage Incised, varieties present early in the phase
include *Akron* (Figure 51a and 56a), *Moon Lake* (Figure 53g), and perhaps a
minor sprinkling of *Carthage* (Figure 52k) and *Fosters*. Late in the phase,
Akron seems to drop out, and *Carthage* (Figures 51o, 52l, 53h, 56d and e, and
62b and e) and *Fosters* (Figures 51m and p, and 56b) rise to greater prominence. Also present in late Moundville II are *Moon Lake* (Figure 51r) and
Poole (Figures 51n and 56c), both of which occur on the highly diagnostic
short-neck bowl form (Figure 27).

Moundville Incised is probably no longer present as a type during this
phase, and its moderate showing in the upper levels of our stratigraphic tests is
best attributed to mixture with earlier material (Figure 60). As evidence, we
can cite the fact that of 29 unburnished jars found in secure Moundville III
gravelots, not one shows this kind of decoration. Also supporting this conclusion is the observation that handles on Moundville Incised jars are consistently
unlike the kind most commonly made during Moundville III, a matter that will
be taken up in much more detail later on. (In light of my contention that the
Moundville Incised in the upper levels is due to mixture, it is of some interest to
note that the one *Carrollton* sherd found in AU.3/8N2E undoubtedly comes
from the same vessel as another found on a house floor in L.20/6N2W.)

Finally, in AU.3A/6N2W occur traces of two varieties that were made
during the protohistoric Alabama River phase: One sherd each was found of
Barton Incised, *variety Demopolis* (Figure 56i) and Alabama River Incised,
variety unspecified (Figure 56h). Their presence 20–30 cm below the surface
rather than at the very top of the deposit is probably the result of an intrusive
feature undetected during excavation—not at all surprising given how pocked
the midden was with postholes and pits.

Representational Motifs (Table 13)

Representational motifs are common in the Moundville III complex, being found on vessels of Moundville Engraved, *variety Hemphill* and Carthage Incised, *variety Fosters*. Within *Hemphill,* the following motifs seem to occur only during the early part of the phase: crested bird (Figure 52r and 62g; Moore 1907:Figure 37), raptor (Figures 52n and 62c), paired wings (Moore 1905:Figure 156), windmill, skull and forearm bones (Figure 62h). Those that seem to occur both early and late are hand and eye (Figure 52j and t and 53d, l, and n; Moore 1905:Figures 123, 153), paired tails (Figures 52q and 53m; Moore 1905:Figure 56), radial fingers (Figures 53c and 55l; Moore 1907: Figure 4), scalp (Figures 52t, 53p, and 55i and j), and winged serpent (Figures 52m and p and 53b; Moore 1907:Figures 51, 57, and 63) (see Table 13 and Figure 28). The one turtle representation in our sample of *Hemphill* vessels belongs to a gravelot containing good diagnostics of late Moundville III (Figure 52i). The one occurrence of the insect motif is on a subglobular bottle with a simple base (Figure 53a), which, judging from its overall shape, probably dates to Moundville III or late Moundville II. The feather motif is found on subglobular bottles with slab bases (Figure 62a), some of which could date to early Moundville III (Figure 28).

Mention should also be made of a peculiar depiction of a bird with a serpent head that appears on a *Hemphill* vessel in Segment 3B (Figure 52h). The vessel in question is a subglobular bottle with a slab base, a predominantly earlier form that got seriated late in the sequence because of its association with a deep flaring-rim bowl. The bowl, however, is a borderline case that could have been almost as easily classified shallow—in which case the gravelot would fit most comfortably in late Moundville II or early Moundville III. The reason for raising this point is that it may have some relevance to understanding the development of the "Southern Cult" style on Moundville pottery—if and when someone actually does a thorough study of it. In general, the more unusual depictions of serpent–bird composites tend to occur on early vessel forms or in early contexts—giving one the impression that the style may have undergone progressive standardization through time. The bird with serpent head in Segment 3B seems to be an exception to this rule, but, in fact, it may not be an exception at all.

The range of representational motifs found in Carthage Incised is considerably smaller than in Moundville Engraved. *Variety Fosters,* which tends to occur late in the phase, exhibits only the hand and forearm bones (Figures 51m and p, 56b, and 62p).

Painted Decoration (Tables 14 and 19)

Both black filming and white filming continued to be practiced during Moundville III. Seventy-three percent of the burnished sherds from the uppermost levels in our excavations are smudged (e.g., Figures 55c–e, g–p, r, and 56a–g, and 58a–i and l–p), and 1.8% are white filmed (Figure 56j and k).

Red filming also persists as an element of the ceramic complex (Figure 56m–p). A significant contrast with earlier complexes is that the great majority of sherds that exhibit this treatment are filmed on the interior surface only; most of these sherds are unburnished on the exterior and probably come from jars. Of the 45 red-filmed sherds in our Moundville III levels, 30 are red on the interior only, 10 on both the interior and exterior, and 5 on the exterior only. Also, one Mississippi Plain, *variety Warrior* jar in Segment 3B has a red-filmed interior (SWG7, bu. 1718/SWG).

The red-and-white treatment appears to be an excellent diagnostic for late Moundville III, since it occurs on four vessels in Segment 3B. Usually the red paint is confined to the area of the lip (Figures 51h and p and 62q), but a few deviations from this standard treatment also exist in the collections. On one flaring-rim bowl, the interior is divided radially into quarters, alternately red and white in color (Figure 62p). Another vessel—a white-slipped bowl classified as Carthage Incised, *variety Poole*—has red paint added to the broad incisions that make up the design (SWG9).

Basic Shapes (Tables 15 and 20)

The principal bottle form in this phase is the subglobular bottle with a simple base (Figures 52a–d, f–g, i–k, and m–t, 53a–d, and 62b–g). Subglobular bottles with slab bases also continue to be made (Figures 52e–h and 62a), but decrease in frequency through time, so that by late Moundville III, they are virtually nonexistent. Cylindrical bottles (early) and narrow-neck bottles (late[?]) are also minor elements within the complex (Figures 52l and 62h).

Simple bowls (Figures 51a, d, and g–k, 53e, and 59g–j), restricted bowls (Figures 51c and 53k and l), and shallow flaring-rim bowls (Figures 53j and 62p) are found throughout the phase. Pedestaled bowls (Figure 53f) and cylindrical bowls (Figure 53n–p) are confined mainly to early Moundville III, although rare examples of the cylindrical form may be found later as well (Figure 53m). Late in the phase, the short-neck bowl first appears (Figures 51n–r, 56c, 58a, and 59b–d), and some flaring-rim bowls become deeper and more curving in profile (Figures 53g–j, 58l–p, and 59k–o). That these two shapes should rise to prominence at the very end of the Moundville sequence is significant because they appear to be direct stylistic predecessors for the "carinated" and "wide-rimmed" bowls so common during the subsequent Alabama River phase (see Sheldon 1974:Figure 7). Also worthy of mention is a wide, straight-sided bowl that seriated very late (SD682, bu. 1515/SD), and is unique in the Moundville sample (Figure 51m). Sherds very similar to this specimen in both shape and decoration have been found at protohistoric–historic sites along the Alabama River in the south-central part of the state (N. J. Jenkins, personal communication). Whether the Moundville example is locally made or an import from this more southerly region is at present unclear.

All unburnished jars in Moundville III contexts are of the standard type (Figure 59p–s). Most unburnished jars have four handles (Figure 54b, c, e–h, and k; Moore 1905:Figures 55 and 154), although two-handled jars continue to be found with declining frequency throughout the phase (Figure 54d, j, and l). Jars with eight or even more handles become common late in the phase (Figure 54a, i, n, and o). Thus, direct stylistic continuity is once again evident with the subsequent Alabama River complex, in which the appliqué fillets and vertical ridges placed on jar rims can be regarded as outgrowths of the late Moundville III multiple handle forms.

Burnished jars are mainly found in the early part of the phase. The one example that occurs in Segment 3B is a rather marginal specimen, hardly burnished at all (Figure 51e and f). These jars invariably have two handles, and are often endowed with frog effigy features (Figure 54m; Moore 1905:Figures 78, and 155).

Double bowls occur in likely Moundville III gravelots (bu. 2390/SW, bu. 3001/SL), one of which fell in Segment 3A of the seriation (Figure 51k). Though there are no composite vessels in contexts that can be securely dated to this phase, it seems rather likely that some, if not all, of the composite shapes found in late Moundville II continued into early Moundville III. This suspicion is upheld by the fact that one composite bowl in our sample (Figure 62k) has fish effigy features—a characteristic generally assigned to Moundville III.

Secondary Shape Features (Tables 16 and 21)

Beaded rims are very common during this phase on simple bowls and burnished jars. This feature may encircle the entire circumference of the rim (Figures 51g–l and 58f–j), or it may be found only along part of the rim, representing the dorsal fin of a fish effigy.

The beaded shoulder may turn up in early Moundville III contexts, since it is used on restricted bowls to depict parts of various effigies, for example, the carapace edge of a turtle (Figure 46h and i) and the dorsal fin of a fish (Figures 51c and 62k).

A notched lip occurs rarely on flaring-rim bowls (Figure 58l). Pedestaled bowls, made early in the phase, inevitably have a notched everted lip (Figure 53f).

Indentations continue to be found on early Moundville III bottles. In contrast to Moundville II examples, which usually have eight or more indentations per vessel, a number of the early Moundville III bottles have only four indentations, spaced equidistantly around the circumference of the vessel at its widest point (e.g., Figure 52e and o; Moore 1905:Figure 80).

A single lug, projecting horizontally from the lip, is an added feature of most cylindrical bowls that date to this phase (Figure 53m, n, and p).

Two, four, or six widely spaced nodes are sometimes found on early Moundville III simple bowls and burnished jars (Figures 53e, 54m, and 58d; Moore 1905:Figure 155). This feature often occurs in combination with a beaded rim, especially on burnished jars. Inasmuch as the band of nodes sometimes occurs on bowls of Moundville Engraved, *variety Havana,* the feature may date to early Moundville III (Rho48, EI2). However, in the absence of better contextual information, this temporal assignment is quite uncertain.

Vertical lugs are found on a single bowl of Carthage Incised, *variety Carthage* (NE461), implying that the feature belongs to the Moundville III complex.

One flaring-rim bowl sherd from AU.3/6N2W exhibits a scalloped rim (Figure 58n). Whether this sherd indeed belongs to the Moundville III complex, or is present as a result of stratigraphic mixture with earlier material, cannot be firmly decided with the data at hand. However, the rim does have a late look to it, in that the flaring part is wide and curving in profile, rather than fairly short and/or straight as in most Moundville I examples.

Downturned lugs are sometimes added to standard jars with two or four handles (Figure 54c, h, and j). Such lugs are often embellished with nodes, similar to the kind found on the handles.

Folded rims from standard jars also show up in the counts from the upper levels of our excavations, but their presence is undoubtedly the result of mixture with earlier midden (Figure 60a). Not one of the 29 jars found in Moundville III gravelots exhibits this mode; nor does a folded rim occur on any jar in the sample with the kind of handles characteristic of this phase.

Handle measurements taken on our (for once) respectable sample of unburnished jars are presented in Tables 25 and 26, for Segments 3A and 3B separately. It can be seen that, in contrast to earlier phases, handles tend to be strongly tapered at the bottom. Their top-width : bottom-width ratio averages 1.9 in early Moundville III, and 2.0 in late Moundville III. Moreover, the handles are generally more straplike than in the previous phases, with a middle-width : thickness ratio averaging 3.1 in the early part, and 2.7 in the late part. One reason that the average ratio drops somewhat at the late end is that jars with eight or more handles become common, and these handles tend to be narrower, more looplike, than the handles on two- and four-handled jars.

In fact, by plotting the middle-width : thickness ratio against the top-width : bottom-width ratio for all our specimens combined, we can clearly see not only the trends in handle shape through time, but also the distinctions among the handles from different phases (Figure 29). Early handles, more looplike and parallel sided, tend to fall in the lower left portion of the scatter, and late handles, more straplike and tapered, tend to fall in the upper right. Differences attributable to time can be highlighted by dividing the scatter into three parts. The zone to the left of line A contains only jars dating to Moundville I; between lines A and B are most of the jars from Moundville II, mixed with some from Moundville I and III; finally, the zone to the right of line

TABLE 25

Handle Measurements of Early Moundville III Unburnished Jars

Catalog number	Type, variety	Burial number	Handles (no.)
SD744	Mississippi Pl., *Warrior*	1525/SD	2
SD746	Mississippi Pl., *Warrior*	1525/SD	4
NE585	Mississippi Pl., *Warrior*	1651/NE	4
SWG1	Mississippi Pl., *Warrior*	1717/SWG	4
SWG4	Mississippi Pl., *Warrior*	1717/SWG	4
SWG5	Mississippi Pl., *Warrior*	1717/SWG	8
SWG25	Mississippi Pl., *Warrior*	1751/SWG	4
EI27	Mississippi Pl., *Warrior*	824/EI	2
NN'39	Mississippi Pl., *Warrior*	2136/NN'	4
WP228	Mississippi Pl., *Warrior*	2496/WP	2
NEC10/M5	Mississippi Pl., *Warrior*	20/NEC/M5	4

TABLE 26

Handle Measurements of Late Moundville III Unburnished Jars

Catalog number	Type, variety	Burial number	Handles (no.)
SD29	Mississippi Pl., *Warrior*	1423/SD	4
SD31	Mississippi Pl., *Warrior*	1423/SD	4
SD32	Mississippi Pl., *Warrior*	1423/SD	2
SD680	Mississippi Pl., *Warrior*	1515/SD	4
SD681	Mississippi Pl., *Warrior*	1515/SD	8
SD837	Mississippi Pl., *Warrior*	1563-64/SD	2
SD838	Mississippi Pl., *Warrior*	1563-64/SD	4
EE88	Mississippi Pl., *Warrior*	1234-37/EE	2
EE124	Mississippi Pl., *Warrior*	1261/EE	4
NG32	Mississippi Pl., *Warrior*	1008/NG	4
SWG7	Mississippi Pl., *Warrior*	1718/SWG	7
EI40	Mississippi Pl., *Warrior*	843/EI	4
NR27	Mississippi Pl., *Warrior*	1089/NR	4
NR28	Mississippi Pl., *Warrior*	1089/NR	5
Rw139	Mississippi Pl., *Warrior*	2733/Rw	8
NR20/M5	Mississippi Pl., *Warrior*	10/NR/M5	4

TABLE 25 (Continued)

Top width (mm)	Middle width (mm)	Bottom width (mm)	Thickness (mm)	Vertical height (mm)	Clearance (mm)	TW:BW ratio[1]	MW:Th ratio[2]
22	18	16	5	35	7	1.4	3.6
20	12	15	5	42	7	1.3	2.4
22	10	13	3	25	7	1.7	3.3
33	19	16	5	38	3	2.1	3.8
26	17	12	4	36	8	2.2	4.3
33	13	13	5	29	8	2.5	2.6
29	12	10	4	29	11	2.9	3.0
13	12	11	8	28	6	1.6	1.5
50	27	22	5	45	9	2.3	5.4
16	13	12	8	30	6	1.3	1.6
—	—	—	—	—	—	—	—
						$\bar{x}=1.9$	$\bar{x}=3.1$

[1] This ratio is the top width divided by the bottom width.
[2] This ratio is the middle width divided by the thickness.

TABLE 26 (Continued)

Top width (mm)	Middle width (mm)	Bottom width (mm)	Thickness (mm)	Vertical height (mm)	Clearance (mm)	TW:BW ratio[1]	MW:Th ratio[2]
27	12	13	6	28	4	2.1	2.0
25	9	7	5	23	6	3.6	1.8
15	10	12	5	25	4	1.3	2.0
45	20	15	5	38	10	3.0	4.0
23	15	16	5	32	9	1.4	3.0
28	15	15	5	35	8	1.9	3.0
21	14	17	5	31	8	1.2	2.8
—	—	6	4	—	—	—	—
31	15	15	5	28	6	2.1	3.0
23	17	18	4	30	4	1.3	4.3
13	7	7	6	30	5	2.4	1.2
13	9	7	5	23	4	1.9	1.8
—	—	—	—	—	—	—	—
27	12	14	4	24	7	1.9	3.0
—	—	—	—	—	—	—	—
—	—	—	—	—	—	—	—
						$\bar{x}=2.0$[3]	$\bar{x}=2.7$[3]
						$\bar{x}=2.0$[4]	$\bar{x}=2.9$[4]

[1] This ratio is the top width divided by the bottom width.
[2] This ratio is the middle width divided by the thickness.
[3] This is the mean for all late Moundville III unburnished jars.
[4] This is the mean for late Moundville III unburnished jars, excluding vessels SWG7 and EI40.

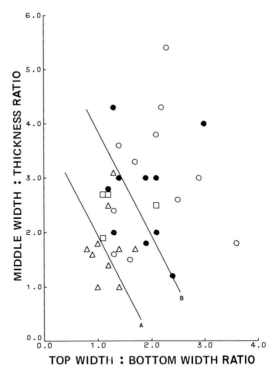

FIGURE 29   Handle-shape ratios of unburnished jars from various phases. (Triangles indicate Moundville I phase; squares indicate Segment 2B, late Moundville II phase; open circles indicate Segment 3A, early Moundville III phase; and filled circles indicate Segment 3B, late Moundville III phase.)

TABLE 27
Handle Measurements of Moundville Incised Jars

Catalog number	Type. variety	Burial number	Handles (no.)
ED54	Moundville Inc., *Carrollton*	2607/ED	2
ED71	Moundville Inc., *Carrollton*	2614/ED	—
SD155	Moundville Inc., *Carrollton*	1437/SD	4
SD265	Moundville Inc., *Carrollton*	1455/SD	2
SEH76	Moundville Inc., *Carrollton*	870/SEH	2
WP21	Moundville Inc., *Moundville*	2179-80/WP	4
NW9	Moundville Inc., *Snows Bend*	1837/NW	4
<I>Rho163	Moundville Inc., *Moundville*	—	—

B contains only Moundville III jars, along with a single specimen from late Moundville II. It is worthwhile to note that of the seven Moundville III examples that fall to the left of line B, two are very late jars with eight or more handles—in general, such handles tend to be more looplike or parallel-sided—and three are two-handled jars that look very much like earlier forms, and probably are either heirlooms, or appear in gravelots that are in fact older than the seriation indicates.

Looking at handle measurements in this way also provides us an opportunity to check the chronological assignment of Moundville Incised. Table 27 presents all the available handle measurements for jars of this type from Moundville; most of these jars come from gravelots that include no other temporally diagnostic vessels. When the two ratios are plotted on the same kind of diagram (Figure 30), we find that all the points fall to the left of line B, a result consistent with my suspicion that Moundville Incised was not locally produced during Moundville III times.

Nodes are a common accoutrement of handles on unburnished jars (Figure 54). Typical patterns include two or three nodes arranged vertically, a single node centered on the front of the handle, and three nodes in a triangular configuration. Handles are luted, not riveted, to the exterior of the vessel, and the top of the handle is often slightly below the level of the lip (e.g., Figures 57b and d and 59q). Also, the handles tend to be straighter, almost vertical in profile, and do not curve outward nearly as much as the typical early form.

Handles on burnished jars are always straplike, and tend to be more parallel sided than those on unburnished jars of this phase. The mean middle-width : thickness ratio of the three handles that were measured is 3.7, and the mean top-width : bottom-width ratio is 1.4 (Table 28).

TABLE 27 (Continued)

Top width (mm)	Middle width (mm)	Bottom width (mm)	Thick-ness (mm)	Vertical height (mm)	Clear-ance (mm)	TW:BW ratio[1]	MW:Th ratio[2]
22	–	13	5	37	–	1.7	–
19	15	16	7	30	7	1.2	2.1
15	13	13	5	30	8	1.2	2.6
10	9	10	5	25	6	1.0	1.8
14	10	11	6	23	5	1.3	1.7
11	9	11	4	31	9	1.0	2.3
19	16	19	5	37	6	1.0	3.2
15	11	10	4	22	7	1.5	2.8
						$\bar{x}=1.2$	$\bar{x}=2.4$

[1] This ratio is the top width divided by the bottom width.
[2] This ratio is the middle width divided by the thickness.

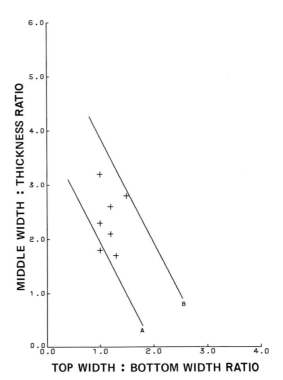

FIGURE 30   Handle-shape ratios, Moundville Incised jars.

TABLE 28
Handle Measurements of Moundville III Burnished Jars

Catalog number	Type, variety	Burial number	Handles (no.)
RW138	Bell Pl., *Hale*	2733/RW	2
SD2/M5	Bell Pl., *Hale*	1/SD/M5	2
SEH10	Bell Pl., *Hale*	18/SEH	2
WP'29	Bell Pl., *Hale*	2166/WP'	2
NR23/M5	Bell Pl., *Hale*	38/NR/M5	2
WR58	Bell Pl., *Hale*	1045/WR	2

Effigy Features (Table 17)

Lug-and-rim-effigy bowls continue to be made in Moundville III. In contrast to earlier examples, particularly those in Moundville I, bird effigy heads tend to be more gracile and naturalistically executed (Figures 51a and 62l; also see DeJarnette and Peebles 1970:111). Another contrast is the fact that the heads invariably face outward rather than inward, and the lug opposite the head often exhibits a series of parallel incisions on top, perpendicular to the lip, that are probably intended to represent tail feathers.

Another lug-and-rim-effigy form dating to this phase is the feline. The one such effigy in our sample (Figure 62q) is painted red and white, implying that it was made in late Moundville III. If and when more data become available, however, I would not at all be surprised to find this form turning up earlier in the phase as well.

One of the most common effigy forms throughout Moundville III is the fish effigy bowl (Figures 51c and 62k). In addition to various appliqué features that represent the head, tail, and ventral fins, these effigies almost always have a notched appliqué band as a dorsal fin—which in sherd collections might be sorted as a beaded rim or a beaded shoulder.

Frog effigies modeled on burnished jars are the second most common effigy form in our Moundville III gravelots, their greatest concentration being early in the phase (Figure 51b and 58q; Moore 1905:Figure 78).

Another contemporary effigy form consists of a simple bowl with a beaded rim, to which have been added four human head medallions spaced equidistantly around the rim (Figure 51g). The one late example in Segment 3B is painted red and white, whereas the two in Segment 3A are simply black filmed.

Three less common effigies that can probably be assigned to early Moundville III are the beaver depicted on a simple bowl (Figure 51d), the turtle

TABLE 28 (Continued)

Top width (mm)	Middle width (mm)	Bottom width (mm)	Thickness (mm)	Vertical height (mm)	Clearance (mm)	TW:BW ratio[1]	MW:Th ratio[2]
—	—	—	—	—	—	—	—
—	—	—	—	—	—	—	—
33	18	17	5	31	9	1.9	3.6
21	19	19	5	22	7	1.1	3.8
—	—	—	—	—	—	—	—
19	15	16	4	32	10	1.2	3.8
						$\bar{x}=1.4$	$\bar{x}=3.7$

[1] This ratio is the top width divided by the bottom width.
[2] This ratio is the middle width divided by the thickness.

depicted on a restricted bowl (Figure 46h and i), and the alligator (as discussed on 114).

Dating

Two radiocarbon dates are available from Moundville III contexts. A sample of charcoal from a hearthlike feature in Level 4, unit 6N2W, yielded an uncorrected date of A.D. 1840±50 (DIC-1242), obviously an inaccurate determination. The only reasonable date comes from Structure 1 at Lubbub (1Pi33), the uncorrected estimate being A.D. 1410±45 (DIC-1233; Jenkins 1981:33, Table 1). Based on the latter date, and the knowledge that Alabama River phase materials have recently been dated to the mid-sixteenth and seventeenth centuries (Curren and Little n.d.), I would estimate that Moundville III lasted from about A.D. 1400 to about A.D. 1550.

SUMMARY AND DISCUSSION

Having just described the ceramic complexes of our newly defined phases in minute detail, it is useful to briefly recapitulate the late prehistoric ceramic sequence in the Warrior Valley as it now stands. The five phases with which we are concerned are now reviewed in chronological order, and a few general points regarding the continuity evident in the sequence as a whole are discussed.

The West Jefferson phase (A.D. 900–1050) exhibits a ceramic complex that is almost entirely grog tempered. The predominant vessel forms are simple bowls and jars, the latter often having two parallel-sided handles. The vast majority of vessels are undecorated, and are classified as Baytown Plain, *variety Roper*. Rarer in the complex are Mulberry Creek Cord-Marked, *variety Aliceville*, Alligator Incised, *variety Geiger*, and Benson Punctate, *variety unspecified*. Shell-tempered ceramics are also found, especially late in the phase, but never in quantities of more than a few percent. The shell-tempered types identified include Mississippi Plain, *variety Warrior* and Moundville Incised, *variety Carrollton*.

It is not until the subsequent Moundville I phase (A.D. 1050–1250) that virtually all vessels become shell tempered. Simple bowls and two-handled jars similar to those in the West Jefferson complex continue to be made, and a number of new shapes are added. Among these new forms are the restricted bowl, the flaring-rim bowl, the slender ovoid bottle, and (late in the phase) the subglobular bottle with a pedestal base. Most of the pottery again is undecorated, falling into the categories Mississippi Plain, *variety Warrior* and Bell Plain, *variety Hale*—the two varieties that remain numerically predominant throughout the rest of the sequence. Decorated bowls and bottles are represented in Carthage Incised, *varieties Akron, Moon Lake*, and *Summerville*, and in Moundville Engraved, *varieties Elliots Creek, Havana*, and *Stewart*. Unburnished jars, when decorated, usually exhibit the arch motif characteristic of Moundville Incised, the most common variety being *Moundville*.

In the Moundville II phase (A.D. 1250–1400), the slender ovoid bottle is replaced by the subglobular form with a pedestal base; late in the phase, slab-base bottles become common as well. The various bowl shapes found in the previous phase continue into Moundville II, and a cylindrical bowl form (often with a single lug) is added to the complex. Jars are generally similar to those in the previous phase, except that most of them have four handles instead of only two. Common secondary shape features include indentations and, late in the phase, beaded rims. The decorated type Moundville Engraved is mainly represented by *varieties Havana, Northport, Taylorville, Hemphill*, and *Tuscaloosa*, the latter two appearing late. Carthage Incised is present as *variety Akron*. Moundville Incised also continues into this phase but with sharply declining popularity as time goes on.

With the start of the Moundville III phase (A.D. 1400–1550) the pedestaled bottle disappears, the slab-base bottle declines in popularity, and the dominant form becomes the subglobular bottle with a simple base. The restricted, simple, cylindrical, and flaring-rim bowl shapes continue to be found; late in the phase, the flaring-rim bowls tend to get deeper and the short-neck bowl first appears. Unburnished jars usually have four handles, but as time goes on, jars with eight or even more handles become commonplace. Moundville III handles, in contrast to most earlier examples, tend to be strap-like and tapered near the bottom. Beaded rims on bowls, which first appeared in Moundville II, attain their greatest frequency in Moundville III. Moundville Engraved is most often represented in the varieties *Wiggins* and *Hemphill*, although *Taylorville, Tuscaloosa*, and *Havana* appear as well, mainly in the early part of the phase. Carthage Incised attains a bit of a resurgence in the varieties *Akron, Carthage, Moon Lake*, and *Poole*. Unburnished jars from this phase are typically undecorated. Late in the phase, red-and-white painted vessels begin to be made.

The Alabama River phase (A.D. 1550–1700), last in the prehistoric sequence, is marked by a ceramic complex that is stylistically a direct outgrowth of the one in late Moundville III. Many of the same vessel forms continue, including the short-neck bowl, the flaring-rim bowl, and the subglobular bottle with a simple base. Standard jars may have 4, 8, or more than 10 handles, but in many cases, the handles are replaced either by appliqué neck fillets or vertical pinched-up ridges of clay. The predominant undecorated varieties continue to be Bell Plain, *variety Hale* and Mississippi Plain, *variety Warrior*. Decorated categories include Alabama River Incised, *variety unspecified*, Barton Incised, *variety Demopolis*, Carthage Incised, *varieties Carthage* and *Fosters*, and certain varieties of Moundville Engraved that have not as yet been formally named. As in late Moundville III, red-and-white painting continues to be used, especially on flaring-rim bowls.

Discussion

The ceramic sequence just presented evidences a great deal of stylistic continuity, especially from Moundville I onward, indicating an uninterrupted local development. This continuity can be traced in the persistence, across phase boundaries, of particular decorative techniques, specific designs, modes of temper, and vessel shapes. Even when the features present in each phase fall into different formal categories, these categories can often be seen as arbitrary divisions along a continuum marked by a gradual set of transformations. For example, the chronological sequence of bottle shapes (slender ovoid bottle, subglobular bottle with a pedestal base, subglobular bottle with a slab base, and subglobular bottle with a simple base) clearly represents a stylistic series marked by a gradual increase in the width of the body, followed by a gradual decrease in the prominence of the basal pedestal.

The only transition in the sequence that appears to be abrupt is that between West Jefferson and Moundville I. A number of major changes took place in this transition, including (a) the wholesale adoption of shell tempering

TABLE 29
Summary Chronology of Types and Varieties[1]

Type, variety	Moundville I	Moundville II		Moundville III	
		Early	Late	Early	Late
Bell Pl., *Hale*	X	X	X	X	X
Mississippi Pl., *Hull Lake*	X	X	X	X	X
Mississippi Pl., *Warrior*	X	X	X	X	X
Carthage Inc., *Akron*	X	X	X	X	
Carthage Inc., *Carthage*				X	X
Carthage Inc., *Fosters*				X	X
Carthage Inc., *Moon Lake*	X	?	?	X	X
Carthage Inc., *Poole*					X
Carthage Inc., *Summerville*	X	?			
Moundville Eng., *Cypress*				X	
Moundville Eng., *Elliots Creek*	X				
Moundville Eng., *Englewood*				X	X
Moundville Eng., *Havana*	X	X	X	X	
Moundville Eng., *Hemphill*		–	X	X	X
Moundville Eng., *Maxwells Crossing*		(X)	X	X	
Moundville Eng., *Northport*	X	X	X		
Moundville Eng., *Prince Plantation*		(X)	(X)		
Moundville Eng., *Stewart*	X	?			
Moundville Eng., *Taylorville*		X	X	X	
Moundville Eng., *Tuscaloosa*			X	X	
Moundville Eng., *Wiggins*			X	X	X
Moundville Inc., *Carrollton*	X	X	–		
Moundville Inc., *Moundville*	X	X	–		
Moundville Inc., *Snows Bend*	X	X	–		
Barton Inc., *unspecified*	X	?	?	?	?

[1] Key: X, present; (X), very likely present; –, present, but in greatly reduced frequency; (–), very likely present, but in greatly reduced frequency; ?, possibly present.

TABLE 30

Summary Chronology of Representational Motifs[1]

Representational motif	Moundville I	Moundville II		Moundville III	
		Early	Late	Early	Late
Bilobed arrow		(X)	X		
Bird with serpent head			?	?	?
Crested bird			?	X	
Feather			(X)	(X)	
Feathered arrow		(X)	(X)	?	
Forearm bones				X	X
Forked eye surround		X	(X)		
Greek cross		(X)	(X)	?	
Hand and eye		(-)	X	X	X
Human head		?	?	?	?
Insect			(X)	(X)	(X)
Ogee		(X)	X		
Paired tails			X	X	X
Paired wings				X	
Radial fingers		?	X	X	X
Raptor		(-)	(-)	X	
Rayed circle		(X)	(X)	?	
Scalp			(-)	X	X
Skull				X	
Turtle					X
Windmill		?	X	X	
Winged serpent				X	X

[1] Key: X, present; (X), very likely present; -, present, but in greatly reduced frequency; (-), very likely present, but in greatly reduced frequency; ?, possibly present.

TABLE 31

Summary Chronology of Painted Decoration[1]

Painted decoration	Moundville I	Moundville II		Moundville III	
		Early	Late	Early	Late
Black film	X	X	X	X	X
Red film	X	X	X	X	X
White film	X	X	X	X	X
Red and black	X	(X)	(X)		
Red and white					X
Black on white	X				
Red and black on white	?	X	?		
Red engraved	X				
White engraved	X				

[1] Key: X, present; (X), very likely present; -, present, but in greatly reduced frequency; (-), very likely present, but in greatly reduced frequency; ?, possibly present.

at the expense of grog tempering, (*b*) the appearance of bottle forms, and (*c*) the appearance of certain decorative techniques such as engraving and black filming. However striking or rapid these changes might have been, it is important to stress that the West Jefferson–Moundville I transition does not represent a total break in the ceramic tradition, whether stylistic or technological. For example, the bowl and two-handled jar shapes made throughout West Jefferson times persist unchanged into Moundville I. Moreover, the shift in tempering practices, though rapid, is by no means absolute or instantaneous. There is clear-cut evidence for the use of shell temper in West Jefferson times; not only do the types Mississippi Plain and Moundville Incised form a consistent minority in late West Jefferson assemblages, but a grog-tempered sherd with shell inclusions has been found in a West Jefferson context dated to A.D. 900, suggesting that West Jefferson potters may have been experimenting with shell temper some 150 years before it came to dominance (see p. 81). Nor does the practice of grog tempering completely stop after Moundville I begins. Grog

TABLE 32
Summary Chronology of Basic Shapes[1]

Basic shape	Moundville I	Moundville II		Moundville III	
		Early	Late	Early	Late
Cylindrical bottle		X	(X)	X	
Narrow-neck bottle				?	X
Slender ovoid bottle	X				
Subglobular bottle, pedestal base	X	X	X		
Subglobular bottle, slab base			X	X	-
Subglobular bottle, simple base	-	?	X	X	X
Cylindrical bowl		X	X	X	-
Flaring-rim bowl:					
(deep)				(X)	X
(shallow)	X	X	X	X	X
Outslanting bowl	?	(X)	(X)	?	
Pedestaled bowl	X	(X)	X	X	
Restricted bowl	X	(X)	X	X	X
Short-neck bowl					X
Simple bowl	X	X	X	X	X
Terraced rectanguloid bowl	?	X	?		
Burnished jar	X	(X)	X	X	-
Neckless jar (unburnished)	X	-			
Standard jar:					
(unburnished, 2 handles)	X	(X)	X	X	-
(unburnished, 4 handles)	?	(X)	X	X	X
(unburnished, 8 handles)				X	X
(unburnished, 10+ handles)					X
Composite bowl			X	(X)	
Composite bowl-jar			X	(X)	
Composite jar-bowl			(X)	(X)	
Double bowl	?	?	(X)	X	?

[1] Key: X, present; (X), very likely present; -, present, but in greatly reduced frequency; (-), very likely present, but in greatly reduced frequency; ?, possibly present.

TABLE 33

Summary Chronology of Secondary Shape Features[1]

Secondary shape feature	Moundville I	Moundville II		Moundville III	
		Early	Late	Early	Late
Band of nodes	(X)	(X)	X	(X)	
Beaded rim			X	X	X
Beaded shoulder	X	(X)	X	X	
Cutout rim	X	?			
Downturned lugs				X	X
Folded rim	X				
Folded-flattened rim	X				
Gadrooning	X	(X)	(X)		
Grouped nodes	X	(X)	X		
Indentations		X	X	X	
Lowered lip	X	X	?		
Notched everted lip		(X)	X	X	
Notched lip		(X)	(X)	X	
Opposing lugs		?	?	?	?
Scalloped rim	X	?	?	(X)	(X)
Single lug		X	X	X	–
Spouts			X		
Vertical lugs				(X)	(X)
Widely spaced nodes:					
(bowl or burnished jar)			X	X	
(unburnished jar)	(X)	(X)	(X)		

[1] Key: X, present; (X), very likely present; –, present, but in greatly reduced frequency; (–), very likely present, but in greatly reduced frequency; ?, possibly present.

TABLE 34

Summary Chronology of Effigy Features[1]

Effigy features	Moundville I	Moundville II		Moundville III	
		Early	Late	Early	Late
Alligator			(X)	(X)	
Beaver			?	X	
Bird:					
(flat head, inward facing)	X	(X)	?		
(flat head, outward facing)	?	(X)	(X)		
(gracile head, outward facing)		?	(X)	X	(X)
Conch shell	X	(X)	(X)		
Feline				?	X
Fish				X	X
Frog				X	X
Frog heads	?	?	?	?	?
Human head medallions			?	X	X
Mammal, unidentified	X	(X)	?	?	
Mussel shell	?	X	X		
Shell spoon	?	?	?	?	?
Turtle			(X)	(X)	
Turtle, inverted			X		

[1] Key: X, present; (X), very likely present; –, present, but in greatly reduced frequency; (–), very likely present, but in greatly reduced frequency; ?, possibly present.

continues to be used throughout the sequence: mixed with shell, it occurs in paste compositions characteristic of Mississippi Plain, *variety Hull Lake* and (sometimes) Bell Plain, *variety Hale.*

The apparent abruptness of the change between West Jefferson and Moundville I has prompted some workers to express the view that the transition was brought about by the in-migration of people bearing a foreign ceramic tradition (Jenkins 1976a). Given the continuities just discussed, however, it seems to me just as plausible, considerably simpler, and therefore preferable to view this transition as being essentially an indigenous process. Undoubtedly, interaction with other regions and other ceramic traditions conditioned the content, and perhaps the rapidity of the ceramic changes that led to Moundville I, but I see no compelling evidence to believe that shell-tempered ceramics necessarily had to be "brought in" by an outside group.

In the same vein, it is important to point out that the abruptness of the ceramic changes between West Jefferson and Moundville I may, at least to some extent, be an illusion created by the nature of the data we have at our disposal. The West Jefferson phase, it will be recalled, was originally defined on the basis of a ceramic assemblage for which the latest dates seemed to fall around A.D. 1050. The current definition of the Moundville I phase, on the other hand, rests primarily on the material excavated from the lower levels of 8N2E and 6N2W. Although the Moundville I deposits encountered in these levels were thick, no ceramic change could be detected stratigraphically within them, suggesting that they may not represent a very long span of time. Given that the top of these Moundville I deposits was dated to about A.D. 1250, it may be that the assemblage from these deposits is more representative of late Moundville I than of the phase as a whole. Thus, our present conception of the differences between West Jefferson and Moundville I may well rest not on a comparison of two assemblages adjacent in time, but rather of two assemblages separated by a gap, thereby artificially accentuating the differences between them. If and when an early Moundville I component is isolated—there is undoubtedly one at Bessemer—I suspect it will contain considerably less engraved ware than late Moundville I, perhaps none at all, and therefore will be stylistically much closer to West Jefferson.[2]

To close this chapter, and to set the stage for the next one, the ceramic chronology for our three newly defined phases is summarized in Tables 29–34.

---

[2]As this book goes to press, a restudy of the Bessemer ceramic collection has been undertaken by Welch (1981b). His preliminary results seem to confirm that the lowest levels in our test excavations at Moundville represent only the late Moundville I phase, bordering on Moundville II. The earliest Moundville I levels at Bessemer are characterized by an assemblage in which the principal decorated types are Barton Incised and Moundville Incised, and the predominant undecorated wares are Mississippi Plain, *variety Warrior* and Bayton Plain, *variety Roper.* Interestingly, engraving is virtually absent, burnished wares are virtually absent, and a relatively large proportion of the unburnished shell-tempered wares contain grog inclusions. Whether *Roper* actually was produced at this time or is present as a result of mixture with earlier deposits is unclear; however, in either case this assemblage does provide a plausible developmental link between West Jefferson and late Moundville I.

5

Community Patterns at Moundville

With the ceramic chronology now established, let us turn to the subject of how the size and configuration of the Moundville site changed through time. All the evidence gathered thus far suggests that people at Moundville were usually buried in close proximity to residential areas—in the floors of dwellings, just outside the dwellings' walls, or in cemeteries nearby (Jones and DeJarnette n.d.:3; Peebles 1978:375–381; 1979). Burials also occur in many of the mounds. Therefore, by plotting the distribution of dated burials and vessels for each time period separately, it should be possible to get at least a rough idea of when different parts of the site were occupied, and when various mounds were built.

The plan of this chapter is as follows: First, I give a brief account of how the ceramic chronology was used to assign relative dates to vessels and the burials with which they were associated. Then, I discuss what is known about the spatial context of these features, and consider some of the limitations in the kinds of spatial interpretations that can be drawn. Finally, the chronological and spatial information are brought together in reconstructing community patterns at Moundville as they existed at various points in time.

RELATIVE DATING OF VESSELS AND BURIALS

The assignment of dates to vessels and burials was a two-step process. All of the whole vessels in the sample were first dated individually, and these dated vessels were then used to chronologically place the burials in which they were found. The actual procedures by which the dates were assigned are described more fully below.

To begin with, each vessel was described in terms of the six classificatory dimensions to which the ceramic chronology refers (see Chapter 3). Each vessel might exhibit features characteristic of a particular type and variety, a particular kind of painted decoration, a basic shape category, certain secondary shape features, and so on. The chronological range of each of these features was usually known (see Tables 29–34 in Chapter 4); logically, therefore, a vessel that exhibited a certain set of features must have been made when the ranges of all these features overlapped. For example, if a vessel had a design that was known to date from Moundville I to late Moundville II, and a basic shape that was diagnostic of the time from late Moundville II to early Moundville III, then the vessel itself could only have been manufactured during late Moundville II.

Once all the vessels had been assigned dates in this manner, these vessels were grouped into gravelots, which could then be used to date the associated burials. A burial containing a single vessel was assigned a date (or date range) identical to that of the vessel. A burial containing more than one vessel was assigned a date corresponding to the span of time in which the date ranges of the individual vessels overlapped. In carrying out this procedure, only local vessels were taken into account, since the chronological positions of nonlocal vessels usually could not be as reliably established.

The resulting temporal assignments for all burials from which ceramic data were available are presented in Table 35. Inasmuch as the spatial distribution of "unassociated" vessels—those that cannot be reliably tied to grave proveniences—may also be of interest, their relative dates are given individually in Table 36.

It is readily apparent from these tables that the above procedures, whether applied to vessels or gravelots, often result in chronological assignments that span more than one phase or phase segment; that is, most vessels and gravelots are dated to a plausible range, rather than to a "point" in time. At first glance this protocol might seem a bit retrogressive, for had not many gravelots already been dated more precisely when they were seriated? The answer is unequivocally no. The seriation did indeed assign each gravelot a best-fit position, but this best fit is by no means the only possible position, nor is it even the only plausible one. Looking back at Figure 25, let us consider gravelot 20/NEC/M5 as an example. This gravelot contained attributes 21 (paired tails) and 7 (subglobular bottle with a simple base), and on this basis it was assigned a best-fit position in Segment 3A (early Moundville III). Yet taking the full chronological range of these two attributes into account (see Figure 26), we see that this burial could actually date anywhere from Segment 2B (late Moundville II) to Segment 3B (late Moundville III). This seeming paradox merely points up the long-recognized (and oft-ignored) fact that the formulation of a ceramic chronology is distinct, both logically and methodologically,

TABLE 35
Temporal Placement of Burials

Burial number(s)[1]	Sample size[2]	Moundville I	Moundville II		Moundville III		Alabama River
			Early	Late	Early	Late	
2914/AdB	1/1			X	X	X	
1894/Rho	1/3	X	X	X	X	X	X
1895/Rho	1/2			X	X		
1896/Rho	1/1	X	X	X	X	X	X
1901/Rho	1/1	X	X	X	X		
1909/Rho	1/1	X	X	X	X		
1923/Rho	2/3			X	X		
1924/Rho	1/1	X	X	X	X	X	X
1931/Rho	2/2			X	X	X	
1934/Rho	3/4	X	X	X	X	X	X
1936/Rho	1/1				X		
1937/Rho	1/1	X	X	X	X	X	X
1939/Rho	1/1			X	X		
1940/Rho	1/2	X	X	X	X	X	X
1943–44/Rho	1/1	X	X	X	X	X	X
1947/Rho	1/1				X	X	
1949/Rho	2/4	X	X	X	X	X	X
1950/Rho	2/3	X	X				
1955/Rho	1/3	X	X	X	X	X	X
1956–57/Rho	2/3					X	
1958/Rho	1/1	X	X	X	X	X	X
1960/Rho	1/1	X	X	X	X	X	X
1964/Rho	1/1	X	X	X	X	X	X
1968/Rho	6/6			X			
1969/Rho	1/3				X	X	
1977/Rho	2/2	X	X				
1978/Rho	7/8	X					
1979/Rho	2/3			X	X	X	
2001/Rho	2/2			X	X	X	
2004/Rho	1/1				X	X	
2008–9/Rho	1/1				X	X	
2011/Rho	1/1	X	X	X	X		
2021/Rho	1/1				X	X	
2025/Rho	1/1			X	X	X	
2042/Rho	2/2	X					
2045/Rho	1/1			X	X	X	
2047/Rho	2/2	X					
2062/Rho	1/2	X	X	X	X	X	X
2068/Rho	4/7					X	
2069–71/Rho	1/2		X	X	X	X	
2079/Rho	1/1	X	X	X	X		
2082/Rho	1/1	X	X	X	X		
2087/Rho	1/3			X	X	X	
2094/Rho	1/1	X	X	X	X	X	X
2096/Rho	1/1			X	X		
2102/Rho	2/2				X		
2110/Rho	2/2			X	X		
2115/Rho	2/3			X			
3/RPB	1/1			X	X	X	

(continued)

TABLE 35 (Continued)

Burial number(s)[1]	Sample size[2]	Moundville I	Moundville II		Moundville III		Alabama River
			Early	Late	Early	Late	
5/RPB	1/1			X	X	X	
8/RPB	1/1			X	X	X	
2664-65/Rw	2/2				X	X	
2673/Rw	1/1	X	X	X			
2687/Rw	1/1		X				
2722/Rw	2/3			X	X		
2725/Rw	2/4			X	X	X	
2726,27,36/Rw	1/1			X	X		
2728-29/Rw	1/1			X	X	X	
2733/Rw	3/3				X	X	
2734/Rw	1/1				X		
2743/Rw	1/3	X	X	X	X	X	X
2747/Rw	1/2	X	X	X	X	X	X
2749/Rw	1/1		X	X	X		
2751/Rw	1/1	X	X	X			
2760/Rw	2/2		X	X	X		
2768/Rw	1/1					X	X
2772/Rw	2/2			X			
2773/Rw	1/1	X	X	X	X	X	X
2774/Rw	1/2	X	X	X	X	X	X
2788/Rw	1/1	X	X	X	X	X	X
2790/Rw	1/1			X	X	X	
2808/Rw	1/1	X	X				
2820/Rw	1/1	X	X	X	X	X	X
2854/Rw	1/1		X	X			
2857/Rw	1/1			X	X		
2859/Rw	1/1		X				
2880/Rw	2/2			X	X		
2882/Rw	1/2		X	X			
2884/Rw	1/1	X					
F.1/WB/M5	1/2	X	X	X	X	X	X
F.1/WB/M5	1/1			X	X		
5,6/C/M5	3/3			X			
F.1/C/M5	2/2			X	X		
F.2/C/M5	2/3			X			
F.3/C/M5	1/2	X	X	X			
2/NEC/M5	1/2					X	X
3/NEC/M5	1/1	X	X	X	X	X	X
11/NEC/M5	1/2	X	X				
20/NEC/M5	2/2				X	X	
F.3/D/M5	1/1			X	X		
F.4/D/M5	1/1			X	X	X	
17/ND	1/1	X	X	X	X		
2172/ND	1/1	X	X	X	X	X	X
2173/ND	1/1				X	X	
F.1/ND/M5	1/2	X	X	X	X	X	X
F.3/ND/M5	1/1			X	X		
F.5/ND/M5	1/1		X	X			
F.6/ND/M5	1/1	X	X	X	X	X	X
F.7/ND/M5	2/2		X	X			

(continued)

TABLE 35 (Continued)

Burial number(s)[1]	Sample size[2]	Moundville I	Moundville II Early	Moundville II Late	Moundville III Early	Moundville III Late	Alabama River
F.8/ND/M5	1/2			X	X		
F.9/ND/M5	1/1			X	X		
13/NED	1/2	X	X	X	X		
18/NED	1/1	X	X	X	X	X	X
20/NED	1/1	X	X	X	X		
26/NED	1/1	X	X	X	X	X	X
8/ED	2/2			X	X		
2598/ED	1/3	X	X	X			
2607/ED	1/2	X	X				
2614/ED	1/2	X	X				
1/SED	1/1	X	X	X	X		
7/SED	1/1			X	X	X	
1/SD	1/1		X				
1423/SD	4/5			X	X	X	
1437/SD	2/2		X	X			
1442/SD	1/1	X	X	X	X	X	X
1443/SD	1/1	X	X	X	X		
1444/SD	2/2	X	X				
1446/SD	1/2	X	X	X	X	X	X
1453/SD	1/2	X	X	X	X		
1455/SD	3/3	X					
1457/SD	2/4	X	X	X	X	X	X
1459/SD	1/1				X		
1462/SD	1/1			X	X	X	
1464/SD	1/1		X	X	X	X	
1468/SD	1/1				X		
1479/SD	1/1		X	X	X	X	
1491/SD	1/1				X		
1495/SD	1/1		X	X	X	X	
1496/SD	4/4			X	X		
1504/SD	3/3			X	X		
1505/SD	2/3			X	X	X	
1514/SD	1/1	X	X	X	X	X	X
1515/SD	5/5				X	X	
1516/SD	3/6			X			
1519/SD	1/1	X	X	X	X	X	X
1520/SD	2/2			X			
1521/SD	1/1	X	X	X	X	X	X
1522/SD	1/1			X	X	X	
1525/SD	6/6				X	X	
1526/SD	2/2	X	X	X	X	X	X
1534/SD	2/5				X	X	
1536/SD	1/1	X	X	X	X	X	X
1537/SD	1/1	X	X	X	X	X	X
1539/SD	5/5				X		
1542-44/SD	5/5			X			
1546/SD	1/1				X	X	
1553/SD	1/1			X	X		
1563-64/SD	3/3				X	X	
1566/SD	1/1			X	X	X	

(continued)

TABLE 35 (Continued)

Burial number(s)[1]	Sample size[2]	Moundville I	Moundville II Early	Moundville II Late	Moundville III Early	Moundville III Late	Alabama River
1567/SD	1/1			X	X		
1569/SD	1/2		X	X	X	X	
1570/SD	1/1				X		
1573/SD	3/3			X	X		
1579-80/SD	1/1			X	X	X	
1582/SD	1/4			X	X		
1,2,5/SD/M5	3/5				X		
23/SD/M5	1/3				X	X	
24/SD/M5	1/2			X	X		
2/SD/M7	1/1				X	X	
8,9/SD/M7	3/5				X	X	
12/SD/M7	1/1			X	X		
13/SD/M7	3/6		X	X			
14/SD/M7	1/1			X	X		
22/SD/M7	1/3				X	X	
27/SD/M7	2/2	X	X	X			
40,41/SD/M7	1/1			X	X		
55/SD/M7	1/1				X	X	
66/SD/M7	1/1				X	X	
71/SD/M7	2/2				X	X	
84/SD/M7	1/1				X	X	
94/SD/M7	1/1	X	X	X	X	X	X
101/SD/M7	1/2			X			
108/SD/M7	1/3				X		
114/SD/M7	1/1				X		
128/SD/M7	1/1				X		
140/SD/M7	1/2				X	X	
150/SD/M7	2/2				X		
151/SD/M7	1/3			X	X	X	
153/SD/M7	1/2			X	X		
156/SD/M7	1/2			X	X	X	
166/SD/M7	1/2	X	X	X			
173/SD/M7	1/5				X	X	
F.1/SD/M7	1/2		X	X	X		
1/NE	1/1	X	X	X	X	X	X
2/NE	3/3			X	X		
15/NE	1/1	X	X	X	X	X	X
17/NE	1/1			X	X	X	
23/NE	1/1		X	X	X	X	
41/NE	1/1		X				
44/NE	1/1	X	X	X	X		
48/NE	1/1			X	X	X	
50/NE	1/1		X	X	X		
53/NE	2/2					X	X
54/NE	2/4			X	X		
55/NE	1/1	X	X	X	X	X	X
59/NE	1/1		X	X			
76/NE	1/1				X	X	
78/NE	1/1				X	X	
79/NE	2/2			X	X	X	

(continued)

TABLE 35 (Continued)

Burial number(s)[1]	Sample size[2]	Moundville I	Moundville II		Moundville III		Alabama River
			Early	Late	Early	Late	
92/NE	1/1	X	X	X	X	X	X
94/NE	1/1	X					
1587/NE	2/2			X	X		
1596/NE	2/2	X	X	X	X	X	X
1600/NE	1/1			X	X	X	
1611/NE	1/1					X	
1620-21/NE	10/12			X	X		
1624/NE	1/1			X	X		
1625/NE	1/1	X	X	X	X	X	X
1628/NE	1/2				X	X	
1631/NE	1/1			X	X	X	
1636/NE	1/1			X	X		
1638/NE	2/2			X	X		
1639/NE	3/4			X	X		
1647-48/NE	3/3			X	X		
1649/NE	1/2			X	X	X	
1651/NE	4/5				X		
1655/NE	1/1			X	X	X	
1655/NE	1/1				X	X	
1668/NE	1/1	X	X				
1673/NE	1/1			X	X		
1674/NE	1/2			X	X	X	
1676/NE	1/1			X	X		
1181-84/EE	6/6					X	
1185/EE	6/6				X	X	
1192/EE	1/1	X	X	X	X	X	X
1198/EE	1/1			X	X	X	
1199-201/EE	1/1			X	X	X	
1202/EE	1/2			X	X	X	
1213/EE	2/3			X	X	X	
1216/EE	1/1	X	X	X	X	X	X
1220/EE	1/1		X	X	X		
1222-23/EE	1/1				X	X	
1225/EE	3/3				X	X	
1227/EE	3/4				X	X	
1228/EE	1/1			X	X		
1229-31/EE	1/2		X	X			
1232/EE	1/1	X	X	X	X	X	X
1234-37/EE	5/9					X	
1238/EE	1/1			X	X		
1243/EE	1/1		X	X	X		
1254/EE	1/1	X	X	X	X	X	X
1255/EE	1/1	X	X	X	X	X	X
1256/EE	1/1		X	X	X		
1261/EE	3/3					X	
1262,65/EE	2/3			X	X		
1263/EE	1/1			X	X	X	
1264/EE	2/2	X	X	X	X		
1267/EE	1/1			X	X	X	
1268/EE	1/1			X	X	X	

(continued)

TABLE 35 (Continued)

Burial number(s)[1]	Sample size[2]	Moundville I	Moundville II Early	Moundville II Late	Moundville III Early	Moundville III Late	Alabama River
1272/EE	1/1			X	X	X	
1275/EE	2/2				X	X	
1276/EE	1/1	X	X	X	X	X	X
1277-78/EE	4/4				X		
1281-82/EE	2/3			X	X		
1283/EE	1/1				X	X	
1284/EE	2/2				X		
1291/EE	2/2					X	
1293,299-301/EE	2/5		X	X	X		
1316/NE	1/1			X	X		
1321/EE	3/3			X	X		
1326-28/EE	1/1			X	X		
1331/EE	1/1				X	X	
1343-44/EE	2/2			X	X	X	
1346/EE	1/1		X	X	X		
1371-72/EE	1/1		X	X	X		
1373-74/EE	4/5			X			
1380/EE	1/1		X	X	X		
1385/EE	1/1	X	X	X			
1387/EE	3/3		X	X	X		
1388/EE	1/1	X	X				
1389-91/EE	1/1			X	X		
1392/EE	2/2		X	X	X		
1394/EE	2/2			X	X		
1399/EE	2/2			X			
1400/EE	1/1	X	X	X	X	X	X
1406/EE	1/1				X		
1407/EE	2/2			X	X		
1409/EE	1/1			X	X	X	
1411/EE	1/1	X	X	X	X	X	X
1412/EE	1/1			X	X	X	
1413/EE	1/1			X	X	X	
1415/EE	1/1				X		
1680/EE	1/1			X	X	X	
1682/EE	1/1			X	X	X	
1380/SE	1/1	X	X	X			
1342/SE	2/2			X	X	X	
2/F/M5	1/1	X	X	X	X	X	X
6/F/M5	1/1		X	X			
11/F/M5	1/1	X	X	X	X	X	X
16/F/M5	1/2	X	X	X			
17/F/M5	1/1	X	X	X	X	X	X
18/F/M5	1/1	X	X	X	X	X	X
1692/EF	2/2	X	X	X			
1693/EF	1/1			X	X	X	
3/NG	4/4	X	X				
8/NG	2/2			X			
9/NG	1/1			X	X		
18/NG	2/2				X	X	
20/NG	1/1			X	X	X	

(continued)

TABLE 35 (Continued)

Burial number(s)[1]	Sample size[2]	Moundville I	Moundville II Early	Moundville II Late	Moundville III Early	Moundville III Late	Alabama River
21/NG	2/2	X	X				
1007-08/NG	3/3				X	X	
1016/NG	1/1		X	X	X		
1017/NG	1/2	X	X	X	X	X	X
1707/SG	1/1	X	X	X	X	X	X
1708/SG	1/1	X	X	X	X	X	X
1732/SG	1/1	X	X	X	X	X	X
1735/SG	2/3			X	X		
1786/SG	2/2		X	X			
1717/SWG	5/5				X		
1718/SWG	2/2					X	
1720/SWG	1/1					X	
1725/SWG	1/2					X	
1728/SWG	2/2	X	X	X	X	X	X
1748-49/SWG	2/2			X			
1751/SWG	2/2			X	X	X	
1754/SWG	1/1			X	X	X	
1758/SWG	1/1						X
1784/SWG	2/2	X	X	X	X	X	X
1788-89/SWG	2/3				X		
1791/SWG	1/1			X	X	X	
1795/SWG	1/1			X	X		
1800/SWG	3/4				X	X	
1801/SWG	1/2				X	X	
1802/SWG	1/3			X	X	X	
1803/SWG	1/1	X	X	X	X	X	X
1805/SWG	2/2			X			
2617/EH	1/2	X	X	X	X		
10/SEH	1/1			X	X	X	
18/SEH	2/2				X		
19/SEH	2/2			X	X	X	
26/SEH	1/1		X	X	X	X	
803/SEH	1/1	X	X				
866/SEH	1/1	X					
869/SEH	3/3				X		
870/SEH	2/2	X	X				
872/SEH	2/2	X	X	X	X	X	X
873/SEH	1/1			X	X		
817/EI	2/3			X	X		
823/EI	1/1			X	X	X	
824/EI	2/3			X	X		
831/EI	1/1	X	X	X	X	X	
839/EI	2/2	X					
843/EI	3/3					X	
851/EI	1/1			X	X	X	
3001/SL	3/4			X	X	X	
3012/SL	1/2			X	X	X	
3014/SL	3/4				X		
3015/SL	1/2	X	X	X	X	X	X
3016/SL	1/1	X	X	X	X		

(continued)

TABLE 35 (Continued)

Burial number(s)[1]	Sample size[2]	Moundville I	Moundville II Early	Moundville II Late	Moundville III Early	Moundville III Late	Alabama River
3020/SL	1/2			X	X	X	
3026/SL	2/4				X	X	
1033/SM	3/3			X	X		
895/SWM	1/1					X	X
907/SWM	1/1	X	X	X	X	X	X
921/SWM	1/1	X	X	X	X	X	X
947/SWM	1/1					X	
950/SWM	1/1			X	X		
952/SWM	2/2	X	X				
961/SWM	2/2		X	X			
964/SWM	1/1		X	X			
965/SWM	2/2		X	X			
966b/SWM	1/1	X	X	X	X	X	X
967/SWM	1/1		X	X	X		
969-70/SWM	1/1	X	X	X	X		
978/SWM	1/1		X	X	X		
979/SWM	1/1	X	X	X	X	X	X
981/SWM	1/1			X	X		
983/SWM	2/2				X	X	
1005/SWM	1/1	X	X	X			
1024/SWM	1/1			X	X	X	
1147/SWM	2/2	X	X	X	X	X	X
1149/SWM	1/1		X	X	X		
1151/SWM	1/1				X	X	
1160/SWM	1/1					X	
9/SWM/M7	3/3		X	X			
14/SWM/M7	1/2			X			
22/SWM/M7	1/1				X	X	
1888/NN'	3/6				X	X	
2125/NN'	3/5	X	X	X	X	X	X
2134/NN'	2/2				X	X	
2136/NN'	4/5				X		
1683/WN	1/1			X	X		
1/WN/M7	1/2	X	X	X	X	X	X
7/O/M5	1/2	X	X	X	X	X	X
9/O/M5	1/1			X	X		
14/O/M5	1/1			X	X		
19/O/M5	1/1				X		
21/O/M5	1/2			X	X		
29/O/M5	1/1	X	X	X	X	X	X
39/O/M5	2/3			X	X		
F.1/O/M5	2/2			X	X		
F.2/O/M5	2/3			X	X		
F.3/O/M5	1/2	X					
1/EO/M5	1/1	X	X	X	X	X	X
2179-80/WP	5/5		X				
2185/WP	2/2			X	X	X	
2187/WP	1/1		X				
2208/WP	1/1	X	X	X	X	X	X
2211/WP	1/1				X		

(continued)

TABLE 35 (Continued)

Burial number(s)[1]	Sample size[2]	Moundville I	Moundville II Early	Moundville II Late	Moundville III Early	Moundville III Late	Alabama River
2223/WP	1/1	X	X	X	X		
2258/WP	1/1				X		
2282/WP	1/2	X					
2289/WP	1/1			X	X		
2314/WP	1/2				X	X	
2317/WP	1/1				X	X	
2326/WP	1/1			X			
2354/WP	1/1	X	X	X	X	X	X
2417/WP	1/1					X	
2421/WP	1/1	X	X	X			
2436/WP	1/1	X	X	X	X	X	X
2447/WP	1/1			X	X	X	
2471/WP	1/1	X	X	X	X		
2476/WP	1/1	X	X	X	X		
2496/WP	3/4			X	X		
2530/WP	1/1	X					
2532/WP	3/4	X					
2538/WP	1/1	X	X	X			
2540/WP	1/1	X	X	X	X	X	X
2544/WP	2/2	X					
2545/WP	1/1	X	X				
2550-51/WP	3/3	X	X	X			
2552-53/WP	2/2	X	X	X			
2555/WP	1/1		X	X	X	X	
2558/WP	1/1			X	X	X	
2559/WP	2/2	X					
2560/WP	2/2	X					
2562-63/WP	3/4	X					
2635/WP	1/1	X	X	X	X	X	X
2636/WP	2/2				X	X	
2640-41/WP	1/2				X	X	
2137/WP′	2/7				X	X	
2152-54/WP′	1/3				X	X	
2165-66/WP′	2/2				X		
2171/WP′	1/1			X	X	X	
1/NQ/M5	1/1	X	X				
12/NR	1/1						X
1083/NR	1/1		X	X	X		
1086/NR	2/2				X	X	
1087,1100/NR	4/5			X	X		
1088/NR	2/2				X		
1089,94-96/NR	3/3			X	X	X	
1098/NR	2/2	X	X	X	X		
1099/NR	1/1		X	X			
1101/NR	2/3			X	X	X	
1102/NR	2/3				X	X	
1103/NR	1/1			X	X	X	
1104-05/NR	3/3		X	X			
1109/NR	5/5			X	X		
1110/NR	2/2				X	X	

(continued)

TABLE 35 (Continued)

Burial number(s)[1]	Sample size[2]	Moundville I	Moundville II		Moundville III		Alabama River
			Early	Late	Early	Late	
1111/NR	1/2	X	X	X	X	X	X
1113/NR	1/1	X	X				
1116/NR	1/2	X	X	X	X	X	X
1117/NR	2/2			X			
1118/NR	1/1		X	X			
1124/NR	2/2	X	X	X	X	X	X
1125-26/NR	2/4			X			
1128/NR	1/1	X	X	X	X	X	X
5/NR/M5	1/1	X	X	X			
8/NR/M5	1/1			X	X		
10/NR/M5	2/3			X	X	X	
11/NR/M5	1/1				X		
14/NR/M5	1/2		X	X			
21/NR/M5	1/2		X	X			
33/NR/M5	1/2				X	X	
38/NR/M5	2/2				X		
48/NR/M5	2/2		X	X			
58/NR/M5	1/1				X	X	
F.1/NR/M5	1/3		X	X			
1/WR	1/1	X	X	X	X	X	X
6/WR	1/1	X	X	X	X	X	X
10/WR	1/1			X	X	X	
15/WR	1/1				X	X	
17/WR	1/1			X	X	X	
1045/WR	5/5				X		
1048/WR	1/1	X	X				
1049-50/WR	3/3	X	X	X	X		
1054/WR	1/1	X	X	X	X	X	X
1057/WR	1/1	X	X	X	X		
1060/WR	1/1	X	X	X	X		X
1065/WR	4/6				X	X	
1068/WR	1/1				X	X	
1/WR/M5	2/2			X	X		
4,5/WR/M7	1/1				X	X	
6/WR/M7	1/1				X	X	
8,9/WR/M7	1/4			X			
20/WR/M7	1/2	X	X	X	X	X	X
2942/W	1/1	X	X				
2947/W	1/1			X	X	X	
2957/W	1/1	X	X	X	X		
2962/W	1/2			X			
2984/W	1/1	X	X				
1833/NW	1/1	X	X	X	X	X	X
1836/NW	2/2			X	X		
1837/NW	2/2		X				
1838/NW	1/1	X	X	X	X		
1840/NW	2/2				X	X	
1841/NW	2/2			X	X		
1842/NW	2/2	X	X	X			
1845/NW	2/2	X	X	X	X	X	X

(continued)

TABLE 35 (Continued)

Burial number(s)[1]	Sample size[2]	Moundville I	Moundville II		Moundville III		Alabama River
			Early	Late	Early	Late	
1846/NW	1/1	X	X	X	X		
1848/NW	1/1	X	X	X	X		
1849/NW	1/1		X	X			
1850/NW	1/2	X					
1853/NW	1/1	X	X	X	X	X	X
1854/NW	3/3	X	X	X			
1856/NW	2/3	X	X	X	X	X	X
1861/NW	1/2	X	X	X	X	X	X
1865/NW	2/2	X	X	X	X		
1869/NW	1/1	X	X	X	X	X	X
2199/SW	3/4			X	X	X	
2022/SW	1/1	X	X	X	X	X	X
2203/SW	1/1			X	X		
2346/SW	1/1	X	X	X	X	X	X
2384/SW	1/1	X	X	X	X	X	X
2386/SW	2/2	X	X	X	X		
2387/SW	1/1	X	X	X	X	X	X
2388/SW	2/2			X	X		
2390/SW	2/2				X	X	
2392/SW	1/2		X	X			
2393/SW	2/5		X	X			
2397/SW	2/2				X	X	
2398/SW	2/2				X	X	
2500/SW	1/1	X	X	X	X		
2501/SW	2/2			X	X		
2504/SW	3/4			X			
2506/SW	2/2	X	X	X	X	X	X
2508/SW	2/2	X	X	X	X	X	X
2509/SW	1/2			X	X		
2513/SW	1/1	X	X	X	X	X	X
2517/SW	1/1			X	X	X	
1821/NWW	1/2	X	X				
1830/NWW	1/2	X	X				

[1] Multiple burials are listed as single gravelots.
[2] The figure to the left of the slash represents the number of vessels recorded in the present sample; the figure to the right of the slash is the number of vessels originally found in the gravelot.

from the assignment of dates once the chronology is established. When building a chronology by means of seriation, it is a formal requirement of the method that each provenience be assigned a single position within the overall sequence. Given this constraint, a provenience is usually placed somewhere near the midpoint of its plausible range, since this is often the best heuristic approximation. But once the ceramic chronology is established, and attention turns from doing a seriation per se to assigning dates for the purposes of interpretation, it becomes preferable, and in many cases more realistic given the state of our knowledge, to make chronological assignments that take the

TABLE 36
Temporal Placement of Unassociated Vessels (Local)

Catalog number	Moundville I	Moundville II Early	Moundville II Late	Moundville III Early	Moundville III Late	Alabama River
Rho1			X			
Rho46	X	X	X	X		
Rho136		X	X			
Rho190	X	X	X	X	X	X
Rho253	X	X	X	X		
Rho302	X	X	X	X	X	X
Rho374	X	X	X	X	X	X
Rw43	X					
Rw182	X	X				
Rw572			X	X		
Rw580			X	X		
Rw878				X	X	
B1				X	X	
B2			X	X	X	
B6		X	X	X		
NB2						X
NB6						X
C6/M5	X	X	X	X	X	X
C12/M5			X			
C13/M5			X			
C21/M5		X	X	X		
NC1			X	X		
NC2			X	X	X	
NC3			X	X	X	
NC5				X	X	
NEC9/M5			X			
D1					X	
ND3				X		
ND4				X	X	
ND5		X	X	X	X	X
ND7			X	X	X	
ND10		X	X	X	X	X
ND11		X	X	X	X	X
ND28	X	X	X	X	X	X
ND6/M5			X	X		
ND20/M5	X	X				
NED10				X	X	
ED2				X	X	
ED3		X	X	X		
ED4	X	X	X	X	X	X
ED6			X	X		
SED1			X	X		
SED2	X	X	X	X	X	X
SED3	X	X	X	X	X	X
SED4				X	X	
SED6			X	X	X	
SED7	X	X	X	X	X	X
SED8			X	X		
SED9			X	X		

(continued)

TABLE 36 (Continued)

Catalog number	Moundville I	Moundville II		Moundville III		Alabama River
		Early	Late	Early	Late	
SED10			X	X		
SED11		X	X	X		
SED13		X	X			
SED14				X	X	
SED15	X	X	X	X	X	X
SED17			X	X	X	
SED18		X	X			
SED19				X	X	
SED27				X		
SED28				X	X	
SED30			X			
SED32	X	X	X	X	X	X
SED33	X	X	X	X	X	X
SED35			X	X		
SED43				X	X	
SD1		X	X			
SD6				X	X	
SD10			X	X	X	
SD27	X	X				
SD3/M5	X	X	X	X	X	X
SD28/M7			X	X		
SD95/M7		X	X	X		
SD103/M7	X	X	X			
SD109/M7		X				
NE1		X				
NE2				X	X	
NE4				X	X	
NE5			X	X		
NE7			X			
NE8			X	X		
NE11			X	X		
NE12			X			
NE17	X	X	X	X	X	X
NE18		X	X	X	X	X
NE19			X	X		
NE25	X	X	X	X		
NE26	X	X	X	X	X	X
NE27	X	X	X	X	X	X
NE30	X	X	X	X	X	X
NE33	X	X	X	X	X	X
NE36	X	X	X	X	X	X
NE37		X	X	X		
NE44	X	X				
NE68				X	X	
NE79			X	X		
NE80				X		
NE85			X	X	X	
NE86				X	X	
NE88				X	X	
NE89				X	X	

(continued)

TABLE 36 (Continued)

Catalog number	Moundville I	Moundville II		Moundville III		Alabama River
		Early	Late	Early	Late	
NE92	X	X	X	X	X	X
NE93	X	X	X	X	X	X
NE95			X	X	X	
NE127				X	X	
NE128			X	X		
NE132	X	X	X	X	X	X
NE133			X	X		
NE134	X	X	X			
NE135	X	X	X	X		
NE136				X	X	
NE138	X	X	X	X	X	X
NE140			X	X	X	
NE145			X	X	X	
NE147			X	X	X	
NE160			X	X	X	
NE192	X	X	X	X	X	X
NE603	X	X	X	X	X	X
EE22			X	X	X	
EE25				X	X	
EE111		X	X	X		
EE112			X	X		
EE166			X	X	X	
EE343				X		
EE377				X	X	
EE383			X	X	X	
EE387	X	X	X	X	X	X
EE446	X	X	X	X		
SE3			X	X		
SE8				X		
SE9		X	X	X	X	X
SE11			X	X	X	
SE12		X	X	X	X	X
SE13			X	X		
SE14			X	X	X	
SE37				X	X	
F4/M5		X	X			
F10/M5		X	X			
NG1		X	X			
NG56			X	X	X	
NG76	X	X	X	X	X	X
SG23	X	X	X	X	X	X
H3/M5		X	X			
SEH18			X	X	X	
SEH19			X	X	X	
SEH20			X	X	X	
SEH22		X	X	X	X	X
SEH82		X	X			
SEH83	X					
SEH85	X					
EI2	X	X	X	X		

(continued)

TABLE 36 (Continued)

Catalog number	Moundville I	Moundville II		Moundville III		Alabama River
		Early	Late	Early	Late	
EI95			X	X	X	
SWM178		X	X			
SWM188			X	X		
SWM189		X	X			
SWM190				X	X	
SWM260	X	X	X	X	X	X
SWM15A/M7			X	X	X	
016/M5		X	X			
020/M5			X	X		
027/M5	X					
037/M5	X	X				
WP16	X	X	X			
WP30		X				
WP32	X	X	X	X		
WP71		X	X	X		
WP73		X				
WP269		X	X			
NR5	X	X	X	X	X	X
NR117	X	X	X	X	X	X
NR31/M5			X	X	X	
WR2			X	X	X	
WR3		X	X	X		
WR9		X	X	X		
WR21					X	
WR46		x	X	X	X	X
WR50	X	X	X	X		
WR51			X			
WR28/M7			X			
W81	X					
W220	X	X	X	X		

entire span of possible dates into account. The resulting chronological estimates may well be conservative in terms of their breadth, but for present purposes little harm can be done if we err on the side of caution.

SPATIAL CONTEXT OF VESSELS AND BURIALS

Obviously, community structure cannot be studied without certain kinds of spatial information. So it is worthwhile to review briefly the kinds and quality of spatial information available for the features that can be dated.

Virtually every Moundville vessel and gravelot comes from a provenience for which the general location within the site is known. During the earlier excavations, including those of Moore, the location of finds was recorded only in rather vague terms, such as "Mound F" or "field north of Mound C." This practice gradually changed, and by the middle to late 1930s the boundaries of each excavated area, and the location of finds within each area, were being recorded with considerably more precision. The important thing to note for present purposes is that, even when descriptions are vague, vessels and gravelots can almost always be reliably located to within 50 m (and usually less) of where they were originally found (Peebles 1979:Figure I–1, passim). In reconstructing spatial patterns that are fairly coarse grained, such errors are hardly noticeable given the large extent of the site as a whole. Thus, this sort of locational information can readily be used to infer the overall size and configuration of the Moundville community at any point in time.

In addition to looking at coarse-grained distributions, one ideally would like to learn something about the finer grained patterning on the site as well. Obviously this would require knowing a great deal more about spatial context than merely the general location of finds; one would also have to know precisely where artifacts and features were found relative to one another within an excavated locality. Given that our chronological attributions apply mainly to whole vessels and burials, it would be particularly valuable to learn in detail how these artifacts and features relate spatially to contemporary mounds, structures, and other activity loci. Unfortunately, patterning at this level is considerably more difficult to approach with the data available from Moundville. Spatial information at this level of detail was often not recorded in the field, and even when it was, its present interpretation is often quite difficult.

To begin with, virtually all the mound excavations were conducted by Moore, who failed to keep any record of horizontal or vertical relationships within the areas he opened. This lack of information makes detailed depositional reconstructions impossible. Our only recourse lies in the fact that dating vessels and gravelots within a mound is tantamount to dating the mound itself: Barring heirlooms, the earliest vessel or gravelot within a mound provides an unequivocal *terminus ante quem* for the onset of constructional activity, even if one does not know precisely where within the mound the vessel or gravelot was found.

With regard to the relationship between burials and other features in off-mound areas, the available data are considerably more variable. In earlier excavations, the presence of off-mound structural features was never recorded, and so the information one would want is simply unavailable. In later excavations, wall trenches, post molds, fire basins, pits and other features were recognized and mapped in relation to burials. Although many of these maps are now published (Peebles 1978, 1979), they still present interpretive problems. Judging from the burials that can be dated by their inclusive vessels, it is clear that many of these maps represent palimpsests of features from several different time periods. If every single feature on such maps could be dated independently, then the palimpsests could be easily sorted out. However, the fact is that less than a third of the burials, and virtually none of the structures, are directly associated with temporally diagnostic vessels. Thus, a typical map might show 3 structures and 20 burials, but only 5 of these burials are likely to contain ceramics that can be unequivocally dated. If the ceramically dated burials fall into different phases (as they often do), then it becomes extremely difficult to infer the chronological positions of the structures and other burials. Except in the relatively infrequent cases of direct superposition, the only avenue of interpretation possible is one that relies on spatial proximity and spatial alignments—lines of evidence that, needless to say, tend to be inconclusive. All one can say for now is that burials quite often do seem to be spatially associated with structures; more detailed interpretations may well be possible in the future, but not until the sherds from these localities are more fully analyzed.

CHANGES IN COMMUNITY PATTERNS THROUGH TIME

The present discussion of community patterns is based principally on a series of maps, each showing the distribution of burials and unassociated vessels belonging to a particular phase of occupation. To assure reliability, only the most narrowly dated vessels and burials were plotted—those that could be securely assigned to a range that spanned no more than two adjacent time segments (e.g., Moundville I–early Moundville II, early Moundville II–late Moundville II, and late Moundville II–early Moundville III, etc.). Thus, one should keep in mind that the number of vessels and burials plotted on these maps actually represents a minimum, since numerous vessels and burials that lacked sufficiently diagnostic features were excluded. For reasons already stated, maps showing the spatial relationships of features within excavated localities will hardly be brought into the discussion, except in the few cases where the features they show can be reliably dated and plausibly interpreted. Given these considerations, I now present the evidence for each phase in turn.

West Jefferson Phase

This component, unlike the others, cannot be defined by plotting the spatial distribution of burials, because West Jefferson gravelots have never been found to contain pottery (see Ensor 1979:12–15). There are literally thousands of burials without ceramics reported at Moundville, but for now it is impossible to tell which date to the West Jefferson phase and which are later.

The principal evidence for a West Jefferson component at Moundville exists in the form of sherds, mostly from the excavations that took place in the 1930s. Although these collections have never been fully analyzed, a number of preliminary reports indicate that most of the grog-tempered pottery was recovered from the western periphery of the site, in the area to the west of Mounds O and P (Walthall and Wimberly 1978:122–123; Wimberly 1956:18–19). Walthall and Wimberly (1978:123) recently estimated that the West Jefferson occupation was a village of approximately 0.5–1.5 ha in size; judging from the

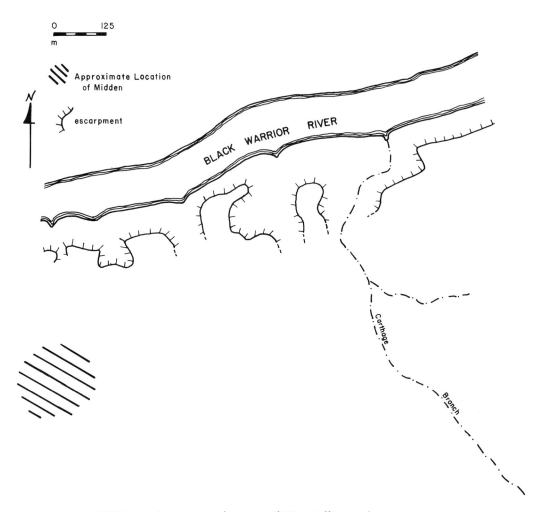

FIGURE 31   Approximate location of West Jefferson phase component.

position of the excavations that produced the greatest number of grog-tempered sherds, this village was located within the area shown on Figure 31.

Moundville I Phase

The greatest concentration of Moundville I burials and vessels occurs in the western part of the site, showing considerable continuity in location from the previous phase (Figure 32). The core of the site at this time appears to have consisted of at least a single mound, an early stage of Mound O. Immediately to the west of this mound was a cluster of burials—probably a small cemetery (Figure 33)—along with some evidence of residential architecture (Figure 34).

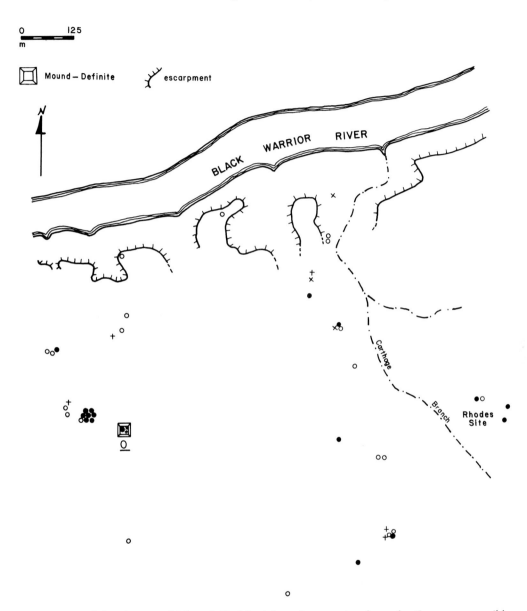

FIGURE 32 Spatial distribution of Moundville I burials and unassociated vessels. (Some may possibly date to early Moundville II.) (Key: ●, Moundville I burial or gravelot; +, Moundville I unassociated vessel; ○, late Moundville I or early Moundville II burial or gravelot; ×, late Moundville I or early Moundville II unassociated vessel.)

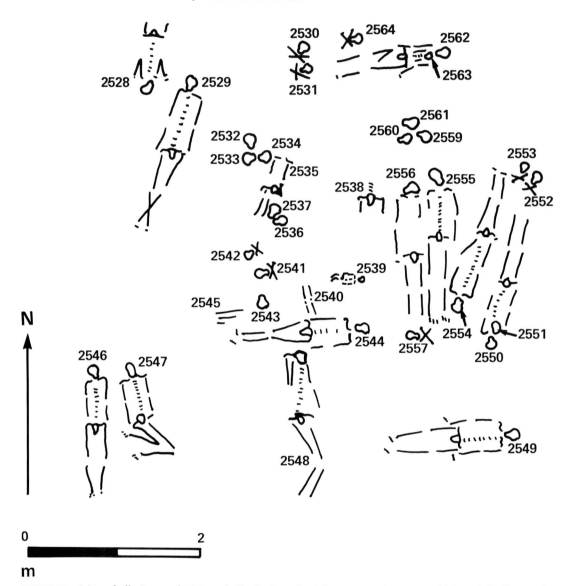

FIGURE 33   Moundville I to early Moundville II phase burial concentration west of Mound O (Excavation WP; after Peebles 1979:Figure VI-3).

The overall distribution of burials also suggests scattered occupation to the north, south, and east of the mound, especially in the areas along Carthage Branch. It is difficult to tell whether the absence of burials and vessels in the central portion of the map represents an actual lack of occupation, or merely the paucity of excavations in the area that was later to become the plaza.

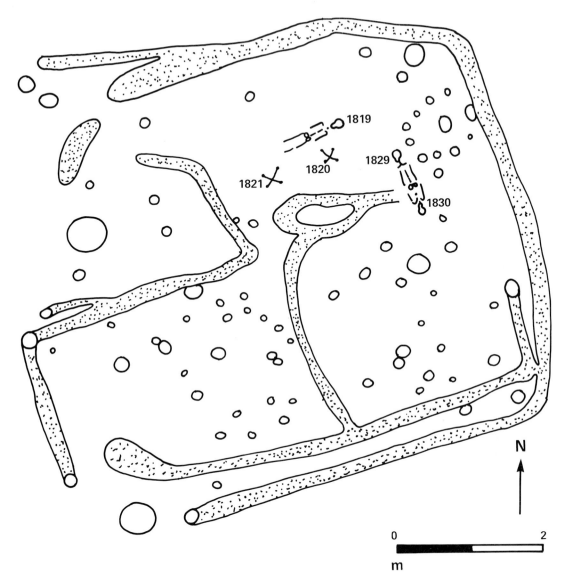

FIGURE 34   Moundville I or early Moundville II phase structure with burials (Excavation NWW; after Peebles 1979:Figure VIII-3).

The community pattern evident in Figure 32 is quite interesting, for it seems to be consistent with patterns found elsewhere in the Black Warrior Valley at the same time. Recent surveys have indicated that during this phase, Moundville was one of a series of small, more or less equivalent political centers, each usually with a single mound, and a number of small hamlets or farmsteads scattered in its immediate vicinity (see Chapter 6). The elaborate three-level settlement hierarchy, which many of our previous models took for granted (e.g., Steponaitis 1978), apparently had not developed by this time.

Moundville II Phase

During the Moundville II phase, the situation changed dramatically as Moundville grew to become a major political center (Figure 35). There were

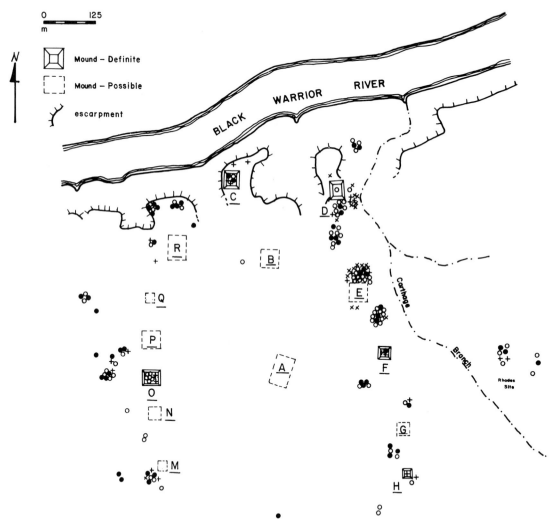

FIGURE 35 Spatial distribution of Moundville II phase burials and unassociated vessels. (Some may possibly date to early Moundville III.) (Key: ●, Moundville II burial or gravelot; +, Moundville II unassociated vessel; ○, late Moundville II or early Moundville III burial or gravelot; ×, late Moundville II or early Moundville III unassociated vessel.)

considerably more burials dating to this phase at the site, probably indicating a much larger population. Moreover, the evidence suggests that this was a time when a considerable amount of public labor was mobilized to build mounds. There is definite evidence in the form of inclusive pottery vessels that at least five mounds (C, D, F, H, and O) were standing by the end of this phase. Moreover, given that the securely dated mounds occur at both the northern

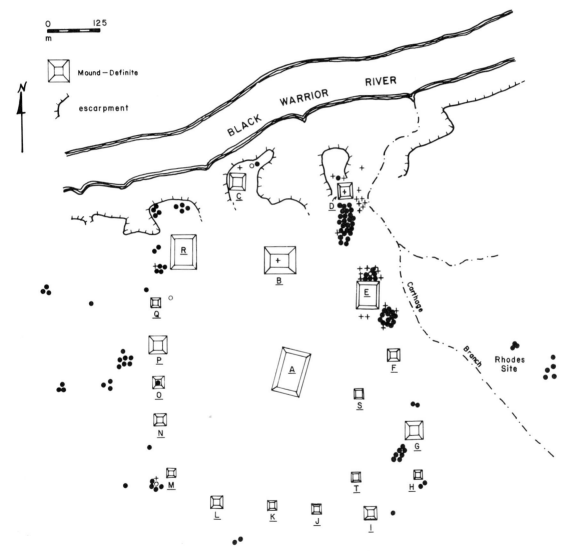

FIGURE 36   Spatial distribution of Moundville III phase burials and unassociated vessels. (Some may possibly date to early Alabama River.) (Key: ●, Moundville III burial or gravelot; +, Moundville III unassociated vessel; ○, late Moundville III or Alabama River burial or gravelot.)

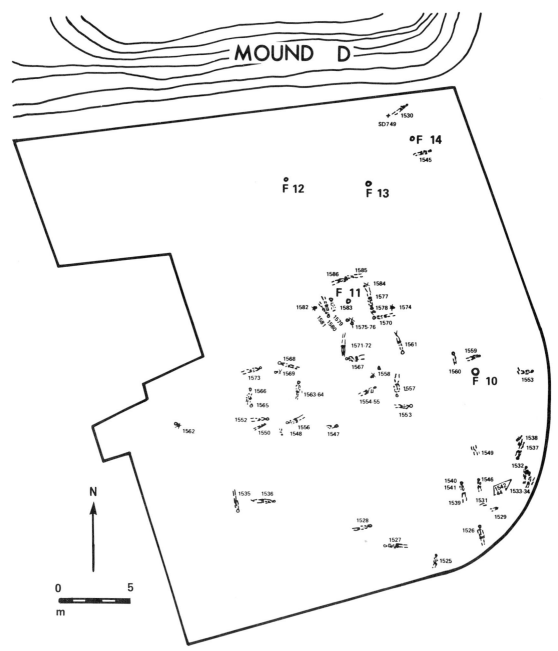

FIGURE 37 Portion of the late Moundville II to early Moundville III phase burial concentration south of Mound D, (Excavation SD; after Peebles 1979:Figure III-11). (Key: F, fire basin or hearth.)

and southern extremities of the site, it seems likely that many of the intervening mounds, from which we have no datable artifacts, were standing as well.

Mortuary activity during this phase continued in the area west of Mound O, and large burial concentrations also began appearing elsewhere on the site, mainly to the east and north. Especially prominent were burial concentrations north of Mound R, southwest of Mound M, and (late in Moundville II) the large cemetery areas near Mounds D and E.

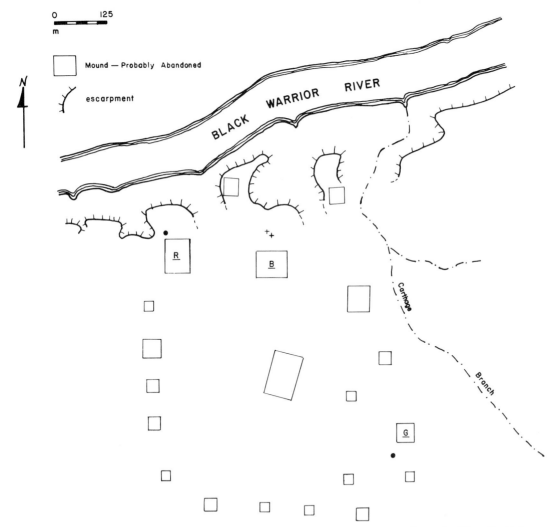

FIGURE 38   Spatial distribution of Alabama River phase burials and unassociated vessels. (Key: ●, Alabama River burial or gravelot; +, Alabama River unassociated vessel.)

Moundville III Phase

Most of the patterns established in Moundville II times continued into Moundville III (Figure 36). Judging from the distribution of burials, the area of settlement may have expanded somewhat farther to the west. Again, the largest concentrations of dated burials occurred in the vicinities of Mounds D and E (Figure 37), with smaller concentrations southwest of Mound G, southwest of Mound M, west of Mounds O and P, west and north of Mound R, and on the Rhodes site east of Carthage Branch. Mound building must have continued apace since vessels definitely of this phase occur in Mounds B, D, and O. Without a doubt, all the mounds reached their final configuration by the end of Moundville III, because by the succeeding Alabama River phase, the site had been virtually abandoned.

Alabama River Phase

That a protohistoric component did exist at Moundville is indicated by the presence of diagnostic vessels and sherds; yet it is abundantly clear that the component was miniscule compared to those that preceded it (Figure 38). Evidence of mortuary activity is minimal: There is one burial southwest of Mound G, another north of Mound R, and two unassociated vessels (which probably came from burials) north of Mound B. Also possibly dating to this phase are two "urn-burials of infants," which Moore reported finding south of Mound D (1907:342–343). All in all, this sparse representation is suggestive of nothing more than a few farmsteads or hamlets scattered over what was once an enormous site.

Summary and Discussion

Summing up the evidence just presented, it appears that Moundville underwent a gradual development through time. The site began as a small nucleated village in the West Jefferson phase, then became a small local center with a single mound in Moundville I, and finally evolved into a large regional center during Moundville II and Moundville III. Decline became evident only in the Alabama River phase, by which time the site had lost its political importance, and was left with only a trace of its former population.

Overall, the sequence is marked by strong continuities in settlement location from one phase to the next, which is especially notable in the transition from West Jefferson to Moundville I. These continuities, together with the continuities in ceramic style (see p. 130), are fully consistent with the notion that the Moundville phases I–III—and the sociopolitical complexity they represent—evolved locally from the indigenous West Jefferson base, and were not the result of any migrations into the valley from outside.

Although the present attempt to reconstruct community patterns from the distributions of whole vessels has been informative, it can only be viewed as a beginning. The vast sherd collections now in the Alabama Museum of Natural History are an invaluable resource with which the interpretations offered here may someday be tested and refined. Hopefully, this resource will not remain untapped much longer.

6

Conclusion: A Regional Perspective

Preceding chapters examined ceramics, technology, classification, chronology, and community patterns from the restricted vantage of a single site. It now remains to expand this perspective by considering the data in a regional framework.

The region I will be concerned with includes the entire Black Warrior drainage, from its headwaters near Birmingham to its confluence with the Tombigbee River near Demopolis. The chapter begins with a brief sketch of the region's late prehistory—outlining the major trends in subsistence, settlement, and organization—and concludes with a consideration of factors that may have helped cause some of the cultural changes observed.

THE LATE PREHISTORY OF THE BLACK WARRIOR DRAINAGE

Until recently, our knowledge of sites in this region other than Moundville and Bessemer was highly limited. Most of the information available consisted of site descriptions compiled in the 1930s (Peebles 1978a:381–388; Sheldon 1974:140–151), supplemented by a 1972 surface reconnaissance that located some sites in the southernmost end of the drainage (Nielsen *et al.* 1973). Although useful in many ways, the information available from these sources was generally insufficient to date the sites in light of the new chronology.

Recent work in the Black Warrior Valley has begun to change this situation, however. In the years between 1975 and 1979, field projects carried out by the Universities of Alabama and Michigan investigated numerous sites south of the fall line at Tuscaloosa. Intensive surveys relocated most of the previously recorded sites, found a number of new sites, and obtained controlled surface collections from each. Also, test excavations were placed in some of the outlying mounds, to provide a basis for dating episodes of construction. Sketchy preliminary reports on these settlement data have already begun to appear (Bozeman 1981; Peebles *et al.* 1979; Walthall and Coblentz 1977; Welch 1979), and more thorough analyses are now underway.[1]

The foregoing, then, provides background not only for the presentation to follow, but also for a disclaimer: Given the recency of the fieldwork, much of the information available remains fragmentary and imprecise—especially that gleaned from preliminary reports, my own (sometimes casual) observations in the field, and personal communications with colleagues. Thus many of the interpretations that follow should be regarded as first approximations, subject to considerable refinement when the data are more fully reported and analyzed.

West Jefferson Phase (A.D. 900—1050)

Components of this phase occur throughout the Warrior drainage, from Locust Fork (near Birmingham) south to the vicinity of Moundville. Components have also been identified on the upper Cahaba River in Jefferson County (Ensor 1979), and on the Sipsey River in Fayette County (Jenkins 1976a).

West Jefferson sites exhibit quite a bit of variation in size. At one extreme are small sites, generally covering an area of less than 0.03 ha. Several of these small sites have been excavated, and have been shown to be seasonal, short-term occupations (Ensor 1979; O'Hear 1975). Such an occupation typically consists of a single (usually circular) dwelling, surrounded by features used for storage, food preparation, and sometimes burial. At the other end of the size scale are a number of larger sites, most covering 0.09–0.50 ha, of which the West Jefferson component at Moundville seems to be an example. Although none of these larger sites is well enough excavated to be sure, it is likely that many of them represent agglomerations of multiple dwellings—communities that could reasonably be called villages (Walthall and Coblentz 1977; Welch 1979). Not a single West Jefferson site shows evidence of contemporary mounds.

Subsistence remains indicate that West Jefferson peoples relied mainly on wild foods, and engaged in agriculture only to a very limited extent. Plant

[1]At this writing, the regional settlement data from the Black Warrior Valley are being studied by Tandy Bozeman (University of California at Santa Barbara), excavated artifacts and features from a small site near Moundville are being analyzed by Paul Welch (University of Michigan), and the floral remains from various sites are being identified by Margaret Scarry (University of Michigan).

foods found in West Jefferson contexts typically include hickory nuts, acorns, walnuts, persimmons, maygrass, sumac, and maize—with the abundance of nuts and wild seeds far outstripping that of maize (Ensor 1979:8; Jenkins and Nielsen 1974:159–161; Scarry 1981b). Although bone preservation at West Jefferson sites has been consistently poor, some idea of which animals were exploited can be gained by looking at evidence from contemporary sites along the central Tombigbee to the west. There, Late Woodland groups preyed on an extremely diverse group of species: principally deer, turkey, rabbit, squirrel, raccoon, drumfish, catfish, and mussels, not to mention a variety of other rodents, reptiles, and amphibians (Curren 1975).

Pulling all these lines of evidence together, Welch (1979, 1981) has proposed a plausible (and still tentative) interpretation of how the West Jefferson settlement system operated. He suggests that each village comprised a more-or-less permanent settlement, which served as a base from which a yearly cycle of economic activities was carried out. Given the importance of wild foods in the West Jefferson diet, some of these activities probably required a seasonal dispersal of population into smaller settlements, but this dispersal need not have entailed a complete abandonment of the village. A similar pattern of large "base camps" and small "transitory camps" has also been suggested for the Late Woodland population on the central Tombigbee (Jenkins *et al.* 1975).

Finally, given the absence of mounds and elaborate burials, it is most reasonable to assume that West Jefferson groups were basically egalitarian in their social and political structure.

Moundville I Phase (A.D. 1050—1250)

At some point after A.D. 1000, a number of far-reaching changes in the Late Woodland lifeway began to take place. These changes manifested themselves in the subsequent Moundville I phase, components of which occur throughout the Warrior drainage and also on the central Tombigbee (Jenkins 1979:273–277).

One set of innovations at this time had to do with subsistence, as the inhabitants of the region greatly intensified their reliance on cultivated plants. The Moundville I levels in the 1978–1979 excavations north of Mound R provide the best evidence of diet. Preliminary examinations have revealed that maize was extremely abundant within these depositis, constituting about 60% by weight of all the plant remains recovered (Scarry 1980, 1981b). This abundance of maize, as compared to its rarity in West Jefferson contexts, stongly implies that the focus of subsistence pursuits had shifted to agriculture. Wild nuts, seeds, and fruits continued to be eaten, but not to the extent that they had been previously. Faunal evidence suggests that hunting remained important, with the emphasis again on deer, squirrel, rabbit, and turkey (Michals 1981). Aquatic resources utilized may have included drumfish, catfish, sucker, and turtle (Michals 1981).

These changes in subsistence were accompanied by some changes in settlement. Despite considerable efforts in the field, not a single village-sized community dating to this phase has been found, either in the Warrior drainage (T. K. Bozeman and P. Welch, personal communication) or on the Tombigbee (Jenkins 1975; Jenkins *et al.* 1975; Nielsen *et al.* 1973). Most of the population probably lived in dispersed farmsteads or small hamlets, sites which show up on the surface as small scatters of shell-tempered pottery (Bozeman 1981: Figure 3). Given the importance that cultigens had achieved in the diet, it seems likely that most of these farmsteads and hamlets would have been permanent, year-round settlements.

Also during the Moundville I phase, the first civic–ceremonial centers appeared, marked by the presence of artifically constructed pyramidal mounds (see Bozeman 1981:Table 2). Among the centers so far identified as dating to this time are 1Tu44 (Peebles 1978:387), 1Tu50 (1978a:381), 1Tu56 (1978a:388), Moundville (Figure 31), and the Bessemer site on Valley Creek, a tributary above the fall line (DeJarnette and Wimberly 1941). It is possible that more early centers will be recognized as analysis of the survey collections proceeds.

The fact that these mounds were built is significant, for it suggests that changes were taking place in social and political organization as well. In native southeastern cultures, flat-topped mounds were generally used as platforms for structures associated with offices of political and religious importance. If the construction of these mounds can be taken to indicate the institution of such offices, then this was the time when the first centralized polities in the region were established.

Most Moundville I phase centers were of modest proportions, having only a single mound. As far as we know, only one site, Bessemer, had as many as three. Bessemer was subjected to large-scale excavations in the 1930s (DeJarnette and Wimberly 1941), and thus provides the most complete picture of what a Moundville I phase center looked like. Each of Bessemer's mounds had a different internal structure: The so-called "domiciliary mound" was rectangular in shape, lacked burials, and supported buildings atop each of its multiple stages; the "ceremonial mound" was oval and flat-topped, yet lacked any evidence of buildings; and the "burial mound" was low, conical in shape, and contained numerous human interments. Many of the buildings found on, beside, and underneath the mounds were rectangular and of wall-trench construction. Many of these buildings were also accompanied by circular enclosures, clay "seats," and small platforms; all of these architectural features are suggestive of civic–ceremonial, rather than domestic, function (see, for example, Lewis and Kneberg 1946:60–72).

Moundville I mortuary practices are relatively well documented at both Moundville and Bessemer. The most common form of burial appears to be the primary supine inhumation, although secondary inhumations of bone "bundles" and individual skulls also occur. Burials often seem to have been placed in or near domestic dwellings, and thus tend to be found spatially scattered along with the dwellings themselves (Figure 34). There also exist some clusters of burials that may represent discrete mortuary areas or cemeteries. These mortuary areas tend to occur at centers, in close proximity to the pyramidal mounds. The clearest examples of such features are the burial mound at Bessemer, and the cemetery at Moundville west of Mound O (Figure 33). Both of these mortuary areas contain at least some (apparently) high-status individuals, their burials accompanied by embossed copper plates (e.g., DeJarnette and Wimberly 1941:Figure 58), shell beads, or carved stone discs. However, none of these burials suggests a mortuary ritual as complex as some of those that were to appear in subsequent phases.

In brief, the Moundville I phase was a time when a number of small local centers were established in the Black Warrior drainage. The typical center had at least one pyramidal mound with an associated mortuary area, and probably served a number of dispersed farmsteads and small hamlets in its immediate vicinity. Each of these centers and its surrounding population probably constituted a somewhat centralized, autonomous polity, analogous to a simple chiefdom (Steponaitis 1978:420).

It is interesting to note that all the known Moundville I centers were built on, or immediately adjacent to, the locations of earlier West Jefferson phase villages. Thus, certain village locations appear to have persisted as focal points of community life, even after most of the former village inhabitants had dispersed into scattered farmsteads and hamlets. This continuity in location through time is thoroughly consistent with the notion that the West Jefferson–Moundville I transition took place in the context of a stable, indigenous population.

Moundville II and Moundville III Phases (A.D. 1250—1550)

Components of the Moundville II and Moundville III phases are known from the lower reaches of the Black Warrior River south of the fall line at Tuscaloosa. It is difficult to say whether the absence of sites above the fall line is due to an actual abandonment of the area, or simply to the lack of adequate survey. Sites with ceramics pertaining to these two phases have also been identified on the central Tombigbee (Jenkins 1979:273–277).

Most aspects of subsistence and settlement established during Moundville I continued into these subsequent phases, with one major exception: Moundville, formerly a small local center, grew tremendously in size and importance. By the end of the Moundville II phase, at least 5, and probably as many as 14, mounds were standing, and the overall size and shape of the plaza had been laid out. At some point during the Moundville III phase, the site achieved its final form, with all 20 mounds complete.

Although Bessemer (above the fall line) had been abandoned by the start of this time period, some of the other small centers (below the fall line) continued to be used. For example, based on a radiocarbon date of A.D. 1340±80, it is likely that the uppermost stages of the mound at 1Tu56 were built during Moundville II. Also, test excavations have revealed that stages were being added to the mounds at 1Tu3 (Snows Bend), 1Tu46, 1Ha14, and 1Ha7 even as late as Moundville III (Bozeman 1981:Table 2).

With the possible exception of Moundville itself, no village-sized communities are known from these phases (T. K. Bozeman and P. Welch, personal communication). It therefore seems reasonable to assume that much of the population remained dispersed in farmsteads and small hamlets.

The degree of social ranking probably reached its zenith during this time, as indicated by the complexity and richness of the mortuary rituals accorded Moundville's elite. Virtually all of the highly elaborate mound burials, which constitute the uppermost tier of Peebles's (1974; Peebles and Kus 1977) "superordinate dimension," took place in Moundville II and early Moundville III. Most of the less elaborate burials at Moundville probably date to this time period as well. Outside of Moundville, it seems that some people were buried in small cemeteries, generally located near the outlying local centers. Examples of such cemeteries have been found at 1Tu3 (DeJarnette and Peebles 1970) and 1Ha8 (Peebles 1978a:368), both of which date to Moundville III.

All in all, the data suggest a three-level settlement hierarchy was in effect: Moundville stood alone as a regional center, unique in both its size and architectural complexity; next came a stratum of local centers, each with only one mound; and lowest were the subordinate farmsteads and hamlets. The fact that only one regional center existed and all the local centers were of equivalent size strongly suggests that the Warrior Valley was politically unified under Moundville's hegemony.

Alabama River Phase (A.D. 1550—1700)

As currently defined, this protohistoric phase extends over much of central, southern, and western Alabama. Major concentrations of sites have been identified along the Black Warrior River south of the fall line, along the lower Tombigbee river, and along the Alabama River between the fall line (at Montgomery) and the confluence with the Tombigbee (Sheldon 1974:Figure 1).

Within the Black Warrior Valley itself, this phase was marked by a considerable decline in social and political complexity, a decline that probably had begun during late Moundville III. By the start of the Alabama River phase, Moundville and all the local centers had been abandoned, their mounds no longer used. Gone, too, were the lavish mortuary rituals that had served to distinguish society's elite. Most adults were interred quite simply: either as primary, extended burials accompanied by a few grave goods, or as disarticulated "bone burials" placed in large ceramic vessels. Thus, both settlement and mortuary data suggest that the society's organization had reverted once again to an egalitarian form.

Subsistence continued to depend heavily on maize, and a similar range of wild foods—both plant and animal—were exploited as previously (Curren and Little n.d., Sheldon 1974:241–246). A major change did occur, however, in the configuration of local communities. For the first time since the West Jefferson phase, large sites—villages—appeared as people moved into larger aggregations. A number of these villages in the Warrior Valley were 1–2 ha in size, and could well have accommodated populations reaching into the hundreds (Sheldon 1974:140–151). Although evidence of small, scattered settlements also exists during this phase (see p. 160), it is likely that most people lived in the larger communities.

In brief, the late prehistoric sequence in the Black Warrior drainage was marked by several major transformations in social and political organization. Beginning with relatively simple, egalitarian societies in West Jefferson times, these transformations apparently took place in three stages. First came the emergence of small hierarchical polities, as evidenced by the appearance of local centers at about A.D. 1050. Later, a number of these small polities were consolidated into a single larger polity as yet another level in the settlement heirarchy emerged. This change was manifested in the building of a large regional center at Moundville, at around A.D. 1250. The resulting political structure persisted for some 250 years, but eventually the system collapsed. Shortly after A.D. 1500, the regional center and the various local centers fell out of use, and the societies in the area once again took on an egalitarian structure.

The nature of the causal processes that underlay these transformations is in many ways still obscure. It is, nevertheless, worthwhile to conclude with a discussion of certain factors that may help to explain, at least in part, why some of these changes occurred.

SOME SPECULATIONS ON THE CAUSES OF CHANGE

Following the work of Rappaport (1968, 1971) and Wright (1977), Peebles and Kus (1977) point out that a fundamental distinction between egalitarian and ranked societies (chiefdoms) lies in the mechanisms of social control and regulation, processes essential to a society's continued existence. These differences in the structure of regulation have important consequences, in that they determine the ability of societies to deal with uncertainties in the environment.

In egalitarian societies, community decisions are arrived at by consensus, and many aspects of economy and external relations are regulated by mechanisms embedded in community ritual. Because achieving community-wide consensus takes time, and because rituals tend to be inflexible, such mechanisms are intrinsically slow in their operation, and limited in their range of response.

Chiefdoms, on the other hand, are characterized by formal offices of leadership, filled by individuals whose authority allows them to make certain decisions for the community as a whole. Not only can directives be issued and carried out more quickly, but individuals in a position of authority can exercise judgment in a way that ritual cycles cannot. Thus, the reaction to any situation can be more rapid, and the range of responses more varied and better suited to the problems at hand.

In short, the transition from egalitaran society to chiefdom entails the emergence of a superordinate level of offices that have important functions in social regulation and control. Peebles and Kus (1977) suggest that such a transition might well occur under conditions where the limited capabilities of the regulatory mechanisms in egalitarian systems are transcended, and hierarchical controls become necessary for continued social reproduction. Such conditions could involve an increase in the uncertainty or unpredictability of certain critical environmental variables. As Rappaport (1968:234) puts it,

> In a stable environment, slow and inflexible regulation may not produce serious problems, but the novel circumstances that are continually presented by rapidly changing environments may require more rapid and flexible regulation.

The establishment of higher-order controls does have certain costs, since office holders and their retinues are often divorced from subsistence production (especially in the more complex chiefdoms), and therefore must be supported by food extracted from the primary producers. Yet as Sahlins (1972: 101–148) argues, such costs tend to be offset by a variety of economic benefits that the existence of a chief can bring. Because of his exalted authority, a chief is able to channel economic activities, accumulate surplus, and distribute surplus in a way that transcends the self-interest of individual households.

> By thus supporting community welfare and organizing activities, the chief creates a collective good beyond the conception and capacity of the society's domestic groups taken separately. He institutes a public economy greater than the sum of its household parts [Sahlins 1972:140].

With these theoretical considerations in mind, let us now turn to some of the specific factors that may help explain the archaeologically observed changes in the late prehistoric societies of the Black Warrior drainage.

One factor that was probably important in the emergence of the earliest local centers (at about A.D. 1050) was the shift to intensive corn agriculture (Ford 1974). West Jefferson groups hunted and gathered a broad spectrum of wild species, and grew relatively little corn. Such a subsistence regime, based on a high diversity of resources, would have been inherently stable, since an unexpected deficit in any one resource could always be compensated for by an increased exploitation of another (i.e., it was extremely unlikely that in a given year all resources would fail at once). By the start of the Moundville I phase,

however, agriculture had increased tremendously in importance as maize became the principal crop. This change in subsistence would have had two immediate consequences. First, it would have increased productivity, allowing
considerably more people to be supported per unit of land. Second, this increase in productivity would have brought about a decrease in the proportional
contribution of other dietary resources, which also implied certain risks.
Whereas previously the failure of any one resource could be compensated for,
now the failure of a crop could mean disaster. These circumstances may have
favored the emergence of leaders who could mobilize a certain portion of each
household's surplus production, and thereby build up communal stores that
could be used to buffer against unexpected losses. These stores could be distributed as needed to correct not only imbalances in production between one
year and the next, but also imbalances between different households or communities within the same political unit.[2]

Another factor that may have been important in the emergence of political
complexity was the need to regulate intercommunity conflict. As Peebles notes,
this factor and the intensification of agriculture were probably interdependent:

> On the one hand as the dependence on agriculture increased, the risk of cata-
> strophic crop failure increased, and the risk of local hostilities increased. On the
> other hand, as local units were integrated into larger political units, the risk of
> hostility from equally large neighboring polities increased and insecurity again
> increased. This left either alliance or large-scale preemptive raids as one strategy to
> eliminate the unpredictable element in a society's environment. Therefore, the

---

[2]Of course, to say that centralized leadership presented certain advantages tells us nothing
about *how* this leadership emerged. But here one can see yet another connection between agriculture and political evolution, in that intensive argiculture provided a means of generating wealth
that individuals or groups could deploy to their political advantage. In primitive societies generally,
an important tool for enhancing personal status and political influence is the gift. The efficacy of
gift giving (or feasting) stems from the social obligations it places on the recipients to repay (Mauss
1967). Not only does gift giving serve to establish and maintain social alliances, but also it can
serve to enhance the donor's prestige. Generosity among kinsmen is a valued trait, and so the more
one gives away, the more respect one accrues. As long as gifts are small and easy to repay,
reciprocity remains balanced, and social relations remain essentially egalitarian. However, to the
extent that certain segments of society succeed in consistently mobilizing and giving away more
goods than others, asymmetric social relations can develop in which differences in prestige and
influence become pronounced. Clearly, the degree to which such differences can develop depends
on the absolute amount of surplus that can be devoted to social and political ends, which in turn
depends on the nature of the productive economy. The broad-spectrum hunting, gathering, and
gardening economy of West Jefferson times probably placed severe constraints on the amount of
surplus that could be mobilized for use in prestige-building transactions. With the shift to intensive
agriculture, however, these constraints were removed (or at least were made less restrictive), and a
new range of political developments became possible. By producing, mobilizing, and ultimately
giving away larger surpluses, certain individuals or groups could enhance their prestige and enlarge
their networks of followers. This process led to increased social differentiation and greater political
centralization—trends that culminated in the institutionalization of chiefly authority and the establishment of formal offices of leadership.

regulatory functions of the chief were to make alliances, or war, as well as to prevent or buffer against the possibility of crop failure.

Such a view might explain the fact that a part of the iconography of the Southern Cult is related to warfare (Brown 1976), and that it served as well as a common set of symbols among several societies. It symbolized the equality of the leaders among allies, equals among enemies, and it emphasized rank within a single polity. Such a view also goes far toward the understanding of warfare among chiefdoms. Such societies engaged in massive raids, but they generally did not take and hold the territory of the group over which they were victorious. Instead they contented themselves with uprooting crops, destroying stored food, taking captives, and generally disrupting their enemies. If warfare was the least predictable element in a chiefdom's environment, and if it could not be rendered predictable by an alliance, then complete disruption of the enemy group would remove it from the contention for at least one seasonal cycle. It seems from the ethnohistoric record of the Southeast that warfare was of this nature and not the result of the territorial ambitions of one group for another's land [Peebles 1978b:59–60].

In support of this line of reasoning, a few more observations can be added. First, it is interesting to note that there seems to be a negative correlation between aggregated settlements and evidence for hierarchical organization. During the West Jefferson and Alabama River phases, when political centralization was absent, nucleated villages were present. Conversely, from Moundville I to Moundville III, when evidence of political centralization was present, aggregated settlements (possibly except for Moundville) were absent, and most of the population lived in dispersed farmsteads. Ethnographic studies have shown that a dispersed pattern is more efficient and often preferred by primitive agriculturalists, since it minimizes the effort expended in walking to and from fields (Chisolm 1968). One reason for aggregation, superseding efficiency and preference, is the need for defense. Thus, the settlement data from the Warrior drainage are consistent with the notion that intercommunity conflict reached a peak at those times when centralized leadership was lacking. This is not to say, of course, that warfare and raiding were ever totally absent—the bastioned palisade and other evidence for warfare at Moundville clearly indicate otherwise (Peebles and Kus 1977:444). However, it may be that chiefly officials, by means of alliances and preemptive raids, could have rendered warfare more *predictable*. With uncertainty thereby lessened, the population could remain dispersed most of the time, retreating to palisaded enclosures only when the threat of attack was greatest (Smith 1978:488–491).

Indeed, there are artifacts at Moundville and elsewhere that can be interpreted as objects that played an important role in rituals of interpolity alliance. Hall (1977) has pointed out that in the aboriginal cultures of the eastern United States, rituals of peacemaking and alliance typically involved exchanges of weapons, either symbolic or real. The most common object of this sort at the time of European contact was the calumet, which Hall argues had symbolic connotations of an arrow or spear-thrower (1977:503–505). Rituals associated with the calumet crosscut cultural boundaries, and were recognized throughout the eastern Woodlands and the Great Plains; in effect, these rituals were a lingua franca for establishing friendly relations between autonomous political units. In this light, it is rather intriguing that many of the distinctive artifacts found with high-status burials at Moundville are ceremonial weapons—copper axes, embossed sheet-copper arrowheads, monolithic axes, chipped stone "swords," maces, and the like. Most of these artifacts seem to date between A.D. 1200 and 1500, and similar artifacts are found in elite burials throughout the southeastern United States, suggesting that these ceremonial weapons were widely exchanged. Given their context and wide geographical distribution, these artifacts could well have been prehistoric analogs of the calumet, functioning in rituals of diplomacy that, for the most part, would have been engaged in by community leaders. And just as calumets were placed on the bier of a dead Natchez chief in commemoration of ceremonies in which he had participated while alive (Swanton 1911:144), so too were ritual weapons included with the mortuary accompaniments of chiefly personages at Moundville and elsewhere.

Thus, it can be argued that two factors—agriculture and the need to regulate interpolity conflicts—contributed to the emergence of sociopolitical complexity in the Black Warrior region. Yet it is also worthwhile to consider what the arguments presented thus far do not explain.

To begin with, we have not dealt with why agriculture was intensified in the first place. On the central Tombigbee, Jenkins *et al.* (1975) have documented a pattern of population increase leading up to the Mississippi period. If such a pattern of growth also occurred along the Warrior, an increase in population density from West Jefferson to Moundville I times could be invoked as a sufficient cause for the change in subsistence. However, the demographic data with which to support such an argument are as yet unavailable.

A second shortcoming in the explanatory sketch is that it does not deal adequately with why the sociopolitical complexity at Moundville advanced to the point that it did. Presumably, a single level of hierarchical offices could have mitigated subsistence risks and carried out alliances. Why, then, did the hierarchy develop even further, as evidenced by the emergence of a regional center that would have consolidated a number of local centers under its hegemony? Here I suspect the answer will not be found in any purely functional explanations that invoke "stresses" in the environment. Rather, it is conceivable that the development resulted from an interaction of social and ideational processes that, in large part, progressed with a momentum that was generated internally. Examples of the sorts of models that may ultimately prove applicable in this regard can be found in the works of Friedman (1975) and Bloch (1978).

Finally, we must address the question of why the elaborate hierarchy that characterized the Moundville system ultimately collapsed. Two hypotheses have been proposed so far. One, perhaps the most commonly alluded to (e.g.,

Ford 1974:408), is that the collapse was engendered by a massive depopulation in the sixteenth century, brought on by the introduction of Old World diseases. Another is that the collapse was due to internal causes, notably that the costs of maintaining the hierarchy eventually proved to be more than the local productive forces could bear (Peebles 1978b:61). Once again, the data crucial to deciding between the two hypotheses are lacking. One important line of evidence would have to be demographic: If no depopulation preceded the decrease in complexity, then the first hypothesis would obviously be false. Other lines of evidence, involving changes in the quality of diet and the intensity of agriculture, would also be relevant, and are now in the process of being examined (Peebles *et al.* 1979; Schoeninger and Peebles 1981).

Vessel and Sherd Illustrations

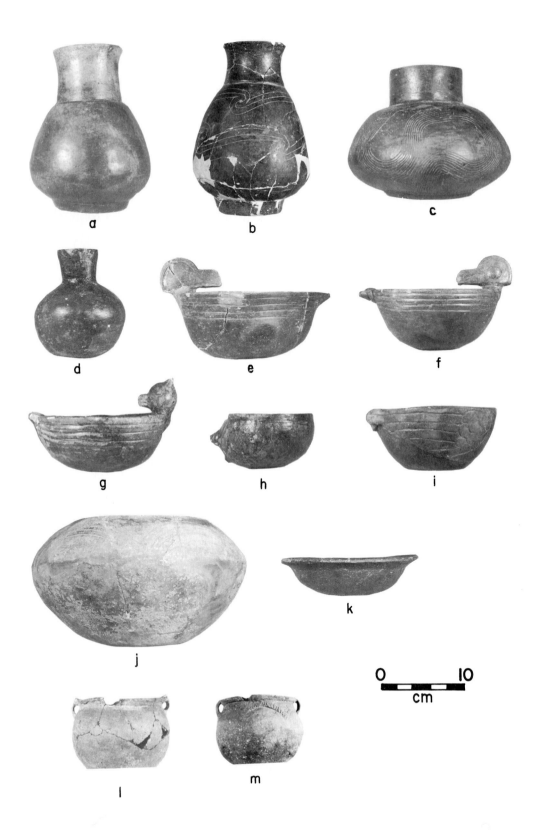

a

b

c

d

e

f

g

h

i

j

k

l

m

0   10
cm

FIGURE 39   Bell Plain, Moundville Engraved, Carthage Incised, and Moundville Incised vessels, Moundville I phase: (a) Bell Plain, *variety Hale,* slender ovoid bottle; (b) Moundville Engraved, *variety Elliots Creek,* slender ovoid bottle; (c) Moundville Engraved, *variety Northport,* subglobular bottle with pedestal base; (d) Bell Plain, *variety Hale,* subglobular bottle with simple base (neck reconstructed); (e and f) Carthage Incised, *variety Akron,* bird effigy bowls with flat, inward facing heads; (g) Carthage Incised, *variety Akron,* unidentified mammal (bear?) effigy bowl; (h) Carthage Incised, *variety Akron,* conch shell effigy; (i) Carthage Incised, *variety unspecified,* bird effigy bowl with incised wings, head missing; (j) Carthage Incised, *variety Summerville,* restricted bowl; (k) Carthage Incised, *variety Moon Lake,* flaring-rim bowl (shallow); (l) Mississippi Plain, *variety Warrior,* standard jar with two handles; and (m) Moundville Incised, *variety Moundville,* standard jar with two handles and folded rim. (Vessel catalog numbers: a, WP213; b, Rw43; c, WP215; d, WP156; e, EI42; f, WP213; g, WP160; h, WP217; i, WP153, j, EI3; k, SD267; l, NG4; m, SD265.)

a

b

c

d

e

f

g

h

i

j

k

l

m

n

o

p

q

r

0　　　　　　　　5
cm

s

FIGURE 40   Moundville Engraved and Carthage Incised sherds, Moundville I phase: (a–d) Moundville Engraved, *variety Elliots Creek*—b is a pedestal base fragment from a bottle, and c is red engraved; (e) Moundville Engraved, *variety Stewart;* (f and g) Moundville Engraved, *variety Havana;* (h–p) Moundville Engraved, *variety unspecified*—h, i, l, o, and p are red engraved and n is white engraved; (q) Carthage Incised, *variety Akron,* bowl rim; (r) Carthage Incised *variety Moon Lake,* flaring-rim bowl rim; and (s) Carthage Incised, *variety unspecified,* sherd from bottle. (Proveniences: a, L.12/8N2E; b, L.26/6N2W; c, L.11/ 8N2E; d, L.16/8N2E; e, L.14/8N2E; f, L.9/6N2W; g, L.27B/6N2W; h, L.23/8N2E; i, L.26/8N2E; j, L.26/6N2W; k, L.14/8N2E; l, L.23/8N2E; m and n, L.14/8N2E; o, L.9/ 8N2E; p, L.17/8N2E; q, L.15/6N2W; r, L.24/6N2W; s, L.13/6N2W.)

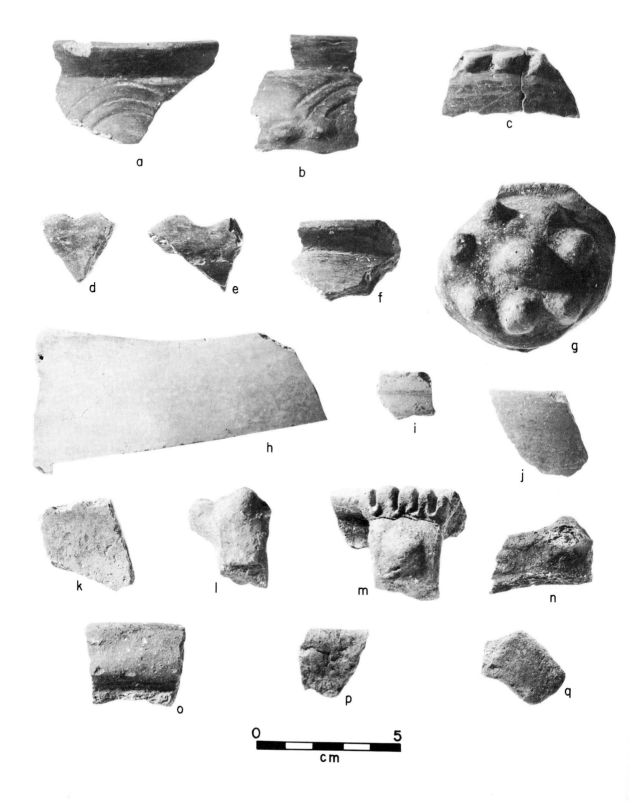

a   b   c

d   e   f   g

h   i   j

k   l   m   n

o   p   q

0   5

cm

FIGURE 41 Carthage Incised, Bell Plain, and Mississippi Plain sherds, some of which show painted decoration, Moundville I phase: (a and b) Carthage Incised, *variety Summerville*, fragments from a burnished jar with grouped nodes; (c) Bell Plain, *variety Hale*, beaded shoulder; (d and e) Bell Plain, *variety Hale*, flaring-rim bowls with scalloped rim; (f) Bell Plain, *variety Hale*, burnished jar rim; (g) Bell Plain, *variety Hale*, conch shell effigy bowl fragment; (h) Bell Plain, *variety Hale*, restricted bowl rim with white slip; (i) Bell Plain, *variety Hale*, black on white; (j) Bell Plain, *variety Hale*, bottle(?) rim, red-filmed interior and exterior; (k) Mississippi Plain, *variety Warrior*, red-filmed interior; (l–o) Mississippi Plain, *variety Warrior*, standard jar rims and handle fragments—o is a folded rim; and (p and q) Mississippi Plain, *variety Hull Lake*—p is a simple bowl rim. (Proveniences: a and b, Rw480; c–e, L.14/8N2E; f, L.12/8N2E; g, L.7A/8N2E; h, L.11/6N2W; i–k, L.14/8N2E; l, L.12/8N2E; m, L.22/6N2W; n, L.25/6N2W; o, L.12/8N2E; p, L.10/8N2E; q, L.12/8N2E.)

a b c d e f g h i j k l m n o

0 5
cm

FIGURE 42 Moundville Incised sherds, Moundville I phase: (a–h) Moundville Incised, *variety Moundville*—h has a folded rim; (i–l) Moundville Incised, *variety Carrollton;* (m and n) Moundville Incised, *variety unspecified*—m has a folded rim; (o) Moundville Incised, *variety Snows Bend.* (Proveniences: a, F.62/6N2W; b, L.14/6N2W; c, L.17,18/ 6N2W; d, L.17/8N2E; e, L.26/6N2W; f, L.15/6N2W; g, L.17,18/6N2W; h, L.14/6N2W; i, F.108/6N2W; j, L.14/6N2W; k, L.7A/8N2E; l, L.15/6N2W; m, L.27A/6N2W; n, L.12/8N2E; o, L.9/6N2W.)

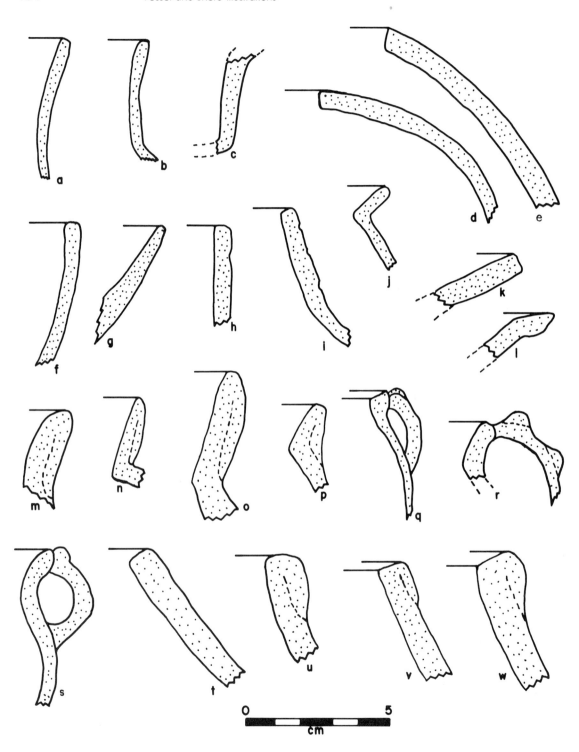

FIGURE 43   Rim and base profiles, Moundville I phase: (a and b) bottle rims; (c) pedestal base fragment from bottle; (d and e) restricted bowl rims; (f–h) simple bowl rims; (i) unusual bowl rim; (j) burnished jar rim; (k and l) flaring-rim bowl rims—l is scalloped; (m–s) standard jar rims (unburnished)—m–p are folded rims, and q is flattened; and (t–w) neckless jar rims (unburnished)—u is folded, and v–w are folded-flattened. (Proveniences: a, L.17, 18/6N2W; b, L.14/6N2W; c, L.26/6N2W; d, surface; e, L.11/6N2W; f, L.14/6N2W; g, L.9/6N2W; h, L.17,18/6N2W; i, L.15/6N2W; j, L.12/8N2E; k, L.24/6N2W; l, L.14/8N2E; m, F.122/6N2W; n, L.9/8N2E; o, L.8/6N2W; p and q, surface; r, L.22/6N2W; s–u, surface; v, L.12/8N2E; w, F.317/8N2E.)

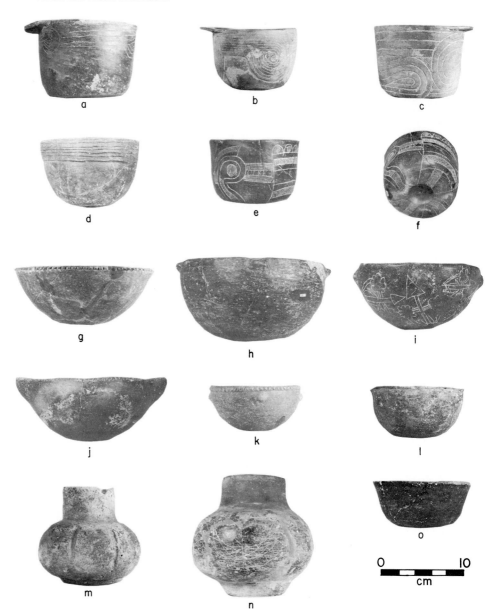

FIGURE 44   Bell Plain and Moundville Engraved vessels, Moundville II phase: (a and b) Moundville Engraved, *variety Havana,* cylindrical bowls with single lugs; (c) Moundville Engraved, *variety Taylorville,* cylindrical bowl with single lug; (d) Moundville Engraved, *variety Havana,* cylindrical bowl; (e and f) Moundville Engraved *variety Hemphill,* paired tails motif, side and bottom view, note indentation on bottom; (g) Bell Plain, *variety Hale,* simple bowl with beaded rim; (h) Bell Plain, *variety Hale,* simple bowl with widely spaced nodes; (i) Moundville Engraved, *variety Hemphill,* bilobed arrow motif, simple bowl with widely spaced nodes; (j) Bell Plain, *variety Hale,* simple bowl with beaded rim and spouts; (k) Bell Plain, *variety Hale,* simple bowl with beaded rim and widely spaced nodes; (l) Moundville Engraved, *variety Hemphill,* rayed circle motif (not visible), simple bowl; (m) Moundville Engraved, *variety Hemphill,* raptor motif (not visible), subglobular bottle with pedestal base and gadrooning; (n) Moundville Engraved, *variety Wiggins,* subglobular bottle with pedestal base; and (o) Moundville Engraved, *variety Hemphill,* Greek cross and scalp motifs (not visible), outslanting bowl. (Vessel catalog numbers: a, SD826; b, SWM142; c, SWM132; d, WP187; e and f, NG3; g, SD822; h, SD827; i, SD48/M7; j, SD821; k, NE453; l, SD733; m, SW34; n, NE68; o, SD154.)

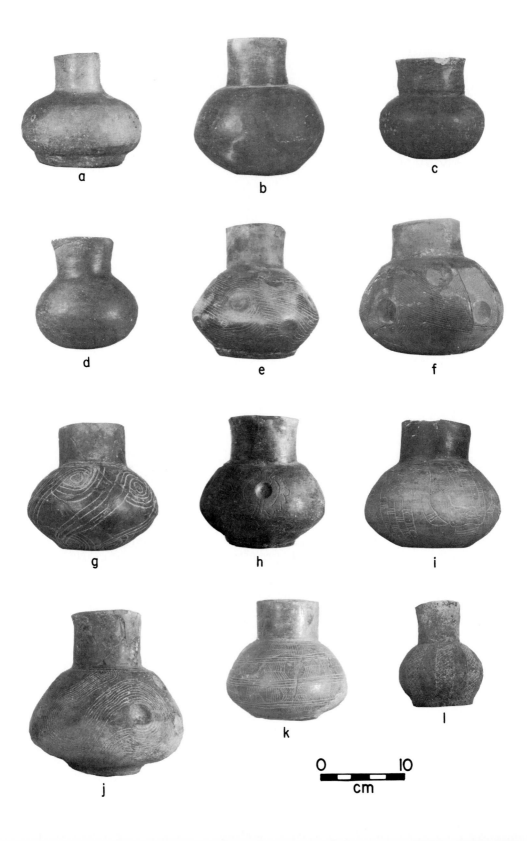

a

b

c

d

e

f

g

h

i

j

k

l

0 _____ 10
cm

FIGURE 45   Bell Plain and Moundville Engraved vessels, Moundville II phase: (a and b) Bell Plain, *variety Hale*, subglobular bottles with pedestal bases; (c and d) Bell Plain, *variety Hale*, subglobular bottles with simple bases; (e) Moundville Engraved, *variety Tuscaloosa*, subglobular bottle with pedestal base and indentations; (f) Moundville Engraved, *variety Tuscaloosa*, subglobular bottle with slab base and indentations; (g) Moundville Engraved, *variety Northport*, subglobular bottle with pedestal base; (h) Moundville Engraved, *variety Hemphill*, bilobed arrow motif, subglobular bottle with pedestal base and indentations; (i) Moundville Engraved, *variety Hemphill*, hand and eye motif, subglobular bottle with pedestal base (neck reconstructed); (j) Moundville Engraved, *variety Northport*, subglobular bottle with pedestal base and indentations; (k) Moundville Engraved, *variety Prince Plantation*, subglobular bottle with pedestal base; and (l) Moundville Engraved, *variety Maxwells Crossing*, subglobular bottle with pedestal base. (Vessel catalog numbers: a, SWM141; b, EE304; c, SD825; d, EE303; e, NG8; f, Rho159; g, SWM131; h, NR11/M5; i, Rho1; j, Rho170; k, NR129; l, SW23.)

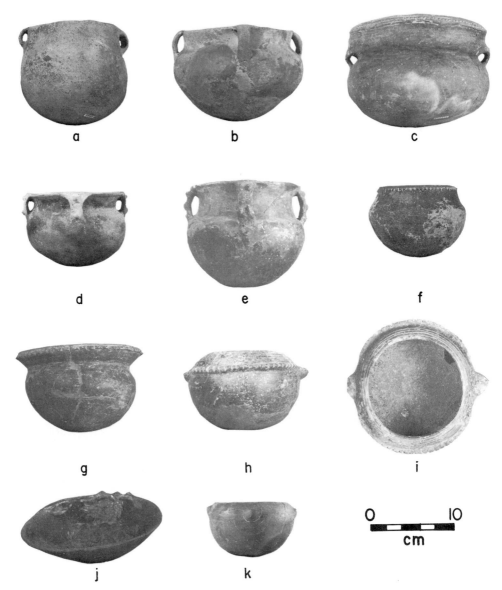

FIGURE 46   Bell Plain, Mississippi Plain, and Moundville Engraved vessels, Moundville II phase: (a) Mississippi Plain, *variety Warrior*, standard jar with two handles; (b) Mississippi Plain, *variety Warrior*, standard jar with four handles; (c) Bell Plain, *variety Hale*, composite bowl–jar with beaded rim; (d) Mississippi Plain, *variety Warrior*, standard jar with four tapered handles (very late Moundville II); (e) Mississippi Plain, *variety Warrior*, standard jar with four handles; (f) Bell Plain, *variety Hale*, burnished jar with no handles and a beaded rim; (g) Bell Plain, *variety Hale*, composite bowl with beaded rim; (h and i) Moundville Engraved, *variety Havana*, turtle effigy bowl, side and top view; (j) Bell Plain, *variety Hale*, mussel shell effigy; and (k) Moundville Engraved, *variety Havana*, restricted bowl with widely spaced nodes. (Vessel catalog numbers: a, SW40; b, NE452; c, Rho371; d, SG15; e, NE444; f, NE450; g, NE445; h and i, NE165; j, WP22; k, O33/M5.)

FIGURE 47   Moundville Engraved and Carthage Incised sherds, Moundville II phase: (a and b) Moundville Engraved, *variety Tuscaloosa;* (c and d), Moundville Engraved, *variety Hemphill;* (e–g) Moundville Engraved, *variety Havana*—f has a notched lip; (h–j) Moundville Engraved, *variety unspecified,* possible examples of *variety Northport;* (k and l) Moundville Engraved, *variety unspecified,* possible examples of *Taylorville* or *Maxwells Crossing;* (m) Moundville Engraved, *variety unspecified,* crosshatched triangles, possibly *Hemphill* or *Wiggins;* (n and o) Moundville Engraved, *variety unspecified;* and (p and q) Carthage Incised, *variety unspecified.* (Proveniences: a, L.6/6N2W; b and c, L.4/8N2E; d and e, L.7/6N2W; f, L.5/8N2E; g, L.4/8N2E; h, L.6/6N2W; i and j, L.4/8N2E; k, L.6/6N2W; l, L.4/8N2E; m, L.7/6N2W; n, L.6/6N2W; o, L.7/6N2W; p, L.7/6N2W; q, L.4/8N2E.)

FIGURE 48 Moundville Incised and Mississippi Plain sherds, Moundville II phase: (a and b) Moundville Incised, *variety Moundville,* standard jar rims; (c and d) Moundville Incised, *variety Snows Bend;* (e) Moundville Incised, *variety Carrollton;* (f and g) Mississippi Plain, *variety Warrior,* standard jar rims; (h–k) Mississippi Plain, *variety Warrior,* jar handle fragments; (l) Mississippi Plain, *variety Warrior,* neckless jar rim; (m) Mississippi Plain, *variety Warrior,* simple bowl rim; (n) Mississippi Plain, *variety Warrior,* flaring-rim bowl rim; and (o) Mississip-

FIGURE 49 Bell Plain sherds, some of which have painted decoration, Moundville II phase: (a–c) Bell Plain, *variety Hale*, flaring-rim bowl rims—c has a notched lip; (d and e) Bell Plain, *variety Hale*, simple bowl beaded rims; (f) Bell Plain, *variety Hale*, pedestal base bottle; (g) Bell Plain, *variety Hale*, outslanting bowl rim; (h) Bell Plain, *variety Hale*, red-filmed exterior; (i and j) Bell Plain, *variety Hale*, white-filmed exterior; and (k) Bell Plain, *variety Hale*, red-on-black, pedestal base bottle. (Proveniences: a–c, L.7/6N2W; d, L.5/8N2W; e, L.4/8N2E; f, L.7/6N2W; g, L.5/8N2E; h, L.4/8N2E; i, L.6/6N2W; j, L.4/8N2E; k, L.4/8N2E.)

pi Plain, *variety Hull Lake*. (Proveniences: a, L.5/8N2E; b, L.6/6N2W; c, L.7/6N2W; d, L.4/8N2E; e, L.7/6N2W; f, L.6/6N2W; g, L.6/6N2W; h, L.5/8N2E; i, L.7/6N2W; j–l, L.6/6N2W; m, L.5/8N2E; n, L.6/6N2W; o, L.7/6N2W.)

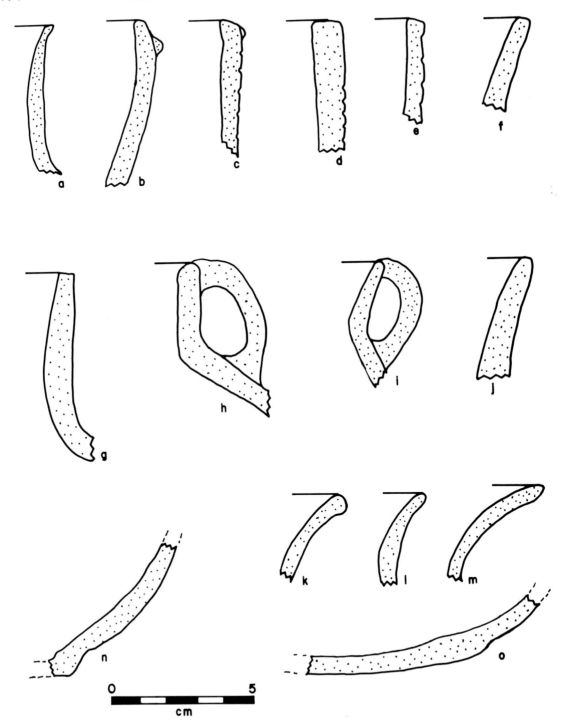

FIGURE 50   Rim and base profiles, Moundville II phase: (a) bottle rim; (b) simple bowl with beaded rim; (c–e) cylindrical bowl rims—c has a notched lip, and d is a thickened rim with a flat lip (probably nonlocal); (f) outslanting bowl rim; (g–m) standard jar rims (unburnished); (n) pedestal base fragment from a bottle; and (o) slab base fragment from a bottle. (Proveniences: a, L.6/6N2W; b, F.36/8N2E; c–e, surface; f, L.5/8N2E; g, L.6/6N2W; h and i, surface; j, L.4/8N2E; k, L.6/6N2W; l, L.5/8N2E; m, L.6A/8N2E; n, L.7/6N2W; o, surface.)

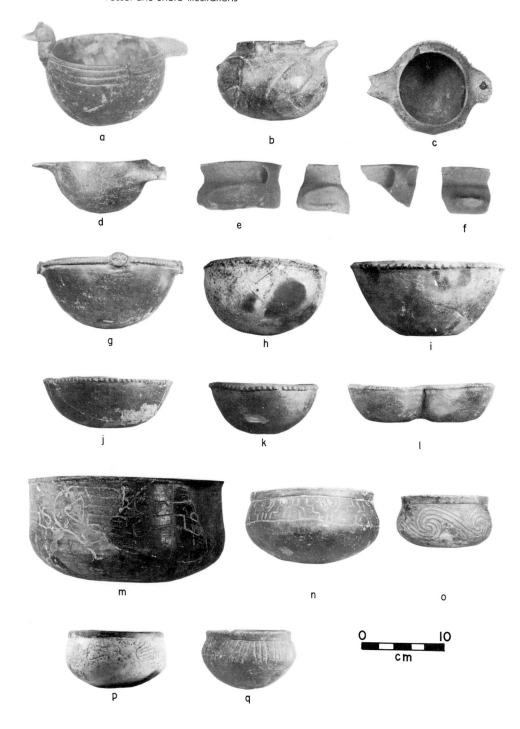

FIGURE 51   Bell Plain and Carthage Incised vessels, Moundville III phase: (a) Carthage Incised, *variety Akron,* bird effigy bowl with a gracile and outward-facing head (not to scale); (b) Bell Plain, *variety Hale,* frog effigy jar; (c) Bell Plain, *variety Hale,* fish effigy bowl; (d) Bell Plain, *variety Hale,* beaver effigy bowl; (e–f), Bell Plain, *variety Hale,* frog effigy jar fragments; (g) Bell Plain, *variety Hale,* simple bowl with beaded rim and human head medallions; (h) Bell Plain, *variety Hale,* simple bowl with beaded rim, red and white; (i–k) Bell Plain, *variety Hale,* simple bowls with beaded rims; (l) Bell Plain, *variety Hale,* double bowl with beaded rim; (m) Carthage Incised, *variety Fosters,* hand and eye motif and forearm bones motif, unusual bowl form; (n) Carthage Incised, *variety Poole,* short-neck bowl; (o) Carthage Incised, *variety Carthage,* short-neck bowl; (p) Carthage Incised, *variety Fosters,* hand motif, forearm bones motif, short-neck bowl; and (q) Carthage Incised, *variety Moon Lake,* short-neck bowl. (Proveniences: a, NR44; b, WP'29; c, EE 187; d, SD816; e–f, Rw138; g, NR118; h, EE87; i, NN'2; j, EE2; k, SD815; l, SL3; m, SD682; n, EI39; o, EE5; p, WP'22; q, NE185.)

a

b

c

d

e

f

g

h

i

j

k

l

m

n

o

p

q

r

s

t

0   10
cm

FIGURE 52   Bell Plain, Carthage Incised, and Moundville Engraved vessels, Moundville III phase: (a) Bell Plain, *variety Hale*, subglobular bottle with simple base; (b) Moundville Engraved, *variety Englewood*, subglobular bottle with simple base; (c–d) Moundville Engraved, *variety Wiggins*, subglobular bottle with simple base; (e) Moundville Engraved, *variety Tuscaloosa*, subglobular bottle with slab base and indentations; (f) Moundville Engraved, *variety Taylorville*, subglobular bottle with simple base; (g) Moundville Engraved, *variety Wiggins*, subglobular bottle with simple base; (h) Moundville Engraved, *variety Hemphill*, bird with serpent head motif, subglobular bottle with slab base; (i) Moundville Engraved, *variety Hemphill*, turtle motif, subglobular bottle with simple base; (j) Moundville Engraved, *variety Hemphill*, hand and eye motif, subglobular bottle with slab base; (k) Carthage Incised, *variety Carthage*, unusual kind of scroll, subglobular bottle with simple base; (l) Carthage Incised, *variety Carthage*, narrow-neck bottle; (m) Moundville Engraved, *variety Hemphill*, winged serpent motif, subglobular bottle with simple base; (n) Moundville Engraved, *variety Hemphill*, raptor motif, subglobular bottle with simple base; (o) Moundville Engraved, *variety Wiggins*, unusual elements (concentric semicircles) within scroll, subglobular bottle with simple base, indentations; (p) Moundville Engraved, *variety Hemphill*, winged serpent motif, subglobular bottle with simple base; (q) Moundville Engraved, *variety Hemphill*, paired tails motif, subglobular bottle with simple base; (r) Moundville Engraved, *variety Hemphill*, crested bird motif (tail element visible, head on other side), subglobular bottle with simple base; (s) Moundville Engraved, *variety Hemphill*, windmill motif, subglobular bottle with simple base; and (t) Moundville Engraved, *variety Hemphill*, scalp motif and hand and eye motif, subglobular bottle with simple base. (Vessel catalog numbers: a, EE129; b, EE10; c, EE85; d, EE86; e, NE572; f, EE429; g, NE574; h, SD805; i, EE4; j, NE61; k, SEH15; l, EE12; m, NN'38; n, SWG63; o, NR40; p, SD836; q, SWG62; r, SEH73; s, EE391; t, NR38.)

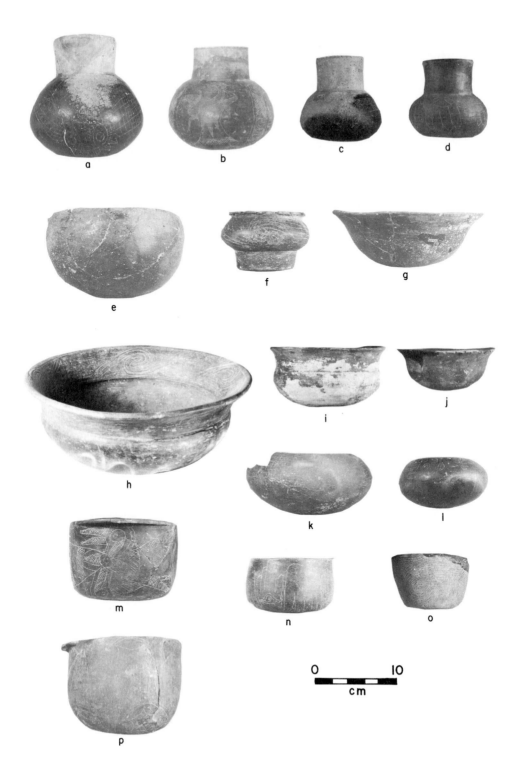

a   b   c   d

e   f   g

h   i   j

k   l

m   n   o

p

0   10
cm

FIGURE 53 Bell Plain, Carthage Incised, and Moundville Engraved vessels, Moundville III phase: (a) Moundville Engraved, *variety Hemphill,* insect motif, subglobular bottle with simple base; (b) Moundville Engraved, *variety Hemphill,* winged serpent motif, subglobular bottle with simple base; (c) Moundville Engraved, *variety Hemphill,* radial fingers motif, subglobular bottle with simple base; (d) Moundville Engraved, *variety Hemphill,* hand and eye motif, subglobular bottle with simple base; (e) Bell Plain, *variety Hale,* simple bowl with widely spaced nodes; (f) Moundville Engraved, *variety Wiggins,* pedestaled bowl with notched everted lip; (g) Bell Plain, *variety Hale,* flaring-rim bowl (shallow); (h) Carthage Incised, *variety Carthage,* flaring-rim bowl (deep); (i) Bell Plain, *variety Hale,* flaring-rim bowl (deep); (j) Carthage Incised, *variety Moon Lake,* flaring-rim bowl (shallow) with notched lip; (k) Moundville Engraved, *variety Hemphill,* radial fingers motif, restricted bowl; (l) Moundville Engraved, *variety Hemphill,* hand and eye motif, restricted bowl; (m) Moundville Engraved, *variety Hemphill,* paired tails motif, cylindrical bowl with single lug; (n) Moundville Engraved, *variety Hemphill,* hand and eye motif, cylindrical bowl with single lug; (o) Moundville Engraved, *variety Havana,* cylindrical bowl; and (p) Moundville Engraved, *Variety Hemphill,* scalp motif, cylindrical bowl with single lug. (Vessel catalog numbers: a, NG10; b, WR81; c, EE7; d, SD32/M7; e, EE392; f, EE160; g, SD723; h, WP121; i, EE77; j, SD745; k, SWG2; l, EE126; m, EE3; n, EE182; o, NE50; p, SWG3.)

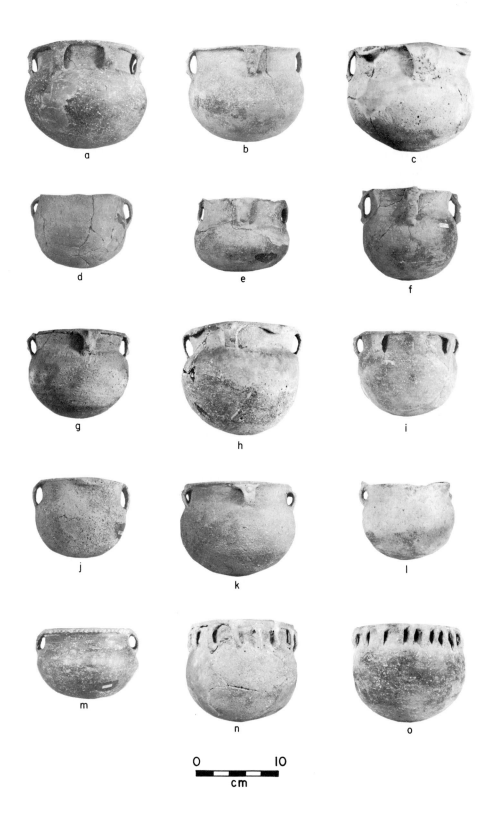

a   b   c

d   e   f

g   h   i

j   k   l

m   n   o

0   10
cm

FIGURE 54   Bell Plain and Mississippi Plain jars, Moundville III phase: (a) Mississippi Plain, *variety Warrior,* standard jar with 8 handles; (b) Mississippi Plain, *variety Warrior,* standard jar with 4 handles; (c) Mississippi Plain, *variety Warrior,* standard jar with 4 handles and downturned lugs; (d) Mississippi Plain, *variety Warrior,* standard jar with 2 handles; (e–g) Mississippi Plain, *variety Warrior,* standard jar with 4 handles; (h) Mississippi Plain, *variety Warrior,* standard jar with 4 handles and downturned lugs; (i) Mississippi Plain, *variety Warrior,* standard jar with 8 handles; (j) Mississippi Plain, *variety Warrior,* standard jar with 2 handles and downturned lugs; (k) Mississippi Plain, *variety Warrior,* standard jar with 4 handles; (l) Mississippi Plain, *variety Warrior,* standard jar with 2 handles (handles look early—may be an heirloom); (m) Bell Plain, *variety Hale,* burnished jar with 2 handles, beaded rim, and widely spaced nodes; and (n and o) Mississippi Plain, *variety Warrior,* standard jars with more than 10 handles. (Vessel catalog numbers: a, SD681; b, SW64; c, NN'39; d, SD744; e, SWG1; f, SD746; g, EE124, h, SD680; i, SWG5; j, SD837; k, NR28; l, WP228; m, SEH10; n, SWG7; o, EI40.)

FIGURE 55 Moundville Engraved sherds from Moundville III Levels: (a and b) *variety Tuscaloosa*; (c) *variety Taylorville*; (d) *variety Maxwells Crossing*; (e and f) *variety Havana*; (g) *variety Wiggins*; (h) *variety Cypress*; (i and j) *variety Hemphill*, scalp motif; (k) *variety Hemphill*, windmill motif; (l) *variety Hemphill*, radial fingers motif; and (m–s) *variety unspecified*. (Proveniences: a–c, L.5/6N2W; d, L.3/6N2W; e, L.3/8N2E; f and g, L.5/6N2W; h, L.3/8N2W, i, L.5/6N2W; j, L.1/8N2W; k, L.4/6N2W; l–n, L.5/6N2W; o, L.4/6N2W; p, L.5/6N2W; q, L.1/8N2E; r, L.4/6N2W; s, L.5/6N2W.)

FIGURE 56   Carthage Incised, Barton Incised, Alabama River Incised, Bell Plain, and Mississippi Plain sherds, some with painted decoration, from Moundville III levels: (a) Carthage Incised, *variety Akron;* (b) Carthage Incised, *variety Fosters,* flaring-rim bowl rim; (c) Carthage Incised, *variety Poole,* short-neck bowl rim; (d and e) Carthage Incised, *variety Carthage*—e is the interior of a flaring-rim bowl; (f and g) Carthage Incised, *variety unspecified;* (h) Alabama River Incised, *variety unspecified,* short-neck bowl rim; (i) Barton Incised, *variety Demopolis,* standard jar rim; (j) Bell Plain, *variety Hale,* white-filmed, flaring-rim bowl rim; (k) Bell Plain, *variety Hale,* white-filmed, restricted bowl rim; (l) Bell Plain, *variety Hale,* red and black (red exterior showing, interior is black-filmed); (m) Bell Plain, *variety Hale,* red-filmed exterior; (n) Mississippi Plain, *variety Warrior,* red-filmed interior and exterior, simple bowl rim; and (o and p) Mississippi Plain, *variety Warrior,* red-filmed interior, standard jar rims—p shows the exterior of the rim (note the red slip appearing over the top of the lip). (Proveniences: a–c, L.1/6N2W; d, L.5/6N2W; e, L.1/6N2W; f, L.2/6N2W; g, L.5/6N2W; h and i, L.3/6N2W; j, L.1/6N2W; k, L.2/6N2W; l, L.4/6N2W; m, L.3/6N2W; n, L.2/6N2W; o, L.1/6N2W; p, L.5/6N2W.)

FIGURE 57   Mississippi Plain sherds from Moundville III levels: (a–d and f–k) *variety War-rior*, standard jar rims—f is noded; (e) *variety Warrior*, handle fragment; (l) *variety War-rior*, bowl rim; (m) *variety Warrior*, flaring-rim bowl rim; and (n and o) *variety Hull Lake.* (Proveniences: a, L.5/6N2W; b, L.3/6N2W; c, L.2/8N2E; d, L.2/6N2W; e, L.3/6N2W; f, L.3/8N2E; g, L.5/6N2W; h and i, L.5/6N2W; j, L.3/6N2W; k, L.3/8N2E; l, L.4/6N2W; m and n, L.2/8N2E; o, L.1/8N2E.)

FIGURE 58   Bell Plain, *variety Hale* sherds from Moundville III levels; (a) short-neck bowl rim; (b–e) simple bowl rims—d has a node; (f–i) simple bowl rims, beaded; (j) burnished jar rim, beaded; (k) restricted bowl rim; (l) deep flaring-rim bowl rim with a notched lip; (m–p) flaring-rim bowl rims—n is scalloped; and (q) jar shoulder with frog effigy features. (Proveniences: a, L.2/6N2W; b, L.4/6N2W; c, L.5/6N2W; d, L.2/8N2E; e, L.2/8N2E; f, L.3/6N2W; g, L.4/6N2W; h, L.2/6N2W; i, L.3/8N2E; j, L.1/8N2E; k and l, L.1/6N2E; m, L.2/8N2E; n, L.5/6N2W; o, L.4/6N2W; p, L.5/6N2W; q, L.1/6N2W.)

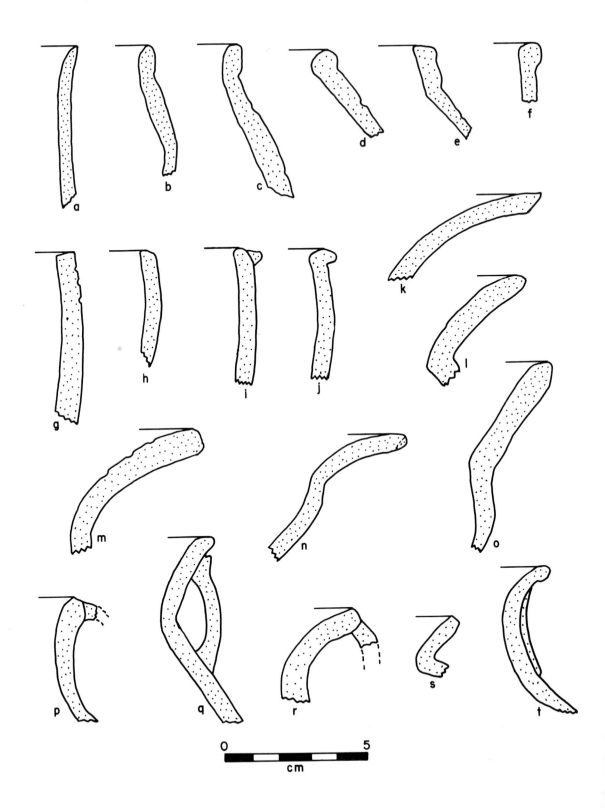

a

b

c

d

e

f

g

h

i

j

k

l

m

n

o

p

q

r

s

t

0   5

cm

FIGURE 59.   Rim profiles of Moundville III and Alabama River phase sherds: (a) bottle; (b–d) short-neck bowls (burnished); (e) short-neck bowl (unburnished), Alabama River Incised; (f) bowl; (g and h) simple bowls; (i and j) simple bowls with beaded rims; (k–o) flaring-rim bowls—o has red and white interior; (p–s) standard jars (unburnished); and (t) standard jar (unburnished) with appliqué neck fillets. (Proveniences: a, L.3/6N2W; b, L.2/6N2W; c, L.1/6N2W; d, L.3/6N2W; e, L.3/6N2W; f, L.5/6N3W; g, L.3/8N2E; h, L.4/6N2W; i, surface; j, L.2/6N2W; k, L.2/8N2E; l and m, surface; n, L.1/6N2W; o, surface; p, L.2/8N2E; q, surface; r, L.5/6N2W; s, L.5/6N2W; t, surface.)

FIGURE 60 Mississippi Plain and Moundville Incised sherds, found in Moundville III levels but probably intrusive from below: (a) Mississippi Plain, *variety Warrior,* folded rim from standard jar; (b–e) Moundville Incised, *variety Moundville;* (f–i) Moundville Incised, *variety Carrollton;* and (j) Moundville Incised, *variety unspecified.* (Proveniences: a, L.2/6N2W; b, L.1/8N2E; c, L.5/6N2W; d, L.1/6N2W; e and f, L.3/8N2E; g and h, L.2/6N2W; i and j, L.5/6N2W.)

FIGURE 61 Unclassified sherds from various levels; (a–e) unclassified decorated (shell-tempered); (f) unclassified engraved (untempered); and (g–j) unclassified plain (untempered)—g is a bowl(?) rim and j appears to be a jar handle. (Proveniences: a, L.2/6N2W; b and c, L.5/6N2W; d, L.6/6N2W; e, L.7/6N2W; f, L.3/6N2W; g, L.1/8N2E; h, L.5/6N2W; i, L.17/8N2E; j, L.4/6N2W.)

a

b

c

d

e

f

g

h

i

j

k

l

m

n

o

p

q

r

0   10

cm

FIGURE 62   Bell Plain, Carthage Incised, Moundville Engraved, and Alabama River Incised vessels, various phases: (a) Moundville Engraved, *variety Hemphill,* feather motif, subglobular bottle with slab base; (b) Carthage Incised, *variety Carthage,* subglobular bottle with simple base; (c) Moundville Engraved, *variety Hemphill,* raptor motif engraved in the round (head visible, wings on sides, and tail in back), subglobular bottle with simple base; (d) Moundville Engraved, *variety Cypress,* subglobular bottle with simple base; (e) Moundville Engraved, *variety Wiggins,* nonconvergent scroll (late), subglobular bottle with simple base; (f) Moundville Engraved, *variety Englewood,* subglobular bottle with simple base; (g) Moundville Engraved, *variety Hemphill,* crested bird motif engraved in the round (head and wing visible, tail and other wing on opposite side), subglobular bottle with simple base; (h) Moundville Engraved, *variety Hemphill,* skull motif and forearm bones motif, cylindrical bottle (not to scale); (i) unclassified plain (untempered), jar with no handles; (j) Bell Plain, *variety Hale,* burnished jar with no handles but with a band of nodes at the shoulder; (k) Bell Plain, *variety Hale,* double bowl with beaded rim and fish effigy features; (l) Carthage Incised, *variety Akron,* cylindrical bowl with bird effigy features, gracile and outward-facing head; (m) Bell Plain, *variety Hale,* simple bowl with alligator effigy features; (n) Moundville Engraved, *variety unspecified,* bowl with effigy features, unidentified mammal; (o) Moundville Engraved, *variety unspecified,* deep flaring-rim bowl (probably Alabama River phase); (p) Carthage Incised, *variety Fosters,* hand motif and forearm bones motif, red and white painted, shallow flaring-rim bowl (rim in bottom half of photograph is reconstructed); (q) Bell Plain, *variety Hale,* red and white, simple bowl with feline effigy features; and (r) Alabama River Incised, *variety unspecified,* standard jar with appliqué neck fillets. (Vessel catalog numbers: a, NE599; b, WP83; c, NE80; d, SED27; e, NE6; f, Rw25; g, SD472; h, NR25; i, WP96; j, Rho220; k, Rho366; l, RPB3; m, NC1; n, SED7; o, NB6; p, Rw25; q, EE203; r, NR7.)

cm

FIGURE 63   Bell Plain, Carthage Incised, Moundville Engraved, and Moundville Incised vessels, various phases: (a) Moundville Engraved, *variety Elliots Creek,* red-engraved, simple bowl; (b) Moundville Engraved, *variety Elliots Creek,* red-engraved, restricted bowl; (c) Moundville Engraved, *variety unspecified,* terraced rectanguloid bowl with lowered lip; (d) Bell Plain, *variety Hale,* red and black on white, terraced rectanguloid bowl with lowered lip; (e) Moundville Engraved, *variety unspecified,* terraced rectanguloid bowl with lowered lip (not to scale); (f) Bell Plain, *variety Hale,* pedestaled bowl with lowered lip and cutout rim; (g) Moundville Engraved, *variety Wiggins,* subglobular bottle with slab base and indentations; (h) Moundville Engraved, *variety Hemphill,* windmill motif, subglobular bottle with slab base and indentations; (i) Moundville Incised, *variety Snows Bend,* standard jar with four handles and widely spaced nodes; (j) Moundville Incised, *variety unspecified,* unusual design, standard jar with two handles and widely spaced nodes; (k) Moundville Incised, *variety Moundville,* standard jar with two handles and widely spaced nodes; (l) Carthage Incised, *variety Akron,* simple bowl with bird effigy features, flat and outward-facing head. (Vessel catalog numbers: a, SEH71; b, SEH83; c, NE1; d, SD3; e, NE67; f, W176; g, Rw572; h, SWM188; i, WP30; j, SD27; k, NE597; l, NR43.)

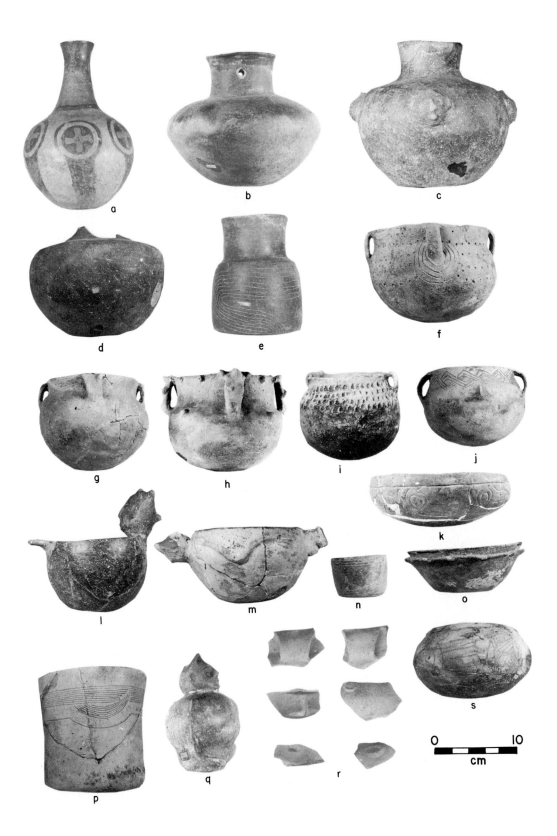

a   b   c

d   e   f

g   h   i   j

k

l   m   n   o

s

p   q   r

0   10
cm

FIGURE 64 Nonlocal vessels: (a) Nashville Negative Painted, *variety unspecified*, carafe-neck bottle; (b) Bell Plain, *variety unspecified*, high-shouldered bottle; (c) Bell Plain, *variety unspecified*, high-shouldered bottle with human head medallions; (d) Bell Plain, *variety unspecified*, high-shouldered bottle; (e) unclassified engraved, cylindrical bottle; (f) unclassified incised and punctated, standard jar with four handles; (g) Mississippi Plain, *variety unspecified*, standard jar with four "eared" handles; (h) Mississippi Plain, *variety unspecified*, standard jar with four handles, and nodes; (i) Parkin Punctated, *variety unspecified*, standard jar with two handles (not to scale); (j) Matthews Incised, *variety Beckwith*, standard jar with two handles and stylized frog effigy features; (k) Pensacola Incised, *variety Little Lagoon*, hand and eye motif, simple bowl; (l) Bell Plain, *variety unspecified*, simple bowl with human head rim effigy; (m) Nodena Red and White, *variety unspecified*, simple bowl with human effigy features (reclining); (n) Andrews Decorated, *variety unspecified*, cylindrical bowl; (o) Bell Plain, *variety unspecified*, bowl with double lip; (p) Mound Place Incised, *variety Mobile*, cylindrical bowl; (q) Walls Engraved, *variety unspecified*, hooded bottle with human effigy features; (r) Mississippi Plain, *variety unspecified*, fragments of standard jar with two handles and stylized frog effigy features; and (s) Pensacola Incised, *variety Little Lagoon*, restricted bowl. (Vessel catalog numbers: a, Rho182; b, Rho178; c, NE448; d, WR83; e, SD813; f, Rho160; g, NN'40; h, SEH10; i, EI16; j, SD848; k, SL24; l, NE444; m, Rho307; n, Rw177; o, WP229; p, SL2; q, WR57; r, EE89; s, NN'3.)

a

b

c

d

e

f

g

h

i

j

k

l

m

n

o

p

q

r

s

t

0   10

cm

FIGURE 65   Nonlocal vessels: (a) Bell Plain, *variety unspecified*, composite bottle with carafe neck; (b) Nodena Red and White, *variety unspecified*, collared bottle; (c) Nodena Red and White, *variety unspecified*, carinated bottle; (d) Holly Fine Engraved, cylindrical bottle; (e) Bell Plain, *variety unspecified*, lobate bottle; (f) Bell Plain, *variety unspecified*, stirrup-neck bottle; (g) Bell Plain, *variety unspecified*, hooded bottle (not to scale); (h) Barton Incised, *variety unspecified*, standard jar with two handles; (i) unclassified engraved, paired tails motif, cylindrical bowl with thickened rim and notched lip; (j) Mound Place Incised, *variety unspecified*, simple bowl with bird effigy features, flat and inward-facing head; (k) Bell Plain, *variety unspecified*, simple bowl with human effigy features (reclining); (l) Pensacola Incised, *variety Strongs Bayou*, cylindrical bottle; (m) unclassified incised (sand-tempered), pedestaled bowl with lowered and notched lip; (n) unclassified engraved (sand-tempered), cylindrical bowl; (o) unclassified engraved (sand-tempered), simple bowl with notched lip; (p) Pensacola Incised, *variety Little Lagoon*, skull motif and forearm bones motif, cylindrical bowl; (q) Pensacola Incised, *variety unspecified*, potbellied bowl; (r) Plaquemine Brushed, *variety unspecified*, jar with no handles; (s) Andrews Decorated, *variety unspecified*, cylindrical bowl; and (t) Bell Plain, *variety unspecified*, restricted bowl with frog effigy features. (Vessel catalog numbers: a, Rho67; b, NED1; c, EE84; d, NE170; e, SW26; f, NN'14; g, ND6; h, W70; i, SE16; j, ND33; k, WR66; l, EE201; m, SD350; n, SD749; o, SD351; p, SEH9; q, NE53; r, WR107; s, SWM166; t, EE67.)

FIGURE 66 Nonlocal sherds from various levels: (a and b) Mound Place Incised, *variety Mobile*, both from the same vessel, simple bowl with thickened rim; (c) Mound Place Incised, *variety unspecified*, cylindrical(?) bowl with thickened rim and flat lip; (d) D'Olive Incised, *variety unspecified*; (e) D'Olive Incised, *variety unspecified*, flaring-rim bowl with thickened rim and notched lip; (f) Lake Jackson Decorated, *variety unspecified*, standard jar rim with three parallel incisions (eroded, but visible on left); (g) McKee Island Cord-Marked; (h) Bell Plain, *variety unspecified*, annular base from bottle; (i) Pouncey Ridge Pinched, *variety unspecified*; (j) Nashville Negative Painted, black (positive?) paint on red slip, bottle fragment. (Provenience: a and b, L.5/6N2W; c, L.2/6N2W; d, L.5/6N2W; e, L.4/8N2E; f, L.4/6N2W; g, L.6A/8N2E; h, L.26/6N2W; i, L.1/8N2E; j, L.23/6N2W.)

FIGURE 67 Woodland period sherds from various levels: (a) Alligator Incised *variety Geiger*; (b) Mulberry Creek Cord-Marked, *variety Aliceville*; (c–h) Baytown Plain, *variety Roper*—c is a simple bowl rim and d is a jar handle fragment; (i) Baldwin Plain, *variety Lubbub*; and (j and k) Baldwin plain, *variety Blubber*, simple bowl rims. (Proveniences: a, L.4/6N2W; b, L.5/8N2E; c, L.15/6N2W; d, L.17/8N2E; e, L.8/6N2W; f and g, L.5/6N2W; h and i, L.14/6N2W; j, L.2/6N2W; k, L.3/6N2W.)

APPENDIXES

A

Individual Vessel Descriptions

The vessel descriptions in this appendix are presented in a standardized format that minimally consists of three lines and may consist of up to six. The first line gives the vessel catalog number, the type, the variety, and, if necessary, additional information on representational motifs, other design characteristics, and painted decoration. Vessels that do not fall into any of the established types are listed as "unclassified"; all such vessels are shell tempered unless otherwise specified. It should also be noted that in compiling data on whole vessels, the presence of black filming was not systematically noted. Thus, the fact that it is not mentioned in the vessel descriptions should not be construed as meaning that it was absent on the vessels.

The second line of each descriptive entry contains information on a vessel's shape. This line generally consists of a basic shape term, followed by the secondary shape features, which in turn may be followed by effigy features. In the present format, secondary shape features are preceded by the preposition "with," and effigy features are preceded by a dash.

The third line gives a vessel's presumed place of manufacture. As noted in Chapter 3, all such attributions are made purely on the basis of style, and therefore should be regarded with caution. Vessels having features of shape, decoration, and paste that commonly occur on the site are classified as "local." Vessels that have many commonly found features, along with a few features that appear to be deviant or unusual, are here listed as "local (questionable)." Vessels exhibiting numerous distinctive and unusual features, especially features known to occur commonly in other regions, are considered nonlocal; wherever possible, style comparisons have been used to name specific geographical areas as the presumed sources of these nonlocal wares.

In addition to the three lines of information just mentioned, several more lines may appear in a descriptive entry as well. If a vessel's burial provenience is known, then the skeleton or feature number is given in the fourth line. If the vessel was illustrated by Moore, then the reference to that illustration is given in the fifth line. Finally, if the vessel is housed in the Museum of the American Indian (MAI) or the National Museum of Natural History (NMNH), then its museum catalog number is given in the sixth line.

The vessels are arranged below according to their locality prefix, using the conventional order of precedence given in Table 1. Within each locality, all vessels excavated during the depression era are listed first, and those excavated by Moore are listed afterward.

The conventions governing vessel catalog numbers and burial numbers are explained in Chapter 1. Classificatory terms that pertain to local vessels are described in Chapter 3; other terms, which pertain to nonlocal vessels only, are treated in Appendix F. The few terms that are not defined in any of these sections are for the most part self-explanatory.

AdB34   Mississippi Plain, *variety unspecified*
         VESSEL SHAPE: Collared bottle with carafe
         neck
         PRESUMED SOURCE: Central Mississippi Valley
         (Clarksdale region)

AdB44   Bell Plain, *variety Hale*
         VESSEL SHAPE: Subglobular bottle with simple
         base
         PRESUMED SOURCE: Local (questionable)
         GRAVELOT PROVENIENCE: Bu. 2914/AdB

Rho1   Moundville Engraved, *variety Hemphill* (hand and
         eye)
         VESSEL SHAPE: Subglobular bottle with
         pedestal base
         PRESUMED SOURCE: Local

Rho18   Mississippi Plain, *variety unspecified*
         VESSEL SHAPE: Flaring-rim bowl with grooved
         lip
         PRESUMED SOURCE: Nonlocal

Rho36   Mississippi Plain, *variety Warrior*
         VESSEL SHAPE: Undiagnostic fragment(s)
         PRESUMED SOURCE: Local
         GRAVELOT PROVENIENCE: Bu. 1894/Rho

Rho38   Moundville Engraved, *variety Maxwells Crossing*
         (crosshatched irregular zones)
         VESSEL SHAPE: Subglobular bottle with slab
         base
         PRESUMED SOURCE: Local
         GRAVELOT PROVENIENCE: Bu. 1895/Rho

Rho39   Mississippi Plain, *variety Warrior*
         VESSEL SHAPE: Simple bowl
         PRESUMED SOURCE: Local
         GRAVELOT PROVENIENCE: Bu. 1896/Rho

Rho46   Mississippi Plain, *variety Warrior*
         VESSEL SHAPE: Standard jar with 2 handles
         PRESUMED SOURCE: Local

Rho48   Moundville Engraved, *variety Havana*
         VESSEL SHAPE: Restricted bowl with band of
         nodes
         PRESUMED SOURCE: Local (questionable)
         GRAVELOT PROVENIENCE: Bu. 1901/Rho

Rho57   Moundville Engraved, *variety Havana*
         VESSEL SHAPE: Simple bowl with single lug
         PRESUMED SOURCE: Local
         GRAVELOT PROVENIENCE: Bu. 1909/Rho

Rho65   Bell Plain, *variety unspecified*
         VESSEL SHAPE: Narrow-neck bottle
         (subglobular)
         PRESUMED SOURCE: Central Mississippi Valley,
         Lower Tennessee-Cumberland area
         GRAVELOT PROVENIENCE: Bu. 1923/Rho

Rho66   Moundville Engraved, *variety Taylorville*
         VESSEL SHAPE: Subglobular bottle with slab
         base
         PRESUMED SOURCE: Local
         GRAVELOT PROVENIENCE: Bu. 1923/Rho

Rho67   Bell Plain, *variety unspecified*
         VESSEL SHAPE: Composite bottle with carafe
         neck
         PRESUMED SOURCE: Central Mississippi Valley
         (Cairo Lowland)
         GRAVELOT PROVENIENCE: Bu. 1924/Rho

Rho84   Mississippi Plain, *variety Warrior*
         VESSEL SHAPE: Standard jar
         PRESUMED SOURCE: Local (questionable)
         GRAVELOT PROVENIENCE: Bu. 1934/Rho

Rho90   Mississippi Plain, *variety Warrior*
         VESSEL SHAPE: Standard jar
         PRESUMED SOURCE: Local
         GRAVELOT PROVENIENCE: Bu. 1934/Rho

Rho100   Bell Plain, *variety Hale*
         VESSEL SHAPE: Burnished jar with 2 handles,
         effigy features—frog
         PRESUMED SOURCE: Local
         GRAVELOT PROVENIENCE: Bu. 1936/Rho

Rho101   Andrews Decorated, *variety unspecified*
         VESSEL SHAPE: Cylindrical bowl

         PRESUMED SOURCE: Lower Chattahoochee Valley
         GRAVELOT PROVENIENCE: Bu. 1937/Rho

Rho102   Moundville Engraved, *variety Wiggins*
         VESSEL SHAPE: Subglobular bottle with simple
         base
         PRESUMED SOURCE: Local
         GRAVELOT PROVENIENCE: Bu. 1931/Rho

Rho104   Moundville Engraved, *variety Tuscaloosa*
         VESSEL SHAPE: Subglobular bottle with slab
         base, indentations
         PRESUMED SOURCE: Local
         GRAVELOT PROVENIENCE: Bu. 1939/Rho

Rho107   Mississippi Plain, *variety Warrior*
         VESSEL SHAPE: Bottle
         PRESUMED SOURCE: Local
         GRAVELOT PROVENIENCE: Bu. 1940/Rho

Rho109   Moundville Engraved, *variety unspecified*
         VESSEL SHAPE: Bottle
         PRESUMED SOURCE: Local
         GRAVELOT PROVENIENCE: Bu. 1943-44/Rho

Rho110   Moundville Engraved, *variety Hemphill* (winged
         serpent)
         VESSEL SHAPE: Bottle
         PRESUMED SOURCE: Local
         GRAVELOT PROVENIENCE: Bu. 1947/Rho

Rho122   Mississippi Plain, *variety Warrior*
         VESSEL SHAPE: Undiagnostic fragment(s)
         PRESUMED SOURCE: Local
         GRAVELOT PROVENIENCE: Bu. 1949/Rho

Rho127   Unclassified Plain (sand tempered)
         VESSEL SHAPE: Pedestaled bowl with notched
         everted lip
         PRESUMED SOURCE: Nonlocal
         GRAVELOT PROVENIENCE: Bu. 1949/Rho

Rho132   Moundville Incised, *variety Carrollton*
         (red-filmed interior)
         VESSEL SHAPE: Standard jar with handles
         PRESUMED SOURCE: Local
         GRAVELOT PROVENIENCE: Bu. 1950/Rho

Rho134   Bell Plain, *variety Hale*
         VESSEL SHAPE: Simple bowl
         PRESUMED SOURCE: Local (questionable)
         GRAVELOT PROVENIENCE: Bu. 1950/Rho

Rho135   Nashville Negative Painted, *variety unspecified*
         VESSEL SHAPE: Subglobular bottle with carafe
         neck
         PRESUMED SOURCE: Central Mississippi Valley
         (Cairo Lowland)
         GRAVELOT PROVENIENCE: Bu. 1931/Rho

Rho136   Bell Plain, *variety Hale*
         VESSEL SHAPE: Bowl with effigy features—
         mussel shell
         PRESUMED SOURCE: Local

Rho138   Unclassified Incised (festoons)
         VESSEL SHAPE: Standard jar with 2 handles
         PRESUMED SOURCE: Lower Tennessee Valley
         GRAVELOT PROVENIENCE: Bu. 1955/Rho

Rho141   Moundville Engraved, *variety Hemphill* (winged
         serpent)
         VESSEL SHAPE: Subglobular bottle with simple
         base
         PRESUMED SOURCE: Local
         GRAVELOT PROVENIENCE: Bu. 1956-57/Rho

Rho142   Bell Plain, *variety Hale* (red and white)
         VESSEL SHAPE: Simple bowl with lug and rim
         effigy—(head missing)
         PRESUMED SOURCE: Local
         GRAVELOT PROVENIENCE: Bu. 1956-57/Rho

Rho148   Bell Plain, *variety Hale*
         VESSEL SHAPE: Bulbous beaker
         PRESUMED SOURCE: Local (questionable)
         GRAVELOT PROVENIENCE: Bu. 1958/Rho

Rho149   Bell Plain, *variety unspecified*
         VESSEL SHAPE: Restricted bowl with everted
         lip, effigy features—fish
         PRESUMED SOURCE: Lower Tennessee-Cumberland
         area
         GRAVELOT PROVENIENCE: Bu. 1960/Rho

Rho153   Unclassified Incised
            VESSEL SHAPE: Bottle
            PRESUMED SOURCE: Nonlocal
            GRAVELOT PROVENIENCE: Bu. 1934/Rho

Rho154   Mississippi Plain, *variety Warrior*
            VESSEL SHAPE: Undiagnostic fragment(s)
            PRESUMED SOURCE: Local
            GRAVELOT PROVENIENCE: Bu. 1964/Rho

Rho156   Bell Plain, *variety Hale*
            VESSEL SHAPE: Bowl with effigy features—
            mussel shell
            PRESUMED SOURCE: Local
            GRAVELOT PROVENIENCE: Bu. 1968/Rho

Rho157   Bell Plain, *variety Hale*
            VESSEL SHAPE: Subglobular bottle with
            pedestal base
            PRESUMED SOURCE: Local
            GRAVELOT PROVENIENCE: Bu. 1968/Rho

Rho158   Bell Plain, *variety Hale*
            VESSEL SHAPE: Bottle
            PRESUMED SOURCE: Local
            GRAVELOT PROVENIENCE: Bu. 1968/Rho

Rho159   Moundville Engraved, *variety Tuscaloosa*
            VESSEL SHAPE: Subglobular bottle with slab
            base, indentations
            PRESUMED SOURCE: Local
            GRAVELOT PROVENIENCE: Bu. 1968/Rho

Rho160   Unclassified Incised and Punctated (festoons)
            VESSEL SHAPE: Standard jar with 4 handles
            PRESUMED SOURCE: Lower Tennessee Valley
            GRAVELOT PROVENIENCE: Bu. 1968/Rho

Rho161   Moundville Engraved, *variety Havana*
            VESSEL SHAPE: Cylindrical bowl with single
            lug
            PRESUMED SOURCE: Local
            GRAVELOT PROVENIENCE: Bu. 1968/Rho

Rho164   Moundville Engraved, *variety Hemphill* (winged
          serpent)
            VESSEL SHAPE: Subglobular bottle with simple
            base
            PRESUMED SOURCE: Local
            GRAVELOT PROVENIENCE: Bu. 1969/Rho

Rho170   Moundville Engraved, *variety Northport*
            VESSEL SHAPE: Subglobular bottle with
            pedestal base, indentations
            PRESUMED SOURCE: Local
            GRAVELOT PROVENIENCE: Bu. 1977/Rho

Rho171   Mississippi Plain, *variety Warrior*
            VESSEL SHAPE: Simple bowl with lug
            PRESUMED SOURCE: Local
            GRAVELOT PROVENIENCE: Bu. 1977/Rho

Rho172   Bell Plain, *variety Hale*
            VESSEL SHAPE: Slender ovoid bottle with
            pedestal base
            PRESUMED SOURCE: Local
            GRAVELOT PROVENIENCE: Bu. 1978/Rho

Rho173   Bell Plain, *variety Hale*
            VESSEL SHAPE: Slender ovoid bottle with
            pedestal base
            PRESUMED SOURCE: Local
            GRAVELOT PROVENIENCE: Bu. 1978/Rho

Rho174   Bell Plain, *variety Hale*
            VESSEL SHAPE: Slender ovoid bottle with
            pedestal base
            PRESUMED SOURCE: Local
            GRAVELOT PROVENIENCE: Bu. 1978/Rho

Rho177   Andrews Decorated, *variety unspecified*
          (multilinear bands at rim and base)
            VESSEL SHAPE: Cylindrical bowl (miniature)
            PRESUMED SOURCE: Lower Chattahoochee Valley
            GRAVELOT PROVENIENCE: Bu. 1978/Rho

Rho178   Bell Plain, *variety unspecified*
            VESSEL SHAPE: High-shouldered bottle
            PRESUMED SOURCE: Central Mississippi Valley
            (Memphis region)
            GRAVELOT PROVENIENCE: Bu. 1978/Rho

Rho182   Nashville Negative Painted, *variety unspecified*

            VESSEL SHAPE: Subglobular bottle with carafe
            neck
            PRESUMED SOURCE: Central Mississippi Valley
            (Cairo Lowland)
            GRAVELOT PROVENIENCE: Bu. 1978/Rho

Rho184   Bell Plain, *variety Hale*
            VESSEL SHAPE: Bottle
            PRESUMED SOURCE: Local (questionable)
            GRAVELOT PROVENIENCE: Bu. 1978/Rho

Rho189   Bell Plain, *variety unspecified*
            VESSEL SHAPE: Hooded bottle (miniature) with
            effigy features—human figure
            PRESUMED SOURCE: Central Mississippi Valley
            (Cairo Lowland)

Rho190   Carthage Incised, *variety Summerville*
            VESSEL SHAPE: Undiagnostic fragment(s)
            PRESUMED SOURCE: Local (questionable)

Rho192   Moundville Engraved, *variety Wiggins*
            VESSEL SHAPE: Bottle (miniature)
            PRESUMED SOURCE: Local
            GRAVELOT PROVENIENCE: Bu. 1979/Rho

Rho193   Matthews Incised, *variety Manly*
            VESSEL SHAPE: Standard jar with 2 handles,
            notched lip
            PRESUMED SOURCE: Central Mississippi Valley
            GRAVELOT PROVENIENCE: Bu. 1979/Rho

Rho212   Mississippi Plain, *variety Warrior*
            VESSEL SHAPE: Standard jar with 4 handles
            PRESUMED SOURCE: Local
            GRAVELOT PROVENIENCE: Bu. 2001/Rho

Rho213   Matthews Incised, *variety Beckwith*
            VESSEL SHAPE: Standard jar
            PRESUMED SOURCE: Central Mississippi Valley
            (Cairo Lowland), Lower Tennessee-Cumberland
            area
            GRAVELOT PROVENIENCE: Bu. 2001/Rho

Rho214   Moundville Engraved, *variety Hemphill* (winged
          serpent)
            VESSEL SHAPE: Subglobular bottle with simple
            base
            PRESUMED SOURCE: Local
            GRAVELOT PROVENIENCE: Bu. 2004/Rho

Rho219   Moundville Engraved, *variety Hemphill* (paired
          tails)
            VESSEL SHAPE: Subglobular bottle with simple
            base
            PRESUMED SOURCE: Local
            GRAVELOT PROVENIENCE: Bu. 2009/Rho

Rho220   Bell Plain, *variety Hale*
            VESSEL SHAPE: Burnished jar with no handles,
            band of nodes
            PRESUMED SOURCE: Local (questionable)
            GRAVELOT PROVENIENCE: Bu. 2011/Rho

Rho226   Carthage Incised, *variety Carthage*
            VESSEL SHAPE: Restricted bowl
            PRESUMED SOURCE: Local
            GRAVELOT PROVENIENCE: Bu. 2021/Rho

Rho227   Bell Plain, *variety Hale*
            VESSEL SHAPE: Simple bowl with beaded rim
            PRESUMED SOURCE: Local
            GRAVELOT PROVENIENCE: Bu. 2025/Rho

Rho228   Unclassified Engraved
            VESSEL SHAPE: Rectanguloid bottle with
            pedestal base
            PRESUMED SOURCE: Nonlocal

Rho251   Carthage Incised, *variety Moon Lake*
            VESSEL SHAPE: Flaring-rim bowl (shallow)
            PRESUMED SOURCE: Local
            GRAVELOT PROVENIENCE: Bu. 2042/Rho

Rho252   Mississippi Plain, *variety unspecified*
            VESSEL SHAPE: Bottle with slab base
            PRESUMED SOURCE: Middle Tennessee Valley
            GRAVELOT PROVENIENCE: Bu. 2042/Rho

Rho253   Mississippi Plain, *variety Warrior*
            VESSEL SHAPE: Standard jar with 2 handles
            PRESUMED SOURCE: Local

Rho255   Bell Plain, *variety Hale*
          VESSEL SHAPE: Simple bowl with beaded rim,
          lug and rim effigy—bird (gracile,
          outward-facing head)
          PRESUMED SOURCE: Local (questionable)
          GRAVELOT PROVENIENCE: Bu. 2045/Rho

Rho256   Bell Plain, *variety unspecified*
          VESSEL SHAPE: Narrow-neck bottle
          (subglobular)
          PRESUMED SOURCE: Central Mississippi Valley
          GRAVELOT PROVENIENCE: Bu. 2047/Rho

Rho257   Carthage Incised, *variety Moon Lake*
          VESSEL SHAPE: Flaring-rim bowl (shallow)
          PRESUMED SOURCE: Local
          GRAVELOT PROVENIENCE: Bu. 2047/Rho

Rho275   Bell Plain, *variety Hale*
          VESSEL SHAPE: Flaring-rim bowl (shallow)
          PRESUMED SOURCE: Local
          GRAVELOT PROVENIENCE: Bu. 2062/Rho

Rho276   Barton Incised, *variety unspecified*
          VESSEL SHAPE: Standard jar
          PRESUMED SOURCE: Nonlocal

Rho302   Bell Plain, *variety Hale* (white filmed)
          VESSEL SHAPE: Restricted bowl
          PRESUMED SOURCE: Local

Rho304   Moundville Engraved, *variety Wiggins*
          VESSEL SHAPE: Subglobular bottle with simple
          base
          PRESUMED SOURCE: Local
          GRAVELOT PROVENIENCE: Bu. 2068/Rho

Rho306   Bell Plain, *variety Hale* (red on white)
          VESSEL SHAPE: Simple bowl with beaded rim,
          effigy features—human head medallions
          PRESUMED SOURCE: Local (questionable)
          GRAVELOT PROVENIENCE: Bu. 2068/Rho

Rho307   Nodena Red and White, *variety unspecified*
          VESSEL SHAPE: Simple bowl with effigy
          features—human figure
          PRESUMED SOURCE: Central Mississippi Valley
          (Clarksdale region)
          GRAVELOT PROVENIENCE: Bu. 2068/Rho

Rho308   Moundville Engraved, *variety Wiggins*
          VESSEL SHAPE: Subglobular bottle with simple
          base
          PRESUMED SOURCE: Local
          GRAVELOT PROVENIENCE: Bu. 2068/Rho

Rho312   Mississippi Plain, *variety Warrior*
          VESSEL SHAPE: Standard jar (miniature) with 4
          handles
          PRESUMED SOURCE: Local (questionable)
          GRAVELOT PROVENIENCE: Bu. 2069-71/Rho

Rho328   Mississippi Plain, *variety Warrior*
          VESSEL SHAPE: Standard jar with 2 handles
          PRESUMED SOURCE: Local
          GRAVELOT PROVENIENCE: Bu. 2079/Rho

Rho329   Mississippi Plain, *variety Warrior*
          VESSEL SHAPE: Standard jar with 2 handles
          PRESUMED SOURCE: Local
          GRAVELOT PROVENIENCE: Bu. 2082/Rho

Rho337   Bell Plain, *variety Hale*
          VESSEL SHAPE: Subglobular bottle with simple
          base
          PRESUMED SOURCE: Local
          GRAVELOT PROVENIENCE: Bu. 2087/Rho

Rho351   Mississippi Plain, *variety Warrior*
          VESSEL SHAPE: Standard jar
          PRESUMED SOURCE: Local
          GRAVELOT PROVENIENCE: Bu. 2094/Rho

Rho364   Moundville Engraved, *variety Taylorville*
          VESSEL SHAPE: Subglobular bottle with simple
          base
          PRESUMED SOURCE: Local
          GRAVELOT PROVENIENCE: Bu. 2096/Rho

Rho366   Bell Plain, *variety Hale*
          VESSEL SHAPE: Composite bowl with beaded rim,
          effigy features—fish
          PRESUMED SOURCE: Local (questionable)
          GRAVELOT PROVENIENCE: Bu. 2102/Rho

Rho367   Bell Plain, *variety Hale*
          VESSEL SHAPE: Simple bowl
          PRESUMED SOURCE: Local
          GRAVELOT PROVENIENCE: Bu. 2102/Rho

Rho368   Bell Plain, *variety Hale*
          VESSEL SHAPE: Burnished jar with 2 handles,
          widely spaced nodes
          PRESUMED SOURCE: Local
          GRAVELOT PROVENIENCE: Bu. 2110/Rho

Rho369   Mississippi Plain, *variety Warrior*
          VESSEL SHAPE: Standard jar
          PRESUMED SOURCE: Local
          GRAVELOT PROVENIENCE: Bu. 2110/Rho

Rho371   Bell Plain, *variety Hale*
          VESSEL SHAPE: Composite bowl-jar with 2
          handles, beaded rim
          PRESUMED SOURCE: Local (questionable)
          GRAVELOT PROVENIENCE: Bu. 2115/Rho

Rho373   Moundville Engraved, *variety Northport*
          VESSEL SHAPE: Subglobular bottle with simple
          base
          PRESUMED SOURCE: Local
          GRAVELOT PROVENIENCE: Bu. 2115/Rho

Rho374   Mississippi Plain, *variety Warrior*
          VESSEL SHAPE: Simple bowl
          PRESUMED SOURCE: Local

RPB(1)   Moundville Engraved, *variety Hemphill* (paired
          tails)
          VESSEL SHAPE: Subglobular bottle with simple
          base
          PRESUMED SOURCE: Local
          GRAVELOT PROVENIENCE: Bu. 3/RPB

RPB(2)   Bell Plain, *variety unspecified*
          VESSEL SHAPE: Carinated bowl with effigy
          features—(distinctive features missing)
          PRESUMED SOURCE: Gulf Coast (Mobile-Pensacola
          region)

RPB(3)   Carthage Incised, *variety Akron*
          VESSEL SHAPE: Cylindrical bowl with lug and
          rim effigy—bird (gracile, outward-facing
          head)

          PRESUMED SOURCE: Local (questionable)
          GRAVELOT PROVENIENCE: Bu. 8/RPB

RPB(4)   Moundville Engraved, *variety Hemphill* (paired
          tails)
          VESSEL SHAPE: Subglobular bottle with simple
          base
          PRESUMED SOURCE: Local
          GRAVELOT PROVENIENCE: Bu. 5/RPB

Rw25   Moundville Engraved, *variety Englewood*
          VESSEL SHAPE: Subglobular bottle with simple
          base
          PRESUMED SOURCE: Local
          GRAVELOT PROVENIENCE: Bu. 2665/Rw

Rw26   Carthage Incised, *variety Akron*
          VESSEL SHAPE: Cylindrical bowl with lug and
          rim effigy—(head missing)
          PRESUMED SOURCE: Local
          GRAVELOT PROVENIENCE: Bu. 2665/Rw

Rw36   Bell Plain, *variety Hale*
          VESSEL SHAPE: Subglobular bottle with
          pedestal base
          PRESUMED SOURCE: Local
          GRAVELOT PROVENIENCE: Bu. 2673/Rw

Rw43   Moundville Engraved, *variety Elliots Creek*
          VESSEL SHAPE: Slender ovoid bottle with
          pedestal base
          PRESUMED SOURCE: Local

Rw64   Moundville Incised, *variety Moundville*
          VESSEL SHAPE: Standard jar with 4 handles
          PRESUMED SOURCE: Local
          GRAVELOT PROVENIENCE: Bu. 2687/Rw

Rw126   Moundville Engraved, *variety Wiggins*
          VESSEL SHAPE: Subglobular bottle with slab
          base
          PRESUMED SOURCE: Local
          GRAVELOT PROVENIENCE: Bu. 2726/Rw

Rw128   Mississippi Plain, *variety Warrior*
         VESSEL SHAPE: Standard jar with 4 handles
         PRESUMED SOURCE: Local
         GRAVELOT PROVENIENCE: Bu. 2725/Rw

Rw129   Mississippi Plain, *variety Warrior*
         VESSEL SHAPE: Standard jar with handles
         PRESUMED SOURCE: Local
         GRAVELOT PROVENIENCE: Bu. 2725/Rw

Rw132   Bell Plain, *variety Hale*
         VESSEL SHAPE: Burnished jar
         PRESUMED SOURCE: Local (questionable)
         GRAVELOT PROVENIENCE: Bu. 2722/Rw

Rw133   Bell Plain, *variety Hale*
         VESSEL SHAPE: Subglobular bottle with slab
         base
         PRESUMED SOURCE: Local (questionable)
         GRAVELOT PROVENIENCE: Bu. 2722/Rw

Rw135   Bell Plain, *variety Hale*
         VESSEL SHAPE: Subglobular bottle with simple
         base
         PRESUMED SOURCE: Local
         GRAVELOT PROVENIENCE: Bu. 2728/Rw

Rw138   Bell Plain, *variety Hale*
         VESSEL SHAPE: Burnished jar with 2 handles,
         effigy features—frog
         PRESUMED SOURCE: Local
         GRAVELOT PROVENIENCE: Bu. 2733/Rw

Rw139   Mississippi Plain, *variety Warrior*
         VESSEL SHAPE: Standard jar with 8 handles
         PRESUMED SOURCE: Local
         GRAVELOT PROVENIENCE: Bu. 2733/Rw

Rw140   Bell Plain, *variety Hale*
         VESSEL SHAPE: Burnished jar with 2 handles,
         effigy features—frog
         PRESUMED SOURCE: Local
         GRAVELOT PROVENIENCE: Bu. 2734/Rw

Rw142   Bell Plain, *variety Hale*
         VESSEL SHAPE: Simple bowl with effigy
         features—fish
         PRESUMED SOURCE: Local
         GRAVELOT PROVENIENCE: Bu. 2733/Rw

Rw145   Mound Place Incised, *variety Mobile*
         VESSEL SHAPE: Potbellied bowl with notched
         lip
         PRESUMED SOURCE: Gulf Coast (Mobile-Pensacola
         region)
         GRAVELOT PROVENIENCE: Bu. 2747/Rw

Rw159   Mississippi Plain, *variety Warrior*
         VESSEL SHAPE: Standard jar
         PRESUMED SOURCE: Local
         GRAVELOT PROVENIENCE: Bu. 2743/Rw

Rw165   Mississippi Plain, *variety Warrior*
         VESSEL SHAPE: Simple bowl (miniature) with
         single lug
         PRESUMED SOURCE: Local
         GRAVELOT PROVENIENCE: Bu. 2749/Rw

Rw168   Mississippi Plain, *variety Warrior*
         VESSEL SHAPE: Standard jar with 2 handles
         PRESUMED SOURCE: Local
         GRAVELOT PROVENIENCE: Bu. 2751/Rw

Rw176   Carthage Incised, *variety Akron*
         VESSEL SHAPE: Simple bowl with grouped nodes
         PRESUMED SOURCE: Local (questionable)
         GRAVELOT PROVENIENCE: Bu. 2760/Rw

Rw177   Bell Plain, *variety Hale*
         VESSEL SHAPE: Simple bowl with single lug
         PRESUMED SOURCE: Local
         GRAVELOT PROVENIENCE: Bu. 2760/Rw

Rw182   Moundville Incised, *variety Moundville*
         VESSEL SHAPE: Standard jar with handles
         PRESUMED SOURCE: Local

Rw195   Carthage Incised, *variety Fosters* (hand and eye
         forearm bones, red and white)
         VESSEL SHAPE: Flaring-rim bowl (shallow)
         PRESUMED SOURCE: Local
         GRAVELOT PROVENIENCE: Bu. 2768/Rw

Rw226   Bell Plain, *variety Hale*

         VESSEL SHAPE: Restricted bowl
         PRESUMED SOURCE: Local
         GRAVELOT PROVENIENCE: Bu. 2774/Rw

Rw227   Moundville Engraved, *variety Wiggins*
         VESSEL SHAPE: Subglobular bottle with
         pedestal base
         PRESUMED SOURCE: Local
         GRAVELOT PROVENIENCE: Bu. 2772/Rw

Rw228   Mississippi Plain, *variety Warrior*
         VESSEL SHAPE: Bottle (miniature)
         PRESUMED SOURCE: Local
         GRAVELOT PROVENIENCE: Bu. 2772/Rw

Rw229   Mississippi Plain, *variety Warrior*
         VESSEL SHAPE: Bottle
         PRESUMED SOURCE: Local
         GRAVELOT PROVENIENCE: Bu. 2773/Rw

Rw245   Mississippi Plain, *variety Warrior*
         VESSEL SHAPE: Standard jar with 4 handles
         PRESUMED SOURCE: Local
         GRAVELOT PROVENIENCE: Bu. 2790/Rw

Rw246   Bell Plain, *variety unspecified*
         VESSEL SHAPE: Bottle with slab base
         PRESUMED SOURCE: Nonlocal
         GRAVELOT PROVENIENCE: Bu. 2788/Rw

Rw260   Moundville Incised, *variety Carrollton*
         VESSEL SHAPE: Standard jar with 2 handles
         PRESUMED SOURCE: Local
         GRAVELOT PROVENIENCE: Bu. 2808/Rw

Rw308   Unclassified Incised (twice-folded scroll)
         VESSEL SHAPE: Simple bowl
         PRESUMED SOURCE: Nonlocal
         GRAVELOT PROVENIENCE: Bu. 2820/Rw

Rw439   Moundville Engraved, *variety Maxwells Crossing*
         (crosshatched vertical bands)
         VESSEL SHAPE: Subglobular bottle with
         pedestal base
         PRESUMED SOURCE: Local
         GRAVELOT PROVENIENCE: Bu. 2854/Rw

Rw440   Moundville Engraved, *variety Tuscaloosa*
         VESSEL SHAPE: Subglobular bottle with slab
         base, indentations
         PRESUMED SOURCE: Local
         GRAVELOT PROVENIENCE: Bu. 2857/Rw

Rw442   Moundville Incised, *variety Carrollton*
         VESSEL SHAPE: Standard jar with 4 handles
         PRESUMED SOURCE: Local
         GRAVELOT PROVENIENCE: Bu. 2859/Rw

Rw470   Mississippi Plain, *variety unspecified*
         VESSEL SHAPE: High-shouldered bottle
         PRESUMED SOURCE: Central Mississippi Valley,
         Lower Tennessee-Cumberland area
         GRAVELOT PROVENIENCE: Bu. 2880/Rw

Rw471   Bell Plain, *variety Hale*
         VESSEL SHAPE: Burnished jar with 2 handles,
         beaded rim
         PRESUMED SOURCE: Local (questionable)
         GRAVELOT PROVENIENCE: Bu. 2880/Rw

Rw473   Bell Plain, *variety Hale*
         VESSEL SHAPE: Outslanting bowl
         PRESUMED SOURCE: Local (questionable)
         GRAVELOT PROVENIENCE: Bu. 2882/Rw

Rw480   Carthage Incised, *variety Summerville*
         VESSEL SHAPE: Burnished jar with grouped
         nodes
         PRESUMED SOURCE: Local (questionable)
         GRAVELOT PROVENIENCE: Bu. 2884/Rw

Rw569   Bell Plain, *variety unspecified*
         VESSEL SHAPE: Subglobular bottle with simple
         base
         PRESUMED SOURCE: Central Mississippi Valley

Rw572   Moundville Engraved, *variety Wiggins*
         VESSEL SHAPE: Subglobular bottle with slab
         base, indentations
         PRESUMED SOURCE: Local

Rw580   Moundville Engraved, *variety Tuscaloosa*
         VESSEL SHAPE: Subglobular bottle with slab
         base
         PRESUMED SOURCE: Local

Rw581   Bell Plain, *variety unspecified*
        VESSEL SHAPE: Subglobular bottle with slab
          base, beveled lip interior
        PRESUMED SOURCE: Central Mississippi Valley
          (Memphis region)

Rw878   Moundville Engraved, *variety Hemphill* (winged
          serpent)
        VESSEL SHAPE: Subglobular bottle with simple
          base
        PRESUMED SOURCE: Local

B1   Carthage Incised, *variety Carthage*
        VESSEL SHAPE: Subglobular bottle with simple
          base
        PRESUMED SOURCE: Local

B2   Bell Plain, *variety Hale*
        VESSEL SHAPE: Simple bowl with beaded rim
        PRESUMED SOURCE: Local

B3   Barton Incised, *variety unspecified*
        VESSEL SHAPE: Simple bowl
        PRESUMED SOURCE: Nonlocal

B6   Moundville Engraved, *variety Havana*
        VESSEL SHAPE: Cylindrical bowl
        PRESUMED SOURCE: Local

NB2   Mississippi Plain, *variety Warrior*
        VESSEL SHAPE: Standard jar with appliqué neck
          fillets
        PRESUMED SOURCE: Local

NB6   Moundville Engraved, *variety unspecified*
        VESSEL SHAPE: Flaring-rim bowl (deep)
        PRESUMED SOURCE: Local

WB1/M5 Bell Plain, *variety Hale*
        VESSEL SHAPE: Simple bowl with effigy
          features—unidentified
        PRESUMED SOURCE: Local (questionable)
        GRAVELOT PROVENIENCE: F.1/WB/M5
        PUBLISHED ILLUSTRATION: Moore 1905:Figure 12
        MAI CATALOG NO.: 17/4371

WB3/M5 Bell Plain, *variety Hale*
        VESSEL SHAPE: Composite bowl with beaded rim
        PRESUMED SOURCE: Local (questionable)
        GRAVELOT PROVENIENCE: Bu. 2/WB/M5
        PUBLISHED ILLUSTRATION: Moore 1905:Figure 13
        MAI CATALOG NO.: 17/4377

C1/M5   Nashville Negative Painted, *variety unspecified*
        VESSEL SHAPE: Subglobular bottle with carafe
          neck
        PRESUMED SOURCE: Central Mississippi Valley
          (Cairo Lowland), Lower Tennessee-Cumberland
          area
        GRAVELOT PROVENIENCE: F.1/C/M5
        PUBLISHED ILLUSTRATION: Moore 1905:Figures
          15-16
        MAI CATALOG NO.: 17/1432

C2/M5   Moundville Engraved, *variety Hemphill* (radial
          fingers)
        VESSEL SHAPE: Cylindrical bowl
        PRESUMED SOURCE: Local
        GRAVELOT PROVENIENCE: F.1/C/M5
        PUBLISHED ILLUSTRATION: Moore 1905:Figure 17
        MAI CATALOG NO.: 18/417

C3/M5   Moundville Engraved, *variety Taylorville*
        VESSEL SHAPE: Subglobular bottle with
          pedestal base
        PRESUMED SOURCE: Local
        GRAVELOT PROVENIENCE: F.2/C/M5
        PUBLISHED ILLUSTRATION: Moore 1905:Figure 20
        MAI CATALOG NO.: 17/3360

C4/M5   Moundville Engraved, *variety Hemphill* (hand and
          eye)
        VESSEL SHAPE: Subglobular bottle with
          pedestal base
        PRESUMED SOURCE: Local
        GRAVELOT PROVENIENCE: F.2/C/M5
        PUBLISHED ILLUSTRATION: Moore 1905:Figures
          21-22
        MAI CATALOG NO.: 18/433

C6/M5   Bell Plain, *variety Hale*
        VESSEL SHAPE: Tall conical vessel
        PRESUMED SOURCE: Local (questionable)

PUBLISHED ILLUSTRATION: Moore 1905:Figure 25
        MAI CATALOG NO.: 17/4367

C7/M5   Moundville Engraved, *variety Havana*
        VESSEL SHAPE: Cylindrical bowl with single
          lug
        PRESUMED SOURCE: Local
        GRAVELOT PROVENIENCE: Bu. 5/C/M5
        PUBLISHED DESCRIPTION: Moore 1905:154
        MAI CATALOG NO.: 17/4393

C8/M5   Moundville Engraved, *variety Hemphill* (windmill)
        VESSEL SHAPE: Subglobular bottle with slab
          base
        PRESUMED SOURCE: Local
        GRAVELOT PROVENIENCE: Bu. 5/C/M5
        PUBLISHED ILLUSTRATION: Moore 1905:Figure 30
        MAI CATALOG NO.: 17/3635

C9/M5   Moundville Engraved, *variety Wiggins*
        VESSEL SHAPE: Subglobular bottle with slab
          base
        PRESUMED SOURCE: Local
        GRAVELOT PROVENIENCE: Bu. 5/C/M5
        PUBLISHED ILLUSTRATION: Moore 1905:Figure 31
        MAI CATALOG NO.: 17/3345

C12/M5 Moundville Engraved, *variety Hemphill* (windmill)
        VESSEL SHAPE: Subglobular bottle with
          pedestal base
        PRESUMED SOURCE: Local
        PUBLISHED ILLUSTRATION: Moore 1905:Figure 35
        MAI CATALOG NO.: 17/3371

C13/M5 Moundville Engraved, *variety Tuscaloosa*
        VESSEL SHAPE: Subglobular bottle with
          pedestal base, indentations
        PRESUMED SOURCE: Local
        PUBLISHED ILLUSTRATION: Moore 1905:Figure 37
        MAI CATALOG NO.: 18/427

C17/M5 Moundville Engraved, *variety Northport*
        VESSEL SHAPE: Subglobular bottle with
          pedestal base, indentations
        PRESUMED SOURCE: Local
        GRAVELOT PROVENIENCE: F.3/C/M5
        PUBLISHED ILLUSTRATION: Moore 1905:Figure 39
        MAI CATALOG NO.: 17/3357

C21/M5 Moundville Engraved, *variety Havana*
        VESSEL SHAPE: Simple bowl with single lug
        PRESUMED SOURCE: Local
        PUBLISHED ILLUSTRATION: Moore 1905:Figure 48
        MAI CATALOG NO.: 17/4390

NC1   Bell Plain, *variety Hale*
        VESSEL SHAPE: Simple bowl with effigy
          features—alligator
        PRESUMED SOURCE: Local

NC2   Bell Plain, *variety Hale*
        VESSEL SHAPE: Subglobular bottle with simple
          base
        PRESUMED SOURCE: Local

NC3   Bell Plain, *variety Hale*
        VESSEL SHAPE: Simple bowl with beaded rim
        PRESUMED SOURCE: Local

NC5   Bell Plain, *variety Hale*
        VESSEL SHAPE: Flaring-rim bowl (deep)
        PRESUMED SOURCE: Local

NEC1/M5 Mississippi Plain, *variety Warrior*
        VESSEL SHAPE: Standard jar with 8 handles
        PRESUMED SOURCE: Local
        GRAVELOT PROVENIENCE: Bu. 2/NEC/M5
        PUBLISHED ILLUSTRATION: Moore 1905:Figure 49
        MAI CATALOG NO.: 17/4385

NEC3/M5 Mississippi Plain, *variety Warrior*
        VESSEL SHAPE: Standard jar with 2 handles
        PRESUMED SOURCE: Local (questionable)
        GRAVELOT PROVENIENCE: Bu. 3/NEC/M5
        PUBLISHED ILLUSTRATION: Moore 1905:Figure 50
        MAI CATALOG NO.: 17/4382

NEC6/M5 Moundville Engraved, *variety Havana*
        VESSEL SHAPE: Simple bowl with lug and rim
          effigy—bird (flat, inward-facing head)
        PRESUMED SOURCE: Local (questionable)
        GRAVELOT PROVENIENCE: Bu. 11/NEC/M5
        PUBLISHED ILLUSTRATION: Moore 1905:Figure 51
        MAI CATALOG NO.: 17/4398

NEC8/M5   Unclassified Incised
           VESSEL SHAPE: Cylindrical bottle with
             indentations
           PRESUMED SOURCE: Nonlocal
           PUBLISHED ILLUSTRATION: Moore 1905:Figure 52
           MAI CATALOG NO.: 17/3374

NEC9/M5   Moundville Engraved, *variety Hemphill* (windmill)
           VESSEL SHAPE: Subglobular bottle with
             pedestal base
           PRESUMED SOURCE: Local
           PUBLISHED ILLUSTRATION: Moore 1905:Figures

             53-54
           MAI CATALOG NO.: 17/3356

NEC10/M5   Mississippi Plain, *variety Warrior*
           VESSEL SHAPE: Standard jar with 4 handles
           PRESUMED SOURCE: Local
           GRAVELOT PROVENIENCE: Bu. 20/NEC/M5
           PUBLISHED ILLUSTRATION: Moore 1905:Figure 55
           MAI CATALOG NO.: 17/4386

NEC11/M5   Moundville Engraved, *variety Hemphill* (paired
           tails)
           VESSEL SHAPE: Subglobular bottle with simple
             base
           PRESUMED SOURCE: Local
           GRAVELOT PROVENIENCE: Bu. 20/NEC/M5
           PUBLISHED ILLUSTRATION: Moore 1905:Figures
             56-57
           MAI CATALOG NO.: 17/1425

D1   Bell Plain, *variety Hale* (red on white)
           VESSEL SHAPE: Short-neck bowl
           PRESUMED SOURCE: Local

D4/M5   Moundville Engraved, *variety Hemphill* (skull,
           hand and eye)
           VESSEL SHAPE: Cylindrical bowl
           PRESUMED SOURCE: Local
           GRAVELOT PROVENIENCE: F.3/D/M5
           PUBLISHED ILLUSTRATION: Moore 1905:Figures
             62-63
           MAI CATALOG NO.: 17/3376

D5/M5   Moundville Engraved, *variety Hemphill* (radial
           fingers)
           VESSEL SHAPE: Subglobular bottle with simple
             base
           PRESUMED SOURCE: Local
           GRAVELOT PROVENIENCE: F.4/D/M5
           PUBLISHED ILLUSTRATION: Moore 1905:Figure 64
           MAI CATALOG NO.: 17/3340

ND3   Moundville Engraved, *variety Hemphill* (skull,
           hand and eye)
           VESSEL SHAPE: Simple bowl
           PRESUMED SOURCE: Local (questionable)

ND4   Moundville Engraved, *variety Hemphill* (scalp)
           VESSEL SHAPE: Subglobular bottle with slab
             base
           PRESUMED SOURCE: Local

ND5   Mississippi Plain, *variety Warrior*
           VESSEL SHAPE: Standard jar with 4 handles
           PRESUMED SOURCE: Local

ND6   Mississippi Plain, *variety unspecified*
           VESSEL SHAPE: Hooded bottle
           PRESUMED SOURCE: Lower Tennessee-Cumberland
             area

ND7   Bell Plain, *variety Hale*
           VESSEL SHAPE: Subglobular bottle with simple
             base
           PRESUMED SOURCE: Local

ND10   Mississippi Plain, *variety Warrior*
           VESSEL SHAPE: Standard jar with 4 handles
           PRESUMED SOURCE: Local

ND11   Mississippi Plain, *variety Warrior*
           VESSEL SHAPE: Standard jar with 4 handles
           PRESUMED SOURCE: Local

ND13   Bell Plain, *variety Hale*
           VESSEL SHAPE: Restricted bowl with band of
             nodes
           PRESUMED SOURCE: Local (questionable)
           GRAVELOT PROVENIENCE: Su. 17/ND

ND14   Mississippi Plain, *variety unspecified*
           VESSEL SHAPE: Standard jar with no handles,
             notched lip
           PRESUMED SOURCE: Nonlocal

ND28   Moundville Engraved, *variety unspecified*
           VESSEL SHAPE: Bottle with pedestal base,
             effigy features—fish
           PRESUMED SOURCE: Local (questionable)

ND33   Mound Place Incised, *variety unspecified*
           VESSEL SHAPE: Simple bowl with lug and rim
             effigy—bird (flat, inward-facing head)
           PRESUMED SOURCE: Gulf Coast (Mobile-Pensacola
             region)
           GRAVELOT PROVENIENCE: Bu. 2172/ND

ND34   Bell Plain, *variety Hale*
           VESSEL SHAPE: Simple bowl with effigy
             features—fish
           PRESUMED SOURCE: Local (questionable)
           GRAVELOT PROVENIENCE: Bu. 2173/ND

ND1/M5   Bell Plain, *variety unspecified*
           VESSEL SHAPE: Flaring-rim bowl with notched
             lip
           PRESUMED SOURCE: Nonlocal
           PUBLISHED ILLUSTRATION: Moore 1905:Figure 67
           MAI CATALOG NO.: 17/3638

ND3/M5   Bell Plain, *variety unspecified*
           VESSEL SHAPE: Subglobular bottle
           PRESUMED SOURCE: Nonlocal
           GRAVELOT PROVENIENCE: F.1/ND/M5
           PUBLISHED ILLUSTRATION: Moore 1905:Figure 68

ND6/M5   Bell Plain, *variety Hale*
           VESSEL SHAPE: Burnished jar with no handles,
             beaded rim, effigy features—alligator
           PRESUMED SOURCE: Local (questionable)
           GRAVELOT PROVENIENCE: F.3/ND/M5
           PUBLISHED ILLUSTRATION: Moore 1905:Figure 69
           MAI CATALOG NO.: 17/4399

ND11/M5   Moundville Engraved, *variety Northport*
           VESSEL SHAPE: Subglobular bottle with
             pedestal base, indentations
           PRESUMED SOURCE: Local (questionable)
           GRAVELOT PROVENIENCE: F.5/ND/M5
           PUBLISHED ILLUSTRATION: Moore 1905:Figure 71
           MAI CATALOG NO.: 18/428

ND12/M5   Bell Plain, *variety unspecified*
           VESSEL SHAPE: Composite bottle
           PRESUMED SOURCE: Central Mississippi Valley
           GRAVELOT PROVENIENCE: F.6/ND/M5
           PUBLISHED ILLUSTRATION: Moore 1905:Figure 72
           MAI CATALOG NO.: 18/439

ND13/M5   Moundville Engraved, *variety Havana*
           VESSEL SHAPE: Cylindrical bowl
           PRESUMED SOURCE: Local
           GRAVELOT PROVENIENCE: F.7/ND/M5
           PUBLISHED ILLUSTRATION: Moore 1905:Figure 73
           MAI CATALOG NO.: 17/4396

ND14/M5   Moundville Engraved, *variety Hemphill* (forked eye
           surround)
           VESSEL SHAPE: Cylindrical bottle
           PRESUMED SOURCE: Local (questionable)
           GRAVELOT PROVENIENCE: F.7/ND/M5
           PUBLISHED ILLUSTRATION: Moore 1905:Figure 74
           MAI CATALOG NO.: 17/3377

ND16/M5   Moundville Engraved, *variety Tuscaloosa*
           VESSEL SHAPE: Subglobular bottle with slab
             base, indentations
           PRESUMED SOURCE: Local
           GRAVELOT PROVENIENCE: F.8/ND/M5
           PUBLISHED DESCRIPTION: Moore 1905:182
           MAI CATALOG NO.: 17/4621

ND17/M5   Moundville Engraved, *variety Wiggins*
           VESSEL SHAPE: Cylindrical bowl
           PRESUMED SOURCE: Local (questionable)
           GRAVELOT PROVENIENCE: F.9/ND/M5
           PUBLISHED ILLUSTRATION: Moore 1905:Figure 75
           MAI CATALOG NO.: 17/3647

ND20/M5   Bell Plain, *variety Hale*
           VESSEL SHAPE: Pedestaled bowl with cutout
             rim, lowered lip
           PRESUMED SOURCE: Local

PUBLISHED ILLUSTRATION: Moore 1905:Figure 76
MAI CATALOG NO.: 18/420

NED1　Nodena Red and White, *variety unspecified*
　　VESSEL SHAPE: Collared bottle with carafe neck
　　PRESUMED SOURCE: Central Mississippi Valley (Clarksdale region)
　　GRAVELOT PROVENIENCE: Bu. 26/NED

NED3　Mississippi Plain, *variety Warrior*
　　VESSEL SHAPE: Simple bowl
　　PRESUMED SOURCE: Local
　　GRAVELOT PROVENIENCE: Bu. 18/NED

NED4　Moundville Engraved, *variety Havana*
　　VESSEL SHAPE: Simple bowl with lug and rim effigy—(head missing)
　　PRESUMED SOURCE: Local
　　GRAVELOT PROVENIENCE: Bu. 20/NED

NED7　Mississippi Plain, *variety Warrior*
　　VESSEL SHAPE: Standard jar with 2 handles
　　PRESUMED SOURCE: Local
　　GRAVELOT PROVENIENCE: Bu. 13/NED

NED10　Moundville Engraved, *variety Hemphill* (winged serpent)
　　VESSEL SHAPE: Subglobular bottle with simple base
　　PRESUMED SOURCE: Local

ED2　Bell Plain, *variety Hale*
　　VESSEL SHAPE: Burnished jar with 2 handles, effigy features—frog
　　PRESUMED SOURCE: Local

ED3　Carthage Incised, *variety Akron*
　　VESSEL SHAPE: Cylindrical bowl
　　PRESUMED SOURCE: Local (questionable)

ED4　Bell Plain, *variety Hale*
　　VESSEL SHAPE: Simple bowl
　　PRESUMED SOURCE: Local (questionable)

ED6　Bell Plain, *variety Hale*
　　VESSEL SHAPE: Burnished jar with 2 handles
　　PRESUMED SOURCE: Local
　　NMNH CATALOG NO.: 377391

ED8　Bell Plain, *variety Hale*
　　VESSEL SHAPE: Simple bowl with lug
　　PRESUMED SOURCE: Local
　　GRAVELOT PROVENIENCE: Bu. 8/ED

ED14　Carthage Incised, *variety Akron*
　　VESSEL SHAPE: Restricted bowl with effigy features—turtle
　　PRESUMED SOURCE: Local
　　GRAVELOT PROVENIENCE: Bu. 8/ED

ED50　Bell Plain, *variety Hale*
　　VESSEL SHAPE: Subglobular bottle with pedestal base
　　PRESUMED SOURCE: Local (questionable)
　　GRAVELOT PROVENIENCE: Bu. 2598/ED

ED54　Moundville Incised, *variety Carrollton*
　　VESSEL SHAPE: Standard jar with 2 handles
　　PRESUMED SOURCE: Local (questionable)
　　GRAVELOT PROVENIENCE: Bu. 2607/ED

ED71　Moundville Incised, *variety Carrollton*
　　VESSEL SHAPE: Standard jar with handles
　　PRESUMED SOURCE: Local
　　GRAVELOT PROVENIENCE: Bu. 2614/ED

SED1　Bell Plain, *variety Hale*
　　VESSEL SHAPE: Burnished jar with 2 handles
　　PRESUMED SOURCE: Local

SED2　Bell Plain, *variety Hale*
　　VESSEL SHAPE: Simple bowl with everted lip
　　PRESUMED SOURCE: Local (questionable)

SED3　Bell Plain, *variety Hale*
　　VESSEL SHAPE: Bowl (miniature) with effigy features—bird
　　PRESUMED SOURCE: Local (questionable)

SED4　Bell Plain, *variety Hale*
　　VESSEL SHAPE: Burnished jar with 2 handles, effigy features—frog
　　PRESUMED SOURCE: Local

SED5　Mississippi Plain, *variety Warrior*
　　VESSEL SHAPE: Standard jar with 2 handles
　　PRESUMED SOURCE: Local
　　GRAVELOT PROVENIENCE: Bu. 1/SED

SED6　Moundville Engraved, *variety Wiggins*
　　VESSEL SHAPE: Subglobular bottle with simple base
　　PRESUMED SOURCE: Local

SED7　Moundville Engraved, *variety unspecified*
　　VESSEL SHAPE: Simple bowl with everted lip, effigy features—unidentified mammal
　　PRESUMED SOURCE: Local (questionable)

SED8　Moundville Engraved, *variety Wiggins*
　　VESSEL SHAPE: Subglobular bottle with simple base, indentations
　　PRESUMED SOURCE: Local

SED9　Carthage Incised, *variety Akron*
　　VESSEL SHAPE: Restricted bowl with effigy features—turtle
　　PRESUMED SOURCE: Local
　　NMNH CATALOG NO.: 377395

SED10　Bell Plain, *variety Hale*
　　VESSEL SHAPE: Burnished jar with 2 handles, beaded rim, widely spaced nodes
　　PRESUMED SOURCE: Local (questionable)

SED11　Mississippi Plain, *variety Warrior*
　　VESSEL SHAPE: Simple bowl with notched lip
　　PRESUMED SOURCE: Local (questionable)

SED13　Moundville Engraved, *variety Havana*
　　VESSEL SHAPE: Cylindrical bowl with lug and rim effigy—bird (flat, outward-facing head)
　　PRESUMED SOURCE: Local (questionable)
　　NMNH CATALOG NO.: 377396

SED14　Bell Plain, *variety Hale*
　　VESSEL SHAPE: Simple bowl with beaded rim, effigy features—human head medallions
　　PRESUMED SOURCE: Local (questionable)

SED15　Mississippi Plain, *variety Warrior*
　　VESSEL SHAPE: Simple bowl
　　PRESUMED SOURCE: Local

SED17　Bell Plain, *variety Hale*
　　VESSEL SHAPE: Subglobular bottle with simple base
　　PRESUMED SOURCE: Local

SED18　Bell Plain, *variety Hale*
　　VESSEL SHAPE: Bowl with effigy features—mussel shell
　　PRESUMED SOURCE: Local (questionable)

SED19　Bell Plain, *variety Hale*
　　VESSEL SHAPE: Simple bowl with effigy features—fish
　　PRESUMED SOURCE: Local (questionable)

SED27　Moundville Engraved, *variety Cypress*
　　VESSEL SHAPE: Subglobular bottle with simple base
　　PRESUMED SOURCE: Local

SED28　Carthage Incised, *variety Fosters* (hand and eye)
　　VESSEL SHAPE: Subglobular bottle with slab base
　　PRESUMED SOURCE: Local

SED30　Bell Plain, *variety Hale*
　　VESSEL SHAPE: Simple bowl with spouts
　　PRESUMED SOURCE: Local

SED32　Bell Plain, *variety Hale*
　　VESSEL SHAPE: Bowl with effigy features—frog heads
　　PRESUMED SOURCE: Local (questionable)

SED33　Bell Plain, *variety Hale*
　　VESSEL SHAPE: Restricted bowl
　　PRESUMED SOURCE: Local
　　NMNH CATALOG NO.: 377400

SED34　Moundville Engraved, *variety Wiggins*
　　VESSEL SHAPE: Subglobular bottle with simple base
　　PRESUMED SOURCE: Local
　　GRAVELOT PROVENIENCE: Bu. 7/SED

SED35   Moundville Engraved, *variety Tuscaloosa*
          VESSEL SHAPE: Subglobular bottle with simple
            base
          PRESUMED SOURCE: Local

SED43   Bell Plain, *variety Hale*
          VESSEL SHAPE: Simple bowl with beaded rim,
            effigy features—human head medallions
          PRESUMED SOURCE: Local (questionable)

SD1   Bell Plain, *variety Hale*
          VESSEL SHAPE: Outslanting bowl
          PRESUMED SOURCE: Local

SD3   Bell Plain, *variety Hale* (red-and-black on white)
          VESSEL SHAPE: Terraced rectanguloid bowl with
            lowered lip
          PRESUMED SOURCE: Local (questionable)
          GRAVELOT PROVENIENCE: Bu. 1/SD

SD6   Mississippi Plain, *variety Warrior*
          VESSEL SHAPE: Standard jar with 8 handles
          PRESUMED SOURCE: Local

SD10   Bell Plain, *variety Hale*
          VESSEL SHAPE: Simple bowl with beaded rim
          PRESUMED SOURCE: Local

SD27   Moundville Incised, *variety unspecified*
          VESSEL SHAPE: Standard jar with 2 handles,
            widely spaced nodes
          PRESUMED SOURCE: Local (questionable)

SD29   Mississippi Plain, *variety Warrior*
          VESSEL SHAPE: Standard jar with 4 handles
          PRESUMED SOURCE: Local
          GRAVELOT PROVENIENCE: Bu. 1423/SD

SD30   Moundville Engraved, *variety Wiggins*
          VESSEL SHAPE: Subglobular bottle with simple
            base
          PRESUMED SOURCE: Local
          GRAVELOT PROVENIENCE: Bu. 1423/SD

SD31   Mississippi Plain, *variety Warrior*
          VESSEL SHAPE: Standard jar with 4 handles
          PRESUMED SOURCE: Local
          GRAVELOT PROVENIENCE: Bu. 1423/SD

SD32   Mississippi Plain, *variety Warrior*
          VESSEL SHAPE: Standard jar with 2 handles
          PRESUMED SOURCE: Local
          GRAVELOT PROVENIENCE: Bu. 1423/SD

SD154   Moundville Engraved, *variety Hemphill* (scalp,
            Greek cross)
          VESSEL SHAPE: Outslanting bowl
          PRESUMED SOURCE: Local (questionable)
          GRAVELOT PROVENIENCE: Bu. 1437/SD

SD155   Moundville Incised, *variety Carrollton*
          VESSEL SHAPE: Standard jar with 4 handles
          PRESUMED SOURCE: Local
          GRAVELOT PROVENIENCE: Bu. 1437/SD

SD169   Bell Plain, *variety Hale*
          VESSEL SHAPE: Bottle
          PRESUMED SOURCE: Local (questionable)
          GRAVELOT PROVENIENCE: Bu. 1442/SD

SD171   Mississippi Plain, *variety Warrior*
          VESSEL SHAPE: Standard jar with 2 handles
          PRESUMED SOURCE: Local
          GRAVELOT PROVENIENCE: Bu. 1443/SD

SD247   Bell Plain, *variety unspecified*
          VESSEL SHAPE: High-shouldered bottle
          PRESUMED SOURCE: Central Mississippi Valley
          GRAVELOT PROVENIENCE: Bu. 1444/SD

SD248   Moundville Engraved, *variety Havana*
          VESSEL SHAPE: Simple bowl with lug and rim
            effigy—bird (flat, inward-facing head)
          PRESUMED SOURCE: Local
          GRAVELOT PROVENIENCE: Bu. 1444/SD

SD251   Bell Plain, *variety Hale*
          VESSEL SHAPE: Undiagnostic fragment(s)
          PRESUMED SOURCE: Local
          GRAVELOT PROVENIENCE: Bu. 1446/SD

SD262   Mississippi Plain, *variety Warrior*
          VESSEL SHAPE: Standard jar with 2 handles

          PRESUMED SOURCE: Local
          GRAVELOT PROVENIENCE: Bu. 1453/SD

SD265   Moundville Incised, *variety Moundville*
          VESSEL SHAPE: Standard jar with 2 handles,
            folded rim
          PRESUMED SOURCE: Local
          GRAVELOT PROVENIENCE: Bu. 1455/SD

SD266   Carthage Incised, *variety unspecified*
          VESSEL SHAPE: Simple bowl with lug and rim
            effigy——(head missing)
          PRESUMED SOURCE: Local (questionable)
          GRAVELOT PROVENIENCE: Bu. 1455/SD

SD267   Carthage Incised, *variety Moon Lake*
          VESSEL SHAPE: Flaring-rim bowl (shallow)
          PRESUMED SOURCE: Local
          GRAVELOT PROVENIENCE: Bu. 1455/SD

SD350   Unclassified Incised (sand tempered) (multilinear
            band at rim)
          VESSEL SHAPE: Pedestaled bowl with notched
            lip, lowered lip
          PRESUMED SOURCE: Nonlocal
          GRAVELOT PROVENIENCE: Bu. 1457/SD

SD351   Unclassified Engraved (sand tempered)
            (multilinear band at rim)
          VESSEL SHAPE: Simple bowl with notched lip
          PRESUMED SOURCE: Nonlocal
          GRAVELOT PROVENIENCE: Bu. 1457/SD

SD362   Moundville Engraved, *variety Hemphill* (raptor in
            the round)
          VESSEL SHAPE: Subglobular bottle with simple
            base
          PRESUMED SOURCE: Local
          GRAVELOT PROVENIENCE: Bu. 1459/SD

SD364   Bell Plain, *variety Hale*
          VESSEL SHAPE: Simple bowl with beaded rim
          PRESUMED SOURCE: Local
          GRAVELOT PROVENIENCE: Bu. 1462/SD

SD365   Mississippi Plain, *variety Warrior*
          VESSEL SHAPE: Standard jar with 4 handles
          PRESUMED SOURCE: Local
          GRAVELOT PROVENIENCE: Bu. 1464/SD

SD472   Moundville Engraved, *variety Hemphill* (crested
            bird in the round)
          VESSEL SHAPE: Subglobular bottle with simple
            base
          PRESUMED SOURCE: Local
          GRAVELOT PROVENIENCE: Bu. 1468/SD

SD473   Mississippi Plain, *variety Warrior*
          VESSEL SHAPE: Standard jar with 4 handles
          PRESUMED SOURCE: Local
          GRAVELOT PROVENIENCE: Bu. 1479/SD

SD482   Bell Plain, *variety Hale*
          VESSEL SHAPE: Burnished jar with 2 handles,
            effigy features—frog
          PRESUMED SOURCE: Local (questionable)
          GRAVELOT PROVENIENCE: Bu. 1491/SD

SD579   Mississippi Plain, *variety Warrior*
          VESSEL SHAPE: Standard jar with 4 handles
          PRESUMED SOURCE: Local
          GRAVELOT PROVENIENCE: Bu. 1495/SD

SD583   Bell Plain, *variety Hale*
          VESSEL SHAPE: Subglobular bottle with simple
            base
          PRESUMED SOURCE: Local
          GRAVELOT PROVENIENCE: Bu. 1496/SD

SD584   Moundville Engraved, *variety Taylorville*
          VESSEL SHAPE: Cylindrical bowl with single
            lug
          PRESUMED SOURCE: Local
          GRAVELOT PROVENIENCE: Bu. 1496/SD

SD585   Moundville Engraved, *variety Englewood*
          VESSEL SHAPE: Subglobular bottle with simple
            base
          PRESUMED SOURCE: Local
          GRAVELOT PROVENIENCE: Bu. 1496/SD

SD586   Moundville Engraved, *variety Hemphill* (raptor in
            the round)

```
          VESSEL SHAPE:  Cylindrical bowl with single
            lug
          PRESUMED SOURCE:  Local
          GRAVELOT PROVENIENCE:  Bu. 1496/SD

SD594    Bell Plain, variety Hale
          VESSEL SHAPE:  Subglobular bottle with concave
            base
          PRESUMED SOURCE:  Local
          GRAVELOT PROVENIENCE:  Bu. 1504/SD

SD595    Mississippi Plain, variety Warrior
          VESSEL SHAPE:  Standard jar with 5 handles
          PRESUMED SOURCE:  Local (questionable)
          GRAVELOT PROVENIENCE:  Bu. 1504/SD

SD596    Bell Plain, variety Hale
          VESSEL SHAPE:  Cylindrical bowl with single
            lug
          PRESUMED SOURCE:  Local
          GRAVELOT PROVENIENCE:  Bu. 1504/SD

SD599    Mississippi Plain, variety Warrior
          VESSEL SHAPE:  Standard jar with 4 handles
          PRESUMED SOURCE:  Local
          GRAVELOT PROVENIENCE:  Bu. 1505/SD

SD600    Bell Plain, variety Hale
          VESSEL SHAPE:  Simple bowl with beaded rim
          PRESUMED SOURCE:  Local
          GRAVELOT PROVENIENCE:  Bu. 1505/SD

SD679    Mississippi Plain, variety Warrior
          VESSEL SHAPE:  Simple bowl
          PRESUMED SOURCE:  Local
          GRAVELOT PROVENIENCE:  Bu. 1514/SD

SD680    Mississippi Plain, variety Warrior
          VESSEL SHAPE:  Standard jar with 4 handles,
            downturned lugs
          PRESUMED SOURCE:  Local
          GRAVELOT PROVENIENCE:  Bu. 1515/SD

SD681    Mississippi Plain, variety Warrior
          VESSEL SHAPE:  Standard jar with 8 handles
          PRESUMED SOURCE:  Local
          GRAVELOT PROVENIENCE:  Bu. 1515/SD

SD682    Carthage Incised, variety Fosters (hand and eye,
          forearm bones)
          VESSEL SHAPE:  Bowl
          PRESUMED SOURCE:  Local (questionable)

          GRAVELOT PROVENIENCE:  Bu. 1515/SD

SD683    Mississippi Plain, variety Warrior
          VESSEL SHAPE:  Standard jar
          PRESUMED SOURCE:  Local
          GRAVELOT PROVENIENCE:  Bu. 1515/SD

SD684    Bell Plain, variety Hale
          VESSEL SHAPE:  Subglobular bottle with slab
            base
          PRESUMED SOURCE:  Local
          GRAVELOT PROVENIENCE:  Bu. 1515/SD

SD687    Bell Plain, variety Hale
          VESSEL SHAPE:  Simple bowl with beaded rim
          PRESUMED SOURCE:  Local
          GRAVELOT PROVENIENCE:  Bu. 1516/SD

SD688    Mississippi Plain, variety Warrior
          VESSEL SHAPE:  Standard jar with 4 handles
          PRESUMED SOURCE:  Local (questionable)
          GRAVELOT PROVENIENCE:  Bu. 1516/SD

SD689    Bell Plain, variety Hale
          VESSEL SHAPE:  Simple bowl with beaded rim,
            spouts
          PRESUMED SOURCE:  Local
          GRAVELOT PROVENIENCE:  Bu. 1516/SD

SD731    Mississippi Plain, variety unspecified
          VESSEL SHAPE:  Standard jar with 2 handles,
            small horizontal lugs, effigy features—
            stylized frog
          PRESUMED SOURCE:  Lower Tennessee-Cumberland
            area
          GRAVELOT PROVENIENCE:  Bu. 1519/SD

SD732    Moundville Engraved, variety Maxwells Crossing
          (crosshatched vertical bands)
          VESSEL SHAPE:  Subglobular bottle with slab
            base
```

```
          PRESUMED SOURCE:  Local
          GRAVELOT PROVENIENCE:  Bu. 1520/SD

SD733    Moundville Engraved, variety Hemphill (rayed
          circle)
          VESSEL SHAPE:  Simple bowl with everted lip
          PRESUMED SOURCE:  Local (questionable)
          GRAVELOT PROVENIENCE:  Bu. 1520/SD

SD734    Bell Plain, variety Hale
          VESSEL SHAPE:  Undiagnostic fragment(s)
          PRESUMED SOURCE:  Local
          GRAVELOT PROVENIENCE:  Bu. 1521/SD

SD736    Bell Plain, variety Hale
          VESSEL SHAPE:  Simple bowl with beaded rim
          PRESUMED SOURCE:  Local
          GRAVELOT PROVENIENCE:  Bu. 1522/SD

SD741    Mississippi Plain, variety Warrior
          VESSEL SHAPE:  Bottle (miniature)
          PRESUMED SOURCE:  Local
          GRAVELOT PROVENIENCE:  Bu. 1525/SD

SD742    Moundville Engraved, variety Hemphill (paired
          tails)
          VESSEL SHAPE:  Subglobular bottle with simple
            base
          PRESUMED SOURCE:  Local
          GRAVELOT PROVENIENCE:  Bu. 1525/SD

SD743    Bell Plain, variety Hale
          VESSEL SHAPE:  Flaring-rim bowl (shallow)
          PRESUMED SOURCE:  Local
          GRAVELOT PROVENIENCE:  Bu. 1525/SD

SD744    Mississippi Plain, variety Warrior
          VESSEL SHAPE:  Standard jar with 2 handles
          PRESUMED SOURCE:  Local
          GRAVELOT PROVENIENCE:  Bu. 1525/SD

SD745    Carthage Incised, variety Moon Lake
          VESSEL SHAPE:  Flaring-rim bowl (shallow) with
            notched lip
          PRESUMED SOURCE:  Local
          GRAVELOT PROVENIENCE:  Bu. 1525/SD

SD746    Mississippi Plain, variety Warrior
          VESSEL SHAPE:  Standard jar with 4 handles
          PRESUMED SOURCE:  Local (questionable)
          GRAVELOT PROVENIENCE:  Bu. 1525/SD

SD747    Bell Plain, variety Hale
          VESSEL SHAPE:  Simple bowl
          PRESUMED SOURCE:  Local
          GRAVELOT PROVENIENCE:  Bu. 1526/SD

SD748    Mississippi Plain, variety Warrior
          VESSEL SHAPE:  Subglobular bottle
          PRESUMED SOURCE:  Local (questionable)
          GRAVELOT PROVENIENCE:  Bu. 1526/SD

SD749    Unclassified Engraved (sand tempered) (festoons)
          VESSEL SHAPE:  Cylindrical bowl
          PRESUMED SOURCE:  Nonlocal

SD805    Moundville Engraved, variety Hemphill (bird with
          serpent head)
          VESSEL SHAPE:  Subglobular bottle with slab
            base
          PRESUMED SOURCE:  Local
          GRAVELOT PROVENIENCE:  Bu. 1534/SD

SD806    Bell Plain, variety Hale
          VESSEL SHAPE:  Flaring-rim bowl (deep)
          PRESUMED SOURCE:  Local
          GRAVELOT PROVENIENCE:  Bu. 1534/SD

SD810    Bell Plain, variety unspecified
          VESSEL SHAPE:  High-shouldered bottle
          PRESUMED SOURCE:  Central Mississippi Valley
          GRAVELOT PROVENIENCE:  Bu. 1536/SD

SD811    Bell Plain, variety Hale
          VESSEL SHAPE:  Bottle
          PRESUMED SOURCE:  Local (questionable)
          GRAVELOT PROVENIENCE:  Bu. 1537/SD

SD813    Unclassified Engraved
          VESSEL SHAPE:  Cylindrical bottle
          PRESUMED SOURCE:  Nonlocal
          GRAVELOT PROVENIENCE:  Bu. 1539/SD

SD814    Moundville Engraved, variety Hemphill (crested
          bird head)
```

VESSEL SHAPE: Subglobular bottle with simple
    base
PRESUMED SOURCE: Local
GRAVELOT PROVENIENCE: Bu. 1539/SD

SD815   Bell Plain, *variety Hale*
        VESSEL SHAPE: Simple bowl with beaded rim
        PRESUMED SOURCE: Local
        GRAVELOT PROVENIENCE: Bu. 1539/SD

SD816   Bell Plain, *variety Hale*
        VESSEL SHAPE: Simple bowl with effigy
            features—beaver
        PRESUMED SOURCE: Local
        GRAVELOT PROVENIENCE: Bu. 1539/SD

SD818   Bell Plain, *variety Hale*
        VESSEL SHAPE: Simple bowl (miniature) with
            beaded rim
        PRESUMED SOURCE: Local
        GRAVELOT PROVENIENCE: Bu. 1539/SD

SD821   Bell Plain, *variety Hale*
        VESSEL SHAPE: Simple bowl with beaded rim,
            spouts
        PRESUMED SOURCE: Local
        GRAVELOT PROVENIENCE: Bu. 1542/SD

SD822   Bell Plain, *variety Hale*
        VESSEL SHAPE: Simple bowl with beaded rim
        PRESUMED SOURCE: Local
        GRAVELOT PROVENIENCE: Bu. 1542/SD

SD825   Bell Plain, *variety Hale*
        VESSEL SHAPE: Subglobular bottle with simple
            base
        PRESUMED SOURCE: Local
        GRAVELOT PROVENIENCE: Bu. 1544/SD

SD826   Moundville Engraved, *variety Havana*
        VESSEL SHAPE: Cylindrical bowl with single
            lug
        PRESUMED SOURCE: Local
        GRAVELOT PROVENIENCE: Bu. 1544/SD

SD827   Bell Plain, *variety Hale*
        VESSEL SHAPE: Simple bowl with widely spaced
            nodes
        PRESUMED SOURCE: Local
        GRAVELOT PROVENIENCE: Bu. 1544/SD
        NMNH CATALOG NO.: 377402

SD832   Bell Plain, *variety Hale*
        VESSEL SHAPE: Simple bowl with effigy
            features—fish
        PRESUMED SOURCE: Local
        GRAVELOT PROVENIENCE: Bu. 1546/SD

SD834   Moundville Engraved, *variety Havana*
        VESSEL SHAPE: Simple bowl with lug and rim
            effigy—bird (gracile, outward-facing head)
        PRESUMED SOURCE: Local (questionable)
        GRAVELOT PROVENIENCE: Bu. 1553/SD

SD836   Moundville Engraved, *variety Hemphill* (winged
            serpent)
        VESSEL SHAPE: Subglobular bottle with simple
            base
        PRESUMED SOURCE: Local
        GRAVELOT PROVENIENCE: Bu. 1563-4/SD

SD837   Mississippi Plain, *variety Warrior*
        VESSEL SHAPE: Standard jar with 2 handles,
            downturned lugs
        PRESUMED SOURCE: Local
        GRAVELOT PROVENIENCE: Bu. 1563-4/SD

SD838   Mississippi Plain, *variety Warrior*
        VESSEL SHAPE: Standard jar with 4 handles
        PRESUMED SOURCE: Local
        GRAVELOT PROVENIENCE: Bu. 1563-4/SD

SD840   Moundville Engraved, *variety Wiggins*
        VESSEL SHAPE: Subglobular bottle with simple
            base
        PRESUMED SOURCE: Local
        GRAVELOT PROVENIENCE: Bu. 1566/SD

SD841   Moundville Engraved, *variety Tuscaloosa*
        VESSEL SHAPE: Subglobular bottle with slab
            base, indentations
        PRESUMED SOURCE: Local
        GRAVELOT PROVENIENCE: Bu. 1567/SD

SD842   Mississippi Plain, *variety Warrior*
        VESSEL SHAPE: Standard jar with 4 handles
        PRESUMED SOURCE: Local
        GRAVELOT PROVENIENCE: Bu. 1569/SD

SD844   Bell Plain, *variety Hale*
        VESSEL SHAPE: Burnished jar with 2 handles,
            effigy features—fish
        PRESUMED SOURCE: Local (questionable)
        GRAVELOT PROVENIENCE: Bu. 1570/SD

SD847   Bell Plain, *variety unspecified*
        VESSEL SHAPE: Simple bowl with effigy
            features—human figure
        PRESUMED SOURCE: Central Mississippi Valley,
            Lower Tennessee-Cumberland area
        GRAVELOT PROVENIENCE: Bu. 1573/SD

SD848   Matthews Incised, *variety Beckwith*
        VESSEL SHAPE: Standard jar with 2 handles,
            effigy features—stylized frog
        PRESUMED SOURCE: Lower Tennessee-Cumberland
            area
        GRAVELOT PROVENIENCE: Bu. 1573/SD

SD849   Moundville Engraved, *variety Hemphill* (feather)
        VESSEL SHAPE: Subglobular bottle with slab
            base
        PRESUMED SOURCE: Local
        GRAVELOT PROVENIENCE: Bu. 1573/SD

SD853   Carthage Incised, *variety Akron*
        VESSEL SHAPE: Simple bowl
        PRESUMED SOURCE: Local (questionable)
        GRAVELOT PROVENIENCE: Bu. 1579-80/SD

SD855   Bell Plain, *variety Hale*
        VESSEL SHAPE: Simple bowl with effigy
            features—turtle
        PRESUMED SOURCE: Local (questionable)
        GRAVELOT PROVENIENCE: Bu. 1582/SD

SD2/M5 Bell Plain, *variety Hale*
        VESSEL SHAPE: Burnished jar with 2 handles,
            beaded rim, effigy features—frog
        PRESUMED SOURCE: Local
        GRAVELOT PROVENIENCE: Bu. 1/SD/M5
        PUBLISHED ILLUSTRATION: Moore 1905:Figure 78
        MAI CATALOG NO.: 17/4617

SD3/M5 Unclassified Plain (untempered)
        VESSEL SHAPE: Bowl (miniature) with effigy
            features—unidentified
        PRESUMED SOURCE: Local
        PUBLISHED ILLUSTRATION: Moore 1905:Figure 79
        MAI CATALOG NO.: 17/2798

SD4/M5 Moundville Engraved, *variety Englewood*
        VESSEL SHAPE: Subglobular bottle with simple
            base, indentations
        PRESUMED SOURCE: Local
        GRAVELOT PROVENIENCE: Bu. 2/SD/M5
        PUBLISHED ILLUSTRATION: Moore 1905:Figure 80
        MAI CATALOG NO.: 17/1427

SD6/M5 Unclassified Engraved
        VESSEL SHAPE: Subglobular bottle with simple
            base
        PRESUMED SOURCE: Nonlocal
        GRAVELOT PROVENIENCE: Bu. 5/SD/M5
        PUBLISHED ILLUSTRATION: Moore 1905:Figure 81
        MAI CATALOG NO.: 17/3366

SD9/M5 Moundville Engraved, *variety Hemphill* (paired
            tails)
        VESSEL SHAPE: Subglobular bottle with simple
            base
        PRESUMED SOURCE: Local
        GRAVELOT PROVENIENCE: Bu. 23/SD/M5
        PUBLISHED ILLUSTRATION: Moore 1905:Figures
            84-85
        MAI CATALOG NO.: 17/3364

SD10/M5 Moundville Engraved, *variety Taylorville*
        VESSEL SHAPE: Subglobular bottle with simple
            base
        PRESUMED SOURCE: Local
        GRAVELOT PROVENIENCE: Bu. 24/SD/M5
        PUBLISHED ILLUSTRATION: Moore 1905:Figure 86
        MAI CATALOG NO.: 17/3354

SD1/M7 Moundville Engraved, *variety Hemphill* (winged
            serpent)

VESSEL SHAPE: Subglobular bottle with simple
    base
PRESUMED SOURCE: Local
GRAVELOT PROVENIENCE: Bu. 2/SD/M7
PUBLISHED ILLUSTRATION: Moore 1907:Figures
    54-55
MAI CATALOG NO.: 17/3365

SD5/M7   Bell Plain, *variety Hale*
    VESSEL SHAPE: Simple bowl with beaded rim,
        effigy features—human head medallions
    PRESUMED SOURCE: Local
    GRAVELOT PROVENIENCE: Bu. 8/SD/M7
    PUBLISHED DESCRIPTION: Moore 1907:346
    MAI CATALOG NO.: 17/4373

SD6/M7   Moundville Engraved, *variety Hemphill* (winged
    serpent)
    VESSEL SHAPE: Subglobular bottle with simple
        base
    PRESUMED SOURCE: Local
    GRAVELOT PROVENIENCE: Bu. 8/SD/M7
    PUBLISHED ILLUSTRATION: Moore 1907:Figures
        51-53
    MAI CATALOG NO.: 18/436

SD7/M7   Moundville Engraved, *variety Hemphill* (radial
    fingers)
    VESSEL SHAPE: Subglobular bottle
    PRESUMED SOURCE: Local
    GRAVELOT PROVENIENCE: Bu. 8/SD/M7
    PUBLISHED ILLUSTRATION: Moore 1907:Figures
        4-5
    MAI CATALOG NO.: 17/3353

SD8/M7   Moundville Engraved, *variety Wiggins*
    VESSEL SHAPE: Subglobular bottle with slab
        base
    PRESUMED SOURCE: Local
    GRAVELOT PROVENIENCE: Bu. 12/SD/M7
    PUBLISHED ILLUSTRATION: Moore 1907:Figures
        66-67
    MAI CATALOG NO.: 17/3338

SD11/M7   Moundville Engraved, *variety Taylorville*
    VESSEL SHAPE: Pedestaled bowl with notched
        everted lip
    PRESUMED SOURCE: Local
    GRAVELOT PROVENIENCE: Bu. 13/SD/M7
    PUBLISHED ILLUSTRATION: Moore 1907:Figures
        15-16
    MAI CATALOG NO.: 17/4378

SD13/M7   Moundville Engraved, *variety Hemphill* (ogee)
    VESSEL SHAPE: Subglobular bottle with
        pedestal base
    PRESUMED SOURCE: Local
    GRAVELOT PROVENIENCE: Bu. 13/SD/M7
    PUBLISHED ILLUSTRATION: Moore 1907:Figure 41
    MAI CATALOG NO.: 17/3341

SD14/M7   Moundville Engraved, *variety Wiggins*
    VESSEL SHAPE: Cylindrical bowl with single
        lug
    PRESUMED SOURCE: Local
    GRAVELOT PROVENIENCE: Bu. 13/SD/M7
    PUBLISHED ILLUSTRATION: Moore 1907:Figures
        68-69
    MAI CATALOG NO.: 17/4391

SD15/M7   Moundville Engraved, *variety Hemphill* (windmill)
    VESSEL SHAPE: Subglobular bottle with simple
        base
    PRESUMED SOURCE: Local
    GRAVELOT PROVENIENCE: Bu. 14/SD/M7
    PUBLISHED ILLUSTRATION: Moore 1907:Figure 12
    MAI CATALOG NO.: 17/3343

SD18/M7   Moundville Engraved, *variety Hemphill* (raptor in
    the round)
    VESSEL SHAPE: Subglobular bottle with simple
        base
    PRESUMED SOURCE: Local
    GRAVELOT PROVENIENCE: Bu. 22/SD/M7
    PUBLISHED ILLUSTRATION: Moore 1907:Figures
        10-11
    MAI CATALOG NO.: 17/4355

SD20/M7   Bell Plain, *variety Hale* (red on black)
    VESSEL SHAPE: Subglobular bottle with
        pedestal base
    PRESUMED SOURCE: Local (questionable)
    GRAVELOT PROVENIENCE: Bu. 27/SD/M7
    PUBLISHED ILLUSTRATION: Moore 1907:Figure 21
    MAI CATALOG NO.: 18/435

SD21/M7   Mississippi Plain, *variety unspecified*
    VESSEL SHAPE: Standard jar with 2 handles
    PRESUMED SOURCE: Central Mississippi Valley
    GRAVELOT PROVENIENCE: Bu. 27/SD/M7
    PUBLISHED ILLUSTRATION: Moore 1907:Figure 33
    MAI CATALOG NO.: 17/4383

SD27/M7   Moundville Engraved, *variety Hemphill* (hand and
    eye)
    VESSEL SHAPE: Cylindrical bowl with single
        lug
    PRESUMED SOURCE: Local
    GRAVELOT PROVENIENCE: Bu. 40/SD/M7
    PUBLISHED DESCRIPTION: Moore 1907:346
    MAI CATALOG NO.: 17/4389

SD28/M7   Moundville Engraved, *variety Hemphill* (radial
    fingers)
    VESSEL SHAPE: Cylindrical bowl with single
        lug
    PRESUMED SOURCE: Local
    PUBLISHED ILLUSTRATION: Moore 1907:Figure 6
    PUBLISHED DESCRIPTION: Moore 1907:349-351
    MAI CATALOG NO.: 17/3377A

SD32/M7   Moundville Engraved, *variety Hemphill* (hand and
    eye)
    VESSEL SHAPE: Subglobular bottle with simple
        base
    PRESUMED SOURCE: Local
    GRAVELOT PROVENIENCE: Bu. 71/SD/M7
    PUBLISHED DESCRIPTION: Moore 1907:346
    MAI CATALOG NO.: 17/4361

SD33/M7   Moundville Engraved, *variety Hemphill* (winged
    serpent)
    VESSEL SHAPE: Subglobular bottle with simple
        base
    PRESUMED SOURCE: Local
    GRAVELOT PROVENIENCE: Bu. 71/SD/M7
    PUBLISHED ILLUSTRATION: Moore 1907:Figures
        57-59
    MAI CATALOG NO.: 17/4356

SD34/M7   Moundville Engraved, *variety Hemphill* (winged
    serpent in the round)
    VESSEL SHAPE: Subglobular bottle with simple
        base (flattened)
    PRESUMED SOURCE: Local
    GRAVELOT PROVENIENCE: Bu. 66/SD/M7
    PUBLISHED ILLUSTRATION: Moore 1907:Figure 56
    PUBLISHED DESCRIPTION: Moore 1907:374
    MAI CATALOG NO.: 17/3361

SD42/M7   Moundville Engraved, *variety Hemphill* (winged
    serpent)
    VESSEL SHAPE: Subglobular bottle with simple
        base
    PRESUMED SOURCE: Local
    GRAVELOT PROVENIENCE: Bu. 84/SD/M7
    PUBLISHED ILLUSTRATION: Moore 1907:Figures
        60-62
    MAI CATALOG NO.: 17/4353

SD44/M7   Moundville Engraved, *variety Hemphill* (winged
    serpent)
    VESSEL SHAPE: Subglobular bottle with simple
        base
    PRESUMED SOURCE: Local
    GRAVELOT PROVENIENCE: Bu. 55/SD/M7
    PUBLISHED ILLUSTRATION: Moore 1907:Figure 65
    PUBLISHED DESCRIPTION: Moore 1907:377
    MAI CATALOG NO.: 17/3355

SD45/M7   Andrews Decorated, *variety unspecified*
    (multilinear bands at rim and base, crosshatched
    rectilinear zones)
    VESSEL SHAPE: Cylindrical bowl
    PRESUMED SOURCE: Lower Chattahoochee Valley
    GRAVELOT PROVENIENCE: Bu. 94/SD/M7
    PUBLISHED ILLUSTRATION: Moore 1907:Figures
        13-14
    MAI CATALOG NO.: 17/1430

SD48/M7   Moundville Engraved, *variety Hemphill* (bilobed
    arrow)
    VESSEL SHAPE: Simple bowl with widely spaced
        nodes
    PRESUMED SOURCE: Local
    GRAVELOT PROVENIENCE: Bu. 101/SD/M7
    PUBLISHED ILLUSTRATION: Moore 1907:Figures
        43-44
    MAI CATALOG NO.: 17/4370

SD54/M7   Moundville Engraved, *variety Hemphill* (raptor
head)
     VESSEL SHAPE: Subglobular bottle with slab
     base
     PRESUMED SOURCE: Local
     GRAVELOT PROVENIENCE: Bu. 108/SD/M7
     PUBLISHED ILLUSTRATION: Moore 1907:Figures
     7-8
     MAI CATALOG NO.: 17/1424

SD55/M7   Bell Plain, *variety unspecified*
     VESSEL SHAPE: Hooded bottle with effigy
     features—human figure
     PRESUMED SOURCE: Central Mississippi Valley
     (Cairo Lowland), Lower Tennessee-Cumberland
     area
     PUBLISHED ILLUSTRATION: Moore 1907:Figure 28
     MAI CATALOG NO.: 17/4403

SD59/M7   Moundville Engraved, *variety Hemphill* (paired
wings)
     VESSEL SHAPE: Subglobular bottle with simple
     base
     PRESUMED SOURCE: Local
     GRAVELOT PROVENIENCE: Bu. 114/SD/M7
     PUBLISHED ILLUSTRATION: Moore 1907:Figures
     49-50
     MAI CATALOG NO.: 17/3344

SD61/M7   Bell Plain, *variety Hale*
     VESSEL SHAPE: Bowl (miniature) with effigy
     features—frog
     PRESUMED SOURCE: Local
     GRAVELOT PROVENIENCE: Bu. 115/SD/M7
     PUBLISHED DESCRIPTION: Moore 1907:346
     MAI CATALOG NO.: 17/3648

SD71/M7   Moundville Engraved, *variety Hemphill* (hand and
eye, raptor head)
     VESSEL SHAPE: Subglobular bottle with slab
     base
     PRESUMED SOURCE: Local
     GRAVELOT PROVENIENCE: Bu. 128/SD/M7
     PUBLISHED ILLUSTRATION: Moore 1907:Figure 9
     MAI CATALOG NO.: 17/3342

SD77/M7   Bell Plain, *variety Hale*
     VESSEL SHAPE: Subglobular bottle with simple
     base, effigy features—frog
     PRESUMED SOURCE: Local (questionable)
     GRAVELOT PROVENIENCE: Bu. 140/SD/M7
     PUBLISHED ILLUSTRATION: Moore 1907:Figure 30
     MAI CATALOG NO.: 17/4402

SD82/M7   Moundville Engraved, *variety Taylorville*
     VESSEL SHAPE: Cylindrical bowl with rim strap
     PRESUMED SOURCE: Local (questionable)
     GRAVELOT PROVENIENCE: Bu. 147/SD/M7
     PUBLISHED ILLUSTRATION: Moore 1907:Figures
     17-18
     MAI CATALOG NO.: 17/4365

SD86/M7   Moundville Engraved, *variety Hemphill* (crested
bird)
     VESSEL SHAPE: Cylindrical bowl
     PRESUMED SOURCE: Local
     GRAVELOT PROVENIENCE: Bu. 150/SD/M7
     PUBLISHED ILLUSTRATION: Moore 1907:Figures
     37-38
     MAI CATALOG NO.: 17/4395

SD87/M7   Moundville Engraved, *variety Hemphill* (winged
serpent)
     VESSEL SHAPE: Subglobular bottle with simple
     base
     PRESUMED SOURCE: Local
     GRAVELOT PROVENIENCE: Bu. 150/SD/M7
     PUBLISHED ILLUSTRATION: Moore 1907:Figures
     63-64
     MAI CATALOG NO.: 17/3350

SD88/M7   Moundville Engraved, *variety Hemphill* (hand and
eye, forearm bones)
     VESSEL SHAPE: Subglobular bottle with simple
     base
     PRESUMED SOURCE: Local
     GRAVELOT PROVENIENCE: Bu. 151/SD/M7
     PUBLISHED ILLUSTRATION: Moore 1907:Figure 45
     MAI CATALOG NO.: 17/4360

SD93/M7   Moundville Engraved, *variety Hemphill* (paired
tails)
     VESSEL SHAPE: Subglobular bottle with slab
     base

     PRESUMED SOURCE: Local
     GRAVELOT PROVENIENCE: Bu. 153/SD/M7
     PUBLISHED ILLUSTRATION: Moore 1907:Figures
     34-36

     MAI CATALOG NO.: 18/432

SD95/M7   Moundville Engraved, *variety Maxwells Crossing*
(crosshatched irregular zones)
     VESSEL SHAPE: Subglobular bottle with slab
     base
     PRESUMED SOURCE: Local
     PUBLISHED ILLUSTRATION: Moore 1907:Figures
     31-32
     MAI CATALOG NO.: 17/3351

SD96/M7   Moundville Engraved, *variety Wiggins*
     VESSEL SHAPE: Subglobular bottle with simple
     base
     PRESUMED SOURCE: Local
     GRAVELOT PROVENIENCE: Bu. 156/SD/M7
     PUBLISHED ILLUSTRATION: Moore 1907:Figures
     70-71
     MAI CATALOG NO.: 17/1423

SD103/M7   Moundville Engraved, *variety unspecified*
     VESSEL SHAPE: Subglobular bottle with
     pedestal base
     PRESUMED SOURCE: Local
     PUBLISHED ILLUSTRATION: Moore 1907:Figures
     24-25
     MAI CATALOG NO.: 17/3347

SD106/M7   Bell Plain, *variety Hale*
     VESSEL SHAPE: Terraced rectanguloid bowl
     PRESUMED SOURCE: Local (questionable)
     GRAVELOT PROVENIENCE: Bu. 165/SD/M7
     PUBLISHED ILLUSTRATION: Moore 1907:Figure 23
     MAI CATALOG NO.: 18/419

SD109/M7   Bell Plain, *variety Hale*
     VESSEL SHAPE: Slender ovoid bottle with
     pedestal base
     PRESUMED SOURCE: Local
     PUBLISHED ILLUSTRATION: Moore 1907:Figure 48
     MAI CATALOG NO.: 17/3368

SD110/M7   Bell Plain, *variety Hale*
     VESSEL SHAPE: Subglobular bottle with simple
     base, effigy features—fish
     PRESUMED SOURCE: Local (questionable)
     GRAVELOT PROVENIENCE: Bu. 173/SD/M7
     PUBLISHED ILLUSTRATION: Moore 1907:Figure 26
     MAI CATALOG NO.: 17/4401

NE1   Moundville Engraved, *variety unspecified*
(multilinear band at rim)
     VESSEL SHAPE: Terraced rectanguloid bowl with
     lowered lip
     PRESUMED SOURCE: Local (questionable)

NE2   Mississippi Plain, *variety Warrior*
     VESSEL SHAPE: Standard jar with 8 handles
     PRESUMED SOURCE: Local

NE4   Bell Plain, *variety Hale*
     VESSEL SHAPE: Restricted bowl with effigy
     features—fish
     PRESUMED SOURCE: Local (questionable)

NE5   Bell Plain, *variety Hale*
     VESSEL SHAPE: Burnished jar with 2 handles,
     beaded rim, widely spaced nodes
     PRESUMED SOURCE: Local (questionable)

NE6   Moundville Engraved, *variety Wiggins*
(nonconvergent scroll)
     VESSEL SHAPE: Subglobular bottle (miniature)
     with simple base
     PRESUMED SOURCE: Local
     GRAVELOT PROVENIENCE: Bu. 53/NE

NE7   Moundville Engraved, *variety Northport*
     VESSEL SHAPE: Subglobular bottle with slab
     base, indentations
     PRESUMED SOURCE: Local

NE8   Moundville Engraved, *variety Taylorville*
     VESSEL SHAPE: Subglobular bottle with simple
     base
     PRESUMED SOURCE: Local

NE9   Bell Plain, *variety unspecified*
     VESSEL SHAPE: Restricted bowl with rim strap,

effigy features—frog
PRESUMED SOURCE: Nonlocal

NE11   Bell Plain, *variety Hale*
        VESSEL SHAPE: Composite jar-bowl with 2
        handles, beaded rim
        PRESUMED SOURCE: Local (questionable)

NE12   Moundville Engraved, *variety Tuscaloosa*
        VESSEL SHAPE: Subglobular bottle with
        pedestal base, indentations
        PRESUMED SOURCE: Local

NE14   Mississippi Plain, *variety Warrior*
        VESSEL SHAPE: Standard jar with more than 10
        handles
        PRESUMED SOURCE: Local
        GRAVELOT PROVENIENCE: Bu. 53/NE

NE15   Bell Plain, *variety unspecified*
        VESSEL SHAPE: Subglobular bottle with carafe
        neck
        PRESUMED SOURCE: Central Mississippi Valley
        (Cairo Lowland), Lower Tennessee-Cumberland
        area

NE17   Bell Plain, *variety Hale*
        VESSEL SHAPE: Restricted bowl
        PRESUMED SOURCE: Local

NE18   Mississippi Plain, *variety Warrior*
        VESSEL SHAPE: Standard jar with 4 handles
        PRESUMED SOURCE: Local

NE19   Bell Plain, *variety Hale*
        VESSEL SHAPE: Simple bowl with widely spaced
        nodes
        PRESUMED SOURCE: Local

NE25   Mississippi Plain, *variety Warrior*
        VESSEL SHAPE: Standard jar with 2 handles
        PRESUMED SOURCE: Local

NE26   Bell Plain, *variety Hale*
        VESSEL SHAPE: Simple bowl with lug and rim
        effigy—(head missing)
        PRESUMED SOURCE: Local

NE27   Mississippi Plain, *variety Warrior*
        VESSEL SHAPE: Bowl
        PRESUMED SOURCE: Local

NE30   Bell Plain, *variety Hale*
        VESSEL SHAPE: Simple bowl
        PRESUMED SOURCE: Local (questionable)

NE31   Bell Plain, *variety Hale*
        VESSEL SHAPE: Restricted bowl with effigy
        features—fish
        PRESUMED SOURCE: Local
        GRAVELOT PROVENIENCE: Bu. 78/NE

NE33   Bell Plain, *variety Hale*
        VESSEL SHAPE: Undiagnostic fragment(s)
        PRESUMED SOURCE: Local

NE36   Bell Plain, *variety Hale*
        VESSEL SHAPE: Restricted bowl
        PRESUMED SOURCE: Local

NE37   Moundville Engraved, *variety Havana*
        VESSEL SHAPE: Cylindrical bowl with single
        lug
        PRESUMED SOURCE: Local

NE38   Moundville Engraved, *variety Havana*
        VESSEL SHAPE: Simple bowl with single lug,
        indentations
        PRESUMED SOURCE: Local
        GRAVELOT PROVENIENCE: Bu. 50/NE

NE39   Bell Plain, *variety Hale*
        VESSEL SHAPE: Restricted bowl with grouped
        nodes
        PRESUMED SOURCE: Local
        GRAVELOT PROVENIENCE: Bu. 1/NE

NE42   Bell Plain, *variety Hale*
        VESSEL SHAPE: Simple bowl with beaded rim
        PRESUMED SOURCE: Local (questionable)
        GRAVELOT PROVENIENCE: Bu. 48/NE

NE44   Bell Plain, *variety Hale*

VESSEL SHAPE: Simple bowl with lug and rim
effigy—bird (flat, inward-facing head)
PRESUMED SOURCE: Local

NE50   Moundville Engraved, *variety Havana*
        VESSEL SHAPE: Cylindrical bowl
        PRESUMED SOURCE: Local
        GRAVELOT PROVENIENCE: Bu. 54/NE

NE53   Pensacola Incised, *variety unspecified*
        VESSEL SHAPE: Potbellied bowl
        PRESUMED SOURCE: Gulf Coast (Mobile-Pensacola
        region)
        GRAVELOT PROVENIENCE: Bu. 92/NE

NE54   Bell Plain, *variety Hale*
        VESSEL SHAPE: Simple bowl with opposing lugs
        PRESUMED SOURCE: Local (questionable)
        GRAVELOT PROVENIENCE: Bu. 79/NE

NE55   Mississippi Plain, *variety Warrior*
        VESSEL SHAPE: Standard jar with 4 handles
        PRESUMED SOURCE: Local
        GRAVELOT PROVENIENCE: Bu. 23/NE

NE56   Bell Plain, *variety Hale*
        VESSEL SHAPE: Subglobular bottle with simple
        base
        PRESUMED SOURCE: Local
        GRAVELOT PROVENIENCE: Bu. 79/NE

NE58   Bell Plain, *variety Hale*
        VESSEL SHAPE: Slender ovoid bottle with
        pedestal base
        PRESUMED SOURCE: Local
        GRAVELOT PROVENIENCE: Bu. 94/NE

NE59   Moundville Engraved, *variety Hemphill* (winged
        serpent)
        VESSEL SHAPE: Subglobular bottle with simple
        base
        PRESUMED SOURCE: Local
        GRAVELOT PROVENIENCE: Bu. 76/NE

NE60   Moundville Engraved, *variety Hemphill* (paired
        tails)
        VESSEL SHAPE: Subglobular bottle with simple
        base
        PRESUMED SOURCE: Local
        GRAVELOT PROVENIENCE: Bu. 17/NE

NE61   Moundville Engraved, *variety Hemphill* (hand and
        eye)
        VESSEL SHAPE: Subglobular bottle with slab
        base
        PRESUMED SOURCE: Local
        GRAVELOT PROVENIENCE: Bu. 54/NE

NE63   Moundville Engraved, *variety Hemphill* (serpent)
        VESSEL SHAPE: Subglobular bottle with
        pedestal base
        PRESUMED SOURCE: Local (questionable)
        GRAVELOT PROVENIENCE: Bu. 59/NE

NE64   Bell Plain, *variety Hale*
        VESSEL SHAPE: Simple bowl with everted lip
        PRESUMED SOURCE: Local (questionable)
        GRAVELOT PROVENIENCE: Bu. 55/NE

NE65   Mississippi Plain, *variety Warrior*
        VESSEL SHAPE: Standard jar with 2 handles
        PRESUMED SOURCE: Local
        GRAVELOT PROVENIENCE: Bu. 44/NE

NE67   Moundville Engraved, *variety unspecified*
        (imbricated festoons)
        VESSEL SHAPE: Terraced rectanguloid bowl with
        lowered lip
        PRESUMED SOURCE: Local (questionable)
        GRAVELOT PROVENIENCE: Bu. 41/NE

NE68   Bell Plain, *variety Hale*
        VESSEL SHAPE: Flaring-rim bowl (deep)
        PRESUMED SOURCE: Local
        NMNH CATALOG NO.: 377401

NE71   Bell Plain, *variety unspecified*
        VESSEL SHAPE: Restricted bowl with effigy
        features—frog
        PRESUMED SOURCE: Nonlocal

NE74   Mississippi Plain, *variety Warrior*
        VESSEL SHAPE: Standard jar with handles
        PRESUMED SOURCE: Local
        GRAVELOT PROVENIENCE: Bu. 2/NE

NE77   Bell Plain, *variety unspecified*
        VESSEL SHAPE: Simple bowl with lug and rim
        effigy—human head
        PRESUMED SOURCE: Central Mississippi Valley
        (Cairo Lowland), Lower Tennessee-Cumberland
        area

NE78   Bell Plain, *variety unspecified*
        VESSEL SHAPE: Subglobular bottle with slab
        base
        PRESUMED SOURCE: Nonlocal
        GRAVELOT PROVENIENCE: Bu. 2/NE

NE79   Moundville Engraved, *variety Hemphill* (windmill)
        VESSEL SHAPE: Subglobular bottle with simple
        base
        PRESUMED SOURCE: Local

NE80   Moundville Engraved, *variety Hemphill* (raptor in
        the round)
        VESSEL SHAPE: Subglobular bottle with simple
        base (flattened)
        PRESUMED SOURCE: Local (questionable)

NE81   Bell Plain, *variety unspecified*
        VESSEL SHAPE: Composite bottle with narrow
        neck
        PRESUMED SOURCE: Central Mississippi Valley
        (Cairo Lowland)

NE82   Bell Plain, *variety unspecified*
        VESSEL SHAPE: Hooded bottle with effigy
        features—human figure
        PRESUMED SOURCE: Central Mississippi Valley
        (Cairo Lowland)

NE85   Bell Plain, *variety Hale*
        VESSEL SHAPE: Simple bowl with beaded rim
        PRESUMED SOURCE: Local

NE86   Bell Plain, *variety Hale*
        VESSEL SHAPE: Simple bowl with beaded rim,
        effigy features—human head medallions
        PRESUMED SOURCE: Local (questionable)

NE88   Mississippi Plain, *variety Warrior*
        VESSEL SHAPE: Standard jar with 8 handles
        PRESUMED SOURCE: Local

NE89   Bell Plain, *variety Hale*
        VESSEL SHAPE: Flaring-rim bowl (deep) with
        scalloped rim
        PRESUMED SOURCE: Local (questionable)

NE90   Moundville Engraved, *variety Hemphill* (winged
        serpent)
        VESSEL SHAPE: Subglobular bottle with simple
        base
        PRESUMED SOURCE: Local

NE92   Bell Plain, *variety Hale*
        VESSEL SHAPE: Bottle
        PRESUMED SOURCE: Local (questionable)

NE93   Bell Plain, *variety Hale*
        VESSEL SHAPE: Simple bowl
        PRESUMED SOURCE: Local

NE95   Bell Plain, *variety Hale*
        VESSEL SHAPE: Simple bowl with beaded rim
        PRESUMED SOURCE: Local

NE122   Bell Plain, *variety unspecified*
        VESSEL SHAPE: Lobate bottle with narrow neck
        (missing)
        PRESUMED SOURCE: Central Mississippi Valley
        (Cairo Lowland)

NE124   Mississippi Plain, *variety unspecified*
        VESSEL SHAPE: Standard jar with 2 handles,
        small horizontal lugs
        PRESUMED SOURCE: Lower Tennessee-Cumberland
        area

NE125   Mississippi Plain, *variety unspecified*
        VESSEL SHAPE: Subglobular bottle with simple
        base
        PRESUMED SOURCE: Nonlocal

NE127   Moundville Engraved, *variety Hemphill* (winged
        serpent)
        VESSEL SHAPE: Cylindrical bottle
        PRESUMED SOURCE: Local

NE128   Moundville Engraved, *variety Hemphill* (radial
        fingers)
        VESSEL SHAPE: Cylindrical bowl
        PRESUMED SOURCE: Local

NE129   Bell Plain, *variety Hale*
        VESSEL SHAPE: Pedestaled bowl with notched
        everted lip
        PRESUMED SOURCE: Local (questionable)
        GRAVELOT PROVENIENCE: Bu. 2/NE

NE130   Bell Plain, *variety unspecified*
        VESSEL SHAPE: Lobate bowl with notched lip
        PRESUMED SOURCE: Central Mississippi Valley
        (Cairo Lowland), Lower Tennessee-Cumberland
        area

NE131   Unclassified Engraved
        VESSEL SHAPE: Bottle
        PRESUMED SOURCE: Nonlocal

NE132   Moundville Engraved, *variety unspecified*
        VESSEL SHAPE: Subglobular bottle
        PRESUMED SOURCE: Local (questionable)

NE133   Moundville Engraved, *variety Taylorville*
        VESSEL SHAPE: Subglobular bottle with slab
        base
        PRESUMED SOURCE: Local

NE134   Bell Plain, *variety Hale*
        VESSEL SHAPE: Simple bowl with grouped nodes
        PRESUMED SOURCE: Local (questionable)

NE135   Carthage Incised, *variety Akron*
        VESSEL SHAPE: Simple bowl
        PRESUMED SOURCE: Local (questionable)

NE136   Mississippi Plain, *variety Warrior*
        VESSEL SHAPE: Standard jar with 8 handles
        PRESUMED SOURCE: Local

NE138   Mississippi Plain, *variety Warrior*
        VESSEL SHAPE: Simple bowl
        PRESUMED SOURCE: Local

NE140   Bell Plain, *variety Hale*
        VESSEL SHAPE: Subglobular bottle with simple
        base
        PRESUMED SOURCE: Local

NE145   Moundville Engraved, *variety Hemphill* (paired
        tails)
        VESSEL SHAPE: Restricted bowl
        PRESUMED SOURCE: Local

NE147   Moundville Engraved, *variety Wiggins*
        VESSEL SHAPE: Subglobular bottle with simple
        base
        PRESUMED SOURCE: Local

NE148   Bell Plain, *variety Hale*
        VESSEL SHAPE: Bottle
        PRESUMED SOURCE: Local (questionable)
        GRAVELOT PROVENIENCE: Bu. 15/NE

NE160   Bell Plain, *variety Hale*
        VESSEL SHAPE: Subglobular bottle with simple
        base
        PRESUMED SOURCE: Local

NE165   Moundville Engraved, *variety Havana*
        VESSEL SHAPE: Restricted bowl with effigy
        features—turtle
        PRESUMED SOURCE: Local
        GRAVELOT PROVENIENCE: Bu. 1587/NE

NE166   Bell Plain, *variety Hale*
        VESSEL SHAPE: Subglobular bottle with simple
        base
        PRESUMED SOURCE: Local (questionable)
        GRAVELOT PROVENIENCE: Bu. 1587/NE

NE169   Bell Plain, *variety unspecified*
        VESSEL SHAPE: High-shouldered bottle
        PRESUMED SOURCE: Nonlocal
        GRAVELOT PROVENIENCE: Bu. 1596/NE

NE170   Holly Fine Engraved
        VESSEL SHAPE: Cylindrical bottle
        PRESUMED SOURCE: Caddoan area
        GRAVELOT PROVENIENCE: Bu. 1596/NE

NE174   Bell Plain, *variety Hale*

VESSEL SHAPE: Simple bowl with beaded rim
PRESUMED SOURCE: Local
GRAVELOT PROVENIENCE: Bu. 1600/NE

NE185 Carthage Incised, *variety Moon Lake*
VESSEL SHAPE: Short-neck bowl
PRESUMED SOURCE: Local
GRAVELOT PROVENIENCE: Bu. 1611/NE

NE192 Mississippi Plain, *variety Warrior*
VESSEL SHAPE: Simple bowl (miniature)
PRESUMED SOURCE: Local

NE443 Mississippi Plain, *variety unspecified*
VESSEL SHAPE: Standard jar with 2 handles,
effigy features—stylized frog
PRESUMED SOURCE: Lower Tennessee-Cumberland
area
GRAVELOT PROVENIENCE: Bu. 1620/NE

NE444 Mississippi Plain, *variety Warrior*
VESSEL SHAPE: Standard jar with 4 handles
PRESUMED SOURCE: Local (questionable)
GRAVELOT PROVENIENCE: Bu. 1620/NE

NE445 Bell Plain, *variety Hale*
VESSEL SHAPE: Composite bowl with beaded rim
PRESUMED SOURCE: Local (questionable)
GRAVELOT PROVENIENCE: Bu. 1620/NE

NE446 Bell Plain, *variety unspecified*
VESSEL SHAPE: Simple bowl with lug and rim
effigy—human head
PRESUMED SOURCE: Central Mississippi Valley
(Cairo Lowland)
GRAVELOT PROVENIENCE: Bu. 1620/NE

NE448 Bell Plain, *variety unspecified*
VESSEL SHAPE: High-shouldered bottle with
effigy features—human head medallions
PRESUMED SOURCE: Central Mississippi Valley
(Memphis region)
GRAVELOT PROVENIENCE: Bu. 1620/NE

NE450 Bell Plain, *variety Hale*
VESSEL SHAPE: Burnished jar with no handles,
beaded rim
PRESUMED SOURCE: Local (questionable)
GRAVELOT PROVENIENCE: Bu. 1620/NE

NE451 Bell Plain, *variety Hale*
VESSEL SHAPE: Simple bowl with effigy
features—inverted turtle
PRESUMED SOURCE: Local (questionable)
GRAVELOT PROVENIENCE: Bu. 1620/NE

NE452 Mississippi Plain, *variety Warrior*
VESSEL SHAPE: Standard jar with 4 handles
PRESUMED SOURCE: Local (questionable)
GRAVELOT PROVENIENCE: Bu. 1620/NE

NE453 Bell Plain, *variety Hale*
VESSEL SHAPE: Simple bowl with beaded rim,
widely spaced nodes
PRESUMED SOURCE: Local
GRAVELOT PROVENIENCE: Bu. 1621/NE

NE454 Mississippi Plain, *variety unspecified*
VESSEL SHAPE: Standard jar with 2 handles,
effigy features—stylized frog
PRESUMED SOURCE: Lower Tennessee-Cumberland
area
GRAVELOT PROVENIENCE: Bu. 1621/NE

NE458 Moundville Engraved, *variety Hemphill* (windmill)
VESSEL SHAPE: Bottle (miniature)
PRESUMED SOURCE: Local
GRAVELOT PROVENIENCE: Bu. 1624/NE

NE460 Mississippi Plain, *variety unspecified*
VESSEL SHAPE: High-shouldered bottle with
effigy features—human head medallions
PRESUMED SOURCE: Central Mississippi Valley
GRAVELOT PROVENIENCE: Bu. 1625/NE

NE461 Carthage Incised, *variety Carthage* (nonconvergent
scroll)
VESSEL SHAPE: Bowl with vertical lugs
PRESUMED SOURCE: Local (questionable)
GRAVELOT PROVENIENCE: Bu. 1628/NE

NE464 Mississippi Plain, *variety Warrior*
VESSEL SHAPE: Standard jar with 4 handles

PRESUMED SOURCE: Local
GRAVELOT PROVENIENCE: Bu. 1631/NE

NE568 Bell Plain, *variety Hale*
VESSEL SHAPE: Subglobular bottle with slab
base
PRESUMED SOURCE: Local
GRAVELOT PROVENIENCE: Bu. 1636/NE

NE570 Bell Plain, *variety Hale*
VESSEL SHAPE: Subglobular bottle with slab
base, indentations
PRESUMED SOURCE: Local
GRAVELOT PROVENIENCE: Bu. .638/NE

NE571 Bell Plain, *variety Hale*
VESSEL SHAPE: Simple bowl with beaded rim
PRESUMED SOURCE: Local
GRAVELOT PROVENIENCE: Bu. 1638/NE

NE572 Moundville Engraved, *variety Tuscaloosa*
VESSEL SHAPE: Subglobular bottle with slab
base, indentations
PRESUMED SOURCE: Local
GRAVELOT PROVENIENCE: Bu. 1639/NE

NE574 Moundville Engraved, *variety Wiggins*
VESSEL SHAPE: Subglobular bottle with simple
base
PRESUMED SOURCE: Local
GRAVELOT PROVENIENCE: Bu. 1639/NE

NE575 Bell Plain, *variety Hale*
VESSEL SHAPE: Simple bowl with effigy
features—fish
PRESUMED SOURCE: Local
GRAVELOT PROVENIENCE: Bu. 1639/NE

NE576 Mississippi Plain, *variety Warrior*
VESSEL SHAPE: Subglobular bottle with simple
base
PRESUMED SOURCE: Local (questionable)
GRAVELOT PROVENIENCE: Bu. 1649/NE

NE581 Bell Plain, *variety Hale*
VESSEL SHAPE: Simple bowl with beaded rim
PRESUMED SOURCE: Local
GRAVELOT PROVENIENCE: Bu. 1651/NE

NE582 Moundville Engraved, *variety Hemphill*
VESSEL SHAPE: Subglobular bottle with simple
base
PRESUMED SOURCE: Local
GRAVELOT PROVENIENCE: Bu. 1651/NE

NE583 Bell Plain, *variety Hale*
VESSEL SHAPE: Cylindrical bowl with single
lug
PRESUMED SOURCE: Local
GRAVELOT PROVENIENCE: Bu. 1651/NE

NE585 Mississippi Plain, *variety Warrior*
VESSEL SHAPE: Standard jar with 4 handles
PRESUMED SOURCE: Local
GRAVELOT PROVENIENCE: Bu. 1651/NE

NE587 Mississippi Plain, *variety Warrior*
VESSEL SHAPE: Standard jar with 4 handles
PRESUMED SOURCE: Local (questionable)
GRAVELOT PROVENIENCE: Bu. 1655/NE

NE591 Mississippi Plain, *variety Warrior*
VESSEL SHAPE: Standard jar with 4 handles
PRESUMED SOURCE: Local
GRAVELOT PROVENIENCE: Bu. 1647-48/NE

NE592 Moundville Engraved, *variety Cypress*
VESSEL SHAPE: Subglobular bottle with simple
base
PRESUMED SOURCE: Local
GRAVELOT PROVENIENCE: Bu. 1647-48/NE

NE593 Mississippi Plain, *variety Warrior*
VESSEL SHAPE: Simple bowl
PRESUMED SOURCE: Local
GRAVELOT PROVENIENCE: Bu. 1647-48/NE

NE596 Moundville Engraved, *variety Hemphill* (winged
serpent)
VESSEL SHAPE: Subglobular bottle with simple
base
PRESUMED SOURCE: Local
GRAVELOT PROVENIENCE: Bu. 1665/NE

NE597   Moundville Incised, *variety Moundville*
         VESSEL SHAPE: Standard jar with 2 handles,
         widely spaced nodes
         PRESUMED SOURCE: Local (questionable)
         GRAVELOT PROVENIENCE: Bu. 1668/NE

NE599   Moundville Engraved, *variety Hemphill* (feather)
         VESSEL SHAPE: Subglobular bottle with slab
         base
         PRESUMED SOURCE: Local
         GRAVELOT PROVENIENCE: Bu. 1673/NE

NE600   Bell Plain, *variety Hale*
         VESSEL SHAPE: Subglobular bottle with simple
         base
         PRESUMED SOURCE: Local
         GRAVELOT PROVENIENCE: Bu. 1674/NE

NE602   Moundville Engraved, *variety Maxwells Crossing*
         (crosshatched vertical bands)
         VESSEL SHAPE: Subglobular bottle with simple
         base
         PRESUMED SOURCE: Local
         GRAVELOT PROVENIENCE: Bu. 1676/NE

NE603   Bell Plain, *variety Hale*
         VESSEL SHAPE: Simple bowl
         PRESUMED SOURCE: Local

EE1   Moundville Engraved, *variety Hemphill* (winged
         serpent)
         VESSEL SHAPE: Subglobular bottle with simple
         base
         PRESUMED SOURCE: Local
         GRAVELOT PROVENIENCE: Bu. 1181-83/EE

EE2   Bell Plain, *variety Hale*
         VESSEL SHAPE: Simple bowl with beaded rim
         PRESUMED SOURCE: Local
         GRAVELOT PROVENIENCE: Bu. 1181-83/EE

EE3   Moundville Engraved, *variety Hemphill* (paired
         tails)
         VESSEL SHAPE: Cylindrical bowl with single
         lug
         PRESUMED SOURCE: Local
         GRAVELOT PROVENIENCE: Bu. 1181-83/EE

EE4   Moundville Engraved, *variety Hemphill* (Turtle)
         VESSEL SHAPE: Subglobular bottle with simple
         base
         PRESUMED SOURCE: Local
         GRAVELOT PROVENIENCE: Bu. 1181-83/EE

EE5   Carthage Incised, *variety Carthage*
         VESSEL SHAPE: Short-neck bowl
         PRESUMED SOURCE: Local
         GRAVELOT PROVENIENCE: Bu. 1181-83/EE

EE6   Moundville Engraved, *variety Wiggins*
         VESSEL SHAPE: Subglobular bottle with simple
         base
         PRESUMED SOURCE: Local
         GRAVELOT PROVENIENCE: Bu. 1184/EE

EE7   Moundville Engraved, *variety Hemphill* (radial
         fingers)
         VESSEL SHAPE: Subglobular bottle with simple
         base (flattened)
         PRESUMED SOURCE: Local
         GRAVELOT PROVENIENCE: Bu. 1185/EE

EE8   Bell Plain, *variety Hale*
         VESSEL SHAPE: Restricted bowl
         PRESUMED SOURCE: Local
         GRAVELOT PROVENIENCE: Bu. 1185/EE

EE9   Moundville Engraved, *variety Wiggins*
         VESSEL SHAPE: Subglobular bottle with simple
         base
         PRESUMED SOURCE: Local
         GRAVELOT PROVENIENCE: Bu. 1185/EE

EE10   Moundville Engraved, *variety Englewood*
         VESSEL SHAPE: Subglobular bottle with simple
         base
         PRESUMED SOURCE: Local
         GRAVELOT PROVENIENCE: Bu. 1185/EE

EE11   Bell Plain, *variety Hale*
         VESSEL SHAPE: Restricted bowl
         PRESUMED SOURCE: Local
         GRAVELOT PROVENIENCE: Bu. 1185/EE

EE12   Carthage Incised, *variety Carthage*
         VESSEL SHAPE: Narrow-neck bottle
         (subglobular)
         PRESUMED SOURCE: Local
         GRAVELOT PROVENIENCE: Bu. 1185/EE

EE13   Bell Plain, *variety Hale*
         VESSEL SHAPE: Subglobular bottle with simple
         base (flattened)
         PRESUMED SOURCE: Local
         GRAVELOT PROVENIENCE: Bu. 1192/EE

EE17   Bell Plain, *variety Hale*
         VESSEL SHAPE: Subglobular bottle with simple
         base
         PRESUMED SOURCE: Local
         GRAVELOT PROVENIENCE: Bu. 1198/EE

EE18   Bell Plain, *variety Hale*
         VESSEL SHAPE: Simple bowl with beaded rim
         PRESUMED SOURCE: Local
         GRAVELOT PROVENIENCE: Bu. 1199-201/EE

EE19   Moundville Engraved, *variety Wiggins*
         VESSEL SHAPE: Subglobular bottle with simple
         base
         PRESUMED SOURCE: Local
         GRAVELOT PROVENIENCE: Bu. 1202/EE

EE22   Bell Plain, *variety Hale*
         VESSEL SHAPE: Subglobular bottle with simple
         base
         PRESUMED SOURCE: Local

EE25   Moundville Engraved, *variety Hemphill* (winged
         serpent)
         VESSEL SHAPE: Subglobular bottle with simple
         base
         PRESUMED SOURCE: Local

EE61   Bell Plain, *variety Hale*
         VESSEL SHAPE: Simple bowl with beaded rim
         PRESUMED SOURCE: Local
         GRAVELOT PROVENIENCE: Bu. 1213/EE

EE64   Bell Plain, *variety Hale*
         VESSEL SHAPE: Undiagnostic fragment(s)
         PRESUMED SOURCE: Local (questionable)
         GRAVELOT PROVENIENCE: Bu. 1213/EE

EE67   Bell Plain, *variety unspecified*
         VESSEL SHAPE: Restricted bowl with effigy
         features—frog
         PRESUMED SOURCE: Lower Tennessee-Cumberland
         area
         GRAVELOT PROVENIENCE: Bu. 1216/EE

EE71   Bell Plain, *variety Hale*
         VESSEL SHAPE: Simple bowl with single lug
         PRESUMED SOURCE: Local
         GRAVELOT PROVENIENCE: Bu. 1220/EE

EE72   Bell Plain, *variety Hale*
         VESSEL SHAPE: Flaring-rim bowl (deep)
         PRESUMED SOURCE: Local
         GRAVELOT PROVENIENCE: Bu. 1222-23/EE

EE74   Bell Plain, *variety Hale*
         VESSEL SHAPE: Subglobular bottle with simple
         base
         PRESUMED SOURCE: Local
         GRAVELOT PROVENIENCE: Bu. 1225/EE
         NMNH CATALOG NO.: 377387

EE75   Moundville Engraved, *variety Hemphill* (winged
         serpent)
         VESSEL SHAPE: Subglobular bottle with simple
         base
         PRESUMED SOURCE: Local
         GRAVELOT PROVENIENCE: Bu. 1225/EE

EE76   Bell Plain, *variety Hale*
         VESSEL SHAPE: Simple bowl with beaded rim
         PRESUMED SOURCE: Local
         GRAVELOT PROVENIENCE: Bu. 1225/EE

EE77   Bell Plain, *variety Hale*
         VESSEL SHAPE: Flaring-rim bowl (deep)
         PRESUMED SOURCE: Local
         GRAVELOT PROVENIENCE: Bu. 1227/EE

EE78   Carthage Incised, *variety Carthage*
         VESSEL SHAPE: Subglobular bottle with simple
         base

PRESUMED SOURCE: Local
GRAVELOT PROVENIENCE: Bu. 1227/EE

EE80   Bell Plain, *variety Hale*
VESSEL SHAPE: Subglobular bottle with simple
base
PRESUMED SOURCE: Local (questionable)
GRAVELOT PROVENIENCE: Bu. 1227/EE

EE81   Moundville Engraved, *variety Taylorville*
VESSEL SHAPE: Subglobular bottle with simple
base
PRESUMED SOURCE: Local
GRAVELOT PROVENIENCE: Bu. 1228/EE

EE82   Bell Plain, *variety Hale*
VESSEL SHAPE: Double bowl with effigy
features—mussel shell
PRESUMED SOURCE: Local (questionable)
GRAVELOT PROVENIENCE: Bu. 1229-31/EE

EE84   Nodena Red and White, *variety unspecified*
VESSEL SHAPE: Carinated bottle with carafe
neck
PRESUMED SOURCE: Central Mississippi Valley
(Clarksdale region)
GRAVELOT PROVENIENCE: Bu. 1232/EE

EE85   Moundville Engraved, *variety Wiggins*
VESSEL SHAPE: Subglobular bottle with simple
base
PRESUMED SOURCE: Local
GRAVELOT PROVENIENCE: Bu. 1234-37/EE

EE86   Moundville Engraved, *variety Wiggins*
VESSEL SHAPE: Subglobular bottle with simple
base
PRESUMED SOURCE: Local
GRAVELOT PROVENIENCE: Bu. 1234-37/EE
NMNH CATALOG NO.: 377386

EE87   Bell Plain, *variety Hale* (red on white)
VESSEL SHAPE: Simple bowl with beaded rim
PRESUMED SOURCE: Local
GRAVELOT PROVENIENCE: Bu. 1234-37/EE

EE88   Mississippi Plain, *variety Warrior*
VESSEL SHAPE: Standard jar with 2 handles
PRESUMED SOURCE: Local
GRAVELOT PROVENIENCE: Bu. 1234-37/EE

EE89   Mississippi Plain, *variety unspecified*
VESSEL SHAPE: Standard jar with 2 handles,
effigy features—stylized frog
PRESUMED SOURCE: Lower Tennessee-Cumberland
area
GRAVELOT PROVENIENCE: Bu. 1234-37/EE

EE94   Moundville Engraved, *variety Wiggins*
VESSEL SHAPE: Subglobular bottle with simple
base, indentations
PRESUMED SOURCE: Local
GRAVELOT PROVENIENCE: Bu. 1238/EE

EE104   Moundville Engraved, *variety Taylorville*
VESSEL SHAPE: Cylindrical bowl with single
lug
PRESUMED SOURCE: Local
GRAVELOT PROVENIENCE: Bu. 1243/EE

EE108   Mississippi Plain, *variety Warrior*
VESSEL SHAPE: Simple bowl
PRESUMED SOURCE: Local
GRAVELOT PROVENIENCE: Bu. 1254/EE

EE109   Bell Plain, *variety unspecified*
VESSEL SHAPE: Simple bowl with effigy
features—fish
PRESUMED SOURCE: Nonlocal
GRAVELOT PROVENIENCE: Bu. 1255/EE

EE110   Bell Plain, *variety Hale*
VESSEL SHAPE: Cylindrical bowl
PRESUMED SOURCE: Local
GRAVELOT PROVENIENCE: Bu. 1256/EE

EE111   Bell Plain, *variety Hale*
VESSEL SHAPE: Simple bowl with single lug
PRESUMED SOURCE: Local

EE112   Bell Plain, *variety Hale*
VESSEL SHAPE: Simple bowl with widely spaced
nodes
PRESUMED SOURCE: Local

EE124   Mississippi Plain, *variety Warrior*
VESSEL SHAPE: Standard jar with 4 handles
PRESUMED SOURCE: Local
GRAVELOT PROVENIENCE: Bu. 1261/EE

EE125   Bell Plain, *variety Hale* (red on white)
VESSEL SHAPE: Short-neck bowl
PRESUMED SOURCE: Local
GRAVELOT PROVENIENCE: Bu. 1261/EE

EE126   Moundville Engraved, *variety Hemphill* (hand and
eye)
VESSEL SHAPE: Restricted bowl
PRESUMED SOURCE: Local
GRAVELOT PROVENIENCE: Bu. 1261/EE

EE129   Bell Plain, *variety Hale*
VESSEL SHAPE: Subglobular bottle with simple
base
PRESUMED SOURCE: Local
GRAVELOT PROVENIENCE: Bu. 1262/EE

EE130   Moundville Engraved, *variety Wiggins*
VESSEL SHAPE: Subglobular bottle with simple
base
PRESUMED SOURCE: Local
GRAVELOT PROVENIENCE: Bu. 1263/EE

EE131   Mississippi Plain, *variety unspecified*
VESSEL SHAPE: Standard jar with 2 handles,
small horizontal lugs, widely spaced nodes
PRESUMED SOURCE: Lower Tennessee-Cumberland
area
GRAVELOT PROVENIENCE: Bu. 1264/EE
NMNH CATALOG NO.: 377390

EE132   Mississippi Plain, *variety Warrior*
VESSEL SHAPE: Standard jar with 2 handles
PRESUMED SOURCE: Local
GRAVELOT PROVENIENCE: Bu. 1264/EE

EE133   Moundville Engraved, *variety Taylorville*
VESSEL SHAPE: Subglobular bottle with slab
base
PRESUMED SOURCE: Local
GRAVELOT PROVENIENCE: Bu. 1265/EE

EE135   Bell Plain, *variety Hale*
VESSEL SHAPE: Simple bowl with beaded rim
PRESUMED SOURCE: Local
GRAVELOT PROVENIENCE: Bu. 1267/EE

EE136   Moundville Engraved, *variety Wiggins*
VESSEL SHAPE: Subglobular bottle with simple
base
PRESUMED SOURCE: Local
GRAVELOT PROVENIENCE: Bu. 1268/EE

EE137   Moundville Engraved, *variety Wiggins*
VESSEL SHAPE: Subglobular bottle with simple
base
PRESUMED SOURCE: Local
GRAVELOT PROVENIENCE: Bu. 1272/EE

EE155   Moundville Engraved, *variety Hemphill* (paired
tails)
VESSEL SHAPE: Subglobular bottle
PRESUMED SOURCE: Local
GRAVELOT PROVENIENCE: Bu. 1275/EE

EE156   Mississippi Plain, *variety Warrior*
VESSEL SHAPE: Flaring-rim bowl (deep)
PRESUMED SOURCE: Local
GRAVELOT PROVENIENCE: Bu. 1275/EE

EE157   Mississippi Plain, *variety Warrior*
VESSEL SHAPE: Undiagnostic fragment(s)
PRESUMED SOURCE: Local
GRAVELOT PROVENIENCE: Bu. 1276/EE

EE159   Mississippi Plain, *variety Warrior*
VESSEL SHAPE: Undiagnostic fragment(s)
PRESUMED SOURCE: Local
GRAVELOT PROVENIENCE: Bu. 1277A/EE

EE160   Moundville Engraved, *variety Wiggins*
VESSEL SHAPE: Pedestaled bowl with notched
everted lip
PRESUMED SOURCE: Local
GRAVELOT PROVENIENCE: Bu. 1277A/EE

EE166   Moundville Engraved, *variety Hemphill* (paired
tails)

VESSEL SHAPE: Subglobular bottle with simple
base
PRESUMED SOURCE: Local

EE179   Bell Plain, *variety Hale*
VESSEL SHAPE: Simple bowl with effigy
features—fish
PRESUMED SOURCE: Local
GRAVELOT PROVENIENCE: Bu. 1278/EE

EE180   Moundville Engraved, *variety Taylorville*
VESSEL SHAPE: Subglobular bottle with simple
base
PRESUMED SOURCE: Local
GRAVELOT PROVENIENCE: Bu. 1278/EE

EE181   Bell Plain, *variety Hale*
VESSEL SHAPE: Restricted bowl
PRESUMED SOURCE: Local
GRAVELOT PROVENIENCE: Bu. 1281/EE

EE182   Moundville Engraved, *variety Hemphill* (hand and
eye)
VESSEL SHAPE: Cylindrical bowl with single
lug
PRESUMED SOURCE: Local
GRAVELOT PROVENIENCE: Bu. 1281/EE

EE186   Bell Plain, *variety Hale*
VESSEL SHAPE: Undiagnostic fragment(s) with
effigy features—frog
PRESUMED SOURCE: Local
GRAVELOT PROVENIENCE: Bu. 1283/EE

EE187   Bell Plain, *variety Hale*
VESSEL SHAPE: Restricted bowl with effigy
features—fish
PRESUMED SOURCE: Local
GRAVELOT PROVENIENCE: Bu. 1284/EE

EE188   Moundville Engraved, *variety Taylorville*
VESSEL SHAPE: Subglobular bottle with simple
base
PRESUMED SOURCE: Local
GRAVELOT PROVENIENCE: Bu. 1284/EE

EE201   Pensacola Incised, *variety Strongs Bayou*
VESSEL SHAPE: Cylindrical bottle
PRESUMED SOURCE: Gulf Coast (Mobile-Pensacola
region)

EE202   Bell Plain, *variety Hale*
VESSEL SHAPE: Bowl
PRESUMED SOURCE: Local
GRAVELOT PROVENIENCE: Bu. 1291/EE

EE203   Bell Plain, *variety Hale* (red on white)
VESSEL SHAPE: Simple bowl with lug and rim
effigy—feline
PRESUMED SOURCE: Local (questionable)
GRAVELOT PROVENIENCE: Bu. 1291/EE

EE204   Moundville Engraved, *variety Wiggins*
VESSEL SHAPE: Subglobular bottle with slab
base
PRESUMED SOURCE: Local
GRAVELOT PROVENIENCE: Bu. 1292/EE

EE206   Unclassified Engraved (multilinear band at rim)
VESSEL SHAPE: Simple bowl with notched lip
PRESUMED SOURCE: Nonlocal
GRAVELOT PROVENIENCE: Bu. 1293/EE

EE210   Moundville Engraved, *variety Havana*
VESSEL SHAPE: Cylindrical bowl with single
lug
PRESUMED SOURCE: Local
GRAVELOT PROVENIENCE: Bu. 1299-301/EE

EE234   Moundville Engraved, *variety Hemphill* (hand and
eye)
VESSEL SHAPE: Cylindrical bowl with single
lug
PRESUMED SOURCE: Local
GRAVELOT PROVENIENCE: Bu. 1316/EE

EE236   Bell Plain, *variety unspecified*
VESSEL SHAPE: High-shouldered bottle
PRESUMED SOURCE: Central Mississippi Valley,
Lower Tennessee Valley
GRAVELOT PROVENIENCE: Bu. 1321/EE

EE237   Bell Plain, *variety Hale*

VESSEL SHAPE: Flaring-rim bowl (shallow)
PRESUMED SOURCE: Local
GRAVELOT PROVENIENCE: Bu. 1321/EE

EE238   Bell Plain, *variety Hale*
VESSEL SHAPE: Simple bowl with widely spaced
nodes
PRESUMED SOURCE: Local
GRAVELOT PROVENIENCE: Bu. 1321/EE

EE242   Bell Plain, *variety Hale*
VESSEL SHAPE: Subglobular bottle with slab
base
PRESUMED SOURCE: Local
GRAVELOT PROVENIENCE: Bu. 1326-28/EE

EE260   Bell Plain, *variety Hale*
VESSEL SHAPE: Simple bowl with effigy
features—fish
PRESUMED SOURCE: Local
GRAVELOT PROVENIENCE: Bu. 1331/EE
NMNH CATALOG NO.: 377394

EE277   Bell Plain, *variety Hale*
VESSEL SHAPE: Simple bowl with beaded rim
PRESUMED SOURCE: Local
GRAVELOT PROVENIENCE: Bu. 1343-44/EE

EE278   Mississippi Plain, *variety unspecified*
VESSEL SHAPE: Standard jar with 2 handles,
small horizontal lugs
PRESUMED SOURCE: Lower Tennessee-Cumberland
area
GRAVELOT PROVENIENCE: Bu. .1343-44/EE

EE281   Bell Plain, *variety Hale* (red filmed)
VESSEL SHAPE: Cylindrical bowl (miniature)
PRESUMED SOURCE: Local (questionable)
GRAVELOT PROVENIENCE: Bu. 1346/EE

EE302   Bell Plain, *variety Hale*
VESSEL SHAPE: Simple bowl with single lug
PRESUMED SOURCE: Local
GRAVELOT PROVENIENCE: Bu. 1371-72/EE

EE303   Bell Plain, *variety Hale*
VESSEL SHAPE: Subglobular bottle with simple
base
PRESUMED SOURCE: Local
GRAVELOT PROVENIENCE: Bu. 1373-74/EE

EE304   Bell Plain, *variety Hale*
VESSEL SHAPE: Subglobular bottle with
pedestal base
PRESUMED SOURCE: Local
GRAVELOT PROVENIENCE: Bu. 1373-74/EE

EE305   Bell Plain, *variety Hale*
VESSEL SHAPE: Subglobular bottle with simple
base (flattened)
PRESUMED SOURCE: Local (questionable)
GRAVELOT PROVENIENCE: Bu. 1373-74/EE

EE307   Unclassified Plain (untempered)
VESSEL SHAPE: Bowl (miniature)
PRESUMED SOURCE: Local
GRAVELOT PROVENIENCE: Bu. 1373-74/EE

EE322   Moundville Engraved, *variety Havana*
VESSEL SHAPE: Cylindrical bowl
PRESUMED SOURCE: Local
GRAVELOT PROVENIENCE: Bu. 1380/EE

EE340   Moundville Engraved, *variety Northport*
VESSEL SHAPE: Subglobular bottle with
pedestal base
PRESUMED SOURCE: Local
GRAVELOT PROVENIENCE: Bu. 1385/EE
NMNH CATALOG NO.: 377383

EE343   Moundville Engraved, *variety Hemphill* (scalp)
VESSEL SHAPE: Subglobular bottle with slab
base
PRESUMED SOURCE: Local

EE377   Bell Plain, *variety Hale*
VESSEL SHAPE: Restricted bowl with effigy
features—fish
PRESUMED SOURCE: Local
NMNH CATALOG NO.: 377393

EE380   Bell Plain, *variety Hale*
VESSEL SHAPE: Pedestaled bowl with notched
everted lip (missing)

PRESUMED SOURCE: Local
GRAVELOT PROVENIENCE: Bu. 1387/EE
NMNH CATALOG NO.: 377392

EE381   Mississippi Plain, *variety Warrior*
VESSEL SHAPE: Simple bowl
PRESUMED SOURCE: Local
GRAVELOT PROVENIENCE: Bu. 1387/EE

EE382   Mississippi Plain, *variety Warrior*
VESSEL SHAPE: Standard jar
PRESUMED SOURCE: Local
GRAVELOT PROVENIENCE: Bu. 1387/EE

EE383   Moundville Engraved, *variety unspecified*
VESSEL SHAPE: Subglobular bottle with simple base
PRESUMED SOURCE: Local (questionable)

EE384   Bell Plain, *variety Hale*
VESSEL SHAPE: Simple bowl with effigy features—conch shell
PRESUMED SOURCE: Local (questionable)
GRAVELOT PROVENIENCE: Bu. 1388/EE

EE385   Moundville Engraved, *variety Taylorville*
VESSEL SHAPE: Subglobular bottle with slab base
PRESUMED SOURCE: Local
GRAVELOT PROVENIENCE: Bu. 1389-91/EE

EE387   Mississippi Plain, *variety Warrior*
VESSEL SHAPE: Simple bowl
PRESUMED SOURCE: Local

EE389   Mississippi Plain, *variety Warrior*
VESSEL SHAPE: Standard jar with 2 handles
PRESUMED SOURCE: Local
GRAVELOT PROVENIENCE: Bu. 1392/EE

EE390   Carthage Incised, *variety Akron*
VESSEL SHAPE: Simple bowl with notched lip
PRESUMED SOURCE: Local (questionable)
GRAVELOT PROVENIENCE: Bu. 1392/EE
NMNH CATALOG NO.: 377398

EE391   Moundville Engraved, *variety Hemphill* (windmill)
VESSEL SHAPE: Subglobular bottle with simple base
PRESUMED SOURCE: Local
GRAVELOT PROVENIENCE: Bu. 1394/EE

EE392   Bell Plain, *variety Hale*
VESSEL SHAPE: Simple bowl with widely spaced nodes
PRESUMED SOURCE: Local
GRAVELOT PROVENIENCE: Bu. 1394/EE
NMNH CATALOG NO.: 377397

EE394   Bell Plain, *variety Hale*
VESSEL SHAPE: Restricted bowl with notched everted lip
PRESUMED SOURCE: Local (questionable)
GRAVELOT PROVENIENCE: Bu. 1399/EE

EE395   Bell Plain, *variety Hale*
VESSEL SHAPE: Simple bowl with beaded rim, spouts, widely spaced nodes
PRESUMED SOURCE: Local
GRAVELOT PROVENIENCE: Bu. 1399/EE

EE396   Bell Plain, *variety Hale*
VESSEL SHAPE: Bowl with effigy features— shell spoon
PRESUMED SOURCE: Local (questionable)
GRAVELOT PROVENIENCE: Bu. 1400/EE

EE416   Moundville Engraved, *variety Hemphill* (raptor in the round)
VESSEL SHAPE: Cylindrical bowl with single lug
PRESUMED SOURCE: Local
GRAVELOT PROVENIENCE: Bu. 1406/EE

EE429   Moundville Engraved, *variety Taylorville*
VESSEL SHAPE: Subglobular bottle with simple base
PRESUMED SOURCE: Local
GRAVELOT PROVENIENCE: Bu. 1407/EE

EE430   Bell Plain, *variety Hale*
VESSEL SHAPE: Simple bowl with beaded rim
PRESUMED SOURCE: Local
GRAVELOT PROVENIENCE: Bu. 1407/EE

EE431   Bell Plain, *variety Hale*
VESSEL SHAPE: Subglobular bottle with simple base
PRESUMED SOURCE: Local (questionable)
GRAVELOT PROVENIENCE: Bu. 1409/EE

EE444   Bell Plain, *variety Hale*
VESSEL SHAPE: Restricted bowl
PRESUMED SOURCE: Local
GRAVELOT PROVENIENCE: Bu. 1411/EE

EE445   Moundville Engraved, *variety Wiggins*
VESSEL SHAPE: Subglobular bottle with simple base
PRESUMED SOURCE: Local
GRAVELOT PROVENIENCE: Bu. 1412/EE

EE446   Carthage Incised, *variety Akron*
VESSEL SHAPE: Simple bowl
PRESUMED SOURCE: Local

EE447   Bell Plain, *variety Hale*
VESSEL SHAPE: Simple bowl with beaded rim
PRESUMED SOURCE: Local
GRAVELOT PROVENIENCE: Bu. 1413/EE

EE475   Bell Plain, *variety Hale*
VESSEL SHAPE: Restricted bowl with effigy features—beaver
PRESUMED SOURCE: Local
GRAVELOT PROVENIENCE: Bu. 1415/EE

EE492   Bell Plain, *variety Hale*
VESSEL SHAPE: Subglobular bottle with simple base
PRESUMED SOURCE: Local
GRAVELOT PROVENIENCE: Bu. 1680/EE

EE495   Bell Plain, *variety Hale*
VESSEL SHAPE: Simple bowl with effigy features—frog heads
PRESUMED SOURCE: Local (questionable)
GRAVELOT PROVENIENCE: Bu. 1682/EE

SE2   Bell Plain, *variety Hale*
VESSEL SHAPE: Simple bowl with effigy features—conch shell
PRESUMED SOURCE: Local
GRAVELOT PROVENIENCE: Bu. 1308/SE

SE3   Moundville Engraved, *variety Taylorville*
VESSEL SHAPE: Subglobular bottle with simple base
PRESUMED SOURCE: Local

SE4   Mississippi Plain, *variety unspecified*
VESSEL SHAPE: Standard jar with 2 handles, small horizontal lugs
PRESUMED SOURCE: Lower Tennessee-Cumberland area

SE8   Moundville Engraved, *variety Hemphill* (raptor in the round)
VESSEL SHAPE: Subglobular bottle with simple base
PRESUMED SOURCE: Local

SE9   Mississippi Plain, *variety Warrior*
VESSEL SHAPE: Standard jar with 4 handles
PRESUMED SOURCE: Local

SE10   Mississippi Plain, *variety unspecified*
VESSEL SHAPE: Standard jar with 4 handles, nodes
PRESUMED SOURCE: Nonlocal

SE11   Bell Plain, *variety Hale*
VESSEL SHAPE: Simple bowl with beaded rim
PRESUMED SOURCE: Local

SE12   Mississippi Plain, *variety Warrior*
VESSEL SHAPE: Standard jar with 4 handles
PRESUMED SOURCE: Local

SE13   Moundville Engraved, *variety Tuscaloosa*
VESSEL SHAPE: Subglobular bottle with slab base, indentations
PRESUMED SOURCE: Local

NMNH CATALOG NO.: 377385

SE14   Bell Plain, *variety Hale*
VESSEL SHAPE: Simple bowl with beaded rim
PRESUMED SOURCE: Local

NMNH CATALOG NO.: 377403

SE16   Unclassified Engraved (paired tails)
        VESSEL SHAPE: Cylindrical bowl with rim
          strap, notched lip
        PRESUMED SOURCE: Nonlocal

SE18   Bell Plain, *variety unspecified*
        VESSEL SHAPE: High-shouldered bottle
        PRESUMED SOURCE: Central Mississippi Valley
          (Memphis region)
        GRAVELOT PROVENIENCE: Bu. 1342/SE

SE19   Bell Plain, *variety Hale*
        VESSEL SHAPE: Simple bowl with beaded rim
        PRESUMED SOURCE: Local
        GRAVELOT PROVENIENCE: Bu. 1342/SE
        NMNH CATALOG NO.: 377399

SE37   Bell Plain, *variety Hale*
        VESSEL SHAPE: Restricted bowl with effigy
          features—frog
        PRESUMED SOURCE: Local (questionable)

F3/M5   Moundville Engraved, *variety Hemphill* (bilobed
        arrow)
        VESSEL SHAPE: Subglobular bottle with
          pedestal base, indentations
        PRESUMED SOURCE: Local
        GRAVELOT PROVENIENCE: Bu. 6/F/M5
        PUBLISHED ILLUSTRATION: Moore 1905:Figures
          87-88
        MAI CATALOG NO.: 18/429

F4/M5   Moundville Engraved, *variety Hemphill* (bird tail)
        VESSEL SHAPE: Subglobular bottle with
          pedestal base
        PRESUMED SOURCE: Local
        PUBLISHED ILLUSTRATION: Moore 1905:Figures
          89-90
        MAI CATALOG NO.: 18/431

F6/M5   D'olive Incised, *variety unspecified*
        VESSEL SHAPE: Flaring-rim bowl with notched
          lip
        PRESUMED SOURCE: Gulf Coast (Mobile-Pensacola
          region)
        GRAVELOT PROVENIENCE: Bu. 11/F/M5
        PUBLISHED ILLUSTRATION: Moore 1905:Figure 92
        MAI CATALOG NO.: 17/3639

F10/M5 Moundville Engraved, *variety Hemphill* (human
        head)
        VESSEL SHAPE: Subglobular bottle with
          pedestal base
        PRESUMED SOURCE: Local (questionable)
        PUBLISHED ILLUSTRATION: Moore 1905:Figure 93

F12/M5 Carthage Incised, *variety Akron*
        VESSEL SHAPE: Simple bowl with effigy
          features—conch shell
        PRESUMED SOURCE: Local
        GRAVELOT PROVENIENCE: Bu. 16/F/M5
        PUBLISHED ILLUSTRATION: Moore 1905:Figure 94

F13/M5 Bell Plain, *variety Hale*
        VESSEL SHAPE: Cylindrical bottle
        PRESUMED SOURCE: Local (questionable)
        GRAVELOT PROVENIENCE: Bu. 17/F/M5
        PUBLISHED ILLUSTRATION: Moore 1905:Figure 96

F14/M5 Bell Plain, *variety unspecified*
        VESSEL SHAPE: High-shouldered bottle with
          lobate protrusions
        PRESUMED SOURCE: Central Mississippi Valley
        GRAVELOT PROVENIENCE: Bu. 2/F/M5
        PUBLISHED ILLUSTRATION: Moore 1905:Figure 97
        MAI CATALOG NO.: 18/424

F15/M5 Bell Plain, *variety Hale*
        VESSEL SHAPE: Subglobular bottle with simple
          base (flattened)
        PRESUMED SOURCE: Local (questionable)
        GRAVELOT PROVENIENCE: Bu. 18/F/M5
        PUBLISHED ILLUSTRATION: Moore 1905:Figure 98
        MAI CATALOG NO.: 17/4363

EF1   Mississippi Plain, *variety Warrior*
        VESSEL SHAPE: Undiagnostic fragment(s)
        PRESUMED SOURCE: Local
        GRAVELOT PROVENIENCE: Bu. 1692/EF

EF2   Moundville Engraved, *variety Northport*

        VESSEL SHAPE: Subglobular bottle with
          pedestal base
        PRESUMED SOURCE: Local
        GRAVELOT PROVENIENCE: Bu. 1692/EF

EF3   Bell Plain, *variety Hale*
        VESSEL SHAPE: Simple bowl with beaded rim
        PRESUMED SOURCE: Local
        GRAVELOT PROVENIENCE: Bu. 1693/EF

NG1   Bell Plain, *variety Hale*
        VESSEL SHAPE: Bowl with effigy features—
          mussel shell
        PRESUMED SOURCE: Local (questionable)

NG2   Bell Plain, *variety unspecified*
        VESSEL SHAPE: Restricted bowl with effigy
          features—frog
        PRESUMED SOURCE: Lower Tennessee-Cumberland
          area

NG3   Moundville Engraved, *variety Hemphill* (paired
        tails)
        VESSEL SHAPE: Cylindrical bowl with
          indentations
        PRESUMED SOURCE: Local
        GRAVELOT PROVENIENCE: Bu. 8/NG

NG4   Mississippi Plain, *variety Warrior*
        VESSEL SHAPE: Standard jar with 2 handles
        PRESUMED SOURCE: Local
        GRAVELOT PROVENIENCE: Bu. 21/NG

NG5   Carthage Incised, *variety Carthage*
        VESSEL SHAPE: Subglobular bottle with simple
          base
        PRESUMED SOURCE: Local
        GRAVELOT PROVENIENCE: Bu. 18/NG

NG6   Moundville Engraved, *variety Wiggins*
        VESSEL SHAPE: Subglobular bottle with simple
          base
        PRESUMED SOURCE: Local
        GRAVELOT PROVENIENCE: Bu. 18/NG

NG8   Moundville Engraved, *variety Tuscaloosa*
        VESSEL SHAPE: Subglobular bottle with
          pedestal base, indentations
        PRESUMED SOURCE: Local
        GRAVELOT PROVENIENCE: Bu. 8/NG

NG9   Bell Plain, *variety Hale*
        VESSEL SHAPE: Subglobular bottle with simple
          base (flattened)
        PRESUMED SOURCE: Local (questionable)
        GRAVELOT PROVENIENCE: Bu. 21/NG

NG10   Moundville Engraved, *variety Hemphill* (insect)
        VESSEL SHAPE: Subglobular bottle with simple
          base (flattened)
        PRESUMED SOURCE: Local
        GRAVELOT PROVENIENCE: Bu. 20/NG

NG11   Moundville Engraved, *variety Havana*
        VESSEL SHAPE: Restricted bowl (miniature)
        PRESUMED SOURCE: Local
        GRAVELOT PROVENIENCE: Bu. 3/NG

NG13   Bell Plain, *variety Hale*
        VESSEL SHAPE: Simple bowl with lug and rim
          effigy—bird (flat, inward-facing head)
        PRESUMED SOURCE: Local
        GRAVELOT PROVENIENCE: Bu. 3/NG

NG23   Bell Plain, *variety Hale*
        VESSEL SHAPE: Undiagnostic fragment(s) with
          pedestal base
        PRESUMED SOURCE: Local
        GRAVELOT PROVENIENCE: Bu. 3/NG

NG24   Bell Plain, *variety Hale*
        VESSEL SHAPE: Undiagnostic fragment(s) with
          beaded shoulder
        PRESUMED SOURCE: Local
        GRAVELOT PROVENIENCE: Bu. 3/NG

NG25   Moundville Engraved, *variety Hemphill* (windmill)
        VESSEL SHAPE: Subglobular bottle with simple
          base (flattened)
        PRESUMED SOURCE: Local
        GRAVELOT PROVENIENCE: Bu. 9/NG

NG30   Moundville Engraved, *variety Hemphill* (winged
        serpent)

VESSEL SHAPE: Subglobular bottle with simple
  base
PRESUMED SOURCE: Local
GRAVELOT PROVENIENCE: Bu. 1007/NG

NG31   Bell Plain, *variety Hale*
       VESSEL SHAPE: Flaring-rim bowl (deep)
       PRESUMED SOURCE: Local
       GRAVELOT PROVENIENCE: Bu. 1007/NG

NG32   Mississippi Plain, *variety Warrior*
       VESSEL SHAPE: Standard jar with 4 handles
       PRESUMED SOURCE: Local
       GRAVELOT PROVENIENCE: Bu. 1008/NG

NG39   Bell Plain, *variety Hale*
       VESSEL SHAPE: Simple bowl with single lug
       PRESUMED SOURCE: Local
       GRAVELOT PROVENIENCE: Bu. 1016/NG

NG44   Bell Plain, *variety unspecified*
       VESSEL SHAPE: Simple bowl with lug and rim
       effigy——human head
       PRESUMED SOURCE: Central Mississippi Valley
       GRAVELOT PROVENIENCE: Bu. 1017/NG

NG56   Bell Plain, *variety Hale*
       VESSEL SHAPE: Subglobular bottle with simple
       base
       PRESUMED SOURCE: Local
       NMNH CATALOG NO.: 377384

NG76   Bell Plain, *variety Hale*
       VESSEL SHAPE: Simple bowl with lug and rim
       effigy——(head missing)
       PRESUMED SOURCE: Local (questionable)

SG4   Mississippi Plain, *variety Warrior*
       VESSEL SHAPE: Undiagnostic fragment(s)
       PRESUMED SOURCE: Local
       GRAVELOT PROVENIENCE: Bu. 1707/SG

SG5   Mississippi Plain, *variety Warrior*
       VESSEL SHAPE: Undiagnostic fragment(s)
       PRESUMED SOURCE: Local
       GRAVELOT PROVENIENCE: Bu. 1708/SG

SG14   Mississippi Plain, *variety Warrior*
       VESSEL SHAPE: Standard jar
       PRESUMED SOURCE: Local
       GRAVELOT PROVENIENCE: Bu. 1732/SG

SG15   Mississippi Plain, *variety Warrior*
       VESSEL SHAPE: Standard jar with 4 handles
       PRESUMED SOURCE: Local
       GRAVELOT PROVENIENCE: Bu. 1735/SG
       NMNH CATALOG NO.: 377389

SG16   Moundville Engraved, *variety Taylorville*
       VESSEL SHAPE: Cylindrical bowl with single
       lug
       PRESUMED SOURCE: Local
       GRAVELOT PROVENIENCE: Bu. 1735/SG

SG23   Bell Plain, *variety Hale*
       VESSEL SHAPE: Bottle
       PRESUMED SOURCE: Local

SG24   Mississippi Plain, *variety Warrior*
       VESSEL SHAPE: Outslanting bowl
       PRESUMED SOURCE: Local
       GRAVELOT PROVENIENCE: Bu. 1786/SG

SG25   Bell Plain, *variety unspecified*
       VESSEL SHAPE: Hooded bottle with effigy
       features——human figure
       PRESUMED SOURCE: Central Mississippi Valley
       (Cairo Lowland)
       GRAVELOT PROVENIENCE: Bu. 1786/SG

SWG1   Mississippi Plain, *variety Warrior*
       VESSEL SHAPE: Standard jar with 4 handles
       PRESUMED SOURCE: Local
       GRAVELOT PROVENIENCE: Bu. 1717/SWG

SWG2   Moundville Engraved, *variety Hemphill* (radial
       fingers)
       VESSEL SHAPE: Restricted bowl
       PRESUMED SOURCE: Local
       GRAVELOT PROVENIENCE: Bu. 1717/SWG

SWG3   Moundville Engraved, *variety Hemphill* (scalp)
       VESSEL SHAPE: Cylindrical bowl with single
       lug

PRESUMED SOURCE: Local
GRAVELOT PROVENIENCE: Bu. 1717/SWG

SWG4   Mississippi Plain, *variety Warrior*
       VESSEL SHAPE: Standard jar with 4 handles
       PRESUMED SOURCE: Local
       GRAVELOT PROVENIENCE: Bu. 1717/SWG

SWG5   Mississippi Plain, *variety Warrior*
       VESSEL SHAPE: Standard jar with 8 handles
       PRESUMED SOURCE: Local
       GRAVELOT PROVENIENCE: Bu. 1717/SWG

SWG6   Moundville Engraved, *variety Wiggins*
       VESSEL SHAPE: Subglobular bottle with simple
       base
       PRESUMED SOURCE: Local
       GRAVELOT PROVENIENCE: Bu. 1718/SWG

SWG7   Mississippi Plain, *variety Warrior* (red-filmed
       interior)
       VESSEL SHAPE: Standard jar with more than 10
       handles
       PRESUMED SOURCE: Local
       GRAVELOT PROVENIENCE: Bu. 1718/SWG

SWG8   Carthage Incised, *variety Moon Lake*
       VESSEL SHAPE: Short-neck bowl
       PRESUMED SOURCE: Local
       GRAVELOT PROVENIENCE: Bu. 1720/SWG

SWG9   Carthage Incised, *variety Poole* (red on white)
       VESSEL SHAPE: Short-neck bowl
       PRESUMED SOURCE: Local
       GRAVELOT PROVENIENCE: Bu. 1725/SWG

SWG16   Leland Incised, *variety unspecified*
       VESSEL SHAPE: Cylindrical bottle
       PRESUMED SOURCE: Lower Mississippi Valley
       GRAVELOT PROVENIENCE: Bu. 1728/SWG

SWG17   Mississippi Plain, *variety Warrior*
       VESSEL SHAPE: Standard jar
       PRESUMED SOURCE: Local
       GRAVELOT PROVENIENCE: Bu. 1728/SWG

SWG21   Bell Plain, *variety unspecified*
       VESSEL SHAPE: Restricted bowl with grouped
       nodes
       PRESUMED SOURCE: Central Mississippi Valley,
       Lower Tennessee-Cumberland area, east
       Tennessee
       GRAVELOT PROVENIENCE: Bu. 1749/SWG

SWG23   Moundville Engraved, *variety Tuscaloosa*
       VESSEL SHAPE: Subglobular bottle with
       pedestal base, indentations
       PRESUMED SOURCE: Local
       GRAVELOT PROVENIENCE: Bu. 1748/SWG

SWG24   Moundville Engraved, *variety Hemphill* (paired
       tails)
       VESSEL SHAPE: Subglobular bottle with simple
       base
       PRESUMED SOURCE: Local
       GRAVELOT PROVENIENCE: Bu. 1751/SWG

SWG25   Mississippi Plain, *variety Warrior*
       VESSEL SHAPE: Standard jar with 4 handles
       PRESUMED SOURCE: Local
       GRAVELOT PROVENIENCE: Bu. 1751/SWG

SWG26   Mississippi Plain, *variety Warrior*
       VESSEL SHAPE: Standard jar with 4 handles
       PRESUMED SOURCE: Local
       GRAVELOT PROVENIENCE: Bu. 1754/SWG

SWG29   Mississippi Plain, *variety Warrior* (red-filmed
       interior)
       VESSEL SHAPE: Standard jar with appliqué neck
       fillets
       PRESUMED SOURCE: Local (questionable)
       GRAVELOT PROVENIENCE: Bu. 1758/SWG

SWG40   Mississippi Plain, *variety unspecified*
       VESSEL SHAPE: Standard jar with 2 handles,
       small horizontal lugs, effigy features——
       stylized frog
       PRESUMED SOURCE: Lower Tennessee-Cumberland
       area
       GRAVELOT PROVENIENCE: Bu. 1784/SWG

SWG41   Mississippi Plain, *variety Warrior*
       VESSEL SHAPE: Undiagnostic fragment(s)

PRESUMED SOURCE: Local
GRAVELOT PROVENIENCE: Bu. 1784/SWG

SWG44   Mississippi Plain, *variety Warrior*
          VESSEL SHAPE: Standard jar with 4 handles
          PRESUMED SOURCE: Local
          GRAVELOT PROVENIENCE: Bu. 1791/SWG

SWG45   Bell Plain, *variety unspecified*
          VESSEL SHAPE: Pedestaled bowl with widely
          spaced nodes
          PRESUMED SOURCE: Nonlocal
          GRAVELOT PROVENIENCE: Bu. 1795/SWG

SWG46   Bell Plain, *variety Hale*
          VESSEL SHAPE: Flaring-rim bowl (shallow)
          PRESUMED SOURCE: Local
          GRAVELOT PROVENIENCE: Bu. 1800/SWG

SWG47   Bell Plain, *variety Hale*
          VESSEL SHAPE: Simple bowl with effigy
          features—fish
          PRESUMED SOURCE: Local
          GRAVELOT PROVENIENCE: Bu. 1800/SWG

SWG49   Bell Plain, *variety Hale*
          VESSEL SHAPE: Subglobular bottle with simple
          base
          PRESUMED SOURCE: Local
          GRAVELOT PROVENIENCE: Bu. 1800/SWG

SWG52   Moundville Engraved, *variety Hemphill* (hand and
          eye)
          VESSEL SHAPE: Restricted bowl
          PRESUMED SOURCE: Local
          GRAVELOT PROVENIENCE: Bu. 1801/SWG

SWG55   Moundville Engraved, *variety Wiggins*
          VESSEL SHAPE: Subglobular bottle with simple
          base
          PRESUMED SOURCE: Local
          GRAVELOT PROVENIENCE: Bu. 1802/SWG

SWG58   Bell Plain, *variety Hale*
          VESSEL SHAPE: Cylindrical bowl with lug and
          rim effigy——(head missing)
          PRESUMED SOURCE: Local
          GRAVELOT PROVENIENCE: Bu. 1803/SWG

SWG62   Moundville Engraved, *variety Hemphill* (paired
          tails)
          VESSEL SHAPE: Subglobular bottle with simple
          base
          PRESUMED SOURCE: Local
          GRAVELOT PROVENIENCE: Bu. 1789/SWG

SWG63   Moundville Engraved, *variety Hemphill* (raptor in
          the round)
          VESSEL SHAPE: Subglobular bottle with simple
          base
          PRESUMED SOURCE: Local

          GRAVELOT PROVENIENCE: Bu. 1788/SWG

SWG66   Bell Plain, *variety Hale*
          VESSEL SHAPE: Simple bowl with beaded rim
          PRESUMED SOURCE: Local
          GRAVELOT PROVENIENCE: Bu. 1805/SWG

SWG67   Bell Plain, *variety Hale*
          VESSEL SHAPE: Double bowl with effigy
          features—mussel shell
          PRESUMED SOURCE: Local (questionable)
          GRAVELOT PROVENIENCE: Bu. 1805/SWG

H3/M5   Bell Plain, *variety Hale*
          VESSEL SHAPE: Subglobular bottle with
          pedestal base
          PRESUMED SOURCE: Local (questionable)
          PUBLISHED ILLUSTRATION: Moore 1905:Figure 100
          MAI CATALOG NO.: 17/3370

EH76   Unclassified Engraved (multilinear band at rim)
          VESSEL SHAPE: Restricted bowl
          PRESUMED SOURCE: Nonlocal
          GRAVELOT PROVENIENCE: Bu. 2617/EH

SEH5   Bell Plain, *variety Hale*
          VESSEL SHAPE: Simple bowl with beaded rim
          PRESUMED SOURCE: Local
          GRAVELOT PROVENIENCE: Bu. 10/SEH

SEH6   Bell Plain, *variety unspecified*

          VESSEL SHAPE: Simple bowl with notched
          everted lip
          PRESUMED SOURCE: Nonlocal

SEH7   Bell Plain, *variety Hale*
          VESSEL SHAPE: Simple bowl with beaded rim
          PRESUMED SOURCE: Local
          GRAVELOT PROVENIENCE: Bu. 19/SEH

SEH8   Mound Place Incised, *variety Mobile*
          VESSEL SHAPE: Cylindrical bowl
          PRESUMED SOURCE: Gulf Coast (Mobile-Pensacola
          region)

SEH9   Pensacola Incised, *variety Little Lagoon* (skull,
          forearm bones)
          VESSEL SHAPE: Cylindrical bowl
          PRESUMED SOURCE: Gulf Coast (Mobile-Pensacola
          region)

SEH10   Bell Plain, *variety Hale*
          VESSEL SHAPE: Burnished jar with 2 handles,
          beaded rim, widely spaced nodes
          PRESUMED SOURCE: Local (questionable)
          GRAVELOT PROVENIENCE: Bu. 18/SEH

SEH11   Mississippi Plain, *variety Warrior*
          VESSEL SHAPE: Standard jar with 4 handles
          PRESUMED SOURCE: Local
          GRAVELOT PROVENIENCE: Bu. 26/SEH

SEH14   Bell Plain, *variety unspecified*
          VESSEL SHAPE: High-shouldered bottle with
          lobate protrusions
          PRESUMED SOURCE: Lower Tennessee-Cumberland
          area
          GRAVELOT PROVENIENCE: Bu. 19/SEH

SEH15   Carthage Incised, *variety Carthage*
          VESSEL SHAPE: Subglobular bottle with simple
          base
          PRESUMED SOURCE: Local
          GRAVELOT PROVENIENCE: Bu. 18/SEH

SEH18   Bell Plain, *variety Hale*
          VESSEL SHAPE: Simple bowl with beaded rim
          PRESUMED SOURCE: Local

SEH19   Moundville Engraved, *variety unspecified*
          VESSEL SHAPE: Subglobular bottle with simple
          base
          PRESUMED SOURCE: Local

SEH20   Bell Plain, *variety Hale*
          VESSEL SHAPE: Subglobular bottle with simple
          base
          PRESUMED SOURCE: Local

SEH22   Mississippi Plain, *variety Warrior*
          VESSEL SHAPE: Standard jar with 4 handles
          PRESUMED SOURCE: Local

SEH45   Moundville Incised, *variety Carrollton*
          VESSEL SHAPE: Standard jar with handles
          PRESUMED SOURCE: Local
          GRAVELOT PROVENIENCE: Bu. 803/SEH

SEH71   Moundville Engraved, *variety Elliots Creek* (red
          engraved)
          VESSEL SHAPE: Simple bowl
          PRESUMED SOURCE: Local (questionable)
          GRAVELOT PROVENIENCE: Bu. 866/SEH

SEH72   Unclassified Plain (untempered)
          VESSEL SHAPE: Undiagnostic fragment(s)
          PRESUMED SOURCE: Local
          GRAVELOT PROVENIENCE: Bu. 869/SEH

SEH73   Moundville Engraved, *variety Hemphill* (crested
          bird in the round)
          VESSEL SHAPE: Subglobular bottle with simple
          base
          PRESUMED SOURCE: Local
          GRAVELOT PROVENIENCE: Bu. 869/SEH

SEH74   Moundville Engraved, *variety Hemphill* (paired
          tails)
          VESSEL SHAPE: Subglobular bottle with simple
          base
          PRESUMED SOURCE: Local
          GRAVELOT PROVENIENCE: Bu. 869/SEH

SEH75   Holly Fine Engraved
          VESSEL SHAPE: Rectanguloid bottle

PRESUMED SOURCE: Caddoan area
GRAVELOT PROVENIENCE: Bu. 870/SEH

SEH76   Moundville Incised, *variety Carrollton*
         VESSEL SHAPE: Standard jar with 2 handles
         PRESUMED SOURCE: Local (questionable)
         GRAVELOT PROVENIENCE: Bu. 870/SEH

SEH82   Bell Plain, *variety Hale*
         VESSEL SHAPE: Simple bowl with lug and rim
         effigy—bird (flat, outward-facing head)
         PRESUMED SOURCE: Local (questionable)

SEH83   Moundville Engraved, *variety Elliots Creek* (red
         engraved)
         VESSEL SHAPE: Restricted bowl with everted
         lip
         PRESUMED SOURCE: Local (questionable)

SEH85   Carthage Incised, *variety Summerville*
         VESSEL SHAPE: Restricted bowl
         PRESUMED SOURCE: Local

SEH86   Pensacola Incised, *variety Little Lagoon* (hand
         and eye)
         VESSEL SHAPE: Cylindrical bowl with rim strap
         PRESUMED SOURCE: Gulf Coast (Mobile-Pensacola
         region)
         GRAVELOT PROVENIENCE: Bu. 872/SEH

SEH87   Bell Plain, *variety Hale*
         VESSEL SHAPE: Subglobular bottle
         PRESUMED SOURCE: Local
         GRAVELOT PROVENIENCE: Bu. 872/SEH

SEH88   Bell Plain, *variety Hale*
         VESSEL SHAPE: Restricted bowl with effigy
         features—(distinctive features missing)
         PRESUMED SOURCE: Local
         GRAVELOT PROVENIENCE: Bu. 873/SEH

EI2   Moundville Engraved, *variety Havana*
         VESSEL SHAPE: Restricted bowl with band of
         nodes
         PRESUMED SOURCE: Local (questionable)

EI15   Moundville Engraved, *variety Taylorville*
         VESSEL SHAPE: Subglobular bottle with simple
         base
         PRESUMED SOURCE: Local
         GRAVELOT PROVENIENCE: Bu. 817/EI

EI16   Parkin Punctated, *variety unspecified*
         VESSEL SHAPE: Standard jar with 2 handles
         PRESUMED SOURCE: Central Mississippi Valley
         GRAVELOT PROVENIENCE: Bu. 817/EI

EI25   Bell Plain, *variety Hale*
         VESSEL SHAPE: Subglobular bottle with simple
         base
         PRESUMED SOURCE: Local
         GRAVELOT PROVENIENCE: Bu. 823/EI

EI26   Bell Plain, *variety Hale*
         VESSEL SHAPE: Subglobular bottle with simple
         base, indentations
         PRESUMED SOURCE: Local
         GRAVELOT PROVENIENCE: Bu. 824/EI

EI27   Mississippi Plain, *variety Warrior*
         VESSEL SHAPE: Standard jar with 2 handles
         PRESUMED SOURCE: Local
         GRAVELOT PROVENIENCE: Bu. 824/EI

EI30   Mississippi Plain, *variety Warrior*
         VESSEL SHAPE: Flaring-rim bowl (shallow)
         PRESUMED SOURCE: Local
         GRAVELOT PROVENIENCE: Bu. 831/EI

EI39   Carthage Incised, *variety Poole*
         VESSEL SHAPE: Short-neck bowl
         PRESUMED SOURCE: Local
         GRAVELOT PROVENIENCE: Bu. 843/EI

EI40   Mississippi Plain, *variety Warrior*
         VESSEL SHAPE: Standard jar with more than 10
         handles
         PRESUMED SOURCE: Local
         GRAVELOT PROVENIENCE: Bu. 843/EI

EI41   Carthage Incised, *variety Carthage*
         VESSEL SHAPE: Subglobular bottle with simple
         base
         PRESUMED SOURCE: Local
         GRAVELOT PROVENIENCE: Bu. 843/EI

EI42   Carthage Incised, *variety Akron*
         VESSEL SHAPE: Simple bowl with lug and rim
         effigy—bird (flat, inward-facing head)
         PRESUMED SOURCE: Local
         GRAVELOT PROVENIENCE: Bu. 839/EI

EI43   Carthage Incised, *variety Summerville*
         VESSEL SHAPE: Restricted bowl
         PRESUMED SOURCE: Local
         GRAVELOT PROVENIENCE: Bu. 839/EI

EI78   Moundville Engraved, *variety Wiggins*
         VESSEL SHAPE: Subglobular bottle with simple
         base
         PRESUMED SOURCE: Local
         GRAVELOT PROVENIENCE: Bu. 851/EI

EI95   Bell Plain, *variety Hale*
         VESSEL SHAPE: Simple bowl with beaded rim
         PRESUMED SOURCE: Local

SL1   Moundville Engraved, *variety Hemphill* (paired
         tails)
         VESSEL SHAPE: Subglobular bottle with slab
         base
         PRESUMED SOURCE: Local
         GRAVELOT PROVENIENCE: Bu. 3001/SL

SL2   Mound Place Incised, *variety Mobile*
         VESSEL SHAPE: Cylindrical bowl
         PRESUMED SOURCE: Gulf Coast (Mobile-Pensacola
         region)
         GRAVELOT PROVENIENCE: Bu. 3001/SL

SL3   Bell Plain, *variety Hale*
         VESSEL SHAPE: Double bowl with beaded rim
         PRESUMED SOURCE: Local (questionable)
         GRAVELOT PROVENIENCE: Bu. 3001/SL

SL21   Moundville Engraved, *variety Hemphill* (paired
         tails)
         VESSEL SHAPE: Subglobular bottle with simple
         base
         PRESUMED SOURCE: Local
         GRAVELOT PROVENIENCE: Bu. 3012/SL

SL24   Pensacola Incised, *variety Little Lagoon* (hand
         and eye)
         VESSEL SHAPE: Simple bowl
         PRESUMED SOURCE: Gulf Coast (Mobile-Pensacola
         region)
         GRAVELOT PROVENIENCE: Bu. 3014/SL

SL25   Moundville Engraved, *variety Tuscaloosa*
         VESSEL SHAPE: Subglobular bottle with simple
         base, indentations
         PRESUMED SOURCE: Local
         GRAVELOT PROVENIENCE: Bu. 3014/SL

SL27   Nashville Negative Painted, *variety unspecified*
         VESSEL SHAPE: Subglobular bottle with carafe
         neck
         PRESUMED SOURCE: Central Mississippi Valley
         (Cairo Lowland)
         GRAVELOT PROVENIENCE: Bu. 3015/SL

SL31   Moundville Engraved, *variety Hemphill* (winged
         serpent in the round)
         VESSEL SHAPE: Subglobular bottle with simple
         base
         PRESUMED SOURCE: Local
         GRAVELOT PROVENIENCE: Bu. 3014/SL

SL33   Bell Plain, *variety Hale*
         VESSEL SHAPE: Simple bowl with beaded rim
         PRESUMED SOURCE: Local
         GRAVELOT PROVENIENCE: Bu. 3020/SL

SL47   Mississippi Plain, *variety Warrior*
         VESSEL SHAPE: Standard jar with 4 handles
         PRESUMED SOURCE: Local
         GRAVELOT PROVENIENCE: Bu. 3026/SL

SL49   Bell Plain, *variety Hale*
         VESSEL SHAPE: Simple bowl with effigy
         features—fish
         PRESUMED SOURCE: Local (questionable)
         GRAVELOT PROVENIENCE: Bu. 3026/SL

SL56   Mississippi Plain, *variety Warrior*
         VESSEL SHAPE: Standard jar with 2 handles
         PRESUMED SOURCE: Local
         GRAVELOT PROVENIENCE: Bu. 3016/SL

SM28   Mississippi Plain, *variety unspecified*
         VESSEL SHAPE: Standard jar with 2 handles,
         small horizontal lugs, effigy features—
         stylized frog
         PRESUMED SOURCE: Lower Tennessee-Cumberland
         area
         GRAVELOT PROVENIENCE: Bu. 1033/SM

SM29   Matthews Incised, *variety Beckwith*
         VESSEL SHAPE: Standard jar with 2 handles
         PRESUMED SOURCE: Central Mississippi Valley
         (Cairo Lowland), Lower Tennessee-Cumberland
         area
         GRAVELOT PROVENIENCE: Bu. 1033/SM

SM30   Moundville Engraved, *variety Hemphill* (paired
         tails)
         VESSEL SHAPE: Cylindrical bowl with single
         lug
         PRESUMED SOURCE: Local
         GRAVELOT PROVENIENCE: Bu. 1033/SM

SWM14   Mississippi Plain, *variety Warrior*
         VESSEL SHAPE: Standard jar with more than 10
         handles
         PRESUMED SOURCE: Local (questionable)
         GRAVELOT PROVENIENCE: Bu. 895/SWM

SWM41   Bell Plain, *variety Hale*
         VESSEL SHAPE: Simple bowl
         PRESUMED SOURCE: Local
         GRAVELOT PROVENIENCE: Bu. 907/SWM

SWM42   Bell Plain, *variety Hale*
         VESSEL SHAPE: Flaring-rim bowl (shallow)
         PRESUMED SOURCE: Local
         GRAVELOT PROVENIENCE: Bu. 921/SWM

SWM87   Bell Plain, *variety Hale* (red on white)
         VESSEL SHAPE: Burnished jar with 2 handles,
         widely spaced nodes
         PRESUMED SOURCE: Local
         GRAVELOT PROVENIENCE: Bu. 947/SWM

SWM92   Unclassified Engraved (multilinear band at rim,
         crosshatched steps)
         VESSEL SHAPE: Restricted bowl
         PRESUMED SOURCE: Nonlocal

SWM93   Bell Plain, *variety Hale*
         VESSEL SHAPE: Subglobular bottle with slab
         base
         PRESUMED SOURCE: Local (questionable)
         GRAVELOT PROVENIENCE: Bu. 950/SWM

SWM94   Bell Plain, *variety Hale*
         VESSEL SHAPE: Simple bowl with lug and rim
         effigy—bird (flat, inward-facing head)
         PRESUMED SOURCE: Local
         GRAVELOT PROVENIENCE: Bu. 952/SWM

SWM95   Carthage Incised, *variety unspecified*
         VESSEL SHAPE: Cylindrical bowl with lug and
         rim effigy—unidentified mammal
         PRESUMED SOURCE: Local (questionable)
         GRAVELOT PROVENIENCE: Bu. 952/SWM

SWM131   Moundville Engraved, *variety Northport*
         VESSEL SHAPE: Subglobular bottle with
         pedestal base
         PRESUMED SOURCE: Local
         GRAVELOT PROVENIENCE: Bu. 961/SWM

SWM132   Moundville Engraved, *variety Taylorville*
         VESSEL SHAPE: Cylindrical bowl with single
         lug
         PRESUMED SOURCE: Local
         GRAVELOT PROVENIENCE: Bu. 961/SWM

SWM140   Moundville Engraved, *variety Northport*
         VESSEL SHAPE: Bottle with indentations
         PRESUMED SOURCE: Local
         GRAVELOT PROVENIENCE: Bu. 964/SWM

SWM141   Bell Plain, *variety Hale*
         VESSEL SHAPE: Subglobular bottle with
         pedestal base
         PRESUMED SOURCE: Local (questionable)
         GRAVELOT PROVENIENCE: Bu. 965/SWM

SWM142   Moundville Engraved, *variety Havana*
         VESSEL SHAPE: Cylindrical bowl with single
         lug

PRESUMED SOURCE: Local
GRAVELOT PROVENIENCE: Bu. 965/SWM

SWM166   Andrews Decorated, *variety unspecified*
         (multilinear bands at rim and base, crosshatched
         triangles)
         VESSEL SHAPE: Cylindrical bowl
         PRESUMED SOURCE: Lower Chattahoochee Valley
         GRAVELOT PROVENIENCE: Bu. 966B/SWM

SWM167   Bell Plain, *variety Hale*
         VESSEL SHAPE: Restricted bowl with notched
         everted lip
         PRESUMED SOURCE: Local (questionable)
         GRAVELOT PROVENIENCE: Bu. 967/SWM

SWM170   Moundville Engraved, *variety Havana*
         VESSEL SHAPE: Cylindrical bowl with single
         lug
         PRESUMED SOURCE: Local
         GRAVELOT PROVENIENCE: Bu. 969-70/SWM

SWM175   Bell Plain, *variety Hale*
         VESSEL SHAPE: Restricted bowl with band of
         nodes
         PRESUMED SOURCE: Local
         GRAVELOT PROVENIENCE: Bu. 971/SWM

SWM178   Bell Plain, *variety Hale*
         VESSEL SHAPE: Outslanting bowl with opposing
         lugs
         PRESUMED SOURCE: Local (questionable)

SWM180   Mississippi Plain, *variety Warrior*
         VESSEL SHAPE: Simple bowl with single lug
         PRESUMED SOURCE: Local
         GRAVELOT PROVENIENCE: Bu. 978/SWM

SWM181   Bell Plain, *variety Hale*
         VESSEL SHAPE: Restricted bowl
         PRESUMED SOURCE: Local
         GRAVELOT PROVENIENCE: Bu. 979/SWM

SWM183   Moundville Engraved, *variety Taylorville*
         VESSEL SHAPE: Subglobular bottle with simple
         base
         PRESUMED SOURCE: Local
         GRAVELOT PROVENIENCE: Bu. 981/SWM

SWM185   Moundville Engraved, *variety Hemphill* (winged
         serpent)
         VESSEL SHAPE: Subglobular bottle with simple
         base
         PRESUMED SOURCE: Local
         GRAVELOT PROVENIENCE: Bu. 983/SWM

SWM186   Bell Plain, *variety Hale*
         VESSEL SHAPE: Simple bowl with beaded rim
         PRESUMED SOURCE: Local
         GRAVELOT PROVENIENCE: Bu. 983/SWM

SWM188   Moundville Engraved, *variety Hemphill* (windmill)
         VESSEL SHAPE: Subglobular bottle with slab
         base, indentations
         PRESUMED SOURCE: Local

SWM189   Bell Plain, *variety Hale*
         VESSEL SHAPE: Subglobular bottle with
         pedestal base
         PRESUMED SOURCE: Local

SWM190   Carthage Incised, *variety Fosters* (hand and eye,
         forearm bones)
         VESSEL SHAPE: Flaring-rim bowl (deep)
         PRESUMED SOURCE: Local

SWM219   Mississippi Plain, *variety Warrior*
         VESSEL SHAPE: Standard jar with handles
         PRESUMED SOURCE: Local
         GRAVELOT PROVENIENCE: Bu. 1005/SWM

SWM220   Moundville Engraved, *variety Wiggins*
         VESSEL SHAPE: Subglobular bottle with simple
         base
         PRESUMED SOURCE: Local
         GRAVELOT PROVENIENCE: Bu. 1024/SWM

SWM222   Bell Plain, *variety Hale*
         VESSEL SHAPE: Restricted bowl
         PRESUMED SOURCE: Local
         GRAVELOT PROVENIENCE: Bu. 1147/SWM

SWM223   Bell Plain, *variety Hale*
         VESSEL SHAPE: Restricted bowl

PRESUMED SOURCE: Local
GRAVELOT PROVENIENCE: Bu. 1147/SWM

SWM226   Bell Plain, *variety Hale*
          VESSEL SHAPE: Simple bowl with single lug,
            expanded lip
          PRESUMED SOURCE: Local (questionable)
          GRAVELOT PROVENIENCE: Bu. 1149/SWM

SWM230   Mississippi Plain, *variety Warrior*
          VESSEL SHAPE: Standard jar with 8 handles
          PRESUMED SOURCE: Local
          GRAVELOT PROVENIENCE: Bu. 1151/SWM

SWM252   Bell Plain, *variety Hale*
          VESSEL SHAPE: Short-neck bowl
          PRESUMED SOURCE: Local
          GRAVELOT PROVENIENCE: Bu. 1160/SWM

SWM260   Bell Plain, *variety Hale*
          VESSEL SHAPE: Bottle
          PRESUMED SOURCE: Local (questionable)

SWM1/M7   Moundville Engraved, *variety Northport*
          VESSEL SHAPE: Subglobular bottle with
            pedestal base
          PRESUMED SOURCE: Local

          GRAVELOT PROVENIENCE: Bu. 9/SWM/M7
          PUBLISHED ILLUSTRATION: Moore 1907:Figure 47
          MAI CATALOG NO.: 17/3358

SWM2/M7   Moundville Engraved, *variety Taylorville*
          VESSEL SHAPE: Cylindrical bottle
          PRESUMED SOURCE: Local
          GRAVELOT PROVENIENCE: Bu. 9/SWM/M7
          PUBLISHED ILLUSTRATION: Moore 1907:Figure 19
          MAI CATALOG NO.: 17/3373

SWM2A/M7 Moundville Engraved, *variety unspecified*
          (multilinear band at rim)
          VESSEL SHAPE: Terraced rectanguloid bowl with
            lowered lip
          PRESUMED SOURCE: Local (questionable)
          GRAVELOT PROVENIENCE: Bu. 9/SWM/M7
          PUBLISHED ILLUSTRATION: Moore 1907:Figure 22
          MAI CATALOG NO.: 17/4404

SWM5/M7   Moundville Engraved, *variety Hemphill* (bilobed
          arrow, feathered arrow, Greek cross, rayed
          circle)
          VESSEL SHAPE: Bowl
          PRESUMED SOURCE: Local (questionable)
          GRAVELOT PROVENIENCE: Bu. 14/SWM/M7
          PUBLISHED ILLUSTRATION: Moore 1907:Figures
            39-40
          MAI CATALOG NO.: 18/421

SWM6/M7   Carthage Incised, *variety Carthage*
          VESSEL SHAPE: Subglobular bottle with simple
            base
          PRESUMED SOURCE: Local
          GRAVELOT PROVENIENCE: Bu. 22/SWM/M7
          PUBLISHED ILLUSTRATION: Moore 1907:Figure 73
          PUBLISHED DESCRIPTION: Moore 1907:379
          MAI CATALOG NO.: 17/3362

SWM15A/M7 Moundville Engraved, *variety Hemphill* (hand and
          eye, forearm bones)
          VESSEL SHAPE: Subglobular bottle with simple
            base
          PRESUMED SOURCE: Local
          PUBLISHED ILLUSTRATION: Moore 1907:Figure 46
          MAI CATALOG NO.: 17/4357

NN'2   Bell Plain, *variety Hale*
          VESSEL SHAPE: Simple bowl with beaded rim
          PRESUMED SOURCE: Local
          GRAVELOT PROVENIENCE: Bu. 1888/NN'

NN'3   Pensacola Incised, *variety Little Lagoon* (hand
          and eye)
          VESSEL SHAPE: Restricted bowl
          PRESUMED SOURCE: Gulf Coast (Mobile-Pensacola
            region)
          GRAVELOT PROVENIENCE: Bu. 1888/NN'

NN'4   Mississippi Plain, *variety Warrior*
          VESSEL SHAPE: Flaring-rim bowl (deep)
          PRESUMED SOURCE: Local (questionable)
          GRAVELOT PROVENIENCE: Bu. 1888/NN'

NN'12   Matthews Incised, *variety Beckwith*
          VESSEL SHAPE: Standard jar with 2 handles,

effigy features—stylized frog
PRESUMED SOURCE: Lower Tennessee-Cumberland
  area
GRAVELOT PROVENIENCE: Bu. 2125/NN'

NN'13   Mississippi Plain, *variety Warrior*
          VESSEL SHAPE: Standard jar (miniature) with 2
            handles
          PRESUMED SOURCE: Local
          GRAVELOT PROVENIENCE: Bu. 2125/NN'

NN'14   Bell Plain, *variety unspecified*
          VESSEL SHAPE: Stirrup-neck bottle
          PRESUMED SOURCE: Central Mississippi Valley
          GRAVELOT PROVENIENCE: Bu. 2125/NN'

NN'18   Moundville Engraved, *variety Hemphill* (winged
          serpent)
          VESSEL SHAPE: Subglobular bottle with simple
            base
          PRESUMED SOURCE: Local
          GRAVELOT PROVENIENCE: Bu. 2134/NN'

NN'19   Carthage Incised, *variety Akron*
          VESSEL SHAPE: Simple bowl
          PRESUMED SOURCE: Local (questionable)
          GRAVELOT PROVENIENCE: Bu. 2134/NN'

NN'38   Moundville Engraved, *variety Hemphill* (winged
          serpent)
          VESSEL SHAPE: Subglobular bottle with simple
            base
          PRESUMED SOURCE: Local
          GRAVELOT PROVENIENCE: Bu. 2136/NN'

NN'39   Mississippi Plain, *variety Warrior*
          VESSEL SHAPE: Standard jar with 4 handles,
            downturned lugs
          PRESUMED SOURCE: Local
          GRAVELOT PROVENIENCE: Bu. 2136/NN'

NN'40   Mississippi Plain, *variety unspecified*
          VESSEL SHAPE: Standard jar with 4 handles
          PRESUMED SOURCE: Nonlocal
          GRAVELOT PROVENIENCE: Bu. 2136/NN'

NN'41   Moundville Engraved, *variety Wiggins*
          VESSEL SHAPE: Subglobular bottle with simple
            base, indentations
          PRESUMED SOURCE: Local
          GRAVELOT PROVENIENCE: Bu. 2136/NN'

WN1   Moundville Engraved, *variety unspecified*
          VESSEL SHAPE: Subglobular bottle with slab
            base
          PRESUMED SOURCE: Local (questionable)
          GRAVELOT PROVENIENCE: Bu. 1683/WN

WN1/M7   Bell Plain, *variety unspecified*
          VESSEL SHAPE: Restricted bowl with effigy
            features—frog
          PRESUMED SOURCE: Nonlocal
          GRAVELOT PROVENIENCE: Bu. 1/WN/M7
          PUBLISHED ILLUSTRATION: Moore 1907:Figure 29
          MAI CATALOG NO.: 17/4400

03/M5   Mississippi Plain, *variety Warrior*
          VESSEL SHAPE: Simple bowl with effigy
            features—unidentified
          PRESUMED SOURCE: Local (questionable)
          GRAVELOT PROVENIENCE: Bu. 7/0/M5
          PUBLISHED ILLUSTRATION: Moore 1905:Figure 108

05/M5   Moundville Engraved, *variety Maxwells Crossing*
          (crosshatched vertical bands)
          VESSEL SHAPE: Subglobular bottle with slab
            base
          PRESUMED SOURCE: Local
          GRAVELOT PROVENIENCE: Bu. 9/0/M5
          PUBLISHED ILLUSTRATION: Moore 1905:Figure 109
          MAI CATALOG NO.: 18/430

06/M5   Moundville Engraved, *variety Hemphill* (paired
          tails)
          VESSEL SHAPE: Subglobular bottle with slab
            base
          PRESUMED SOURCE: Local
          GRAVELOT PROVENIENCE: Bu. 14/0/M5
          PUBLISHED ILLUSTRATION: Moore 1905:Figures
            112-113
          MAI CATALOG NO.: 17/3363

09/M5   Moundville Engraved, *variety Hemphill* (raptor

head with wing)
  VESSEL SHAPE: Subglobular bottle with slab
   base
  PRESUMED SOURCE: Local
  GRAVELOT PROVENIENCE: Bu. 19/0/M5
  PUBLISHED ILLUSTRATION: Moore 1905:Figures
   114-115
  MAI CATALOG NO.: 17/3339

010/M5 Moundville Engraved, *variety Hemphill* (paired
  tails)
   VESSEL SHAPE: Subglobular bottle with slab
    base
   PRESUMED SOURCE: Local
   GRAVELOT PROVENIENCE: Bu. 21/0/M5
   PUBLISHED ILLUSTRATION: Moore 1905:Figures
    117-118
   MAI CATALOG NO.: 17/3359

014/M5 Moundville Engraved, *variety Tuscaloosa*
   VESSEL SHAPE: Subglobular bottle with slab
    base, indentations
   PRESUMED SOURCE: Local
   GRAVELOT PROVENIENCE: F.1/0/M5
   PUBLISHED ILLUSTRATION: Moore 1905:Figure 119
   MAI CATALOG NO.: 18/426

015/M5 Moundville Engraved, *variety Havana*
   VESSEL SHAPE: Cylindrical bowl with single
    lug
   PRESUMED SOURCE: Local
   GRAVELOT PROVENIENCE: F.1/0/M5
   PUBLISHED ILLUSTRATION: Moore 1905:Figure 120
   MAI CATALOG NO.: 17/4387

016/M5 Moundville Engraved, *variety Hemphill* (ogee)
   VESSEL SHAPE: Subglobular bottle with
    pedestal base
   PRESUMED SOURCE: Local
   PUBLISHED ILLUSTRATION: Moore 1905:Figures
    121-122
   MAI CATALOG NO.: 18/440

018/M5 Moundville Engraved, *variety Hemphill* (hand and
  eye)
   VESSEL SHAPE: Subglobular bottle with slab
    base
   PRESUMED SOURCE: Local
   GRAVELOT PROVENIENCE: F.2/0/M5
   PUBLISHED ILLUSTRATION: Moore 1905:Figure 123
   MAI CATALOG NO.: 17/3352

019/M5 Moundville Engraved, *variety Wiggins*
   VESSEL SHAPE: Cylindrical bowl with single
    lug
   PRESUMED SOURCE: Local
   GRAVELOT PROVENIENCE: F.2/0/M5
   PUBLISHED ILLUSTRATION: Moore 1905:Figure 124

020/M5 Moundville Engraved, *variety Hemphill* (radial
  fingers)
   VESSEL SHAPE: Subglobular bottle with slab
    base
   PRESUMED SOURCE: Local
   PUBLISHED ILLUSTRATION: Moore 1905:Figures
    125-126
   MAI CATALOG NO.: 17/3346

026/M5 Unclassified Incised
   VESSEL SHAPE: Collared bottle with narrow
    neck, pedestal base
   PRESUMED SOURCE: Nonlocal
   GRAVELOT PROVENIENCE: Bu. 29/0/M5
   PUBLISHED ILLUSTRATION: Moore 1905:Figure 128
   MAI CATALOG NO.: 17/3380

027/M5 Bell Plain, *variety Hale*
   VESSEL SHAPE: Slender ovoid bottle with
    pedestal base
   PRESUMED SOURCE: Local
   PUBLISHED ILLUSTRATION: Moore 1905:Figure 129

028/M5 Bell Plain, *variety Hale*
   VESSEL SHAPE: Slender ovoid bottle with
    pedestal base
   PRESUMED SOURCE: Local
   GRAVELOT PROVENIENCE: F.3/0/M5
   PUBLISHED ILLUSTRATION: Moore 1905:Figure 130

031/M5 Moundville Engraved, *variety Taylorville*
   VESSEL SHAPE: Cylindrical bowl with single
    lug
   PRESUMED SOURCE: Local

   GRAVELOT PROVENIENCE: Bu. 39/0/M5
   PUBLISHED ILLUSTRATION: Moore 1905:Figure 133
   MAI CATALOG NO.: 17/4392

033/M5 Moundville Engraved, *variety Havana*
   VESSEL SHAPE: Simple bowl with widely spaced
    nodes
   PRESUMED SOURCE: Local (questionable)
   GRAVELOT PROVENIENCE: Local
   PUBLISHED DESCRIPTION: Moore 1905:217
   MAI CATALOG NO.: 18/415

037/M5 Bell Plain, *variety Hale*
   VESSEL SHAPE: Pedestaled bowl with lowered
    lip, noded rim
   PRESUMED SOURCE: Local (questionable)
   PUBLISHED ILLUSTRATION: Moore 1905:Figure 135
   MAI CATALOG NO.: 17/4375

E01/M5 Unclassified Engraved
   VESSEL SHAPE: Bowl
   PRESUMED SOURCE: Nonlocal
   GRAVELOT PROVENIENCE: Bu. 1/E0/M5
   PUBLISHED ILLUSTRATION: Moore 1905:Figure 136
   MAI CATALOG NO.: 17/4372

WP16 Bell Plain, *variety Hale*
   VESSEL SHAPE: Simple bowl with grouped nodes
   PRESUMED SOURCE: Local

WP19 Mississippi Plain, *variety Warrior*
   VESSEL SHAPE: Standard jar with 2 handles
   PRESUMED SOURCE: Local (questionable)
   GRAVELOT PROVENIENCE: Bu. 2179/WP

WP20 Mississippi Plain, *variety Warrior*
   VESSEL SHAPE: Standard jar with 2 handles
   PRESUMED SOURCE: Local
   GRAVELOT PROVENIENCE: Bu. 2179/WP

WP21 Moundville Incised, *variety Moundville*
   VESSEL SHAPE: Standard jar with 4 handles
   PRESUMED SOURCE: Local
   GRAVELOT PROVENIENCE: Bu. 2179/WP

WP22 Bell Plain, *variety Hale*
   VESSEL SHAPE: Bowl with effigy features—
    mussel shell
   PRESUMED SOURCE: Local
   GRAVELOT PROVENIENCE: Bu. 2180/WP

WP23 Bell Plain, *variety Hale*
   VESSEL SHAPE: Restricted bowl
   PRESUMED SOURCE: Local
   GRAVELOT PROVENIENCE: Bu. 2180/WP

WP27 Bell Plain, *variety Hale*
   VESSEL SHAPE: Subglobular bottle with simple
    base
   PRESUMED SOURCE: Local (questionable)
   GRAVELOT PROVENIENCE: Bu. 2185/WP

WP28 Bell Plain, *variety Hale*
   VESSEL SHAPE: Simple bowl (miniature)
   PRESUMED SOURCE: Local
   GRAVELOT PROVENIENCE: Bu. 2185/WP

WP29 Carthage Incised, *variety Carthage*
   VESSEL SHAPE: Short-neck bowl
   PRESUMED SOURCE: Local
   GRAVELOT PROVENIENCE: Bu. 2187/WP

WP30 Moundville Incised, *variety Snows Bend*
   VESSEL SHAPE: Standard jar with 4 handles,
    widely spaced nodes
   PRESUMED SOURCE: Local (questionable)

WP32 Moundville Engraved, *variety Havana*
   VESSEL SHAPE: Simple bowl
   PRESUMED SOURCE: Local (questionable)

WP47 Moundville Engraved, *variety Havana*
   VESSEL SHAPE: Bowl (miniature)
   PRESUMED SOURCE: Local (questionable)
   GRAVELOT PROVENIENCE: Bu. 2223/WP

WP52 Moundville Engraved, *variety Havana*
   VESSEL SHAPE: Restricted bowl with effigy
    features—fish
   PRESUMED SOURCE: Local
   GRAVELOT PROVENIENCE: Bu. 2211/WP

WP61 Moundville Engraved, *variety Elliots Creek*

VESSEL SHAPE:　Slender ovoid bottle with
　pedestal base
PRESUMED SOURCE:　Local
GRAVELOT PROVENIENCE:　Bu. 2282/WP

WP65　Moundville Engraved, *variety Prince Plantation*
　VESSEL SHAPE:　Subglobular bottle with slab
　　base
　PRESUMED SOURCE:　Local
　GRAVELOT PROVENIENCE:　Bu. 2326/WP

WP67　Bell Plain, *variety Hale*
　VESSEL SHAPE:　Subglobular bottle with slab
　　base
　PRESUMED SOURCE:　Local
　GRAVELOT PROVENIENCE:　Bu. 2289/WP

WP71　Moundville Engraved, *variety Havana*
　VESSEL SHAPE:　Double bowl (cylindrical)
　PRESUMED SOURCE:　Local

WP72　Bell Plain, *variety Hale*
　VESSEL SHAPE:　Burnished jar (miniature) with
　　2 handles, effigy features—frog
　PRESUMED SOURCE:　Local
　GRAVELOT PROVENIENCE:　Bu. 2258/WP

WP73　Bell Plain, *variety Hale*
　VESSEL SHAPE:　Pedestaled bowl with notched
　　everted lip, lowered lip
　PRESUMED SOURCE:　Local

WP83　Carthage Incised, *variety Carthage*
　VESSEL SHAPE:　Subglobular bottle with simple
　　base
　PRESUMED SOURCE:　Local
　GRAVELOT PROVENIENCE:　Bu. 2314/WP

WP85　Carthage Incised, *variety Carthage*
　VESSEL SHAPE:　Subglobular bottle with simple
　　base
　PRESUMED SOURCE:　Local
　GRAVELOT PROVENIENCE:　Bu. 2317/WP

WP94　Bell Plain, *variety Hale*
　VESSEL SHAPE:　Restricted bowl
　PRESUMED SOURCE:　Local
　GRAVELOT PROVENIENCE:　Bu. 2354/WP

WP96　Unclassified Plain (untempered)
　VESSEL SHAPE:　Standard jar with no handles
　PRESUMED SOURCE:　Local
　GRAVELOT PROVENIENCE:　Bu. 2208/WP

WP104　Mississippi Plain, *variety Warrior*
　VESSEL SHAPE:　Standard jar with 4 handles
　PRESUMED SOURCE:　Local (questionable)
　GRAVELOT PROVENIENCE:　Bu. 2447/WP

WP119　Moundville Engraved, *variety Northport*
　VESSEL SHAPE:　Subglobular bottle with
　　pedestal base
　PRESUMED SOURCE:　Local
　GRAVELOT PROVENIENCE:　Bu. 2421/WP

WP121　Carthage Incised, *variety Carthage*
　VESSEL SHAPE:　Flaring-rim bowl (deep)
　PRESUMED SOURCE:　Local
　GRAVELOT PROVENIENCE:　Bu. 2417/WP

WP122　Carthage Incised, *variety Fosters* (hand and eye,
　forearm bones, red on white)
　VESSEL SHAPE:　Short-neck bowl
　PRESUMED SOURCE:　Local
　GRAVELOT PROVENIENCE:　Bu. 2417/WP

WP135　Mississippi Plain, *variety Warrior*
　VESSEL SHAPE:　Flaring-rim bowl (shallow)
　PRESUMED SOURCE:　Local
　GRAVELOT PROVENIENCE:　Bu. 2436/WP

WP149　Bell Plain, *variety Hale*
　VESSEL SHAPE:　Slender ovoid bottle with
　　pedestal base
　PRESUMED SOURCE:　Local
　GRAVELOT PROVENIENCE:　Bu. 2530/WP

WP152　Bell Plain, *variety Hale*
　VESSEL SHAPE:　Slender ovoid bottle with
　　pedestal base
　PRESUMED SOURCE:　Local
　GRAVELOT PROVENIENCE:　Bu. 2532/WP

WP153　Carthage Incised, *variety unspecified*

VESSEL SHAPE:　Simple bowl with lug and rim
　effigy—bird (head missing)
PRESUMED SOURCE:　Local (questionable)
GRAVELOT PROVENIENCE:　Bu. 2532/WP

WP156　Bell Plain, *variety Hale*
　VESSEL SHAPE:　Subglobular bottle
　PRESUMED SOURCE:　Local (questionable)
　GRAVELOT PROVENIENCE:　Bu. 2532/WP

WP158　Bell Plain, *variety Hale*
　VESSEL SHAPE:　Subglobular bottle with
　　pedestal base
　PRESUMED SOURCE:　Local
　GRAVELOT PROVENIENCE:　Bu. 2538/WP

WP159　Bell Plain, *variety Hale*
　VESSEL SHAPE:　Subglobular bottle with simple
　　base (flattened)
　PRESUMED SOURCE:　Local (questionable)
　GRAVELOT PROVENIENCE:　Bu. 2540/WP

WP160　Carthage Incised, *variety Akron*
　VESSEL SHAPE:　Simple bowl with lug and rim
　　effigy—unidentified mammal
　PRESUMED SOURCE:　Local (questionable)
　GRAVELOT PROVENIENCE:　Bu. 2544/WP

WP161　Bell Plain, *variety Hale*
　VESSEL SHAPE:　Slender ovoid bottle with
　　pedestal base
　PRESUMED SOURCE:　Local
　GRAVELOT PROVENIENCE:　Bu. 2544/WP

WP165　Carthage Incised, *variety Akron*
　VESSEL SHAPE:　Simple bowl with lug and rim
　　effigy—(head missing)
　PRESUMED SOURCE:　Local
　GRAVELOT PROVENIENCE:　Bu. 2545/WP

WP170　Mississippi Plain, *variety Warrior*
　VESSEL SHAPE:　Undiagnostic fragment(s)
　PRESUMED SOURCE:　Local
　GRAVELOT PROVENIENCE:　Bu. 2550/WP

WP171　Bell Plain, *variety Hale*
　VESSEL SHAPE:　Subglobular bottle with
　　pedestal base
　PRESUMED SOURCE:　Local
　GRAVELOT PROVENIENCE:　Bu. 2550/WP

WP173　Mississippi Plain, *variety Warrior*
　VESSEL SHAPE:　Standard jar
　PRESUMED SOURCE:　Local
　GRAVELOT PROVENIENCE:　Bu. 2550/WP

WP186　Bell Plain, *variety Hale*
　VESSEL SHAPE:　Subglobular bottle with
　　pedestal base
　PRESUMED SOURCE:　Local (questionable)
　GRAVELOT PROVENIENCE:　Bu. 2553/WP

WP187　Moundville Engraved, *variety Havana*
　VESSEL SHAPE:　Simple bowl
　PRESUMED SOURCE:　Local
　GRAVELOT PROVENIENCE:　Bu. 2553/WP

WP207　Mississippi Plain, *variety Warrior*
　VESSEL SHAPE:　Standard jar with 4 handles
　PRESUMED SOURCE:　Local
　GRAVELOT PROVENIENCE:　Bu. 2555/WP

WP208　Moundville Engraved, *variety Hemphill* (hand and
　eye)
　VESSEL SHAPE:　Subglobular bottle with simple
　　base
　PRESUMED SOURCE:　Local
　GRAVELOT PROVENIENCE:　Bu. 2558/WP

WP212　Carthage Incised, *variety Akron*
　VESSEL SHAPE:　Simple bowl with lug and rim
　　effigy—bird (flat, inward-facing head)
　PRESUMED SOURCE:　Local
　GRAVELOT PROVENIENCE:　Bu. 2559/WP

WP213　Bell Plain, *variety Hale*
　VESSEL SHAPE:　Slender ovoid bottle with
　　pedestal base
　PRESUMED SOURCE:　Local
　GRAVELOT PROVENIENCE:　Bu. 2559/WP

WP214　Bell Plain, *variety Hale*
　VESSEL SHAPE:　Slender ovoid bottle with
　　pedestal base

PRESUMED SOURCE: Local
GRAVELOT PROVENIENCE: Bu. 2560/WP

WP215   Moundville Engraved, *variety Northport*
     VESSEL SHAPE: Subglobular bottle with
     pedestal base
     PRESUMED SOURCE: Local
     GRAVELOT PROVENIENCE: Bu. 2560/WP

WP216   Bell Plain, *variety Hale*
     VESSEL SHAPE: Slender ovoid bottle with
     pedestal base
     PRESUMED SOURCE: Local
     GRAVELOT PROVENIENCE: Bu. 2562/WP

WP217   Carthage Incised, *variety Akron*
     VESSEL SHAPE: Simple bowl with effigy
     features—conch shell
     PRESUMED SOURCE: Local
     GRAVELOT PROVENIENCE: Bu. 2562/WP

WP218   Moundville Engraved, *variety unspecified*
     VESSEL SHAPE: Simple bowl with lug and rim
     effigy—bird (head missing)
     PRESUMED SOURCE: Local (questionable)
     GRAVELOT PROVENIENCE: Bu. 2562/WP

WP221   Mississippi Plain, *variety Warrior*
     VESSEL SHAPE: Standard jar with 2 handles
     PRESUMED SOURCE: Local
     GRAVELOT PROVENIENCE: Bu. 2471/WP

WP223   Mississippi Plain, *variety Warrior*
     VESSEL SHAPE: Standard jar with 2 handles
     PRESUMED SOURCE: Local
     GRAVELOT PROVENIENCE: Bu. 2476/WP

WP228   Mississippi Plain, *variety Warrior*
     VESSEL SHAPE: Standard jar with 2 handles
     PRESUMED SOURCE: Local
     GRAVELOT PROVENIENCE: Bu. 2496/WP

WP229   Bell Plain, *variety unspecified*
     VESSEL SHAPE: Bowl with double lip
     PRESUMED SOURCE: Nonlocal
     GRAVELOT PROVENIENCE: Bu. 2496/WP

WP230   Moundville Engraved, *variety Taylorville*
     VESSEL SHAPE: Subglobular bottle with simple
     base
     PRESUMED SOURCE: Local
     GRAVELOT PROVENIENCE: Bu. 2496/WP

WP258   Mississippi Plain, *variety Warrior*
     VESSEL SHAPE: Flaring-rim bowl (shallow)
     PRESUMED SOURCE: Local
     GRAVELOT PROVENIENCE: Bu. 2635/WP

WP259   Carthage Incised, *variety Carthage*
     VESSEL SHAPE: Cylindrical bowl
     PRESUMED SOURCE: Local (questionable)
     GRAVELOT PROVENIENCE: Bu. 2636/WP

WP260   Bell Plain, *variety Hale*
     VESSEL SHAPE: Bowl
     PRESUMED SOURCE: Local (questionable)
     GRAVELOT PROVENIENCE: Bu. 2636/WP

WP264   Bell Plain, *variety Hale*
     VESSEL SHAPE: Flaring-rim bowl (deep)
     PRESUMED SOURCE: Local
     GRAVELOT PROVENIENCE: Bu. 2640-41/WP

WP269   Bell Plain, *variety Hale*
     VESSEL SHAPE: Subglobular bottle with
     pedestal base
     PRESUMED SOURCE: Local

WP'19   Moundville Engraved, *variety Hemphill* (winged
     serpent)
     VESSEL SHAPE: Subglobular bottle with simple
     base
     PRESUMED SOURCE: Local
     GRAVELOT PROVENIENCE: Bu. 2152-54/WP'

WP'29   Bell Plain, *variety Hale*
     VESSEL SHAPE: Burnished jar with 2 handles,
     effigy features—frog
     PRESUMED SOURCE: Local
     GRAVELOT PROVENIENCE: Bu. 2166/WP'

WP'30   Moundville Engraved, *variety Hemphill* (raptor)
     VESSEL SHAPE: Subglobular bottle with slab
     base

PRESUMED SOURCE: Local
GRAVELOT PROVENIENCE: Bu. 2165/WP'

WP'32   Bell Plain, *variety Hale*
     VESSEL SHAPE: Simple bowl with beaded rim
     PRESUMED SOURCE: Local
     GRAVELOT PROVENIENCE: Bu. 2137/WP'

WP'34   Bell Plain, *variety Hale*
     VESSEL SHAPE: Simple bowl with effigy
     features—fish
     PRESUMED SOURCE: Local
     GRAVELOT PROVENIENCE: Bu. 2137/WP'

WP'39   Moundville Engraved, *variety Hemphill* (hand and
     eye)
     VESSEL SHAPE: Subglobular bottle with simple
     base (flattened)
     PRESUMED SOURCE: Local
     GRAVELOT PROVENIENCE: Bu. 2171/WP'

NQ1/M5   Moundville Incised, *variety Carrollton*
     VESSEL SHAPE: Standard jar with 2 handles,
     lobate protrusions
     PRESUMED SOURCE: Local
     GRAVELOT PROVENIENCE: Bu. 1/NQ/M5
     PUBLISHED ILLUSTRATION: Moore 1905:Figure 140
     MAI CATALOG NO.: 17/4380

NR5   Bell Plain, *variety Hale*
     VESSEL SHAPE: Tall cylindrical vessel
     PRESUMED SOURCE: Local (questionable)

NR7   Alabama River Incised, *variety unspecified*
     VESSEL SHAPE: Standard jar with appliqué neck
     fillets
     PRESUMED SOURCE: Local (questionable)
     GRAVELOT PROVENIENCE: Bu. 12/NR

NR9   Moundville Engraved, *variety Havana*
     VESSEL SHAPE: Cylindrical bowl
     PRESUMED SOURCE: Local (questionable)
     GRAVELOT PROVENIENCE: Bu. 1083/NR

NR20   Bell Plain, *variety Hale*
     VESSEL SHAPE: Subglobular bottle with simple
     base, effigy features—frog
     PRESUMED SOURCE: Local (questionable)
     GRAVELOT PROVENIENCE: Bu. 1086/NR

NR21   Bell Plain, *variety Hale*
     VESSEL SHAPE: Subglobular bottle with simple
     base
     PRESUMED SOURCE: Local
     GRAVELOT PROVENIENCE: Bu. 1086/NR

NR23   Bell Plain, *variety Hale*
     VESSEL SHAPE: Subglobular bottle with simple
     base
     PRESUMED SOURCE: Local (questionable)
     GRAVELOT PROVENIENCE: Bu. 1087/NR

NR24   Moundville Engraved, *variety Wiggins*
     VESSEL SHAPE: Cylindrical bowl
     PRESUMED SOURCE: Local
     GRAVELOT PROVENIENCE: Bu. 1088/NR

NR25   Moundville Engraved, *variety Hemphill* (skull,
     forearm bones)
     VESSEL SHAPE: Cylindrical bottle
     PRESUMED SOURCE: Local (questionable)
     GRAVELOT PROVENIENCE: Bu. 1088/NR

NR27   Mississippi Plain, *variety Warrior*
     VESSEL SHAPE: Standard jar with 4 handles
     PRESUMED SOURCE: Local
     GRAVELOT PROVENIENCE: Bu. 1089/NR

NR28   Mississippi Plain, *variety Warrior*
     VESSEL SHAPE: Standard jar with 4 handles
     PRESUMED SOURCE: Local
     GRAVELOT PROVENIENCE: Bu. 1089/NR

NR38   Moundville Engraved, *variety Hemphill* (hand and
     eye, scalp)
     VESSEL SHAPE: Subglobular bottle with simple
     base
     PRESUMED SOURCE: Local
     GRAVELOT PROVENIENCE: Bu. 1094-96/NR

NR40   Moundville Engraved, *variety Wiggins*
     VESSEL SHAPE: Subglobular bottle with simple
     base, indentations

PRESUMED SOURCE: Local
GRAVELOT PROVENIENCE: Bu. 1087/NR

NR41 Mississippi Plain, *variety Warrior*
    VESSEL SHAPE: Standard jar with 2 handles
    PRESUMED SOURCE: Local
    GRAVELOT PROVENIENCE: Bu. 1098/NR

NR42 Mississippi Plain, *variety Warrior*
    VESSEL SHAPE: Standard jar
    PRESUMED SOURCE: Local
    GRAVELOT PROVENIENCE: Bu. 1098/NR

NR43 Carthage Incised, *variety Akron*
    VESSEL SHAPE: Simple bowl with lug and rim
    effigy—bird (flat, outward-facing head)
    PRESUMED SOURCE: Local (questionable)
    GRAVELOT PROVENIENCE: Bu. 1099/NR

NR44 Carthage Incised, *variety Akron*
    VESSEL SHAPE: Simple bowl with lug and rim
    effigy—bird (gracile, outward-facing head)
    PRESUMED SOURCE: Local (questionable)
    GRAVELOT PROVENIENCE: Bu. 1100/NR

NR46 Carthage Incised, *variety Akron*
    VESSEL SHAPE: Simple bowl with lug and rim
    effigy—(head missing)
    PRESUMED SOURCE: Local
    GRAVELOT PROVENIENCE: Bu. 1101/NR

NR47 Bell Plain, *variety Hale*
    VESSEL SHAPE: Subglobular bottle with simple
    base
    PRESUMED SOURCE: Local (questionable)
    GRAVELOT PROVENIENCE: Bu. 1101/NR

NR96 Mississippi Plain, *variety Warrior*
    VESSEL SHAPE: Standard jar with 8 handles
    PRESUMED SOURCE: Local
    GRAVELOT PROVENIENCE: Bu. 1102/NR

NR97 Carthage Incised, *variety Akron*
    VESSEL SHAPE: Simple bowl with lug and rim
    effigy—bird (gracile, outward-facing head)
    PRESUMED SOURCE: Local (questionable)
    GRAVELOT PROVENIENCE: Bu. 1102/NR

NR98 Moundville Engraved, *variety Tuscaloosa*
    VESSEL SHAPE: Subglobular bottle with slab
    base, indentations
    PRESUMED SOURCE: Local
    GRAVELOT PROVENIENCE: Bu. 1087/NR

NR99 Moundville Engraved, *variety Hemphill* (serpent)
    VESSEL SHAPE: Subglobular bottle with simple
    base
    PRESUMED SOURCE: Local
    GRAVELOT PROVENIENCE: Bu. 1103/NR

NR100 Moundville Engraved, *variety Northport*
    VESSEL SHAPE: Subglobular bottle with
    pedestal base, indentations
    PRESUMED SOURCE: Local
    GRAVELOT PROVENIENCE: Bu. 1104/NR

NR101 Carthage Incised, *variety Akron*
    VESSEL SHAPE: Simple bowl with lug and rim
    effigy—(head missing)
    PRESUMED SOURCE: Local
    GRAVELOT PROVENIENCE: Bu. 1104/NR

NR102 Bell Plain, *variety Hale*
    VESSEL SHAPE: Simple bowl with lug and rim
    effigy—(head missing)
    PRESUMED SOURCE: Local
    GRAVELOT PROVENIENCE: Bu. 1105/NR

NR106 Mississippi Plain, *variety Warrior*
    VESSEL SHAPE: Simple bowl with grouped nodes
    PRESUMED SOURCE: Local (questionable)
    GRAVELOT PROVENIENCE: Bu. 1109/NR

NR107 Plaquemine Brushed, *variety unspecified*
    VESSEL SHAPE: Standard jar with no handles
    PRESUMED SOURCE: Lower Mississippi Valley
    GRAVELOT PROVENIENCE: Bu. 1109/NR

NR112 Bell Plain, *variety Hale*
    VESSEL SHAPE: Bottle
    PRESUMED SOURCE: Local (questionable)
    GRAVELOT PROVENIENCE: Bu. 1111/NR

NR114 Moundville Engraved, *variety Hemphill* (windmill)

    VESSEL SHAPE: Bowl
    PRESUMED SOURCE: Local
    GRAVELOT PROVENIENCE: Bu. 1109/NR

NR115 Mississippi Plain, *variety Warrior*
    VESSEL SHAPE: Standard jar with 2 handles
    PRESUMED SOURCE: Local
    GRAVELOT PROVENIENCE: Bu. 1109/NR

NR116 Mississippi Plain, *variety Warrior*
    VESSEL SHAPE: Standard jar with 4 handles
    PRESUMED SOURCE: Local
    GRAVELOT PROVENIENCE: Bu. 1109/NR

NR117 Mississippi Plain, *variety Warrior*
    VESSEL SHAPE: Simple bowl
    PRESUMED SOURCE: Local

NR118 Bell Plain, *variety Hale*
    VESSEL SHAPE: Simple bowl with beaded rim,
    effigy features—human head medallions
    PRESUMED SOURCE: Local (questionable)
    GRAVELOT PROVENIENCE: Bu. 1110/NR

NR119 Bell Plain, *variety Hale*
    VESSEL SHAPE: Subglobular bottle with simple
    base
    PRESUMED SOURCE: Local
    GRAVELOT PROVENIENCE: Bu. 1110/NR

NR121 Bell Plain, *variety Hale*
    VESSEL SHAPE: Simple bowl with lug and rim
    effigy—(head missing)
    PRESUMED SOURCE: Local (questionable)
    GRAVELOT PROVENIENCE: Bu. 1113/NR

NR124 Bell Plain, *variety Hale*
    VESSEL SHAPE: Flaring-rim bowl (shallow)
    PRESUMED SOURCE: Local
    GRAVELOT PROVENIENCE: Bu. 1116/NR

NR127 Moundville Engraved, *variety Northport*
    VESSEL SHAPE: Subglobular bottle with slab
    base
    PRESUMED SOURCE: Local
    GRAVELOT PROVENIENCE: Bu. 1117/NR

NR128 Mississippi Plain, *variety Warrior*
    VESSEL SHAPE: Simple bowl
    PRESUMED SOURCE: Local
    GRAVELOT PROVENIENCE: Bu. 1117/NR

NR129 Moundville Engraved, *variety Prince Plantation*
    VESSEL SHAPE: Subglobular bottle with
    pedestal base
    PRESUMED SOURCE: Local
    GRAVELOT PROVENIENCE: Bu. 1118/NR

NR152 Mississippi Plain, *variety unspecified*
    VESSEL SHAPE: Subglobular bottle
    PRESUMED SOURCE: Nonlocal
    GRAVELOT PROVENIENCE: Bu. 1124/NR

NR153 Mississippi Plain, *variety Warrior*
    VESSEL SHAPE: Cylindrical bowl
    PRESUMED SOURCE: Local
    GRAVELOT PROVENIENCE: Bu. 1124/NR

NR160 Bell Plain, *variety Hale*
    VESSEL SHAPE: Simple bowl
    PRESUMED SOURCE: Local

NR161 Bell Plain, *variety Hale*
    VESSEL SHAPE: Bowl
    PRESUMED SOURCE: Local
    GRAVELOT PROVENIENCE: Bu. 1126/NR

NR162 Moundville Engraved, *variety Tuscaloosa*
    VESSEL SHAPE: Subglobular bottle with
    pedestal base, indentations
    PRESUMED SOURCE: Local
    GRAVELOT PROVENIENCE: Bu. 1126/NR

NR189 Mississippi Plain, *variety Warrior*
    VESSEL SHAPE: Simple bowl
    PRESUMED SOURCE: Local
    GRAVELOT PROVENIENCE: Bu. 1128/NR

NR1/M5 Moundville Engraved, *variety Hemphill* (radial
fingers)
    VESSEL SHAPE: Subglobular bottle with
    pedestal base, indentations
    PRESUMED SOURCE: Local

GRAVELOT PROVENIENCE: F.1/NR/M5
PUBLISHED ILLUSTRATION: Moore 1905:Figures
  143-144
MAI CATALOG NO.: 17/3375

NR4/M5   Bell Plain, *variety Hale*
          VESSEL SHAPE: Subglobular bottle with
            pedestal base
          PRESUMED SOURCE: Local
          GRAVELOT PROVENIENCE: Bu. 5/NR/M5
          PUBLISHED ILLUSTRATION: Moore 1905:Figure 145
          MAI CATALOG NO.: 17/1428

NR6/M5   Moundville Engraved, *variety Cypress*
          VESSEL SHAPE: Restricted bowl
          PRESUMED SOURCE: Local
          GRAVELOT PROVENIENCE: Bu. 8/NR/M5
          PUBLISHED DESCRIPTION: Moore 1905:223
          MAI CATALOG NO.: 17/3643

NR9/M5   Moundville Engraved, *variety Hemphill* (scalp,
          skull, forearm bones, hand and eye)
          VESSEL SHAPE: Subglobular bottle with simple
            base (flattened)
          PRESUMED SOURCE: Local
          GRAVELOT PROVENIENCE: Bu. 11/NR/M5
          PUBLISHED ILLUSTRATION: Moore 1905:Figures
            146-147
          MAI CATALOG NO.: 17/1426

NR11/M5   Moundville Engraved, *variety Hemphill* (bilobed
          arrow)
          VESSEL SHAPE: Subglobular bottle with
            pedestal base, indentations
          PRESUMED SOURCE: Local
          GRAVELOT PROVENIENCE: Bu. 14/NR/M5
          PUBLISHED ILLUSTRATION: Moore 1905:Figure 148
          MAI CATALOG NO.: 18/425

NR15A/M5 Bell Plain, *variety Hale*
          VESSEL SHAPE: Restricted bowl with widely
            spaced nodes
          PRESUMED SOURCE: Local
          GRAVELOT PROVENIENCE: Bu. 21/NR/M5
          PUBLISHED ILLUSTRATION: Moore 1905:Figure 150
          MAI CATALOG NO.: 17/4369

NR17/M5   Moundville Engraved, *variety Hemphill* (winged
          serpent)
          VESSEL SHAPE: Subglobular bottle with simple
            base
          PRESUMED SOURCE: Local
          GRAVELOT PROVENIENCE: Bu. 33/NR/M5

          PUBLISHED ILLUSTRATION: Moore 1905:Figures
            151-152
          MAI CATALOG NO.: 17/4359

NR19/M5   Moundville Engraved, *variety Hemphill* (hand and
          eye)
          VESSEL SHAPE: Subglobular bottle with simple
            base
          PRESUMED SOURCE: Local
          GRAVELOT PROVENIENCE: Bu. 10/NR/M5
          PUBLISHED ILLUSTRATION: Moore 1905:Figure 153
          MAI CATALOG NO.: 17/3649

NR20/M5   Mississippi Plain, *variety Warrior*
          VESSEL SHAPE: Standard jar with 4 handles
          PRESUMED SOURCE: Local
          GRAVELOT PROVENIENCE: Bu. 10/NR/M5
          PUBLISHED ILLUSTRATION: Moore 1905:Figure 154
          MAI CATALOG NO.: 17/3644

NR23/M5   Bell Plain, *variety Hale*
          VESSEL SHAPE: Burnished jar with 2 handles,
            beaded rim, widely spaced nodes
          PRESUMED SOURCE: Local
          GRAVELOT PROVENIENCE: Bu. 38/NR/M5
          PUBLISHED ILLUSTRATION: Moore 1905:Figure 155
          MAI CATALOG NO.: 17/3645

NR24/M5   Moundville Engraved, *variety Hemphill* (paired
          wings)
          VESSEL SHAPE: Subglobular bottle
          PRESUMED SOURCE: Local
          GRAVELOT PROVENIENCE: Bu. 38/NR/M5
          PUBLISHED ILLUSTRATION: Moore 1905:Figure 156

NR26/M5   Moundville Engraved, *variety unspecified*
          VESSEL SHAPE: Subglobular bottle with
            pedestal base
          PRESUMED SOURCE: Local
          GRAVELOT PROVENIENCE: Bu. 48/NR/M5

PUBLISHED ILLUSTRATION: Moore 1905:Figures
  157-158
MAI CATALOG NO.: 17/1422

NR27/M5   Unclassified Incised (hand)
          VESSEL SHAPE: Narrow-neck bottle
            (subglobular)
          PRESUMED SOURCE: Central Mississippi Valley
          GRAVELOT PROVENIENCE: Bu. 48/NR/M5
          PUBLISHED ILLUSTRATION: Moore 1905:Figure 159
          MAI CATALOG NO.: 18/438

NR30/M5   Moundville Engraved, *variety Hemphill* (winged
          serpent in the round)
          VESSEL SHAPE: Subglobular bottle with simple
            base
          PRESUMED SOURCE: Local
          GRAVELOT PROVENIENCE: Bu. 58/NR/M5
          PUBLISHED ILLUSTRATION: Moore 1905:Figures
            160-161
          MAI CATALOG NO.: 17/3378

NR31/M5   Moundville Engraved, *variety Wiggins*
          VESSEL SHAPE: Subglobular bottle with simple
            base
          PRESUMED SOURCE: Local
          PUBLISHED ILLUSTRATION: Moore 1905:Figure 162
          MAI CATALOG NO.: 17/4358

WR1   Bell Plain, *variety unspecified*
          VESSEL SHAPE: Bottle
          PRESUMED SOURCE: Nonlocal

WR2   Moundville Engraved, *variety Wiggins*
          VESSEL SHAPE: Subglobular bottle
          PRESUMED SOURCE: Local

WR3   Bell Plain, *variety Hale*
          VESSEL SHAPE: Cylindrical bowl
          PRESUMED SOURCE: Local (questionable)

WR9   Moundville Engraved, *variety Taylorville*
          VESSEL SHAPE: Simple bowl with single lug
          PRESUMED SOURCE: Local

WR10   Moundville Engraved, *variety Hemphill* (hand and
          eye)
          VESSEL SHAPE: Subglobular bottle with simple
            base
          PRESUMED SOURCE: Local
          GRAVELOT PROVENIENCE: Bu. 17/WR

WR11   Unclassified Engraved (sand tempered) (festoons)
          VESSEL SHAPE: Cylindrical bowl with rim
            strap, grooved lip
          PRESUMED SOURCE: Nonlocal
          GRAVELOT PROVENIENCE: Bu. 6/WR

WR12   Bell Plain, *variety Hale*
          VESSEL SHAPE: Flaring-rim bowl (deep)
          PRESUMED SOURCE: Local
          GRAVELOT PROVENIENCE: Bu. 15/WR

WR13   Moundville Engraved, *variety Hemphill* (paired
          tails)
          VESSEL SHAPE: Subglobular bottle with simple
            base
          PRESUMED SOURCE: Local
          GRAVELOT PROVENIENCE: Bu. 10/WR

WR21   Bell Plain, *variety Hale*
          VESSEL SHAPE: Short-neck bowl
          PRESUMED SOURCE: Local (questionable)

WR24   Unclassified Engraved
          VESSEL SHAPE: Standard jar with no handles
          PRESUMED SOURCE: Nonlocal

WR46   Mississippi Plain, *variety Warrior*
          VESSEL SHAPE: Standard jar with 4 handles
          PRESUMED SOURCE: Local

WR50   Carthage Incised, *variety Akron*
          VESSEL SHAPE: Simple bowl with lug and rim
            effigy——(head missing)
          PRESUMED SOURCE: Local

WR51   Moundville Engraved, *variety Tuscaloosa*
          VESSEL SHAPE: Subglobular bottle with
            pedestal base, indentations
          PRESUMED SOURCE: Local

WR52   Bell Plain, *variety unspecified*

VESSEL SHAPE: Bottle
PRESUMED SOURCE: Nonlocal

WR53   Barton Incised, *variety unspecified*
        VESSEL SHAPE: Standard jar with 2 handles,
          small horizontal lugs
        PRESUMED SOURCE: Central Mississippi Valley,
          Lower Tennessee Valley
        GRAVELOT PROVENIENCE: Bu. 1/WR

WR56   Mississippi Plain, *variety unspecified*
        VESSEL SHAPE: Standard jar with 2 handles,
          small horizontal lugs, effigy features—
          stylized frog
        PRESUMED SOURCE: Lower Tennessee-Cumberland
          area
        GRAVELOT PROVENIENCE: Bu. 1045/WR

WR57   Walls Engraved, *variety unspecified*
        VESSEL SHAPE: Hooded bottle with effigy
          features—human figure
        PRESUMED SOURCE: Central Mississippi Valley
          (Cairo Lowland)
        GRAVELOT PROVENIENCE: Bu. 1045/WR

WR58   Bell Plain, *variety Hale*
        VESSEL SHAPE: Burnished jar with 2 handles,
          effigy features—frog
        PRESUMED SOURCE: Local (questionable)
        GRAVELOT PROVENIENCE: Bu. 1045/WR

WR59   Moundville Engraved, *variety Hemphill* (winged
          serpent)
        VESSEL SHAPE: Subglobular bottle with simple
          base
        PRESUMED SOURCE: Local
        GRAVELOT PROVENIENCE: Bu. 1045/WR

WR60   Moundville Engraved, *variety Taylorville*
        VESSEL SHAPE: Pedestaled bowl with notched
          everted lip
        PRESUMED SOURCE: Local
        GRAVELOT PROVENIENCE: Bu. 1045/WR

WR65   Carthage Incised, *variety Akron*
        VESSEL SHAPE: Simple bowl with lug and rim
          effigy—bird (flat, inward-facing head)
        PRESUMED SOURCE: Local
        GRAVELOT PROVENIENCE: Bu. 1048/WR

WR66   Bell Plain, *variety unspecified*
        VESSEL SHAPE: Simple bowl with effigy
          features—human figure
        PRESUMED SOURCE: Lower Tennessee-Cumberland
          area
        GRAVELOT PROVENIENCE: Bu. 1049/WR

WR68   Unclassified Punctated
        VESSEL SHAPE: Standard jar with 2 handles
        PRESUMED SOURCE: Nonlocal
        GRAVELOT PROVENIENCE: Bu. 1050/WR

WR69   Mississippi Plain, *variety Warrior*
        VESSEL SHAPE: Standard jar with 2 handles
        PRESUMED SOURCE: Local
        GRAVELOT PROVENIENCE: Bu. 1050/WR

WR70   Unclassified Engraved
        VESSEL SHAPE: Carinated bottle
        PRESUMED SOURCE: Nonlocal
        GRAVELOT PROVENIENCE: Bu. 1054/WR

WR72   Mississippi Plain, *variety Warrior*
        VESSEL SHAPE: Standard jar with 2 handles
        PRESUMED SOURCE: Local
        GRAVELOT PROVENIENCE: Bu. 1057/WR

WR74   Bell Plain, *variety Hale*
        VESSEL SHAPE: Cylindrical bowl with single
          lug
        PRESUMED SOURCE: Local
        GRAVELOT PROVENIENCE: Bu. 1060/WR

WR80   Bell Plain, *variety Hale*
        VESSEL SHAPE: Simple bowl with beaded rim
        PRESUMED SOURCE: Local
        GRAVELOT PROVENIENCE: Bu. 1065/WR

WR81   Moundville Engraved, *variety Hemphill* (winged
          serpent in the round)
        VESSEL SHAPE: Subglobular bottle with simple
          base
        PRESUMED SOURCE: Local
        GRAVELOT PROVENIENCE: Bu. 1065/WR

WR82   Bell Plain, *variety Hale*
        VESSEL SHAPE: Flaring-rim bowl (deep)
        PRESUMED SOURCE: Local
        GRAVELOT PROVENIENCE: Bu. 1065/WR

WR83   Bell Plain, *variety unspecified*
        VESSEL SHAPE: High-shouldered bottle
        PRESUMED SOURCE: Central Mississippi Valley,
          Lower Tennessee-Cumberland area
        GRAVELOT PROVENIENCE: Bu. 1065/WR

WR85   Carthage Incised, *variety Carthage*
        VESSEL SHAPE: Subglobular bottle with simple
          base
        PRESUMED SOURCE: Local
        GRAVELOT PROVENIENCE: Bu. 1068/WR

WR1/M5 Bell Plain, *variety unspecified*
        VESSEL SHAPE: Bottle with podal supports
        PRESUMED SOURCE: Nonlocal
        GRAVELOT PROVENIENCE: Bu. 1/WR/M5
        PUBLISHED ILLUSTRATION: Moore 1905:Figure 172
        MAI CATALOG NO.: 17/4405

WR2/M5 Moundville Engraved, *variety Hemphill* (hand and
          eye)
        VESSEL SHAPE: Bottle
        PRESUMED SOURCE: Local (questionable)
        GRAVELOT PROVENIENCE: Bu. 1/WR/M5
        PUBLISHED ILLUSTRATION: Moore 1905:Figure 173
        MAI CATALOG NO.: 17/4366

WR2/M7 Mississippi Plain, *variety Warrior* (red-filmed
          interior)
        VESSEL SHAPE: Standard jar with 8 handles
        PRESUMED SOURCE: Local
        GRAVELOT PROVENIENCE: Bu. 4/WR/M7
        PUBLISHED DESCRIPTION: Moore 1907:346
        MAI CATALOG NO.: 17/4384

WR3/M7 Carthage Incised, *variety Carthage*
        VESSEL SHAPE: Narrow-neck bottle
          (subglobular)
        PRESUMED SOURCE: Local (questionable)
        GRAVELOT PROVENIENCE: Bu. 6/WR/M7
        PUBLISHED ILLUSTRATION: Moore 1907:Figure 72
        MAI CATALOG NO.: 17/3634

WR8/M7 Moundville Engraved, *variety Hemphill* (hand and
          eye)
        VESSEL SHAPE: Subglobular bottle with
          pedestal base
        PRESUMED SOURCE: Local
        GRAVELOT PROVENIENCE: Bu. 9/WR/M7
        PUBLISHED DESCRIPTION: Moore 1907:346
        MAI CATALOG NO.: 17/4364

WR15/M7 Bell Plain, *variety unspecified*
        VESSEL SHAPE: Simple bowl with effigy
          features—fish
        PRESUMED SOURCE: Lower Tennessee-Cumberland
          area
        GRAVELOT PROVENIENCE: Bu. 20/WR/M7
        PUBLISHED ILLUSTRATION: Moore 1907:Figure 27
        MAI CATALOG NO.: 17/3641

WR18/M7 Nashville Negative Painted, *variety unspecified*
        VESSEL SHAPE: Subglobular bottle with carafe
          neck
        PRESUMED SOURCE: Lower Tennessee-Cumberland
          area
        PUBLISHED ILLUSTRATION: Moore 1907:Figure 20
        MAI CATALOG NO.: 17/3381

WR28/M7 Moundville Engraved, *variety Hemphill* (ogee)
        VESSEL SHAPE: Subglobular bottle with simple
          base
        PRESUMED SOURCE: Local
        PUBLISHED ILLUSTRATION: Moore 1907:Figure 42
        MAI CATALOG NO.: 17/4618

W70   Barton Incised, *variety unspecified*
        VESSEL SHAPE: Standard jar with 2 handles
        PRESUMED SOURCE: Nonlocal

W81   Bell Plain, *variety Hale*
        VESSEL SHAPE: Slender ovoid bottle with
          pedestal base
        PRESUMED SOURCE: Local

W176   Bell Plain, *variety Hale*
        VESSEL SHAPE: Pedestaled bowl with cutout
          rim, lowered lip

PRESUMED SOURCE: Local
GRAVELOT PROVENIENCE: Bu. 2942/W

W186   Bell Plain, *variety Hale*
VESSEL SHAPE: Simple bowl with beaded rim
PRESUMED SOURCE: Local
GRAVELOT PROVENIENCE: Bu. 2947/W

W192   Mississippi Plain, *variety Warrior*
VESSEL SHAPE: Standard jar with 2 handles
PRESUMED SOURCE: Local (questionable)
GRAVELOT PROVENIENCE: Bu. 2957/W

W219   Moundville Engraved, *variety Wiggins*
VESSEL SHAPE: Subglobular bottle with
pedestal base
PRESUMED SOURCE: Local
GRAVELOT PROVENIENCE: Bu. 2962/W

W220   Mississippi Plain, *variety Warrior*
VESSEL SHAPE: Standard jar with 2 handles
PRESUMED SOURCE: Local

W239   D'olive Incised, *variety unspecified*
VESSEL SHAPE: Flaring-rim bowl (shallow) with
notched lip
PRESUMED SOURCE: Gulf Coast (Mobile-Pensacola
region)

W310   Moundville Incised, *variety Moundville*
VESSEL SHAPE: Standard jar with 2 handles
PRESUMED SOURCE: Local
GRAVELOT PROVENIENCE: Bu. 2984/W

NW5   Mississippi Plain, *variety Warrior*
VESSEL SHAPE: Undiagnostic fragment(s)
PRESUMED SOURCE: Local
GRAVELOT PROVENIENCE: Bu. 1833/NW

NW7   Bell Plain, *variety Hale*
VESSEL SHAPE: Subglobular bottle with slab
base
PRESUMED SOURCE: Local
GRAVELOT PROVENIENCE: Bu. 1836/NW

NW8   Mississippi Plain, *variety Warrior*
VESSEL SHAPE: Undiagnostic fragment(s)
PRESUMED SOURCE: Local
GRAVELOT PROVENIENCE: Bu. 1836/NW

NW9   Moundville Incised, *variety Snows Bend*
VESSEL SHAPE: Standard jar with 4 handles
PRESUMED SOURCE: Local (questionable)
GRAVELOT PROVENIENCE: Bu. 1837/NW

NW11   Mississippi Plain, *variety Warrior*
VESSEL SHAPE: Standard jar with 2 handles
PRESUMED SOURCE: Local
GRAVELOT PROVENIENCE: Bu. 1837/NW

NW12   Mississippi Plain, *variety Warrior*
VESSEL SHAPE: Standard jar with 2 handles
PRESUMED SOURCE: Local
GRAVELOT PROVENIENCE: Bu. 1838/NW

NW14   Mississippi Plain, *variety Warrior*
VESSEL SHAPE: Standard jar with 8 handles
PRESUMED SOURCE: Local
GRAVELOT PROVENIENCE: Bu. 1840/NW

NW15   Mississippi Plain, *variety Warrior*
VESSEL SHAPE: Standard jar with 2 handles
PRESUMED SOURCE: Local
GRAVELOT PROVENIENCE: Bu. 1840/NW

NW16   Moundville Engraved, *variety Havana*
VESSEL SHAPE: Restricted bowl with lug and
rim effigy—bird (gracile, outward-facing
head)
PRESUMED SOURCE: Local (questionable)
GRAVELOT PROVENIENCE: Bu. 1841/NW

NW17   Bell Plain, *variety Hale*
VESSEL SHAPE: Flaring-rim bowl (shallow)
PRESUMED SOURCE: Local (questionable)
GRAVELOT PROVENIENCE: Bu. 1841/NW

NW18   Bell Plain, *variety Hale*
VESSEL SHAPE: Subglobular bottle with
pedestal base
PRESUMED SOURCE: Local
GRAVELOT PROVENIENCE: Bu. 1842/NW

NW19   Mississippi Plain, *variety Warrior*

VESSEL SHAPE: Undiagnostic fragment(s)
PRESUMED SOURCE: Local
GRAVELOT PROVENIENCE: Bu. 1842/NW

NW21   Mississippi Plain, *variety Warrior*
VESSEL SHAPE: Undiagnostic fragment(s)
PRESUMED SOURCE: Local
GRAVELOT PROVENIENCE: Bu. 1845/NW

NW22   Mississippi Plain, *variety Warrior*
VESSEL SHAPE: Undiagnostic fragment(s)
PRESUMED SOURCE: Local
GRAVELOT PROVENIENCE: Bu. 1845/NW

NW23   Mississippi Plain, *variety Warrior* (red-filmed
interior)
VESSEL SHAPE: Standard jar with 2 handles
PRESUMED SOURCE: Local
GRAVELOT PROVENIENCE: Bu. 1846/NW

NW24   Mississippi Plain, *variety Warrior*
VESSEL SHAPE: Standard jar with 2 handles
PRESUMED SOURCE: Local
GRAVELOT PROVENIENCE: Bu. 1848/NW

NW25   Carthage Incised, *variety Akron*
VESSEL SHAPE: Outslanting bowl with lug and
rim effigy—(head missing)
PRESUMED SOURCE: Local (questionable)
GRAVELOT PROVENIENCE: Bu. 1849/NW

NW26   Moundville Incised, *variety Moundville*
VESSEL SHAPE: Standard jar with handles,
folded rim
PRESUMED SOURCE: Local
GRAVELOT PROVENIENCE: Bu. 1850/NW

NW30   Mississippi Plain, *variety Warrior*
VESSEL SHAPE: Undiagnostic fragment(s)
PRESUMED SOURCE: Local
GRAVELOT PROVENIENCE: Bu. 1853/NW

NW31   Bell Plain, *variety Hale*
VESSEL SHAPE: Subglobular bottle with
pedestal base
PRESUMED SOURCE: Local (questionable)
GRAVELOT PROVENIENCE: Bu. 1854/NW

NW32   Pensacola Incised, *variety unspecified*
VESSEL SHAPE: Subglobular bottle
PRESUMED SOURCE: Gulf Coast (Mobile-Pensacola
region)
GRAVELOT PROVENIENCE: Bu. 1854/NW

NW33   Mississippi Plain, *variety Warrior*
VESSEL SHAPE: Undiagnostic fragment(s)
PRESUMED SOURCE: Local
GRAVELOT PROVENIENCE: Bu. 1854/NW

NW35   Mississippi Plain, *variety Warrior*
VESSEL SHAPE: Undiagnostic fragment(s)
PRESUMED SOURCE: Local
GRAVELOT PROVENIENCE: Bu. 1856/NW

NW36   Bell Plain, *variety Hale*
VESSEL SHAPE: Bottle (miniature)
PRESUMED SOURCE: Local
GRAVELOT PROVENIENCE: Bu. 1856/NW

NW39   Mississippi Plain, *variety Warrior*
VESSEL SHAPE: Standard jar with handles
PRESUMED SOURCE: Local
GRAVELOT PROVENIENCE: Bu. 1861/NW

NW42   Mississippi Plain, *variety Warrior*
VESSEL SHAPE: Standard jar with 2 handles
PRESUMED SOURCE: Local
GRAVELOT PROVENIENCE: Bu. 1865/NW

NW43   Bell Plain, *variety Hale*
VESSEL SHAPE: Simple bowl with band of nodes
PRESUMED SOURCE: Local (questionable)
GRAVELOT PROVENIENCE: Bu. 1865/NW

NW46   Bell Plain, *variety Hale*
VESSEL SHAPE: Simple bowl with lug and rim
effigy—(head missing)
PRESUMED SOURCE: Local (questionable)
GRAVELOT PROVENIENCE: Bu. 1869/NW

SW2   Mississippi Plain, *variety Warrior*
VESSEL SHAPE: Standard jar with 4 handles
PRESUMED SOURCE: Local
GRAVELOT PROVENIENCE: Bu. 2199/SW

SW4   Bell Plain, *variety Hale*
        VESSEL SHAPE: Simple bowl with beaded rim
        PRESUMED SOURCE: Local
        GRAVELOT PROVENIENCE: Bu. 2199/SW

SW5   Mississippi Plain, *variety Warrior*
        VESSEL SHAPE: Bottle
        PRESUMED SOURCE: Local (questionable)
        GRAVELOT PROVENIENCE: Bu. 2199/SW

SW9   Mississippi Plain, *variety Warrior*
        VESSEL SHAPE: Flaring-rim bowl (shallow)
        PRESUMED SOURCE: Local
        GRAVELOT PROVENIENCE: Bu. 2202/SW

SW10   Moundville Engraved, *variety Maxwells Crossing*
        (crosshatched vertical bands)
        VESSEL SHAPE: Subglobular bottle with slab
          base
        PRESUMED SOURCE: Local
        GRAVELOT PROVENIENCE: Bu. 2203/SW

SW11   Barton Incised, *variety unspecified*
        VESSEL SHAPE: Bowl
        PRESUMED SOURCE: Nonlocal
        GRAVELOT PROVENIENCE: Bu. 2346/SW

SW13   Mississippi Plain, *variety Warrior*
        VESSEL SHAPE: Bottle
        PRESUMED SOURCE: Local
        GRAVELOT PROVENIENCE: Bu. 2384/SW

SW14   Mississippi Plain, *variety Warrior*
        VESSEL SHAPE: Simple bowl (miniature) with
          undulating rim
        PRESUMED SOURCE: Local (questionable)
        GRAVELOT PROVENIENCE: Bu. 2386/SW

SW15   Mississippi Plain, *variety Warrior*
        VESSEL SHAPE: Standard jar with 2 handles
        PRESUMED SOURCE: Local
        GRAVELOT PROVENIENCE: Bu. 2386/SW

SW17   Mississippi Plain, *variety Warrior*
        VESSEL SHAPE: Standard jar with 2 handles
        PRESUMED SOURCE: Local
        GRAVELOT PROVENIENCE: Bu. 2500/SW

SW18   Mississippi Plain, *variety Warrior*
        VESSEL SHAPE: Cylindrical bowl (miniature)
          with notched everted lip
        PRESUMED SOURCE: Local (questionable)
        GRAVELOT PROVENIENCE: Bu. 2506/SW

SW19   Andrews Decorated, *variety unspecified*
        (multilinear bands at rim and base)
        VESSEL SHAPE: Cylindrical bowl
        PRESUMED SOURCE: Lower Chattahoochee Valley
        GRAVELOT PROVENIENCE: Bu. 2506/SW

SW20   Bell Plain, *variety Hale*
        VESSEL SHAPE: Restricted bowl with effigy
          features—fish
        PRESUMED SOURCE: Local
        GRAVELOT PROVENIENCE: Bu. 2390/SW

SW21   Bell Plain, *variety Hale*
        VESSEL SHAPE: Double bowl (rectanguloid)
        PRESUMED SOURCE: Local (questionable)
        GRAVELOT PROVENIENCE: Bu. 2390/SW

SW23   Moundville Engraved, *variety Maxwells Crossing*
        (crosshatched vertical bands)
        VESSEL SHAPE: Subglobular bottle with
          pedestal base
        PRESUMED SOURCE: Local
        GRAVELOT PROVENIENCE: Bu. 2392/SW

SW25   Bell Plain, *variety Hale*
        VESSEL SHAPE: Restricted bowl with effigy
          features—turtle
        PRESUMED SOURCE: Local
        GRAVELOT PROVENIENCE: Bu. 2501/SW

SW26   Bell Plain, *variety unspecified*
        VESSEL SHAPE: Lobate bottle with carafe neck
        PRESUMED SOURCE: Central Mississippi Valley
        GRAVELOT PROVENIENCE: Bu. 2501/SW

SW31   Moundville Engraved, *variety Havana*
        VESSEL SHAPE: Cylindrical bowl with single
          lug
        PRESUMED SOURCE: Local
        GRAVELOT PROVENIENCE: Bu. 2393/SW

SW34   Moundville Engraved, *variety Hemphill* (raptor
        head)
        VESSEL SHAPE: Subglobular bottle with
          pedestal base, gadrooning
        PRESUMED SOURCE: Local (questionable)
        GRAVELOT PROVENIENCE: Bu. 2393/SW

SW39   Moundville Engraved, *variety Tuscaloosa*
        VESSEL SHAPE: Subglobular bottle with
          pedestal base
        PRESUMED SOURCE: Local
        GRAVELOT PROVENIENCE: Bu. 2504/SW

SW40   Mississippi Plain, *variety Warrior*
        VESSEL SHAPE: Standard jar with 2 handles
        PRESUMED SOURCE: Local
        GRAVELOT PROVENIENCE: Bu. 2504/SW

SW41   Bell Plain, *variety Hale*
        VESSEL SHAPE: Simple bowl with beaded rim
        PRESUMED SOURCE: Local
        GRAVELOT PROVENIENCE: Bu. 2504/SW

SW45   Mississippi Plain, *variety Warrior*
        VESSEL SHAPE: Terraced rectanguloid bowl with
          simple base
        PRESUMED SOURCE: Local (questionable)
        GRAVELOT PROVENIENCE: Bu. 2517/SW

SW46   Bell Plain, *variety unspecified*
        VESSEL SHAPE: Narrow-neck bottle
          (subglobular)
        PRESUMED SOURCE: Nonlocal
        GRAVELOT PROVENIENCE: Bu. 2513/SW

SW50   Mississippi Plain, *variety Warrior*
        VESSEL SHAPE: Bottle with slab base
        PRESUMED SOURCE: Local (questionable)
        GRAVELOT PROVENIENCE: Bu. 2509/SW

SW52   Bell Plain, *variety Hale*
        VESSEL SHAPE: Burnished jar with no handles
        PRESUMED SOURCE: Local (questionable)
        GRAVELOT PROVENIENCE: Bu. 2508/SW

SW53   Mississippi Plain, *variety Warrior*
        VESSEL SHAPE: Undiagnostic fragment(s)
        PRESUMED SOURCE: Local
        GRAVELOT PROVENIENCE: Bu. 2508/SW

SW55   Mississippi Plain, *variety Warrior*
        VESSEL SHAPE: Simple bowl with everted lip
        PRESUMED SOURCE: Local (questionable)
        GRAVELOT PROVENIENCE: Bu. 2398/SW

SW57   Mississippi Plain, *variety Warrior*
        VESSEL SHAPE: Restricted bowl with effigy
          features—fish
        PRESUMED SOURCE: Local
        GRAVELOT PROVENIENCE: Bu. 2398/SW

SW60   Unclassified Incised
        VESSEL SHAPE: Bottle (miniature)
        PRESUMED SOURCE: Local
        GRAVELOT PROVENIENCE: Bu. 2397/SW

SW61   Mississippi Plain, *variety Warrior*
        VESSEL SHAPE: Simple bowl with effigy
          features—frog
        PRESUMED SOURCE: Local (questionable)
        GRAVELOT PROVENIENCE: Bu. 2397/SW

SW62   Moundville Engraved, *variety Cypress*
        VESSEL SHAPE: Subglobular bottle with slab
          base
        PRESUMED SOURCE: Local
        GRAVELOT PROVENIENCE: Bu. 2388/SW

SW63   Mississippi Plain, *variety Warrior*
        VESSEL SHAPE: Simple bowl with expanded lip
        PRESUMED SOURCE: Local (questionable)
        GRAVELOT PROVENIENCE: Bu. 2388/SW

SW64   Mississippi Plain, *variety Warrior*
        VESSEL SHAPE: Undiagnostic fragment(s)
        PRESUMED SOURCE: Local
        GRAVELOT PROVENIENCE: Bu. 2387/SW

NWW1   Moundville Engraved, *variety Havana*
        VESSEL SHAPE: Simple bowl with lug and rim
          effigy—bird (flat, inward-facing head)
        PRESUMED SOURCE: Local (questionable)
        GRAVELOT PROVENIENCE: Bu. 1821/NWW

NWW7   Carthage Incised, *variety Akron*
            VESSEL SHAPE: Simple bowl with lug and rim
              effigy—bird (flat, inward-facing head)
            PRESUMED SOURCE: Local
            GRAVELOT PROVENIENCE: Bu. 1830/NWW

Mi37   Moundville Engraved, *variety unspecified*
            VESSEL SHAPE: Terraced bowl
            PRESUMED SOURCE: Local (questionable)

Mi61   Unclassified Red on Buff
            VESSEL SHAPE: Bottle
            PRESUMED SOURCE: Nonlocal

Mi62   Moundville Engraved, *variety Hemphill* (winged
              serpent)
            VESSEL SHAPE: Subglobular bottle with simple
              base
            PRESUMED SOURCE: Local

Mi397   Mississippi Plain, *variety unspecified*
            VESSEL SHAPE: Standard jar with 2 handles,
              small horizontal lugs, effigy features—
              stylized frog
            PRESUMED SOURCE: Lower Tennessee-Cumberland
              area

Mi430   Mississippi Plain, *variety Warrior*
            VESSEL SHAPE: Simple bowl with lug and rim
              effigy—(head missing)
            PRESUMED SOURCE: Local

Mi431   Moundville Engraved, *variety Hemphill* (winged
              serpent)
            VESSEL SHAPE: Narrow-neck bottle
              (subglobular), with slab base
            PRESUMED SOURCE: Local (questionable)
            NMNH CATALOG NO.: 377382

Mi434   Bell Plain, *variety Hale*
            VESSEL SHAPE: Bowl with effigy features—
              mussel shell
            PRESUMED SOURCE: Local (questionable)

Mi435   Bell Plain, *variety Hale*
            VESSEL SHAPE: Simple bowl with single lug
            PRESUMED SOURCE: Local

Mi438   Bell Plain, *variety Hale*
            VESSEL SHAPE: Restricted bowl with effigy
              features—alligator
            PRESUMED SOURCE: Local

Mi440   Mississippi Plain, *variety unspecified*
            VESSEL SHAPE: Simple bowl with beaded rim
            PRESUMED SOURCE: Nonlocal

Mi456   Moundville Engraved, *variety Havana*
            VESSEL SHAPE: Restricted bowl with lug and
              rim effigy—(head missing)
            PRESUMED SOURCE: Local

Mi462   Bell Plain, *variety unspecified*
            VESSEL SHAPE: Simple bowl with large flat
              nodes
            PRESUMED SOURCE: Nonlocal

Mi1015   Moundville Incised, *variety Carrollton*
            VESSEL SHAPE: Standard jar with 2 handles
            PRESUMED SOURCE: Local

<I>NR25   Mississippi Plain, *variety Warrior*
            VESSEL SHAPE: Standard jar with 2 handles,
              downturned lugs
            PRESUMED SOURCE: Local

<I>NR25   Nashville Negative Painted, *variety unspecified*
            VESSEL SHAPE: Subglobular bottle with carafe
              neck
            PRESUMED SOURCE: Lower Tennessee-Cumberland
              area

<I>NW13   Mississippi Plain, *variety Warrior*
            VESSEL SHAPE: Bowl
            PRESUMED SOURCE: Local (questionable)

<I>Rho163   Moundville Incised, *variety Moundville*
            VESSEL SHAPE: Standard jar with 2 handles
            PRESUMED SOURCE: Local

<I>SD15   Mississippi Plain, *variety unspecified*
            VESSEL SHAPE: Standard jar (miniature) with 2
              handles, small horizontal lugs, effigy
              features—stylized frog

            PRESUMED SOURCE: Lower Tennessee-Cumberland
              area

<I>SW353   Moundville Engraved, *variety unspecified*
            VESSEL SHAPE: Simple bowl
            PRESUMED SOURCE: Local (questionable)

<I>SWG2   Carthage Incised, *variety Moon Lake*
            VESSEL SHAPE: Short-neck bowl
            PRESUMED SOURCE: Local
            NMNH CATALOG NO.: 377388

<I>W50   Moundville Engraved, *variety Wiggins*
            VESSEL SHAPE: Subglobular bottle with
              pedestal base
            PRESUMED SOURCE: Local

<I>W50   Moundville Incised, *variety Moundville*
            VESSEL SHAPE: Standard jar with 2 handles
            PRESUMED SOURCE: Local

<I>WP1   Mississippi Plain, *variety unspecified*
            VESSEL SHAPE: Standard jar with 2 handles,
              small horizontal lugs, effigy features—
              stylized frog
            PRESUMED SOURCE: Lower Tennessee-Cumberland
              area

<M>2   Moundville Engraved, *variety Wiggins*
            VESSEL SHAPE: Subglobular bottle with simple
              base, indentations
            PRESUMED SOURCE: Local

<M>3   Mississippi Plain, *variety Warrior*
            VESSEL SHAPE: Standard jar (miniature) with 2
              handles
            PRESUMED SOURCE: Local

<M>4   Bell Plain, *variety Hale*
            VESSEL SHAPE: Bottle with beaded shoulder
            PRESUMED SOURCE: Local (questionable)

<M>5   Carthage Incised, *variety unspecified*
            VESSEL SHAPE: Flaring-rim bowl (deep) with
              notched lip
            PRESUMED SOURCE: Local (questionable)

<M>6   Bell Plain, *variety Hale*
            VESSEL SHAPE: Outslanting bowl
            PRESUMED SOURCE: Local (questionable)

<M>7   Bell Plain, *variety Hale*
            VESSEL SHAPE: Simple bowl with effigy
              features—conch shell
            PRESUMED SOURCE: Local

<M>8   Bell Plain, *variety Hale*
            VESSEL SHAPE: Simple bowl with notched
              everted lip
            PRESUMED SOURCE: Local (questionable)

<M>9   Bell Plain, *variety Hale*
            VESSEL SHAPE: Simple bowl
            PRESUMED SOURCE: Local

<M>10   Bell Plain, *variety Hale*
            VESSEL SHAPE: Subglobular bottle with simple
              base, effigy features—frog
            PRESUMED SOURCE: Local (questionable)

<M>11   Mississippi Plain, *variety Warrior*
            VESSEL SHAPE: Standard jar with 2 handles
            PRESUMED SOURCE: Local (questionable)

<M>12   Bell Plain, *variety Hale*
            VESSEL SHAPE: Burnished jar with 2 handles
            PRESUMED SOURCE: Local (questionable)

<M>13   Bell Plain, *variety Hale*
            VESSEL SHAPE: Restricted bowl with beaded
              shoulder
            PRESUMED SOURCE: Local (questionable)

<M>14   Mississippi Plain, *variety Warrior*
            VESSEL SHAPE: Standard jar with 2 handles
            PRESUMED SOURCE: Local (questionable)

<M>15   Mississippi Plain, *variety Warrior*
            VESSEL SHAPE: Standard jar with 4 handles
            PRESUMED SOURCE: Local

<M>19   Carthage Incised, *variety Carthage*
            VESSEL SHAPE: Short-neck bowl
            PRESUMED SOURCE: Local

<M> Bell Plain, *variety Hale*
     VESSEL SHAPE: Subglobular bottle with simple
     base
     PRESUMED SOURCE: Local
     MAI CATALOG NO.: 17/1429

<M> Bell Plain, *variety Hale*
     VESSEL SHAPE: Burnished jar with 2 handles,
     beaded rim, effigy features—frog
     PRESUMED SOURCE: Local
     MAI CATALOG NO.: 17/1431

<M> Moundville Engraved, *variety Northport*
     VESSEL SHAPE: Subglobular bottle with
     pedestal base
     PRESUMED SOURCE: Local
     MAI CATALOG NO.: 17/3348

<M> Bell Plain, *variety Hale*
     VESSEL SHAPE: Subglobular bottle with
     pedestal base
     PRESUMED SOURCE: Local (questionable)
     MAI CATALOG NO.: 17/3367

<M> Bell Plain, *variety Hale*
     VESSEL SHAPE: Slender ovoid bottle with
     pedestal base
     PRESUMED SOURCE: Local (questionable)
     MAI CATALOG NO.: 17/3369

<M> Unclassified Engraved (multilinear band at rim)
     VESSEL SHAPE: Simple bowl with notched lip,
     opposing lugs
     PRESUMED SOURCE: Nonlocal
     MAI CATALOG NO.: 17/3375A

<M> Matthews Incised, *variety Beckwith*
     VESSEL SHAPE: Standard jar with 2 handles,
     effigy features—stylized frog
     PRESUMED SOURCE: Lower Tennessee-Cumberland
     area
     MAI CATALOG NO.: 17/3379

<M> Bell Plain, *variety Hale*
     VESSEL SHAPE: Simple bowl with beaded rim
     PRESUMED SOURCE: Local
     MAI CATALOG NO.: 17/3637

<M> Carthage Incised, *variety Carthage*
     VESSEL SHAPE: Simple bowl
     PRESUMED SOURCE: Local
     MAI CATALOG NO.: 17/3642

<M> Mississippi Plain, *variety unspecified*
     VESSEL SHAPE: Standard jar with 2 handles,
     nodes
     PRESUMED SOURCE: Lower Tennessee-Cumberland
     area
     MAI CATALOG NO.: 17/3646

<M> Moundville Engraved, *variety Englewood*
     VESSEL SHAPE: Subglobular bottle with simple
     base
     PRESUMED SOURCE: Local (questionable)
     MAI CATALOG NO.: 17/4354

<M> Bell Plain, *variety Hale*
     VESSEL SHAPE: Subglobular bottle with simple
     base
     PRESUMED SOURCE: Local (questionable)
     MAI CATALOG NO.: 17/4362

<M> Moundville Engraved, *variety Northport*

     VESSEL SHAPE: Subglobular bottle with slab
     base
     PRESUMED SOURCE: Local (questionable)
     MAI CATALOG NO.: 17/4368

<M> Mississippi Plain, *variety Warrior*
     VESSEL SHAPE: Simple bowl with grouped nodes
     PRESUMED SOURCE: Local (questionable)
     MAI CATALOG NO.: 17/4374

<M> Bell Plain, *variety Hale*
     VESSEL SHAPE: Simple bowl with effigy
     features—conch shell
     PRESUMED SOURCE: Local
     MAI CATALOG NO.: 17/4376

<M> Carthage Incised, *variety unspecified*
     VESSEL SHAPE: Burnished jar with 2 handles,
     widely spaced nodes
     PRESUMED SOURCE: Local (questionable)
     MAI CATALOG NO.: 17/4379

<M> Moundville Incised, *variety Moundville*
     VESSEL SHAPE: Standard jar with 2 handles
     PRESUMED SOURCE: Local (questionable)
     MAI CATALOG NO.: 17/4381

<M> Bell Plain, *variety Hale*
     VESSEL SHAPE: Simple bowl with notched lip
     PRESUMED SOURCE: Local (questionable)
     MAI CATALOG NO.: 17/4394

<M> Bell Plain, *variety Hale*
     VESSEL SHAPE: Restricted bowl
     PRESUMED SOURCE: Local
     MAI CATALOG NO.: 17/4397

<M> Barton Incised, *variety unspecified*
     VESSEL SHAPE: Standard jar with 2 handles,
     effigy features—stylized frog
     PRESUMED SOURCE: Lower Tennessee-Cumberland
     area
     MAI CATALOG NO.: 17/4616

<M> Moundville Engraved, *variety Tuscaloosa*
     VESSEL SHAPE: Subglobular bottle with slab
     base, indentations
     PRESUMED SOURCE: Local
     MAI CATALOG NO.: 17/4619

<M> Moundville Engraved, *variety Tuscaloosa*
     VESSEL SHAPE: Subglobular bottle with
     pedestal base, indentations
     PRESUMED SOURCE: Local
     MAI CATALOG NO.: 17/4620

<M> Moundville Engraved, *variety Englewood*
     VESSEL SHAPE: Simple bowl with rolled lip
     PRESUMED SOURCE: Local (questionable)
     MAI CATALOG NO.: 18/414

<M> Moundville Engraved, *variety unspecified*
     VESSEL SHAPE: Subglobular bottle with
     pedestal base
     PRESUMED SOURCE: Local (questionable)
     MAI CATALOG NO.: 18/434

<M> Moundville Engraved, *variety Wiggins*
     VESSEL SHAPE: Subglobular bottle with simple
     base
     PRESUMED SOURCE: Local
     MAI CATALOG NO.: 18/437

B

Vessels Indexed by Burial Number

The following table includes all burials from the 1905–1941 excavations that were accompanied by pottery vessels as grave offerings. Entries are arranged in order by burial number, with the catalog numbers of the associated vessels appearing immediately to the right of each burial number. Nonburial proveniences, prefixed with F., are found at the very end of the list. An asterisk next to a catalog number indicates that the vessel is nonlocal. Vessels that were originally associated with burials, but were not located for inclusion in the present sample, are entered below in parentheses. Individual descriptions of all vessels included in the sample can be found in Appendix A.

TABLE A.1
Vessels Arranged by Burial Number

Burial	Associated vessels
1/A/M7	(A1/M7), (A2/M7)
1/NC/M7	(NC1/M7), (NC2/M7), (NC3/M7)
1/ED	(ED9)
1/SED	SED5
1/SD	SD3
1/SD/M5	(SD1/M5), SD2/M5
1/NE	NE39
1/L	(L1)
1/WN/M7	WN1/M7*, (WN2/M7)
1/EO/M5	EO1/M5*
1/NQ/M5	NQ1/M5
1/WR	WR53*
1/WR/M5	WR1/M5*, WR2/M5

(continued)

TABLE A.1 (Continued)

Burial	Associated vessels
2/WB/M5	WB3/M5
2/NEC/M5	NEC1/M5, (NEC2/M5)
2/SD/M5	SD4/M5
2/SD/M7	SD1/M7
2/NE	NE74, NE78*, NE129
2/F/M5	(F1/M5), F14/M5+
2/L	(L2)
3/RPB	RPB(1)
3/NEC/M5	NEC3/M5
3/SD/M7	(SD2/M7)
3/NG	NG11, NG13, NG23, NG24
3/WR/M7	(WR1/M7)
4/WR/M7	WR2/M7
5/RPB	RPB(4)
5,6/C/M5	C7/M5, C8/M5, C9/M5
5/SD/M5	(SD5/M5), SD6/M5*
5/NR/M5	NR4/M5
6/NEC/M5	(NEC4/M5)
6/F/M5	F3/M5
6/O/M5	(O1/M5)
6/WR	WR11*
6/WR/M7	WR3/M7
7/SED	SED34
7/O/M5	O3/M5, (O4/M5)
7/WR/M7	(WR5/M7), (WR6/M7)
8/RPB	RPB(3)
8/ED	ED8, ED14
8,9/SD/M7	(SD3/M7), (SD4/M7), SD5/M7, SD6/M7, SD7/M7
8/NG	NG3, NG8
8/NR/M5	NR6/M5
8/WR/M7	(WR4/M7), (WR7/M7)
9/WR/M7	WR8/M7, (WR9/M7)
9/F/M5	(F7/M5)
9/NG	NG25
9/SWM/M7	SWM1/M7, SWM2/M7, SWM2A/M7
9/O/M5	O5/M5
9/NR/M5	(NR7/M5)
9/WR/M7	WR8/M7, (WR9/M7)
10/F/M5	(F5/M5)
10/SEH	SEH5
10/NR/M5	(NR8/M5), (NR18/M5), NR19/M5, NR20/M5
10/WR	WR13
11/NC/M7	(NC4/M7), (NC5/M7)
11/NEC/M5	NEC6/M5, (NEC7/M5)
11/F/M5	F6/M5*
11/SWM/M7	(SWM3/M7)
11/NR/M5	NR9/M5
12/C/M5	(C9A/M5), (C10/M5)
12/SD/M7	SD8/M7
12/NR	NR7
13/NED	(NED2), NED7

(continued)

TABLE A.1 (Continued)

Burial	Associated vessels
13/SD/M7	(SD9/M7), (SD10/M7), SD11/M7, (SD12/M7), SD13/M7, SD14/M7
13/F/M5	(F9/M5)
13/NR/M5	(NR10/M5)
14/SD/M7	SD15/M7
14/SWM/M7	(SWM4/M7), SWM5/M7
14/O/M5	O6/M5
14/NR/M5	NR11/M5, (NR12/M5)
15/NE	NE148
15/NR/M5	(NR14/M5)
15/WR	WR12
16/F/M5	(F11/M5), F12/M5
16/WR/M7	(WR12/M7)
17/NEC/M5	(NEC12/M5), (NEC13/M5)
17/ND	ND13
17/NE	NE60
17/F/M5	F13/M5
17/WR	WR10
18/NED	NED3
18/F/M5	F15/M5
18/NG	NG5, NG6
18/SEH	SEH10, SEH15
19/SD/M7	(SD16/M7)
19/SEH	SEH7, SEH14*
19/O/M5	O9/M5
20/NEC/M5	NEC10/M5, NEC11/M5
20/NED	NED4
20/NG	NG10
20/WR/M7	WR15/M7*, (WR16/M7)
21/NED	(NED12)
21/SD/M7	(SD16A/M7)
21/NG	NG4, NG9
21/O/M5	O10/M5, (O11/M5)
21/NR/M5	(NR15/M5), NR15A/M5
22/SD/M7	(SD17/M7), SD18/M7, (SD18A/M7)
22/SWM/M7	SWM6/M7
22/WR/M7	(WR17/M7), (WR19/M7), (WR20/M7)
23/SD/M5	(SD7/M5), (SD8/M5), SD9/M5
23/SD/M7	(SD19/M7)
23/NE	NE55
23/WR/M7	(WR13/M7), (WR14/M7)
24/SD/M5	SD10/M5, (SD11/M5)
25/NEC/M5	(NEC15/M5)
25/O/M5	(O12/M5), (O13/M5)
26/NED	NED1*
26/SEH	SEH11
27/SD/M7	SD20/M7, SD21/M7*
28/SD/M7	(SD22/M7)
29/O/M5	O26/M5*
29/WR/M7	(WR25/M7)
30/SD/M7	(SD23/M7)
30/WR/M7	(WR21/M7), (WR22/M7), (WR23/M7)

(continued)

TABLE A.1 (Continued)

Burial	Associated vessels
32/WR/M7	(WR24/M7)
33/NR/M5	NR17/M5, (NR21/M5)
35/SD/M7	(SD24/M7)
37/NR/M5	(NR22/M5)
38/NR/M5	NR23/M5, NR24/M5
39/O/M5	O31/M5, (O32/M5), O33/M5
40,41/SD/M7	(SD26/M7), SD27/M7
40/O/M5	(O34/M5), (O35/M5), (O36/M5)
40/WR/M7	(WR26/M7)
41/NE	NE67
41/NR/M5	(NR25/M5)
44/NE	NE65
48/NE	NE42
48/NR/M5	NR26/M5, NR27/M5*
50/NE	NE38
50/NR/M5	(NR28/M5)
53/NE	NE6, NE14
54/NE	N50, NE61, (NE62), (NE70)
55/SD/M7	SD44/M7
55/NE	NE64
58/SWM/M7	(SWM9/M7)
58/NR/M5	NR30/M5
59/NE	NE63
64/SD/M7	(SD30/M7)
66/SD/M7	SD34/M7
70/SD/M7	(SD31/M7)
71/SD/M7	SD32/M7, SD33/M7
75/SD/M7	(SD36/M7), (SD37/M7)
76/NE	NE59
77/SD/M7	(SD40/M7)
78/NE	NE31
79/NE	NE54, NE56
80/SD/M7	(SD39/M7)
84/SD/M7	SD42/M7
86/SD/M7	(SD43/M7)
92/NE	NE53*
94/SD/M7	SD45/M7*
94/NE	NE58
100/SD/M7	(SD46/M7)
101/SD/M7	(SD47/M7), SD48/M7
104/SD/M7	(SD49/M7)
105/SD/M7	(SD50/M7)
107/SD/M7	(SD51/M7)
108/SD/M7	(SD52/M7), (SD53/M7), SD54/M7
114/SD/M7	SD59/M7
115/SD/M7	(SD60/M7), SD61/M7
120/SD/M7	(SD63/M7)
122/SD/M7	(SD64/M7)
126/SD/M7	(SD65/M7)
127/SD/M7	(SD66/M7), (SD67/M7)
128/SD/M7	SD71/M7, (SD115/M7), (SD116/M7)
129/SD/M7	(SD68/M7), (SD69/M7), (SD117/M7)

(continued)

TABLE A.1 (Continued)

Burial	Associated vessels
131/SD/M7	(SD70/M7)
133/SD/M7	(SD72/M7), (SD73/M7), (SD74/M7)
134/SD/M7	(SD75/M7)
135/SD/M7	(SD76/M7)
140/SD/M7	SD77/M7, (SD78/M7)
141/SD/M7	(SD79/M7)
147/SD/M7	(SD80/M7)
149/SD/M7	(SD84/M7)
150/SD/M7	(SD85/M7), SD86/M7, SD87/M7
151/SD/M7	SD88/M7, (SD89/M7), (SD90/M7)
153/SD/M7	SD93/M7, (SD94/M7)
154/SD/M7	(SD92/M7)
156/SD/M7	SD96/M7, (SD97/M7)
161/SD/M7	(SD98/M7)
162/SD/M7	(SD99/M7)
165/SD/M7	(SD105/M7), SD106/M7
166/SD/M7	(SD102/M7)
167/SD/M7	(SD104/M7)
169/SD/M7	(SD107/M7)
173/SD/M7	SD110/M7, (SD111/M7), (SD112/M7), (SD113/M7), (SD114/M7)
802/SEH	(SEH39)
803/SEH	SEH45
815/EI	(EI14A)
817/EI	EI15, EI16*, (EI17)
823/EI	EI25
824/EI	EI26, EI27, (EI28)
831/EI	EI30
833/EI	(EI34)
839/EI	EI42, EI43
843/EI	EI39, EI40, EI41
851/EI	EI78
864/SEH	(SEH69)
866/SEH	SEH71
869/SEH	SEH72, SEH73, SEH74
870/SEH	SEH75*, SEH76
872/SEH	SEH86*, SEH87
873/SEH	SEH88,
895/SWM	SWM14
907/SWM	SWM41
921/SWM	SWM42
943/SWM	(SWM82)
947/SWM	SWM87
50/SWM	SWM93
952/SWM	SWM94, SWM95
961/SWM	SWM131, SWM132
963/SWM	(SWM139)
964/SWM	SWM140
965/SWM	SWM141, SWM142
966B/SWM	SWM166*
967/SWM	SWM167
968/SWM	(SWM169)

(continued)

TABLE A.1 (Continued)

Burial	Associated vessels
969-70/SWM	SWM170
971/SWM	SWM175
975/SM	(SM3)
978/SWM	SWM180
979/SWM	SWM181
981/SWM	SM183
983/SWM	SWM185, SWM186
1002/SWM	(SWM212)
1005/SWM	SWM219
1007/NG	NG30, NG31
1008/NG	NG32
1016/NG	NG39
1017/NG	(NG43), NG44*
1024/SWM	SWM220
1032/SWM	(SM26)
1033/SM	SM28*, SM29*, SM30
1045/WR	WR56*, WR57*, WR58, WR59, WR60
1048/WR	WR65
1049/WR	WR66*
1050/WR	WR68*, WR69
1054/WR	WR70*
1057/WR	WR72
1060/WR	WR74
1065/WR	(WR79), WR80, WR81, WR82, WR83*, (WR84)
1068/WR	WR85
1083/NR	NR9
1086/NR	NR20, NR21
1087/NR	NR23, (NR26), NR40, NR98
1088/NR	NR24, NR25
1089/NR	NR27, NR28
1094-96/NR	NR38
1098/NR	NR41, NR42
1099/NR	NR43
1100/NR	NR44
1101/NR	NR46, NR47, (NR49)
1102/NR	(NR95), NR96, NR97
1103/NR	NR99
1104/NR	NR100, NR101
1105/NR	NR102
1106/NR	(NR104)
1109/NR	NR106, NR107*, NR114, NR115, NR116
1110/NR	NR118, NR119
1111/NR	NR112, (NR113)
1113/NR	NR121
1116/NR	NR124, (NR125)
1117/NR	NR127, NR128
1118/NR	NR129
1124/NR	NR152*, NR153
1125/NR	(NR159)
1126/NR	NR161, NR162, (NR163)
1128/NR	NR189
1147/SWM	SWM222, SWM223

(continued)

TABLE A.1 (Continued)

Burial	Associated vessels
1149/SWM	SWM226
1151/SWM	SWM230
1160/SWM	SWM252
1174/NE	(NE691)
1178/NE	(NE693)
1181-83/EE	EE1, EE2, EE3, EE4, EE5
1184/EE	EE6
1185/EE	EE7, EE8, EE9, EE10, EE11, EE12
1192/EE	EE13
1198/EE	EE17
1199-201/EE	EE18
1202/EE	EE19, (EE20)
1213/EE	EE61, (EE63), EE64
1216/EE	EE67*
1220/EE	EE71
1222-23/EE	EE72
1224/EE	(EE73)
1225/EE	EE74, EE75, EE76
1227/EE	EE77, EE78, (EE79), EE80
1228/EE	EE81
1229-31/EE	EE82, (EE83)
1232/EE	EE84*
1234-37/EE	EE85, EE86, EE87, EE88, EE89*, (EE90), (EE91), (EE92), (EE93)
1238/EE	EE94
1243/EE	EE104
1254/EE	EE108
1255/EE	EE109*
1256/EE	EE110
1261/EE	EE124, EE125, EE126
1262/EE	EE129
1263/EE	EE130
1264/EE	EE131*, EE132
1265/EE	EE133, (EE134)
1267/EE	EE135
1268/EE	EE136
1272	EE137
1275/EE	EE155, EE156
1276/EE	EE157
1277A/EE	EE159, EE160
1278/EE	EE179, EE180
1281/EE	EE181, EE182
1282/EE	(EE183)
1283/EE	EE186
1284/EE	EE187, EE188
1291/EE	EE202, EE203
1292/EE	EE204
1293/EE	EE206*
1299-301/EE	(EE209), EE210, (EE211), (EE213)
1308/SE	SE2
1316/EE	EE234
1321/EE	EE236*, EE237, EE238

(continued)

TABLE A.1 (**Continued**)

Burial	Associated vessels
1324/EE	(EE246)
1326-28/EE	EE242
1331/EE	EE260
1333-40/EE	(EE275)
1342/SE	SE18*, SE19
1343-44/EE	EE277, EE278*
1346/EE	EE281
1348/EE	(EE292)
1371-72/EE	EE302
1373-74/EE	EE303, EE304, EE305, (EE306), EE307
1377/EE	(EE310), (EE311), (EE314)
1379/EE	(EE317)
1380/EE	EE322
1385/EE	EE340
1387/EE	EE380, EE381, EE382
1388/EE	EE384
1389-91/EE	EE385
1392/EE	EE389, EE390
1394/EE	EE391, EE392
1399/EE	EE394, EE395
1400/EE	EE396
1405/EE	(EE415)
1406/EE	EE416
1407/EE	EE429, EE430
1409/EE	EE431
1411/EE	EE444
1412/EE	EE445
1413/EE	EE447
1415/EE	EE475
1423/SD	SD29, SD30, SD31, SD32, (SD33)
1437/SD	SD154, SD155
1439/SD	(SD157)
1442/SD	SD169
1443/SD	SD171
1444/SD	SD247*, SD248
1446/SD	SD251, (SD252)
1453/SD	SD262, (SD263)
1455/SD	SD265, SD266, SD267
1457/SD	SD350*, SD152*, (SD352), (SD353)
1459/SD	SD362
1462/SD	SD364
1464/SD	SD365
1465/SD	(SD366)
1468/SD	SD472
1479/SD	SD473
1491/SD	SD482
1495/SD	SD579
1496/SD	SD583, SD584, SD585, SD586
1500/SD	(SD589), (SD590)
1504/SD	SD594, SD595, SD596
1505/SD	SD599, SD600, (SD603)
1513/SD	(SD678)

(continued)

TABLE A.1 (Continued)

Burial	Associated vessels
1514/SD	SD679
1515/SD	SD680, SD681, SD682, SD683, SD684
1516/SD	(SD686), SD687, SD688, SD689, (SD690), (SD691)
1519/SD	SD731*
1520/SD	SD732, SD733
1521/SD	SD734
1522/SD	SD736
1525/SD	SD741, SD742, SD743, SD744, SD745, SD746
1526/SD	SD747, SD748
1534/SD	SD805, SD806, (SD807), (SD808), (SD809)
1536/SD	SD810*
1537/SD	SD811
1539/SD	SD813*, SD814, SD815, SD816, SD818
1542/SD	SD821, SD822
1544/SD	SD825, SD826, SD827
1546/SD	SD832
1552/SD	(SD833)
1553/SD	SD834
1563-4/SD	SD836, SD837, SD838
1566/SD	SD840
1567/SD	SD841
1569/SD	SD842, (SD843)
1570/SD	SD844
1571-2/SD	(SD846)
1573/SD	SD847*, SD848*, SD849
1579-80/SD	SD853
1581/SD	(SD854)
1582/SD	SD855, (SD856), (SD857), (SD858)
1587/NE	NE165, NE166
1596/NE	NE169*, NE170*
1600/NE	NE174
1605/NE	(NE184)
1611/NE	NE185
1612/NE	(NE186)
1620/NE	NE443*, NE444, NE445, NE446*, (NE447), NE448*, NE450, NE451, NE452
1621/NE	NE453, NE454*
1624/NE	NE458
1625/NE	NE460*
1628/NE	NE461, (NE462)
1631/NE	NE464
1636/NE	NE568
1638/NE	NE570, NE571
1639/NE	NE572, (NE573), NE574, NE575
1647-48/NE	NE591, NE592, NE593
1649/NE	NE576, (NE577)
1651/NE	NE581, NE582, NE583, (NE584), NE585
1655/NE	NE587, NE596
1688/NE	NE597
1673/NE	NE599
1674/NE	NE600, (NE601)

(continued)

TABLE A.1 (Continued)

Burial	Associated vessels
1676/NE	NE602
1680/EE	EE492
1682/EE	EE495
1683/WN	WN1
1692/EF	EF1, EF2
1693/EF	EF3
1696/EF	(EF4), (EF5)
1707/SG	SG4
1708/SG	SG5
1714/SG	(SG8)
1717/SWG	SWG1, SWG2, SWG3, SWG4, SWG5
1718/SWG	SWG6, SWG7
1720/SWG	SWG8
1725/SWG	SWG9, (SWG10)
1728/SWG	SWG16*, SWG17
1731/SG	(SG11)
1732/SG	(SG14)
1735/SG	SG15, SG16, (SG17)
1748/SWG	SWG23
1749/SWG	SWG21*
1751/SWG	SWG24, SWG25
1754/SWG	SWG26
1758/SWG	SWG29
1784/SWG	SWG40*, SWG41
1786/SG	SG24, SWG25*
1788/SWG	SWG63, (SWG64)
1789/SWG	SWG62
1791/SWG	SWG44
1793/SWG	(SWG42), (SWG43)
1795/SWG	SWG45*
1800/SWG	SWG46, SWG47, (SWG48), SWG49
1801/SWG	SWG52, (SWG53)
1802/SWG	(SWG55), (SWG56), (SWG57)
1803/SWG	SWG58
1805/SWG	SWG66, SWG67
1821/NWW	NWW1, (NWW2)
1830/NWW	NNW7, (NWW8)
1832/NW	(NW1)
833/NW	NW5
1836/NW	NW7, NW8
1837/NW	NW9, NW11
1838/NW	NW12
1840/NW	NW14, NW15
1841/NW	NW16, NW17
1842/NW	NW18 NW19
1845/NW	NW21, NW22
1846/NW	NW23
1848/NW	NW24
1849/NW	NW25
1850/NW	NW26, (NW47)
1851/NW	(NW27)
1852/NW	(NW29)

(continued)

TABLE A.1 (Continued)

Burial	Associated vessels
1853/NW	NW30
1854/NW	NW31, NW32*, MW33
1856/NW	NW35, NW36, (NW37)
1859/NW	(NW41)
1861/NW	NW39, (NW40)
1865/NW	NW42, NW43
1869/NW	NW46
1885/NW	(NG79)
1888/NN′	(NN′1), NN′2, NN′3*, NN′4, (NN′5), NN′6
1894/Rho	(Rho34), (Rho35), Rho36
1895/Rho	(Rho37), Rho38
1896/Rho	Rho39
1901/Rho	Rho48
1909/Rho	Rho57
1923/Rho	Rho65*, Rho66, (Rho73)
1924/Rho	Rho67*
1931/Rho	Rho102, Rho135*
1934/Rho	Rho84, (Rho85), Rho90, Rho153*
1936/Rho	Rho100
1937/Rho	Rho101*
1939/Rho	Rho104
1940/Rho	Rho107, (Rho108)
1943-44/Rho	Rho109
1947/Rho	Rho110
1949/Rho	(Rho121), Rho122, Rho127*, (Rho155)
1950/Rho	Rho132, (Rho133), Rho134
1955/Rho	(Rho137), RhoW138*, (Rho139)
1956-57/Rho	Rho141, Rho142, (Rho143)
1958/Rho	Rho148
1960/Rho	Rho149*
1964/Rho	Rho154
1968/Rho	Rho156, Rho157, Rho158, Rho159, Rho160*, Rho161
1969/Rho	(Rho162), Rho163, Rho164
1977/Rho	Rho170, Rho171
1978/Rho	Rho172, Rho173, Rho174, Rho177*, Rho178, Rho182, Rho184, (Rho185)
1979/Rho	(Rho191), Rho192, Rho193*
1989/Rho	(Rho201)
1996/Rho	(Rho211)
2001/Rho	Rho212, Rho213*
2004/Rho	Rho214
2009/Rho	Rho219
2011/Rho	Rho220
2021/Rho	Rho226
2025/Rho	Rho227
2035/Rho	(Rho242)
2042/Rho	Rho251, Rho252*,
2045/Rho	Rho255
2047/Rho	Rho256*, Rho257
2054/Rho	(Rho265)
2056/Rho	(Rho266)

(continued)

TABLE A.1 (Continued)

Burial	Associated vessels
2060/Rho	(Rho271), (Rho272)
2062/Rho	Rho275, (Rho275A)
2068/Rho	Rho304, (Rho305), Rho306, Rho307*, Rho308, (Rho309), (Rho310)
2069-71/Rho	Rho312, (Rho315)
2072/Rho	(Rho316)
2079/Rho	Rho328
2082/Rho	Rho329
2087/Rho	(Rho333), (Rho336), Rho337
2089/Rho	(Rho338)
2091/Rho	(Rho341)
2093/Rho	(Rho350)
2094/Rho	Rho351
2096/Rho	Rho364
2100-01/Rho	(Rho370)
2102/Rho	Rho366, Rho367
2110/Rho	Rho368, Rho369
2115/Rho	Rho371, Rho372, Rho373
2125/NN'	NN'12*, NN'13, (NN'15), (NN'16), NN'14*
2134/NN'	NN'18, NN'19
2135/NN'	(NN'20), (NN'22)
2136/NN'	NN'38, NN'39, NN'40*, NN'41, (NN'42)
2137/WP'	WP'32, (WP'33), WP'34, (WP'35), (WP'36) (WP'37), (WP'38)
2148/WP'	(WP'6)
2152-54	WP'19, (WP'21), (WP'22)
2159/WP'	(WP'23)
2160/WP'	(WP'24)
2165/WP'	WP'30
2166/WP'	WP'29
2167/WP'	(WP'31)
2171/WP'	WP'39
2172/ND	ND33*
2173/ND	NE34
2179/WP	WP19, WP20, WP21
2180/WP	WP22, WP23
2184/WP	(WP26)
2185/WP	WP27, WP28
2187/WP	WP29
2199/SW	SW2, (SW3), SW4, SW5
2201/SW	(SW8)
2202/SW	SW9
2203/SW	SW10
2208/WP	WP96
2211/WP	WP52
2223/WP	WP47
2224/SW	(SW43), (SW44)
2252/WP	(WP53)
2258/WP	WP72
2273/WP	(WP81)
2282/WP	(WP60), WP61
2289/WP	WP67

(continued)

TABLE A.1 (Continued)

Burial	Associated vessels
2304/WP	(WP49)
2310/WP	(WP139)
2314/WP	WP83, (WP84)
2317/WP	WP85
2318/WP	(WP137)
2326/WP	WP65
2330/WP	(WP93)
2337/WP	(WP91)
2341/WP	(WP97)
2346/SW	SW11*
2354/WP	WP94
2358/WP	(WP94A)
2374/SW	(SW54)
2384/SW	(SW12), SW13
2386/SW	SW14, SW15
2387/SW	SW64
2388/SW	SW62, SW63
2390/SW	SW20, SW21
2391/SW	(SW28)
2392/SW	(SW22), SW23
2393/SW	(SW29), (SW30), SW31, (SW32), SW34
2397/SW	SW60, SW61
2398/SW	SW55, SW57
2414/WP	(WP108)
2417/WP	WP121, WP122
2421/WP	WP119
2436/WP	WP135
2447/WP	WP104
2469/WP	(WP219A)
2471/WP	(WP220), WP221
2476/WP	WP223
2496/WP	(WP227), WP228, WP229*, WP230
2498/WP	(WP231)
2500/SW	SW17
2501/SW	SW25, SW26*
2503/SW	(SW37)
2504/SW	SW39, SW40,, SW41, (SW42)
2506/SW	SW18, SW19*
2508/SW	SW52, SW53
2509/SW	SW50, (SW51)
2513/SW	SW46*
2514/SW	(SW47)
2517/SW	SW45
2530/WP	WP149
2532/WP	WP152, WP153, (WP155), WP156
2538/WP	WP158
2540/WP	WP159
2544/WP	WP160, WP161
2545/WP	WP165
2550/WP	WP170, WP171, WP173
2553/WP	WP186, WP187, WP207
2558/WP	WP208

(continued)

TABLE A.1 (Continued)

Burial	Associated vessels
2559/WP	WP212, WP213
2560/WP	WP214, WP215
2562/WP	WP216, WP217, WP218
2563/WP	(WP219)
2569/WP	(WP245)
2575/ED	(ED18), (ED24)
2582/ED	(ED26)
2597/ED	(ED46), (ED47)
2598/ED	(ED49), ED50, (ED51)
2600/ED	(ED52), (ED53)
2607/ED	ED54, (ED55)
2608/ED	(ED68)
2614/ED	ED71, (ED72)
2617/EH	(EH75), EH76*
2619/K	(K77)
2633/WP	(WP254)
2634/WP	(WP257)
2635/WP	WP258
2636/WP	WP259, WP260
2640-41/WP	(WP263), WP264
2645/WP	(WP267)
2662/Rw	(Rw24)
2665/Rw	Rw25, Rw26
2671/Rw	(Rw32)
2672/Rw	(Rw38)
2673/Rw	Rw36
2687/Rw	Rw64
2688/Rw	(Rw62)
2690/Rw	(Rw83)
2722/Rw	(Rw131), Rw132, Rw133
2725/Rw	(Rw127), Rw128, Rw129, (Rw130)
2726/Rw	Rw126
2728/Rw	Rw135
2732/Rw	(Rw134)
2733/Rw	Rw138, Rw139, Rw142
2734/Rw	Rw140
2739/Rw	(Rw150)
2740/Rw	(Rw152), (Rw153)
2743/Rw	(Rw157), (Rw158), Rw159
2746/Rw	(Rw162), (Rw175)
2747/Rw	Rw145*, (<I>Rho163)
2748/Rw	(Rw154)
2749/Rw	Rw165
2750/Rw	(Rw166)
2751/Rw	Rw168
2760/Rw	Rw176, Rw177
2765/Rw	(Rw190), (Rw191)
2766/Rw	(Rw193)
2767/Rw	(Rw194)
2768/Rw	Rw195
2772/Rw	Rw227, Rw228
2773/Rw	Rw229

(continued)

TABLE A.1 (Continued)

Burial	Associated vessels
2774/Rw	Rw226, (Rw239)
2778/Rw	(Rw238)
2779/Rw	(Rw244)
2788/Rw	Rw246*
2790/Rw	Rw245
2808/Rw	Rw260
2820/Rw	Rw308*
2823/Rw	(Rw309)
2854/Rw	Rw439
2857/Rw	Rw440
2859/Rw	Rw442
2880/Rw	Rw470*, Rw471
2882/Rw	(Rw472), Rw473
2884/Rw	Rw480
2887/Rw	(Rw502), (Rw508)
2890/Rw	(Rw507)
2894/Rw	(Rw512)
2895/Rw	(Rw511)
2906/W	(W50), (W53)
2914/AdB	AdB44
2942/W	W176
2947/W	W186
2948/W	(W188)
2957/W	W192
2962/W	(W215), W219
2984/W	(W309), W310
3001/SL	SL1, SL2*, SL3, (SL4)
3005/SL	(SL8), (SL9), (SL11)
3008/SL	(SL12)
3010/SL	(SL14)
3010'/MPA	(MPA133)
3011/SL	(SL15), (SL16)
3012/SL	SL21, (SL22)
3014/SL	SL24*, SL25, (SL29), SL31
3015/SL	SL27*, (SL28)
3016/SL	SL56
3020/SL	SL33, (SL34)
3021/SL	SL38
3025/SL	(SL44), (SL45), (SL46)
3026/SL	SL47, (SL48), SL49, (SL50)
F.1/WB/M5	WB1/M5, (WB2/M5)
F.1/C/M5	C1/M5*, C2/M5
F.1/NEC/M5	(NEC14/M5)
F.1/D/M5	(D1/M5), (D2/M5), (D10/M5), (D11/M5), (D12/M5)
F.1/ND/M5	(ND2/M5), ND3/M5*
F.1/SD/M7	SD82/M7, (SD83/M7)
F.1/F/M5	(F2/M5)
F.1/H/M5	(H1/M5), (H2/M5)
F.1/O/M5	O14/M5, O15/M5
F.1/NR/M5	NR1/M5, (NR2/M5), (NR3/M5)
F.2/C/M5	C3/M5, C4/M5, (C5/M5)

(continued)

TABLE A.1 (Continued)

Burial	Associated vessels
F.2/ND/M5	(ND5/M5)
F.2/SD/M7	(SD91/M7)
F.2/O/M5	(O17/M5), O18/M5, O19/M5
F.2/NR/M5	(NR13/M5)
F.3/C/M5	C17/M5, (C18/M5)
F.3/D/M5	D4/M5
F.3/ND/M5	ND6/M5
F.3/O/M5	O28/M5
F.3/NR/M5	(NR16/M5)
F.4/C/M5	(C14A/M5), (C15/M5)
F.4/D/M5	D5/M5
F.4/ND/M5	(ND7/M5), (ND8/M5), (ND9/M5), (ND10/M5)
F.4/O/M5	(O7/M5), (O8/M5)
F.5/C/M5	(C16/M5)
F.5/D/M5	(D6/M5), (D7/M5), (D8/M5)
F.5/ND/M5	ND11/M5
F.5/O/M5	(O23/M5), (O24/M5), (O25/M5)
F.6/C/M5	(C19/M5), (C20/M5)
F.6/D/M5	(D9/M5)
F.6/ND/M5	ND12/M5*
F.7/ND/M5	ND13/M5, ND14/M5
F.8/ND/M5	(ND15/M5), ND16/M5
F.9/ND/M5	ND17/M5
F.10/ND/M5	(ND19/M5)

C

Stratigraphic Level Descriptions

Below is a summary of the levels excavated in the two test units north of Mound R; it was from these units that the sherds analyzed in the present study were obtained. Tables A.2 and A.3 provide level-by-level descriptions of the depositional sequence within units 6N2W and 8N2E, respectively (for profile drawings, see Scarry 1981a:Figures 1 and 2). Table A.4 correlates the levels in one unit with those in the other. All the information in this appendix was kindly supplied by C. Margaret Scarry, who directed the excavations. It should be noted that levels are numbered in the order they were excavated, that is, from the top down.

TABLE A.2
Excavated Levels in Unit 6N2W

Level number	Type	Thickness (cm)	Depositional interpretation
1	Arbitrary	10	Midden and/or fill, probably includes some backfill from previous excavations in the area, along with traces of a plow zone
2	Arbitrary	10	Midden and/or fill
3	Arbitrary	10	Midden and/or fill
4	Arbitrary	10	Midden and/or fill, with scattered occupational features (2 possible hearths), but no definite floors
5	Natural	10-12	Midden and/or fill, interspersed with discontinuous remnants of a sand floor that was not stratigraphically separated
6	Natural	4-8	Midden and/or fill, along with remnants of about 3 superimposed sand floors that did not cover the full horizontal extent of the excavation
7	Natural	7	Midden and/or fill
8	Natural	5-9	At least 1, and probably 2 superimposed sand floors
9	Natural	3-6	Daub layer, consisting of collapsed wall debris. This stratum corresponds to Level 8B in 8N2E
10	Natural	2-4	Sand floor with some trampled-in midden debris
11	Natural	6-8	Sand floor, partially covered by a thin lense of daub and charcoal
12	Natural	3-5	Sand floor
13	Natural	3-4	Sand floor; it was noted during excavation that many of the artifacts came from an area later discovered to be the top of a pit starting at this level
14	Natural	10	Sand floor, or possibly 2 indistinct floors superimposed, including an area of greyish ash

(continued)

TABLE A.2 (Continued)

Level number	Type	Thickness (cm)	Depositional interpretation
15	Natural	10	Midden and/or fill
16	Natural	2	Sand floor
17, 18	Natural	6-12	Sand floor, covered by a discontinuous lense of pink clay
19	Natural	1-2	Thin lense of midden, trampled into the sand floor below (i.e., Level 20)
20	Natural	2-3	Sand floor
21	Natural	2-3	Sand floor
22	Natural	13	Fill
23	Natural	10	Several thin sand floors, interspersed with lenses of ash and midden
24	Natural	5-10	Sand floor in north end of square, midden and/or fill in south portion of square
25	Arbitrary	10	Fill
26	Arbitrary	10	Midden and fill, some of the latter being within the sunken house feature
27A	Natural		Fill within a rectangular(?) sunken house
27B	Natural		Fill within a pit feature, originating at the same level as, and apparently associated with, the sunken house
28	Natural		Compacted sand floor of sunken house

TABLE A.3
Excavated Levels in Unit 8N2E

Level number	Type	Thickness (cm)	Depositional interpretation
1	Natural	5-12	Midden and/or fill, with considerable recent and nineteenth-century disturbance
2	Arbitrary	10	Midden and/or fill, with some nineteenth-century disturbance
3	Arbitrary	10	Midden and/or fill, with some nineteenth-century disturbance
4	Arbitrary	10	Midden and/or fill, interspersed with discontinuous traces of sand floors; some nineteenth-century disturbance is evident
5	Natural	10	Sand floor (or perhaps several closely superimposed floors) with most, but not all, recent disturbances separated out
6	Natural	2-5	Midden and/or fill; sand floor remnants within this level were excavated separately as Level 6A
6A	Natural		Discontinuous remnants of 1 or more sand floors within Level 6
7	Natural	6-9	Midden and/or fill; sand floor remnants within this level were excavated separately as Level 7A
7A	Natural		Discontinuous remnants of 1 or more sand floors within Level 7
8A	Natural	3-6	Sand floor (above Level 8B)
8B	Natural	6-10	Daub layer, consisting of collapsed wall debris; this stratum corresponds to Level 9 in 6N2W
9	Natural	4-5	Sand floor with a charcoal lense just above it
10	Natural	2-4	Sand floor
11	Natural	10-12	Sand floor (or possibly more than 1 floor closely superimposed)
12	Natural	4-6	Sand floor (or possibly more than 1 floor closely superimposed)

(continued)

TABLE A.3 (Continued)

Level number	Type	Thickness (cm)	Depositional interpretation
13	Natural	2-3	Sand floor
14	Natural	20	Midden and/or fill
15	Natural	3-4	Sand floor, along with a thin lense of midden just below it
16	Natural	5	Sand floor (or possibly more than 1 floor closely superimposed)
17	Natural	7-8	Midden and/or fill
18	Natural	2-3	Sand floor, along with some of the midden associated with the floor below it
19	Natural	2-3	Sand floor, with a thin lense of midden above it
20	Natural	2-3	Sand floor, with a thin lense of midden trampled into it
21	Natural	2-5	Two sand floors with a thin lense of midden between them
22	Natural	2-5	Hard-packed sand floor
23	Natural	3-8	A series of thin sand floors interspersed with ash and midden lenses
24	Natural	2-4	A series of thin sand floors interspersed with ash and midden lenses (actually part of the same deposit as Level 23 above)
25	Natural	2-5	Sandy fill, consisting of numerous thin sand lenses interspersed with ash and burned sand
26	Natural	2-10	Compacted ashy midden and/or fill

TABLE A.4
Depositional Correlation between
Levels in Units 6N2W and 8N2E

6N2W		8N2E
L.1-L.4	with	L.1-L.3
L.5[1]	with	L.4[1]
L.6-L.8	with	L.5-L.8A
L.9[1]	with	L.8[1]
L.10-L.11[1]	with	L.9[1]
L.12[1]	with	L.10[1]
L.13-L.14	with	L.11-L.13
L.15-L.17[1]	with	L.14[1]
L.18-L.19	with	L.15
L.20-L.21	with	L.16
L.22[1]	with	L.17[1]
L.23	with	L.18-L.22
L.24-L.25	with	L.23-L.24
L.26	with	L.25-L.26
L.27		—[2]
L.28		—[2]

[1] In these levels the stratigraphic correspondence between the two units is clear and certain.
[2] There is no equivalent deposit in this unit.

D

Sherd Frequencies by Level

Tables A.5 and A.6 present sherd frequencies from the two test units excavated north of Mound R in 1978 and 1979 (Scarry 1980, 1981a). A brief description of these excavations, which were directed by Scarry, has already been presented in Chapter 1, and a synopsis of the depostional context within each level is given in Appendix C. It should be noted that the counts presented here generally exclude material found in pits, post molds, wall trenches, and other features that intruded into earlier midden and thus were stratigraphically mixed. The categories according to which the sherds were classified are defined in Chapter 3.

TABLE A.5
Sherd Frequencies by Level, Unit 6N2W

Level	Bell Pl., Hale	Mississippi Pl., Hull Lake	Mississippi Pl., Warrior	Carthage Inc., Akron	Carthage Inc., Carthage	Carthage Inc., Fosters	Carthage Inc., Moon Lake	Carthage Inc., Poole	Carthage Inc., Summerville	Carthage Inc., unspecified	Moundville Eng., Elliots Creek	Moundville Eng., Havana	Moundville Eng., Hemphill	Moundville Eng., Maxwells Crossing	Moundville Eng., Taylorville	Moundville Eng., Tuscaloosa	Moundville Eng., Wiggins	Moundville Eng., unspecified	Moundville Inc., Carrollton	Moundville Inc., Moundville	Moundville Inc., Snows Bend	Moundville Inc., unspecified	Alabama River Inc., unspecified	Barton Inc., Demopolis
1	113	1	261	1	3	1	—	1	—	8	—	—	3	—	—	—	1	5	1	2	—	1	—	—
2	128	3	338	—	—	1	—	—	—	6	—	—	3	1	—	—	—	7	5	2	—	—	1	1
3	100	—	272	1	—	—	—	—	—	6	—	—	—	—	2	—	—	6	—	1	—	1	—	—
4	126	—	214	—	3	—	—	—	1	6	—	1	4	—	1	2	3	18	2	4	1	—	—	—
5	243	1	497	—	6	1	—	—	—	4	—	1	6	—	—	1	2	23	3	2	—	2	—	—
6	68	—	187	—	2	—	—	—	—	3	—	—	1	—	—	—	—	9	—	7	—	—	—	—
7	117	1	241	—	—	—	—	—	—	3	—	1	1	—	—	—	—	1	1	—	1	1	—	—
8	17	1	32	—	—	—	—	—	—	—	—	—	—	—	—	—	—	—	—	3	—	—	—	—
9	85	—	97	—	—	—	—	—	—	—	—	—	—	—	—	—	—	—	—	1	—	1	—	—
10	2	—	5	1	—	—	—	—	—	—	—	—	—	—	—	—	—	4	—	—	—	—	—	—
11	8	—	9	—	—	—	—	—	—	—	—	—	—	—	—	—	—	1	—	5	—	1	—	—
12	24	—	30	1	—	—	—	—	—	3	—	—	—	—	—	—	—	3	—	2	—	—	—	—
13	11	—	16	—	—	—	—	—	—	2	—	—	—	—	—	—	—	5	2	7	—	2	—	—
14	92	—	84	—	—	—	—	—	—	—	—	—	—	—	—	—	—	1	—	9	—	—	—	—
15	151	1	161	—	—	—	—	—	—	—	—	—	—	—	—	—	—	—	—	—	—	—	—	—
16	5	—	10	—	—	—	—	—	—	—	—	—	—	—	—	—	—	—	—	2	—	—	—	—
17,18	28	—	35	—	—	—	—	—	—	—	—	—	—	—	—	—	—	2	—	1	—	—	—	—
19	3	1	14	—	—	—	—	—	—	—	—	—	—	—	—	—	—	1	—	3	—	—	—	—
20	28	—	21	—	—	—	—	—	—	—	—	—	—	—	—	—	—	—	—	2	—	—	—	—
21	24	3	34	1	—	—	—	—	—	—	—	—	—	—	—	—	—	2	—	2	—	—	—	—
22	32	—	22	—	—	—	—	—	—	—	—	—	—	—	—	—	—	—	—	1	—	2	—	—
23	40	—	46	—	—	—	—	—	—	—	—	—	—	—	—	—	—	—	—	1	—	1	—	—
24	5	—	16	—	—	—	—	—	—	—	1	—	—	—	—	—	—	—	—	—	—	4	—	—
25	17	—	52	—	—	—	1	—	—	—	—	—	—	—	—	—	—	—	—	6	—	2	—	—
26	20	—	47	—	—	—	—	—	—	—	1	—	—	—	—	—	—	—	—	3	—	—	—	—
27A	32	—	53	—	—	—	—	—	—	—	—	2	—	—	—	—	—	—	—	—	—	1	—	—
27B	2	—	10	—	—	—	—	—	—	—	—	—	—	—	—	—	—	—	—	—	—	—	—	—
28	2	—	1	—	—	—	—	—	—	—	—	—	—	—	—	—	—	—	—	1	—	—	—	1

Mississippian types and varieties (local)

(continued)

TABLE A.5 (Continued)

Level	Mississippian types and varieties (nonlocal) D'Olive Inc., unspecified	Lake Jackson Dec., unspecified	Mound Place Inc., Mobile	Mound Place Inc., unspecified	Bell Pl., unspecified	Woodland types and varieties Alligator Inc., Geiger	Baytown Pl., Roper	Baldwin Pl., Blubber	Baldwin Pl., Lubbub	Unclassified	Total sherd count	Total sherd weight (g)	Painted decoration Black film	Red film	White film	Red and black	Red engraved
1	—	—	—	—	—	—	1	—	—	5	406	1376	101	6	3	—	—
2	—	—	1	1	—	—	—	1	—	4	499	1388	107	6	5	—	—
3	—	—	3	—	—	1	1	—	—	8	499	1228	84	8	2	—	—
4	1	—	9	—	—	—	—	1	—	13	376	1325	124	7	5	—	—
5	—	1	—	—	—	—	5	—	—	1	823	2765	218	6	4	—	—
6	—	—	—	—	—	—	1	—	—	2	273	1071	57	—	3	—	—
7	—	—	—	—	—	—	1	—	—	1	384	1425	89	2	2	—	—
8	—	—	—	—	—	—	1	—	—	—	50	255	9	—	1	—	—
9	—	—	—	—	—	—	—	—	—	—	190	841	55	—	1	—	—
10	—	—	—	—	—	—	—	—	1	1	8	127	1	—	—	—	—
11	—	—	—	—	—	—	—	—	—	—	18	109	6	1	1	—	—
12	—	—	—	—	—	—	—	—	—	—	64	167	17	—	—	—	1
13	—	—	—	—	—	—	—	—	—	1	35	170	10	2	1	—	—
14	—	—	—	—	—	—	1	—	—	—	192	807	62	1	—	—	—
15	—	—	—	—	—	—	—	—	—	—	334	1592	102	—	4	—	—
16	—	—	—	—	—	—	—	—	—	—	16	38	5	1	—	—	—
17,18	—	—	—	—	—	—	1	—	—	—	65	308	18	—	—	—	—
19	—	—	—	—	—	—	—	—	—	—	18	64	3	—	—	—	—
20	—	—	—	—	—	—	—	—	—	—	55	202	22	—	—	—	—
21	—	—	—	—	—	—	—	—	—	—	61	325	15	1	—	—	—
22	—	—	—	—	—	—	—	—	—	—	57	365	27	—	—	—	—
23	—	—	—	—	—	—	1	—	—	—	93	263	36	—	—	—	—
24	—	—	—	—	—	—	1	—	—	—	28	152	8	—	—	—	—
25	—	—	—	—	—	—	—	—	—	1	72	387	18	—	—	—	—
26	—	—	—	—	1	—	1	—	—	—	80	432	21	1	—	—	—
27A	—	—	—	—	—	—	—	—	—	—	91	453	30	—	—	—	—
27B	—	—	—	—	—	—	1	—	—	—	15	101	4	—	—	—	—
28	—	—	—	—	—	—	—	—	—	—	2	5	—	—	—	—	—

(continued)

291

TABLE A.5 (Continued)

Level	Rim and base fragments														Secondary shape features					
	Bottle (rims)	Bottle (pedestal-base fragments)	Bottle (slab-base fragments)	Cylindrical bowl (rims)	Flaring-rim bowl (rims)	Outslanting bowl (rims)	Restricted bowl (rims)	Short-neck bowl (rims)	Simple bowl (rims)	Burnished jar (rims)	Neckless jar (unburnished, rims)	Standard jar (unburnished, rims)	Miscellaneous rims	Total rims	Beaded rim	Folded rim	Folded-flattened rim	Indentations	Notched lip	Scalloped rim
1	1				4		3	1	1			17	9	35	2	4			1	
2	1			1	3		2	4	4			12	6	33	1	1				
3	1				2		2		2			14	7	28	2					
4	3		1	1	5		4		7			12	14	43	2	1		1		1
5	2	2			3			1	3			21	12	45				1		
6	1	1		1	2		2					9	5	18						
7	1				4				1	1		3	7	18						
8							1				1	4	1	9		2			1	
9	2			1					1			3	2	1						
10													1							
11														4						
12									2			2		6		2				
13	1				4		1					5		13		2				
14					1				5			3	1	15		3				1
15									1		1	5		1						
16	2								1			1	7	4			1			
17, 18											1		1	3		2				
19					1		2					2		6						1
20	1											3	2	9		2				
21	1				1				1			2	1	3		1				1
22		1			1				1			2		3		2				
23					1				2			4	3	12		1	1			1
24	1				1							1	1	3						
25												1	1	5						
26		1										2		3		2				
27A												1	1	3		2				
27B													1	1						
28																				

292

TABLE A.6
Sherd Frequencies by Level, Unit 8N2E

Mississippian types and varieties (local)

Level	Bell Pl., Hale	Mississippi Pl., Hull Lake	Mississippi Pl., Warrior	Carthage Inc., Akron	Carthage Inc., Carthage	Carthage Inc., Moon Lake	Carthage Inc., Poole	Carthage Inc., unspecified	Moundville Eng., Cypress	Moundville Eng., Elliots Creek	Moundville Eng., Havana	Moundville Eng., Hemphill	Moundville Eng., Stewart	Moundville Eng., Taylorville	Moundville Eng., Tuscaloosa	Moundville Eng., Wiggins	Moundville Eng., unspecified	Moundville Inc., Carrollton	Moundville Inc., Moundville	Moundville Inc., Snows Bend	Moundville Inc., unspecified
1	120	3	344	—	1	—	—	7	—	—	1	4	—	1	—	—	13	—	3	—	—
2	109	1	305	—	—	—	—	5	—	—	1	1	—	—	1	—	2	2	1	—	1
3	135	3	331	1	—	—	—	4	1	—	1	—	—	—	1	—	6	—	6	1	—
4	147	1	337	—	—	—	—	5	—	—	1	1	—	—	2	—	18	—	6	—	1
5	49	—	79	—	—	—	—	1	—	—	—	1	—	—	—	—	3	—	1	1	—
6	21	1	55	—	—	—	1	—	—	—	—	1	—	—	—	1	1	1	—	—	1
6A	11	1	23	—	—	—	—	—	—	—	—	—	—	—	—	—	—	—	—	—	—
7	17	—	51	—	—	—	—	—	—	—	—	—	—	—	—	—	—	—	—	—	—
7A	22	—	54	—	—	—	—	1	—	—	—	—	—	—	—	—	2	—	1	—	—
8A	15	—	55	—	—	—	—	—	—	—	—	—	—	—	—	—	—	—	—	—	—
8B	8	—	22	—	—	—	—	—	—	—	—	—	—	—	—	—	2	—	—	—	—
9	21	1	33	—	—	—	—	—	—	—	—	—	—	—	—	—	3	—	8	—	2
10	16	—	28	—	—	—	—	—	—	—	—	—	—	—	—	—	—	—	2	—	3
11	18	1	28	—	—	—	—	—	—	—	—	—	—	—	—	—	6	—	8	—	—
12	44	—	97	1	—	—	—	—	—	1	—	—	—	—	—	—	—	—	—	—	1
13	1	—	2	—	—	—	—	—	—	1	—	—	1	—	—	—	5	—	—	—	—
14	90	—	204	—	—	—	1	—	—	—	—	—	—	—	—	—	1	—	—	—	—
15	4	—	8	—	—	—	—	—	—	1	—	—	—	—	—	—	2	—	3	—	—
16	6	—	22	—	—	1	—	—	—	—	—	—	—	—	—	—	5	—	—	—	3
17	38	—	92	—	—	1	—	—	—	—	—	—	—	—	—	—	2	—	—	—	—
18	3	—	3	—	—	—	—	—	—	—	—	—	—	—	—	—	—	—	1	—	—
19	—	—	6	—	—	—	—	—	—	—	—	—	—	—	—	—	—	—	—	—	—
20	2	—	15	—	—	—	—	—	—	—	—	—	—	—	—	—	—	—	—	—	—
21	—	—	19	—	—	—	—	—	—	—	—	—	—	—	—	—	—	—	—	—	—
22	2	—	31	—	—	—	—	—	—	2	—	—	—	—	—	—	—	—	—	—	—
23	12	—	12	—	—	—	—	—	—	—	—	—	—	—	—	—	—	—	—	—	—
24	14	—	3	—	—	—	—	—	—	—	—	—	—	—	—	—	—	—	—	—	—
25	5	—	3	—	—	—	—	—	—	—	—	—	—	—	—	—	—	—	—	—	—
26	1	—	—	—	—	—	—	—	—	—	—	—	—	—	—	—	—	—	—	—	—
Mixed:																					
15–17	4	—	20	—	—	—	—	—	—	—	—	1	—	—	—	—	1	—	1	—	—
18–21	2	—	7	—	—	—	—	—	—	—	—	—	—	—	—	—	—	—	—	—	—
22–25	4	—	6	—	—	—	—	—	—	—	—	—	—	—	—	—	—	—	—	—	—

(continued)

293

TABLE A.6 (Continued)

Level	Mississippian types and varieties (nonlocal) D'Olive Inc., unspecified	McKee Island C.M., unspecified	Pouncey Pinched, unspecified	Woodland types and varieties Mulberry Creek C.M., Aliceville	Baytown Pl., Roper	Baytown Pl., unspecified	Unclassified	Total sherd count	Total sherd weight (g)	Painted decoration Black film	Red film	White film	Red and black	Black on white	Red engraved	White engraved
1	—	—	1	—	—	—	5	502	1288	117	7	3	—	—	—	—
2	—	—	—	—	1	—	5	429	1279	82	1	—	—	—	—	—
3	—	—	—	1	—	—	7	501	1523	114	4	2	2	—	—	—
4	—	—	—	—	—	1	6	528	1728	128	2	1	—	—	—	—
5	1	—	—	—	1	—	1	139	436	36	1	1	—	—	—	—
6	—	—	—	—	1	—	2	83	338	16	—	—	—	—	—	—
6A	—	1	—	—	1	—	1	39	129	3	—	—	—	—	—	—
7	—	—	—	—	—	—	—	71	270	11	—	—	—	—	1	—
7A	—	—	—	—	—	—	1	81	332	18	—	—	—	—	—	—
8A	—	—	—	—	—	—	—	72	303	9	—	—	—	—	1	—
8B	—	—	—	—	1	—	—	30	144	3	—	—	—	—	—	—
9	—	—	—	—	—	—	—	55	290	17	—	—	—	—	—	—
10	—	—	—	—	—	—	—	47	148	9	2	1	—	—	1	—
11	—	—	—	—	1	1	—	51	156	16	—	—	—	—	—	—
12	—	—	—	—	—	—	1	151	653	45	—	2	1?	—	1	1
13	—	—	—	—	1	—	—	8	8	—	—	—	—	—	—	—
14	—	—	—	—	—	—	—	315	1538	75	—	1	—	2	—	—
15	—	—	—	—	—	—	—	14	84	2	2	2	—	1	—	—
16	—	—	—	—	2	—	2	35	197	10	—	—	—	—	2	—
17	—	—	—	—	—	—	—	150	875	40	—	—	—	—	—	—
18	—	—	—	—	—	—	—	3	32	—	—	—	—	—	—	—
19	—	—	—	—	—	—	—	9	53	3	—	—	—	—	—	—
20	—	—	—	—	—	—	—	1	2	1	—	—	—	—	—	—
21	—	—	—	—	—	—	—	21	59	1	—	—	—	—	—	—
22	—	—	—	—	—	—	—	31	106	12	—	—	—	—	4	—
23	—	—	—	—	—	—	—	58	188	15	—	—	—	—	—	—
24	—	—	—	—	—	—	—	17	47	3	—	—	—	—	2	—
25	—	—	—	—	—	—	—	4	10	—	—	—	—	—	—	—
26	—	—	—	—	—	—	—	6	22	3	—	—	—	—	—	—
Mixed: 15–17	—	—	—	—	—	—	1	26	114	4	1	1	—	—	—	—
18–21	—	—	—	—	—	—	—	9	43	2	—	—	—	—	—	—
21–25	—	—	—	—	—	—	—	10	31	4	1	—	—	—	—	—

(continued)

Level	Bottle (rims)	Bottle (pedestal-base fragments)	Bottle (slab-base fragments)	Cylindrical bowl (rims)	Flaring-rim bowl (rims)	Outslanting bowl (rims)	Restricted bowl (rims)	Short-neck bowl (rims)	Simple bowl (rims)	Burnished jar (rims)	Neckless jar (unburnished, rims)	Standard jar (unburnished, rims)	Miscellaneous rims	Total rims	Beaded rim	Beaded shoulder	Folded rim	Folded-flattened rim	Indentations	Notched lip	Scalloped rim
1	1		1	1	1			1	2			8	10	24	1		1			1	1
2					8		1	1	5			7	14	35	1		1		1	1	
3	1		3		1				5			11	12	26	3				1	1	
4	1			1	1	1	2		1			10	4	25	1				1	1	
5		3							2			2	3	10							
6									1			1	1	7							
6A																					
7												2	2	2							
7A	1											1		1							
8A											2	2	1	2							
8B												1		4							3
9												1	1								
10									2					2			1				
11	1								2			6	1	2			3				
12		2												3			1		1		1
13										1						2	10				
14					2				2	1		10	3	15			1				1
15	2				4		1		2					21			2				
16									1												
17		1			1	1			1			3	3	9			1	1	1		1
18												1									
19																	1				
20																					
21									2			2	2	2							
22	2				1							1	1	4			1				
23														1							
24																					
25																					
26																					
Mixed: 15-17					1							1		1			1				
18-21																					
22-25																					

E

Methods for Measuring Physical Properties

TENSILE STRENGTH

This property was measured with a three-point bending test, carried out on an Instron load frame. The slab of pottery was placed on a pair of transverse supports, 3 cm apart. A constantly increasing load was then applied to the slab from above, by means of a transverse knife edge situated midway between the supports. The load at which the slab broke was recorded, and this value was used to evaluate the modulus of rupture using the general formula:

$$S = \frac{3kl}{2bd^2}$$

where:

S = modulus of rupture (kg/cm^2)
k = breaking load (kg)
l = distance between the supports (cm)
d = depth of the slab (cm)
b = breadth of the slab (cm)

The slabs used in making the measurements were cut from sherds with a mineralogical saw, and the cut faces were polished on a lap in order to remove any large flaws that may have been introduced by the saw. Generally the slabs were about 0.7–1.0 cm in breadth, and were always cut so that their long dimension was parallel to the orientation of the coils (i.e., horizontal on the original vessel). In testing strength, the slab was always positioned so that the load was applied to the surface that represented the original exterior of the vessel.

POROSITY

The porosity of sherds was measured as follows: First, a test piece was boiled for two hours to saturate its pores with water. While still saturated, the piece was weighed and its volume was determined with a pycnometer. Next, the piece was placed in a dessicating oven, and, when thoroughly dry, the piece was weighed again. The apparent porosity, as a percentage of total volume, was calculated with the following formula:

$$P = \frac{100(W_s - W_d)}{V}$$

where:

P = apparent porosity (percent of volume)
W_s = saturated weight (g)
W_d = dessicated weight (g)
V = volume (cm^2).

The test pieces were small fragments of the slabs that had been cut for measuring tensile strength. Two pieces were processed from every sherd to ensure that the results obtained were reliable. The test pieces averaged about 1.0 cm^3 in volume.

It should be noted that the procedure described above measures only the "apparent" porosity, that is, the volume fraction of pores that are accessible to water from the surface. However, small pieces of low-fired pottery are likely to have relatively few sealed pores, and so in this case the apparent porosity is probably very close to the true porosity (Shepard 1956:126).

THERMAL DIFFUSIVITY

The procedure used to measure diffusivity was designed by Alan Franklin and C. K. Chiang of the National Bureau of Standards. Although this procedure was probably not accurate to more than absolute determinations, it was quite easy to set up and eminently suited to the purposes at hand.

The equipment consisted of a jerry-built frame to which were added a soldering iron and a thermocouple. The thermocouple was hooked up to a graphic $x-y$ recorder capable of producing a plot of temperature (y axis) as a function of time (x axis).

A sherd was mounted horizontally in the frame, the thermocouple held against the bottom of the sherd with a spring. The hot soldering iron was then lowered from above, so that its tip came in contact with the upper surface of the sherd, directly opposite where the thermocouple touched the bottom surface. As the sherd was gradually heated, the $x-y$ recorder produced a graph showing the temperature change through time. It was from this graph that the diffusivity could be calculated.

Ideally, the graph should have showed a pattern of no temperature change, followed abruptly by an increase in temperature, which continued to rise in proportion to the square root of time. The delay time—the interval between the contact of the soldering iron at the upper surface and the abrupt increase in temperature at the lower surface—was measured, and used to compute a relative estimate of diffusivity as follows:

$$D = \frac{d^2}{t}$$

where:

    D = diffusivity
    d = distance between the heat source and the thermocouple (i.e., the thickness of the sherd in mm)
    t = delay time

In practice, it was sometimes difficult, when looking at the graph, to determine the precise point at which the temperature rise began. This difficulty stemmed from the fact that the initial rise was often gradual, not abrupt as theory would predict. To overcome the problem, a square root transformation was applied to the x axis (time) and the curve was replotted. The linear portion of the resulting curve was then extrapolated to the point where it met the x axis, and this point was regarded as the terminus of the delay time.

ELASTICITY

This property was measured by means of a three-point bending test, identical to the one used in determining tensile strength. In fact, the very same test results from each slab were used to calculate both tensile strength and elasticity.

Using the graphical data provided by the Instron machine, Young's modulus of elasticity was calculated as follows:

$$E = \frac{Sl^2}{6yd}$$

where:

E = Young's modulus (kg/cm²)
S = modulus of rupture (kg/cm²)
l = distance between the supports (cm)
d = depth of the slab (cm)
y = vertical displacement of the slab when fracture occurs (cm).

F

Type–Variety Descriptions

It is the purpose of this appendix to describe all of the types and varieties—both local and nonlocal—that appear in the whole vessel and sherd samples from Moundville. Much of the information on local ceramics has, of course, already been presented, but in somewhat scattered fashion. The technological characteristics of the Mississippian ceramics were discussed in Chapter 2, many of the classificatory categories were briefly defined in Chapter 3, and chronological relationships were presented in Chapter 4. Here, these data and more are gathered together and collated by type and variety, the intent being to provide the reader with a useful and concise summary of the Moundville assemblage.

The appendix is divided into two major sections, treating local ceramics first, and nonlocal ceramics second. The types within each section are arranged alphabetically, with the "unclassified" categories last. The named varieties under each type heading are also ordered alphabetically, with *variety unspecified* last. Individual vessels pertaining to each category can be located using the index in Appendix G, supplemented if necessary by the one in Appendix H. Descriptions of these individual vessels, including information on provenience, appear in Appendix A.

LOCAL TYPES

ALABAMA RIVER INCISED

When first proposed by Cottier (1970:21-23), this type subsumed material exhibiting a tremendous range of formal variation. Indeed, it was much easier to characterize this type in spatial and temporal terms, rather than in formal ones, for it lumped together all the incised, shell-tempered wares found on late prehistoric sites along the Warrior, lower Tombigbee, and Alabama rivers. Sheldon subsequently curtailed its formal range somewhat by splitting off a second type, Foster Filmed Incised (1974:208-210), and now the process of curtailment has been carried even further. Alabama River Incised is here understood to refer to vessels of unburnished, shell-tempered ware decorated with curvilinear, wet-paste incisions. The characteristic designs are scrolls (not arches), which are usually found on jars in the area below the neck. Vessels with burnished surfaces and broad-line incision, formerly included in Alabama River Incised, are here subsumed within the type Carthage Incised.

Examples of Alabama River Incised are very rare at Moundville, and in the absence of a good comparative sample, I have not attempted to set up varieties. Presumably, the type's rarity is attributable to its very late position in time, postdating the bulk of Moundville's occupation.

Alabama River Incised, *variety unspecified*
(Figures 56h; 62r)

Sample. 1 vessel, 1 sherd.

Description. The one whole vessel in the sample is a standard jar with appliqué neck fillets, decorated with a two-line running scroll. The one sherd comes from a short-neck bowl, and is not large enough to accurately reconstruct the design.

Chronological Position. Alabama River phase.

References. Cottier 1970:21-23; Sheldon 1974:208-210.

ALLIGATOR INCISED

This type was originally defined with reference to sherds from the Lower Mississippi Valley (Phillips 1970:38-40). Recently, however, its range has been extended to the central Tombigbee region (Jenkins 1981:82-85), and so it would seem appropriate to use it here as well. The type includes ceramics decorated with rectilinear designs, executed with sloppy, wet-paste incisions. The paste, by definition, is tempered predominantly with grog. Only one variety has been recognized in our sample.

Alligator Incised, *variety Geiger*
(Figure 67a)

Sample.   1 sherd.

Description.   Conforming to Jenkins's definition, the sherd is decorated with a series of parallel oblique lines placed just below the lip.   The lip itself is thickened with a flange to the exterior.

Chronological Position.   West Jefferson phase, and possibly slightly earlier.

References.   Jenkins 1981:84-85.

BALDWIN PLAIN

The earliest use of this name was to describe certain undecorated Miller II (Middle Woodland) ceramics in northeast Mississippi (Jennings 1941:200; Cotter and Corbett 1951:17-18).   Most recently, Jenkins (1981:123-127) has extended the concept to refer to all pre-Mississippian, sand-tempered plainware in the Tombigbee drainage, and has recognized several varieties based on differences in paste and rim form.
A few sherds of this type were found in the 1978-1979 excavations north of Mound R.   Their presence attests to some scattered, early components in the vicinity, predating Moundville's major occupation.

Baldwin Plain, *variety Blubber*
(Figure 67j-k)

Sample.   2 sherds.

Description.   As defined by Jenkins, the sherds are tempered with medium to fine sand.   Both specimens in the sample are simple bowl rims.

Chronological Position.   On the Tombigbee, the variety is predominantly associated with the span between Early Miller I and Early Miller III, or from about 100 B.C. to A.D. 900.

References.   Jenkins 1981:124-125.

Baldwin Plain, *variety Lubbub*
(Figure 67i)

Sample.   1 sherd.

Description.   An undecorated ware, tempered with coarse

sand.

Chronological Position.   The ware of this variety is the local equivalent of the Alexander Series, and therefore dates to the Early Woodland period (ca. 500-100 B.C.).

References. Jenkins 1981:125-126.

BARTON INCISED

Following the usage established by Phillips (1970:43-44), this type includes unburnished, shell-tempered pottery, decorated with rectilinear patterns that consist of multiple parallel lines. The lines themselves typically have "burred" edges, indicating that they were incised when the paste was in a wet, highly plastic state.

Local (or apparently local) examples of Barton Incised are rare at Moundville. Although the one named variety falls very late in the ceramic sequence, there are reasons to believe that a local version of this type was manufactured earlier as well. Sites in the immediate vicinity of Moundville have been known to produce occasional examples of Barton Incised, *variety unspecified* with a folded-flattened rim—a very distinctive local feature that dates to Moundville I. No such sherds have yet been observed in the collections from Moundville, however.

Barton Incised, *variety Demopolis*
(Figure 56i)

Sample. 1 sherd.

Description. The decoration is confined to the neck of a standard jar, and consists of multiple parallel lines that are incised vertically (or almost vertically) from a point just below the lip.

Chronological Position. Alabama River phase.

References. Jenkins 1981:62-63.

BAYTOWN PLAIN

This is another type, long established in the Mississippi Valley (Phillips 1970:47-48), which was recently adopted on the Tombigbee (Jenkins 1981:87-91). By definition, it includes undecorated ceramics with a paste that is predominantly "clay tempered," and may contain some sand as well.

Baytown Plain, *variety Roper*
(Figure 67c-h)

Sample. 26 sherds.

Description. This variety is tempered with grog alone, and lacks deliberate sand inclusions. Temper particles are large enough to be readily visible, often more than 1 mm in width. Colors tend to warm shades of brown, with the temper particles often appearing lighter than the matrix. Among the vessel shapes recognized in the sample are simple bowls and standard jars, the latter often exhibiting handles. Note that this variety is equivalent to what has elsewhere been called West Jefferson Plain (Jenkins and Nielsen 1974:146-148).

Chronological Position. West Jefferson phase, and probably extending back in time to Late Miller II (ca. A.D. 600).

References. Jenkins 1981:89-90; Jenkins and Nielsen 1974:146-148 (described as West Jefferson Plain).

Baytown Plain, *variety unspecified*

Sample. 1 sherd.

Description. This designation was applied to a single unusual sherd that is considerably harder than most examples of *Roper*, and has a more finely textured paste. The exterior surface is fired to a whitish color, whereas the core and interior surface are black.

Chronological Position. Unknown.

BELL PLAIN

Bell Plain was originally the name given to the shell-tempered "polished" plainware found in the area from northeast Arkansas to northwest Mississippi (Phillips *et al.* 1951:122-126). Later the concept was expanded, both taxonomically and geographically, when Phillips made it *the* polished, shell-tempered plainware for the entire Central and Lower Mississippi Valley, subsuming a number of distinctive regional varieties (Phillips 1970:58-61). Given the logic of the type-variety system, and given the general similarity of Moundville ceramics to those of the Mississippi Valley, it seems most reasonable to make the local smooth-surfaced plainware a variety of Bell Plain, as Jenkins (1981:63-65) has already done.

Traditionally, two characteristics have been associated with Bell Plain. One, as previously mentioned, is the smooth surface produced by burnishing the vessel before firing. The second is a paste that is tempered with very fine shell. There is no question that these two features are, in a statistical sense, associated. Most burnished vessels have a fine paste, and vice versa. However, the fact that this association is not invariant brings with it a classificatory problem: to wit, what to do about the not insignificant proportion of fine-paste vessels that are unburnished, and coarse-paste vessels that are burnished? Here the problem is circumvented by relying on surface finish, not temper particle size, as the primary sorting criterion. Such a rule has several things to recommend it. First of all, I suspect that the burnished-unburnished distinction separates vessels along functional lines (i.e., bottles and bowls versus jars) much more cleanly than does the fine-coarse distinction in paste. Besides, there is no practical alternative to relying on surface finish when dealing with whole vessels, since in most cases it is not possible to get a good look at the paste.

In brief, Bell Plain is here defined to include shell tempered ceramics that lack tooled decoration but have a burnished surface. Locally, the type includes ceramics that were formerly classified as Moundville Black Filmed (McKenzie 1965:56-58), along with some whose light surface color precluded their assignment to the latter type.

Bell Plain, *variety Hale*
(Figures 39a, d; 41c-j; 44g-h, j-k; 45a-d; 46c,
f-g, j; 49a-k; 51b-l; 52a; 53e, g, i; 54m;
56j-m; 58a-q; 62j-k, m, q; 63d, f)

Sample. 346 vessels, 2460 sherds.

Description. New variety.

Sorting Criteria. A shell-tempered ware with a burnished (though not necessarily lustrous) surface. *Hale* tends to have somewhat smaller temper particles than Mississippi Plain, *variety Warrior*; however, the particle size is in itself not distinctive because the two varieties overlap quite a bit in this respect. *Hale* may also occasionally exhibit particles of grog as an added, but not exclusive, tempering agent.

Additional Characteristics. Most vessels belonging to this variety are bottles and bowls; jars are quite rare. A wide range of secondary shape features occur, most common among them being beaded rims (on bowls), indentations (on bottles), single lug (on bowls), widely spaced nodes (on bowls and jars), spouts (on bowls), and handles (on jars). Effigy features are also a common accoutrement of *Hale*, the most frequently occuring kinds being the fish, frog, bird, and mussel shell, in that order. The vast majority of *Hale* vessels are black filmed. The other painted treatments that occur are white film, red film, red on white, red on black, black on white, and red and black on white.

Distribution. Reported from the Black Warrior drainage and the central Tombigbee.

Published Illustrations. Moore 1905:Figures 12, 13,

25, 69, 76, 78, 96, 98, 100, 129, 130, 135, 145, 150, 155, 1907:Figures 21, 23, 26, 30, 48; Jones and DeJarnette n.d.:Plate 1f; DeJarnette and Wimberly 1941:Figures 63 (top row), 65 (4), 65 (12); Webb and DeJarnette 1942:Plates 60 (1), 125 (1); McKenzie 1966:Figures 6, 7, 11c, 13, 14; DeJarnette and Peebles 1970:97 (bottom), 100 (top), 114 (top); Nielsen and Jenkins 1973:Plate 2a, d-f; Peebles 1979:Figures III-7, III-15, III-17, III-18, III-20, III-24, III-25, IV-1, IV-3, IV-10, IV-11, IV-14, IV-29, V-3, VII-11, VII-14; Jenkins 1981:Figures 57, 58.

Chronological Position. Moundville I phase to Alabama River phase. Finer chronological distinctions can be made on the basis of vessel shapes, secondary shape features, effigy features, and painted decoration (see Chapter 4).

References. Steponaitis 1980:49 (described as a variety of Mississippi Plain); Jenkins 1981:65-66 (*Hale*, as defined here, also subsumes Jenkins's variety *Big Sandy*).

CARTHAGE INCISED

This category is approximately equivalent to the old type Moundville Filmed Incised (DeJarnette and Wimberly 1941:84; McKenzie 1965:60-61), differing only in that specimens need not be black filmed to be included. The elimination of black filming as a defining criterion obviously necessitated that the name of the old type be changed. The simplest solution would have been to rechristen it Moundville Incised, but this name was already being used to refer to another type. So Carthage Incised was decided upon as a reasonable alternative.

Carthage Incised is defined to include shell-tempered vessels with a burnished surface that are decorated with broad, "trailed" incisions. Typically, these incisions are from 1.5 to 2.0 mm wide, and are U-shaped in cross section, having been executed when the paste was in a leather-hard state of dryness. By far the most common vessel forms in this type are bowls and bottles, with jars being extremely rare.

Carthage Incised, *variety Akron*
(Figures 39e-h; 40q; 51a; 56a; 621; 631)

Sample. 26 vessels, 8 sherds.

Description. New variety.

Sorting Criteria. A design whose major feature is a horizontal band of two or more lines running parallel to and just below the lip. The band of lines is commonly embellished with loops and/or folds. The ware is equivalent to that of Bell Plain, *variety Hale*.

Additional Characteristics. In virtually all cases the

band that makes up the design consists of either three or four lines; only a single example of a two-line band is known (ED14). The decorated portion of the rim on one vessel (NW25) is visibly thickened on the exterior.

By far the most common vessel form is the simple bowl. Cylindrical bowls, restricted bowls, and outslanting bowls appear less frequently. Of the 26 whole vessels in the sample, 19 sport effigy features of some sort. Most of these effigy vessels are of the lug-and-rim-adorno type, usually depicting a bird. A few turtle and conch shell effigies occur also. With regard to secondary shape features, grouped nodes and a notched lip are found on one vessel each.

All but four of the vessels in the sample are black filmed, as are all the sherds.

Distribution.   The Black Warrior drainage, the central and upper Tombigbee drainage, and possibly as far north as the Pickwick Basin on the Middle Tennessee River. Actually, burnished, shell-tempered ceramics with this sort of design are widely distributed over the Southeast, and where the distribution of *Akron* should end is, at this stage, a somewhat arbitrary decision.

Published Illustrations.   Moore 1905:Figure 94; DeJarnette and Wimberly 1941:Figures 63 (bottom middle), 64 (top right); McKenzie 1966:Figure 11a; DeJarnette and Peebles 1970:102 (top), 111 (bottom); Peebles 1979:Figures III-26, VII-13; Jenkins 1981:Figure 4a-d.

Chronological Position.   Moundville I through early Moundville III. Temporal distinctions within this span are recognizable on the basis of effigy features, secondary shape features, and (to a lesser extent) basic shape (see Chapter 4).

References.   Steponaitis 1980:50; Jenkins 1981:79 (described as a variety of Mound Place Incised).

Carthage Incised, *variety Carthage*
(Figures 49k-1; 51o; 53h; 56d-e; 62b)

Sample.   19 vessels, 21 sherds.

Description.   New variety.

Sorting Criteria.   A design consisting of a two- to four-line scroll, which runs entirely around the vessel's circumference. The paste and surface finish are like those of Bell Plain, *variety Hale.*

Additional Characteristics.   The distinctive shapes represented in the whole vessel sample are the subglobular bottle with simple base, short-neck bowl, narrow-neck bottle, flaring-rim bowl, simple bowl, restricted bowl, and cylindrical bowl. One rather unusual, straight-sided bowl (NE461) is embellished with vertical lugs.

On most vessels, the scroll making up the design consists of three lines; the two-line and four-line treatments are rare. The nature of the scroll is usually such that it converges into a swirl at intervals around the vessel's circumference. Only two variations on this sort of convergent scroll are known to occur: One vessel (SEH15) exhibits a concatenated series of scrolls, each of which ends in a loop (Figure 52k). Another (NE461) exhibits a continuous, nonconvergent scroll (similar to the one in Figure 62e). These two variants probably have chronological significance, the former being early (i.e., early Moundville III) and the latter being late (i.e., late Moundville III to Alabama River phase).

Fourteen of the *Carthage* vessels are black filmed, and five are not.

Distribution. *Carthage* has been reported from the Black Warrior Valley, the central Tombigbee Valley, and the Alabama River Valley below Montgomery.

Published Illustrations. Moore 1899:Figure 68, 1907:Figure 72, 1915:Figure 24; Nance 1976:Figure 32e; Jenkins 1981:Figure 3a-d.

Chronological Position. Moundville III and Alabama River phases.

References. Steponaitis 1980:50; Jenkins 1981:67-68.

Carthage Incised, *variety Fosters*
(Figures 51m, p; 56b; 62p)

Sample. 5 vessels, 3 sherds.

Description. New variety.

Sorting Criteria. A design consisting of free-standing representational motifs, usually depicting the hand and/or forearm bones. The ware is comparable to Bell Plain, *variety Hale.*

Additional Characteristics. This variety includes mostly flaring-rim bowls (having the design on the interior), and short-neck bowls (having the design on the exterior). Also in the sample is one subglobular bottle with a slab base, and an unusually large, straight-sided bowl (SD682).

The hand motif in this variety is always executed in a highly simplified manner, so that it is really nothing more than an outline. The hand itself may or may not exhibit a stylized eye. In only one instance (SED28) are forearm bones missing from the design. Sometimes the representational motifs are interspersed with "hanging" scrolls (see, for example, DeJarnette and Peebles 1970:113 [bottom]).

The surface of these vessels is frequently either black filmed, or painted red and white.

   Distribution.   *Fosters* is known from the Black Warrior
Valley, the central Tombigbee Valley, and the Alabama River
Valley below Montgomery.

   Published   Illustrations.   Moore   1899:Figure   41;
DeJarnette   and   Peebles   1970:113   (bottom);   Jenkins
1981:Figure 3i-j.

Chronological   Position.   Moundville   III   (especially   late
Moundville III) and Alabama River phases.

References. Steponaitis 1980:50; Jenkins 1981:68.

                Carthage Incised, *variety Moon Lake*
                    (Figures 39k; 40r; 51q; 53j)

Sample.   7 vessels, 3 sherds.

Description.   New variety.

   Sorting Criteria.   Zones of parallel (usually oblique)
line segments, arranged in chevronlike patterns that form a
band around the vessel.   The design may occur either on the
interior   or   the   exterior   of   a   vessel   whose   ware   is
equivalent to Bell Plain, *variety Hale.*

   Additional Characteristics.   The variety seems to occur
only on shallow flaring-rim bowls and short-neck bowls.   In
the former case, the design is confined to a band that
follows the interior of the rim; in the latter case, the
design is placed on the exterior shoulder.   Vessels of *Moon
Lake* are usually black filmed.   One flaring-rim bowl in the
sample exhibits a notched lip.

   Distribution.   The variety occurs both in the Warrior
drainage and on the central Tombigbee.

   Published   Illustrations.   DeJarnette   and   Wimberly
1941:Figures 63 (bottom left),   64 (bottom left); McKenzie
1966:Figure 3 (top); Jenkins 1981:Figure 3e-h.

Chronological Position.   Moundville I phase to Moundville
III phase.   Shallow flaring-rim bowls of this variety were
most common during Moundville I, although some may have been
made as late as early Moundville III.   The variety then
seems to have had a resurgence of popularity during late
Moundville III, when the design was placed on short-neck
bowls.

References. Steponaitis 1980:50; Jenkins 1981:68-69.

                Carthage Incised, *variety Poole*
                    (Figures 51n; 56c)

Sample. 2 vessels, 2 sherds.

Description. New variety.

Sorting Criteria. The characteristic design consists of step motifs enclosing (or alternating with) concentric rayed semicircles, all within a band that encircles the vessel. The ware is comparable to Bell Plain, *variety Hale.*

Additional Characteristics. The variety is known to occur only on short-neck bowls. Most examples are black filmed; one is red and white, the red slip being placed on the neck and within the incised lines.

Distribution. Thus far the variety is known from the Black Warrior Valley and from the Alabama River Valley in the vicinity of Montgomery. One can expect it to turn up on the central Tombigbee as well.

Published Illustrations. None.

Chronological Position. Late Moundville III, probably extending into the Alabama River phase.

References. Steponaitis 1980:50.

Carthage Incised, *variety Summerville*
(Figures 39j; 41a-b)

Sample. 4 vessels, 1 sherd.

Description. New variety.

Sorting Criteria. Decoration consists of incised arches arranged end to end around the vessel's circumference. The paste and surface finish are like those of Bell Plain, *variety Hale.*

Additional Characteristics. The variety is known to occur on restricted bowls, burnished jars, and subglobular bottles with a pedestal base. Whatever the shape, the design is invariably placed on the vessel's shoulder. The arches themselves may consist of from one to four concentric lines. Grouped nodes are often positioned at the points where adjacent arches meet. The vessels are usually black filmed.

Distribution. Known from the Black Warrior drainage and from the central Tombigbee Valley.

Published Illustrations. Jenkins 1981:Figure 63.

Chronological Position. Moundville I phase, perhaps also extending into early Moundville II.

References. Steponaitis 1980:50; Jenkins 1981:69.

Carthage Incised, *variety unspecified*
(Figures 39i; 40j; 47p-q; 56f-q)

Sample. 5 vessels, 59 sherds.

Description. Most of the sherds in this category are specimens that show too little of the original design to be reliably placed in any of the established varieties. The vessels, however, are all rather distinctive and deserve individual description.

One (<M>MAI-17/4379) is a burnished jar decorated with three horizontal incisions that encircle the vessel at the shoulder. The incisions dip below each of four widely spaced nodes, positioned at equal intervals around the circumference.

Another (WP153) is a bird effigy bowl, with incisions on the sides depicting wings.

The third (SD266) may be an unfinished example of *Akron.* It is a bird effigy bowl with three concentric U-shaped lines incised on the rim below the lug, but these lines do not continue around the circumference.

The fourth (SWM95) is a lug-and-rim-effigy bowl with a design that resembles *Carthage.* It is decorated with two distinct three-line scrolls, one placed on each side of the vessel (McKenzie 1966:Figure 11b).

The last (<M>5) is a deep flaring-rim bowl with a curvilinear incised design on the interior of the rim. The design is highly eroded, and its exact pattern is difficult to make out, but it does appear to contain some areas of punctation as well. Overall, the character of the vessel and the design (insofar as it can be made out) suggest the specimen dates to the Alabama River phase.

MISSISSIPPI PLAIN

Following Phillips (1970:130-131), the "coarse" Mississippian plainwares in the Black Warrior region are best considered varieties of the type Mississippi Plain. This type is defined by the following characteristics: (*a*) a paste tempered predominantly with shell, (*b*) a surface that, though it may be smoothed, is not burnished, and (*c*) a lack of tooled decoration. The shell-temper particles in Mississippi Plain tend to be coarser than those in Bell Plain, but this attribute in itself is not definitive (see remarks under Bell Plain).

As presently constituted, Mississippi Plain subsumes a number of previously recognized local types: Warrior Plain (DeJarnette and Wimberly 1941:82-83; McKenzie 1965:55-56), Alabama River Plain (Sheldon 1974:201-203), and, since it lacks tooled decoration, Alabama River Appliqué (Sheldon 1974:205-206).

Mississippi Plain, *variety Hull Lake*
(Figures 41p-q; 48o; 57n-o)

Sample. 24 sherds.

Description. This variety was provisionally set up by workers on the central Tombigbee, in order to record the presence of coarse, unburnished sherds tempered with both shell and grog. A number of such sherds have been found at Moundville, so the variety is adopted here as well. Most of the sherds in the Moundville sample have rough surfaces, considerably more bumpy than is usual for *Warrior*, and exhibit colors that tend to reddish brown. The grog particles in the paste tend to be quite coarse, commonly 2 mm or more in width and sometimes as large as 5 mm. The shell particles are usually somewhat finer.
It should be noted that this variety is difficult to separate from *variety Warrior*, unless one can see the paste in cross section. Thus, the absence of *Hull Lake* among the whole vessels could be due to lack of recognition.

Distribution. Reported from the Black Warrior drainage, the upper Cahaba Valley, and the central Tombigbee Valley.

Chronological Position. This variety appears as a consistent minority throughout the Moundville sequence, beginning in the West Jefferson phase (Ensor 1979:Figure 13d), and continuing into the Alabama River phase.

References. Jenkins 1981:72.

Mississippi Plain, *variety Warrior*
(Figures 39l; 41k-o; 46a-b, d-e; 48f-n; 54a-l,
n-o; 56n-p; 57a-m; 60a)

Sample. 198 vessels, 5101 sherds.

Description. New variety.

Sorting Criteria. *Warrior* includes undecorated ceramics that are tempered soley with shell, and have smoothed, but not burnished surfaces. The temper particles tend to be coarser than those of Bell Plain, *variety Hale*, but this in itself is not necessarily definitive since the two varieties overlap quite a bit in this respect.

Additional Characteristics. Most vessels of this variety are jars, almost invariably equipped with handles, and sometimes with downturned lugs. The number of handles is variable, usually 2, 4, or 8, but sometimes more than 10. The number of handles tends to increase through time, and in the Alabama River phase, functional handles are often superseded by appliqué neck fillets. Other vessel shapes that occasionally turn up in this variety are simple bowls, flaring-rim bowls, and bottles.
Warrior usually lacks painted decoration, and tends to

exhibit surface colors in the range from buff to reddish brown. When painted decoration does occur, it is either red or (in Alabama River phase contexts) red and white.

Distribution. Primarily found in the Warrior drainage and the central Tombigbee Valley.

Published Illustrations. Moore 1905:Figures 49, 50, 55, 108, 154; DeJarnette and Wimberly 1941:Figures 62 (top row), 64 (top left); McKenzie 1966:Figure 4; DeJarnette and Peebles 1970:99 (top), 102 (bottom), 103, 105, 108 (top), 109 (bottom), 111 (top), 113 (top), 114 (bottom); Nielsen and Jenkins 1973:Plates 1f, 2i-j; Jenkins 1981:Figures 59-61, 65; Peebles 1979:Figure III-8.

Chronological Position. Moundville I to Alabama River phase. Finer chronological distinctions can be made on the basis of vessel shape and secondary shape features (see Chapter 4).

References. Steponaitis 1980:49-50; Jenkins 1981:71-72.

MOUNDVILLE ENGRAVED

This type is defined to include shell-tempered vessels with burnished surfaces that are decorated with either post-fired engraving or fine, dry-paste incision. The lines that make up the design are always less than 1.5 mm wide and usually no more than 1 mm wide. In effect, this type combines the old types Moundville Filmed Hemagraved (DeJarnette and Wimberly 1941:84), Moundville Filmed Engraved (McKenzie 1965:58-59), and Moundville Engraved Indented (McKenzie 1965:59-60), while at the same time eliminating "black filming" as a defining attribute.

In an earlier paper (Steponaitis 1980), I referred to the present type as "Hemphill Engraved." The latter name was originally chosen in hopes that it would prevent the newly redefined category from being confused with the many versions of "Moundville Engraved" already in the literature (e.g., Willey 1949:466; see also references just cited). In retrospect, however, its seems that the original choice created more confusion than it prevented; so the sooner Hemphill Engraved is forgotten, the better.

Moundville Engraved, *variety Cypress*
(Figures 55h; 62d)

Sample. 4 vessels, 1 sherd.

Description. New variety.

Sorting Criteria. A design characterized by scrolls contained within rectangular panels. The horizontal and vertical bands that border the panels are often filled in with lines, concentric semicircles, punctations, and other elements that sometimes occur in the representational designs of Moundville Engraved, *variety Hemphill*. The ware is equivalent to Bell Plain, *variety Hale*.

Additional Characteristics. The variety usually is found on subglobular bottles with a simple or slab base. One rather marginal example, a simple bowl, has a design that lacks true panels; instead the design consists of a single horizontal band (filled in with lines and concentric circles) along the rim, beneath which hang festoons made up of concentric semicircles.

Vessels of this variety are generally black filmed.

Distribution. Recognized thus far only at the Moundville site.

Published Illustrations. None.

Chronological Position. Early Moundville III. It would not be surprising if, with additional evidence, the range of this variety were found to extend into late Moundville II as well.

References. None.

Moundville Engraved, *variety Elliots Creek*
(Figures 39b; 40a–d; 63a–b)

Sample. 4 vessels, 8 sherds.

Description. New variety.

Sorting Criteria. Engraved designs that are embellished with areas of excision. The designs themselves may consist of either curvilinear scrolls or rectilinear patterns, the latter usually made up of numerous closely spaced lines. The ware is comparable to Bell Plain, *variety Hale*.

Additional Characteristics. The variety occurs on slender ovoid bottles, simple bowls, and restricted bowls. The vessels are usually black filmed, and many are red engraved.

It should be noted that on some bowls, the upper portion of the design field is defined by a multilinear band —the motif that, when found alone, characterizes Moundville Engraved, *variety Havana*.

Distribution. Thus far reported only from the Black Warrior drainage.

Published Illustrations. DeJarnette and Wimberly 1941:Figure 63 (bottom right); McKenzie 1966:Figure 8a.

Chronological Position. Moundville I phase. I suspect the type is late within the phase, and, with more evidence, may be found to extend into early Moundville II.

References.   Steponaitis 1980:50 (described as a variety of
Hemphill Engraved).

Moundville Engraved, *variety Englewood*
(Figures 52b; 62f)

Sample.   6 vessels.

Description.   New variety.

   Sorting Criteria.   A curvilinear scroll, consisting of
6-10 lines,   that   runs   entirely around   the vessel's
circumference.   The ware is like that of Bell Plain, *variety
Hale.*

   Additional Characteristics.   The variety usually occurs
on subglobular bottles with simple bases,   sometimes with
indentations.   In one case it is found on a simple bowl with
a lip that is "rolled" to the exterior.   Vessels are usually
black filmed.

   Distribution.   Thus far observed only at sites in the
Black Warrior drainage,   including both Moundville and Snows
Bend.

   Published Illustrations.   Moore 1905:Figure 80.

Chronological Position.   Moundville III phase.

References.   None.

Moundville Engraved, *variety Havana*
(Figures 40f-g; 44a-b, d; 46h, k; 47e-g; 53o;
55e-f)

Sample.   37 vessels, 10 sherds.

Description.   New variety.

   Sorting Criteria.   A design whose major feature is a
horizontal band of two or more lines running parallel to and
just   below   the   lip.   The   band of lines is usually
embellished with loops and/or folds.   Comparable to Bell
Plain, *variety Hale* in paste and surface finish.

   Additional Characteristics.   Havana occurs exclusively
on bowl forms—mostly cylindrical, simple, and restricted.
Often these bowls are embellished either with a single lug,
or with a lug-and-rim-effigy depicting a bird.   Secondary
shape features that occur less commonly are a band of nodes,
widely spaced nodes,   and indentations.   Among the less
common effigy types are the turtle and the fish.
   Generally the design consists of from 3 to 8 parallel
lines, although in some cases there are up to 15.   On about
a third of the vessels,   the bottom of the decorated portion
of the rim is defined by a broad, "overhanging" line, and

sometimes the vessel wall above that line is visibly thickened.
     Most vessels in this variety are black filmed.

     Distribution. The variety is known to occur in the Warrior drainage and on the central Tombigbee.

     Published Illustrations. Moore 1905:Figures 48, 51, 73, 120; McKenzie 1966:Figure 5; DeJarnette and Peebles 1970:108 (bottom); Jenkins 1981:Figure 4b-c, e-f; Peebles 1979:Figure IV-8.

Chronological Position. Moundville I (probably beginning late in this phase) through early Moundville III.

References. Steponaitis 1980:50 (described under Hemphill Engraved); Jenkins 1981:87.

          Moundville Engraved, *variety Hemphill*
     (Figures 44e-f, i, 1-m, o; 45h-i; 47c-d; 52h-j,
       m-n, p-t; 53a-d, k-n, p; 55i-1; 62a, c, g-h;
                         63h)

Sample. 138 vessels, 25 sherds.

Description. New variety.

     Sorting Criteria. A design consisting of free-standing or representational motifs, most of which have at one time or another been considered part of the Southeastern Ceremonial Complex. A wide range of specific motifs are included in this variety (see section on representational motifs in Chapter 3). The ware is comparable to Bell Plain, *variety Hale.*

     Additional Characteristics. Subglobular bottles with simple, slab, and pedestal bases constitute the most abundant shape categories in *Hemphill.* Considerably less common are cylindrical bowls, simple bowls, restricted bowls, cylindrical bottles and narrow-neck bottles. A few of the bottles in the sample are embellished with indentations, and bowls occasionally exhibit a single lug, widely spaced nodes, or indentations. One pedestaled bottle is gadrooned.
     Most of the *Hemphill* vessels at Moundville and elsewhere are black filmed.

     Distribution. This variety is known from sites on the Black Warrior River, on the central Tombigbee, and as far north as the Pickwick Basin on the Middle Tennessee River.

     Published Illustrations. Moore 1905:Figures 17, 21, 22, 30, 35, 56, 57, 62-64, 74, 84, 87-90, 93, 112-115, 117, 118, 121-123, 125, 126, 143, 144, 146-148, 151-153, 156, 160, 161, 173, 1907:Figures 4-12, 34-40, 42-46, 49-51, 53-65; Jones and DeJarnette n.d.:Plates 1c, 2g, 3g; Webb and DeJarnette 1942:Plates 67 (1), 119, 262 (2), 263 (2 right),

268;   DeJarnette 1952:Figure   152 (bottom);   McKenzie
1966:Figures 8b, 18, 19; DeJarnette and Peebles 1970:Figures
99 (bottom), 100 (bottom); Peebles 1979:Figures III-2,
III-21, IV-4, IV-16, IV-17, V-1, V-5, VII-2, VII-3, VII-9,
VII-12; Jenkins 1981:Figure 6a-g.

Chronological Position.   Moundville II and Moundville III
phases.   Finer temporal distinctions can be drawn on the
basis of vessel shape and motif (see Chapter 4).

References.   Steponaitis 1980:50 (described as a variety of
Hemphill Engraved); Jenkins 1981:73-74.

Moundville Engraved, *variety Maxwells Crossing*
(Figures 451; 55d)

Sample.   8 vessels, 1 sherd.

Description.   New variety.

Sorting Criteria.   The design consists mainly of
crosshatched vertical bands, spaced at intervals around the
vessel's circumference.   Occasional variations can occur in
this basic theme as described below.   The ware is comparable
to Bell Plain, *variety Hale.*

Additional Characteristics.   The variety occurs on
subglobular bottles,   usually with slab or pedestal bases,
but sometimes with simple bases.
Four vessels in the sample have designs that consist
solely of the crosshatched vertical bands.   On one vessel
(Rw439),   the design is embellished with crosshatched
terraced-shape elements in the space between the bands (see
Fundaburk and Foreman 1957:Plate 38 [lower left corner]).
On two other vessels (Rho38, SD95/M7), some of the vertical
bands on the design have an irregular boundary on one side
(see Moore 1907:Figure 31).
Most examples of *Maxwells Crossing* are black filmed.

Distribution.   Known from the Black Warrior drainage
and from the central Tombigbee.

Published Illustrations.   Moore 1905:Figure   109,
1907:Figures 31, 32.

Chronological Position.   Moundville II to early Moundville
III.

References.   Steponaitis 1980:50 (described as a variety of
Hemphill Engraved, and defined somewhat more broadly than it
is here).

Moundville Engraved, *variety Northport*
(Figures 39c; 45g, j)

Sample.   16 vessels.

Description.   New variety.

Sorting Criteria.   The design consists of 4- to 15-line vertical scrolls, that is, scrolls that begin at the upper boundary of the design field and end at the lower.   The ware is comparable to Bell Plain, *variety Hale.*

Additional Characteristics.   Northport occurs only on subglobular bottles, usually with pedestal or slab bases, rarely with a simple base.   Indentations are frequently present as a secondary shape feature.
The number of lines in the scroll varies, usually from 6 to 10, although some examples exist with as few as 2, or as many as 13.   The chronologically earlier vessels tend to have a scroll that is continuous from top to bottom (e.g., Figure 39c).   On some of the later vessels, the vertical scroll forms a guilloche (e.g., Figure 45g).   Also on some of the later vessels, the scroll is embellished with fill-in cross-hatching and crosshatched fins (e.g., Peebles 1979:Figure IV-12)

Distribution.   The variety occurs in the Black Warrior Valley and on the central Tombigbee.

Published Illustrations.   Moore 1905:Figures 39, 71, 1907:Figure 47; Peebles 1979:Figure IV-12.

Chronological Position.   Late Moundville I and Moundville II phases.   There are some minor variations in the design that have chronological significance, as just discussed.

References.   Steponaitis 1980:50 (described under Hemphill Engraved, as a variant of the then more broadly defined *variety Tuscaloosa*).

Moundville Engraved, *variety Prince Plantation*
(Figure 45k)

Sample.   2 vessels.

Description.   New variety.

Sorting Criteria.   The design is a herringbone pattern, consisting of horizontal bands that are filled in with zones of vertical and oblique parallel lines.   The boundaries between adjacent bands are made up of one or several closely spaced horizontal lines.   The ware is equivalent to Bell Plain, *variety Hale.*

Additional Characteristics.   The variety occurs on subglobular bottles with pedestal or slab bases.   One of the two vessels at Moundville is black filmed.

Distribution.   So far known only from the Moundville site.

Published Illustrations.   None.

Chronological Position.   Late Moundville II to early Moundville III.

References.   Steponaitis 1980:50 (described as a distinctive variant of Hemphill Engraved, *variety Maxwells Crossing*).

Moundville Engraved, *variety Stewart*
(Figure 40e)

Sample. 1 sherd.

Description. New variety.

   Sorting Criteria.   Zones of oblique parallel line segments, forming either chevrons or line-filled triangles. The design is confined to a band encircling the vessel. The ware is comparable to Bell Plain, *variety Hale.*

   Additional Characteristics.   The variety occurs on flaring-rim bowls, with the decoration confined to a band on the interior of the rim. The one example from Moundville is black filmed.

   Distribution.   Thus far identified only at Moundville, but undoubtedly it will turn up elsewhere in the Warrior drainage and on the central Tombigbee as analysis of collections proceeds.

   Published Illustrations. None.

Chronological Position.   Definitely found in Moundville I contexts, it would not be surprising to find it continuing later as the fine-line equivalent of Carthage Incised, *variety Moon Lake.*

References. None.

Moundville Engraved, *variety Taylorville*
(Figures 44c; 52f; 55c)

Sample. 26 vessels, 4 sherds.

Description. New variety.

   Sorting Criteria.   The design that chracterizes this variety is made up of a three- to four-line running scroll, superimposed on a crosshatched background.   The ware is comparable to Bell Plain, *variety Hale.*

   Additional Characteristics.   *Taylorville* most commonly occurs on subglobular bottles with simple and slab bases, rarely with pedestal bases. Other shapes represented in the sample are the pedestaled bowl, cylindrical bowl, and cylindrical bottle. The pedestaled bowls generally exhibit a notched everted lip, and the cylindrical bowls often have a single lug.

Two basic variants of the *Taylorville* design occur. One has a scroll that consists of conjoined, S-shaped segments (e.g., Figure 44c); the other has a scroll that is continuous, the lines encircling the vessel in unbroken fashion (e.g., Figure 52f). On the whole, I suspect that the former treatment tends to be chronologically earlier than the latter. It should also be noted that about half the vessels with the continuous scroll have radial fingers "hanging" from the upper and lower boundaries of the design field. In such cases, the outlines of these fingers form the upper and lower boundaries of the crosshatched background (Figure 52f).

Taylorville vessels are almost invariably black filmed.

Distribution. Known from the Black Warrior drainage and from the central Tombigbee.

Published Illustrations. Moore 1905:Figures 17, 18, 20, 80, 133, 1907:Figure 19; Peebles 1979:Figures IV-19, VII-7.

Chronological Position. Moundville II and early Moundville III phases.

References. Steponaitis 1980:50 (described as a variety of Hemphill Engraved).

Moundville Engraved, variety Tuscaloosa
(Figures 45e-f; 47a-b; 52e; 55a-b)

Sample. 21 vessels, 7 sherds.

Description. New variety.

Sorting Criteria. The design is a curvilinear scroll made up of 15-40 closely spaced lines. The scroll encircles the vessel and is wide enough to take up almost the entire design field. The ware is comparable to Bell Plain, *variety Hale.*

Additional Characteristics. This variety occurs almost exclusively on subglobular bottles with pedestal or slab bases. Occasionally, an example turns up on a subglobular bottle with simple base. All but three of the whole vessels in the sample have indentations. Vessels of this variety are usually black filmed.

Distribution. The "core area" of this variety probably includes the Black Warrior drainage and the central Tombigbee. Examples virtually identical to those found at Moundville have also been reported from the Pickwick Basin on the Middle Tennessee River (Webb and DeJarnette 1942) and also from Arkansas (Holmes 1903). I suspect that the presence of *Tuscaloosa* in the latter two areas is the result of trade.

Published Illustrations. Holmes 1903:Plate 13b; Moore

1905:Figures 37, 119; Webb and DeJarnette 1942:Plates 122 (1), 261 (1 left), 267 (2); McKenzie 1966:Figure 22; Peebles 1979:Figures IV-13, VII-6.

Chronological Position. Late Moundville II to early Moundville III.

References. Steponaitis 1980:50 (described as a variety of Hemphill Engraved, and defined somewhat more broadly than it is here).

Moundville Engraved, *variety Wiggins*
(Figures 44n; 52c-d, g, o; 53; 55g; 62e; 63g)

Sample. 47 vessels, 7 sherds.

Description. New variety.

Sorting Criteria. The design consists of a two- to five-line scroll encircling the vessel's circumference. Not infrequently, the scroll is embellished with fill-in crosshatching or with crosshatched triangular projections. Paste and surface finish are similar to Bell Plain, *variety Hale*.

Additional Characteristics. *Wiggins* is usually found on subglobular bottles with simple bases. Subglobular bottles with slab or pedestal bases, cylindrical bowls, and pedestaled bowls occur less frequently. Secondary shape features that sometimes appear on these vessels are indentations (on bottles), single lug (on cylindrical bowls), and notched everted lip (on pedestaled bowls).
As previously noted the engraved scroll may consist of from two to five lines, but the modal number is three. More often than not, the scroll converges into a series of "swirls" as it encircles the vessel, and is embellished with crosshatched fins. There are, however, a number of variations on this basic *Wiggins* design that appear to have chronological significance. Cross-hatching within the scroll itself (e.g., Figure 63g) is an early trait (late Moundville II), as is a four-line scroll consisting of conjoined S-shaped segments (e.g., Moore 1905:Figures 31, 124). A nonconvergent scroll, such as the one in Figure 62e, seems to be a late characteristic (late Moundville III).
Virtually all *Wiggins* vessels are black filmed.

Distribution. Principally the Black Warrior drainage and the central Tombigbee. One possible trade sherd is illustrated from site 1Ma4 in the Wheeler Basin on the Tennessee River (Webb 1939).

Published Illustrations. Moore 1905:Figures 31, 75, 124, 162; Webb 1939:Plate 106b (7); McKenzie 1966:Figure 9; Peebles 1979:Figure VII-5; Jenkins 1981:Figure 6h-i.

Chronological Position. Late Moundville II through late Moundville III.

References.   Steponaitis 1980:50 (described as a variety of Hemphill Engraved); Jenkins 1981:74.

              Moundville Engraved, *variety unspecified*
              (Figures 40h-p; 47h-o; 55m-s; 62n-o; 63c, e)

Sample.   18 vessels, 170 sherds.

Description.   The bulk of the sample within this category consists of sherds that do not show enough of the design to be reliably assigned elsewhere. In addition, there are a number of vessels that do exhibit a complete design but do not conform to the definition of any of the established varieties. A few of these vessels are described in more detail below.
       One (WP218) is a bird effigy bowl with engraved lines on the sides depicting wings.
       Another (NB6) is a deep flaring-rim bowl with concentric semicircles crudely engraved on the interior of the rim. Judging from the shape and the character of the design, this vessel undoubtedly dates to the Alabama River phase.
       Four vessels in this category are terraced rectanguloid bowls (Figures 63c, e; Moore 1907:Figure 22). One (NE67) is decorated with imbricated festoons; two (NE1, SWM2A/M7) have multilinear bands along the irregularly shaped rim; and the fourth (Mi37) has a multilinear band together with a hand and eye motif, the latter raised in relief.
       Several other vessels are decorated with designs of various sorts that appear to be totally idiosyncratic (SED7 [Figure 24n], SD103/M7 [Moore 1907:Figure 24], NE132, SEH19, WN1, NR26/M5 [Moore 1905:Figure 157], <M>MAI-18/0434]).
       Finally, two vessels (ND28, EE383) exhibit a few random engraved lines, almost as though a design were started but never completed.

                    MOUNDVILLE INCISED

       The present concept of Moundville Incised corresponds closely to the original definition by DeJarnette and Wimberly (1941:83). The characteristic design consists of incised arches arranged end to end around a vessel's upper portion. The surface is smoothed but not burnished, and the paste is tempered predominantly with shell. The incision is typically done in a wet paste. Three local varieties have been defined on the basis of differences in the way the arch is executed.

              Moundville Incised, *variety Carrollton*
                    (Figures 42i-l; 48e; 60f-i)

Sample.   10 vessels, 21 sherds.

Description.   New variety.

Sorting Criteria. A design in which one or more arches occur alone, not embellished with radiating incisions or punctations. The ware is comparable to Mississippi Plain, *variety Warrior*.

Additional Characteristics. This variety occurs only on jars with two or four handles. All jars in the present sample are standard jars.
The arches that make up the design usually consist of from one to three concentric lines. Sometimes the lowest line is made with a broad square-ended stylus, so as to produce an "overhanging" incision. In a few cases (NQ1/M5, Mi1015), the vessel wall below each arch is pushed out somewhat, resulting in a series of lobate protrusions. On one vessel (ED54), the area where adjacent arches meet is further decorated with a series of short vertical incisions. Painted decoration is rare; only one vessel (Rho132) has a red filmed interior.

Distribution. Abundant in the Warrior drainage and along the central Tombigbee. Similar material occurs in the Middle Tennessee drainage, but whether or not that material should be included in this variety cannot be decided until more about it is known.

Published Illustrations. Moore 1905:Figure 40; DeJarnette and Wimberly 1941:Figure 62 (bottom left); Bohannon 1972:Figure 11 (bottom); Jenkins and Nielsen 1974:Plate 14e; Jenkins 1981:Figure 5a-f.

Chronological Position. Predominantly found in Moundville I and early Moundville II, although some may continue into late Moundville II as well.

References. Steponaitis 1980:50; Jenkins 1981:76-77.

Moundville Incised, *variety Moundville*
(Figures 39m; 42a-h; 48a-b; 60b-e; 63k)

Sample. 10 vessels, 122 sherds.

Description. New variety.

Sorting Criteria. The design in this variety is embellished with numerous short incisions that radiate upward from the arch. The ware is comparable to Mississippi Plain, *variety Warrior*.

Additional Characteristics. Variety *Moundville* occurs only on jars with either two or four handles. It is not uncommon for these vessels to have folded or folded-flattened rims. Widely spaced nodes may sometimes appear on the shoulder, at the points where adjacent arches meet.
The arch itself almost invariably consists of a single line. This line is often (although not always) incised with a broad, flat stylus, producing an "overhanging" effect. The line segments that radiate upward from the arch show

some variation within the sample, and at least some of the variation is apparently related to time. The earliest examples of *Moundville* (well represented at Bessemer) tend to have rays that are narrow, relatively long, and closely spaced. As time goes on, the rays have a tendency to get shorter, broader, and more widely spaced.

Distribution. Moundville is found throughout the Black Warrior and central Tombigbee drainages. Typologically very similar pottery also occurs in the Pickwick and Wheeler Basins on the Tennessee River.

Published Illustrations. DeJarnette and Wimberly 1941:Figure 62 (bottom middle); McKenzie 1966:Figure 2; Bohannon 1972:Figure 9d; Blakeman 1975:Plate 16; Jenkins 1981:Figures 4g-k, 62, 66.

Chronological Position. Moundville I to early Moundville II, possibly continuing with greatly diminished frequency into late Moundville II.

References. Steponaitis 1980:50; Jenkins 1981:77.

Moundville Incised, *variety Snows Bend*
(Figures 42o; 48c-d; 63i)

Sample. 2 vessels, 5 sherds.

Description. New variety.

Sorting Criteria. The design has incised arches that are embellished with punctations. The ware is comparable to Mississippi Plain, *variety Warrior.*

Additional Characteristics. The variety occurs only on jars. Both vessels in the Moundvlle sample are standard jars with four handles. One has widely spaced nodes at the places where adjacent arches meet.
The arch itself generally consists of either one or two lines. In about half the cases, the punctations are round and have raised centers, as though they were made with a hollow instrument. One marginal specimen seems to have an arch made up of punctations without an accompanying line (Figure 48c); in the future it may prove worthwhile to accomodate such specimens in a different typological category.

Distribution. As with the other varieties of this type, *Snows Bend* occurs in the Black Warrior and Tombigbee drainages, and its range may ultimately be extended to subsume similar material on the Middle Tennessee River as well.

Published Illustrations. DeJarnette and Wimberly 1941:Figure 62 (bottom right); Jenkins 1981:Figure 6j-l.

Chronological Position. Moundville I and Moundville II

phases. Judging from its extreme rarity in Moundville I levels, its relative abundance in the sherd collections from Lubbub (which has a strong Moundville II component), and the fact that all *Snows Bend* vessels in the sample are four-handle jars, I strongly suspect that this variety reached its greatest popularity during Moundville II, probably in the early portion of the phase.

References. Steponaitis 1980:50; Jenkins 1981:78.

Moundville Incised, *variety unspecified*
(Figures 42m-n; 60j; 63)

Sample. 1 vessel, 29 sherds.

Description. Only two specimens in this category have enough of their design showing to warrant an individual description. One is a sherd on which the arch consists of two lines, with the area between the lines crosshatched (Figure 42m). The other is a standard jar with two handles and widely spaced nodes, on which the design is embellished with vertical line segments below the arch (Figure 63j). The latter design seems to occur more frequently in areas to the south of the Warrior drainage (e.g., Nance 1976:113), and so it is not inconceivable that the vessel is an import.

MULBERRY CREEK CORD MARKED

Here we follow Jenkins (1981:99-100) in treating the local cord-marked, grog-tempered pottery as a variety of this type, long recognized both in the Tennessee Valley to the north (Haag 1939), and the Mississippi Valley to the west (Phillips 1970:136-139, and references therein).

Mulberry Creek Cord Marked, *variety Aliceville*
(Figure 67b)

Sample. 1 sherd.

Description. As defined by Jenkins, this variety includes cord-marked ceramics tempered exclusively with grog, having no significant sand inclusions.

Chronological Position. Present in the West Jefferson phase, but considerably more popular in the preceding Late Miller III period.

References. Jenkins 1981:100-102.

UNCLASSIFIED DECORATED

A number of the more distinctive sherds that may (or may not) be of local manufacture are illustrated in Figure 61a-f.

UNCLASSIFIED PLAIN (UNTEMPERED)

This category seems to be a consistent minority throughout the Mississippian sequence at Moundville, as represented in the test excavations north of Mound R. More than 50 sherds of this type were recovered; all seem to come from relatively small vessels, and characteristically tend to be fired to a greyish color (Figure 61g-i). Three whole vessels are included in the sample also. Two are miniature bowls (Moore 1905:Figure 79), and one is a small jar without handles (WP96).

.

NONLOCAL TYPES

ANDREWS DECORATED

This type has been recently set up on the basis of ceramics from the Lower Chattahoochee Valley (Schnell *et al*. 1981:175-177). By definition it is restricted to cylindrical bowls, "beakers," that are decorated by incision and/or excision. The temper is usually sand, but sometimes may include grit or shell. I cannot be positive that the specimens in the Moundville collection come from the Lower Chattahoochee Valley proper, but their similarity to the illustrated examples from Cemochechobee (Schnell *et al*. 1981:Plates 4.9-4.11) does at least suggest a source somewhere in the noncoastal portion of the Fort Walton culture area.

Andrews Decorated, *variety unspecified*
(Figures 64n, 65s; Moore 1907:Figure 130)

Sample. 5 vessels.

Description. Three of the vessels are decorated only with engraved multilinear bands at the rim and base (Rho101, Rho177, SW19). Two other vessels have the multilinear bands at rim and base, with crosshatched rectilinear designs in between (SD45/M7, SWM166).

Chronological Position. Schnell *et al*. (1981:177) assign Andrews Decorated a range of A.D. 900-1350. This placement is consistent with the fact that one of the vessels at

Moundville occurs in a gravelot (bu. 1978/Rho) that can be independently dated to the Moundville I phase.

BARTON INCISED

As most recently defined by Phillips (1970:43-47), this type includes shell-tempered, unburnished vessels decorated with simple rectilinear designs, such as bands of parallel lines, line-filled triangles, or cross-hatching. Characteristically, the lines were incised while the paste was fairly wet, leaving them with burred margins. The name Barton Incised has generally been used in the Mississippi Valley, but vessels that in all respects fit the definition occur in the Tennessee-Cumberland drainage as well.

Barton Incised, *variety unspecified*
(Figure 65h)

Sample. 6 vessels.

Description. Two vessels in the sample are standard jars, each with two strap handles and two small horizontal lugs positioned at the lip (WR53, <M>MAI-17/4616). These features suggest an origin somewhere in the Lower Tennessee or Cumberland drainage. The four other vessels (Rho276, B3, W70, SW11) all appear to be nonlocal, but their specific source areas are unknown.

Chronological Position. Taken over its entire geographical range, Barton Incised spans almost the entire Mississippi period, from about A.D. 1000 to 1700.

BELL PLAIN

This shell-tempered ware is usually defined in terms of two characteristics: very fine-grained temper particles and a burnished surface. Griffin, in his original definition (Phillips et al. 1951:122-126), seemed to rely on the former as the primary sorting criterion; Phillips, in his more recent definition (1970:58-59), seemed to rely mainly on the latter. Here I follow Phillips in placing the primary emphasis on surface finish, not only because this is more consistent with the distinctions I have drawn in the local classification, but also because determining the size of temper particles in whole vessels is often extremely difficult. As with its unburnished counterpart Mississippi Plain, Bell Plain is here regarded as having a very broad geographical scope, referring to burnished shell-tempered pottery wherever it occurs in the southeastern states. Local vessels of the type are assigned to the variety *Hale*, which has already been described. Nonlocal vessels, on the other hand, are here lumped together under *variety unspecified*, despite the fact that numerous individual specimens have distinctive features that can be identified with specific regions, among them the Central Mississippi Valley, the Lower Tennessee-Cumberland drainage, and the Mobile-Pensacola region on the Gulf Coast.

Bell Plain, *variety unspecified*
(Figures 64b-d, l, o; 65a, e, f, k, t; 66h; Moore 1905:Figures 68, 72, 97, 172, 1907:Figures 27-29; Peebles 1979:Figures III-22, IV-9, IV-18, IV-20, V-4, VII-8)

Sample. 53 vessels, 1 sherd.

Description. Given that this category includes vessels from many different regions, it is not surprising to find an extreme diversity of shapes and effigy features represented in the sample. Only some of the more distinctive of these vessels are described below:

Three of the vessels are composite bottles, that is, vessels built to appear as though a bottle were set inside a jar (Figure 65a; Moore 1905:Figure 72; Peebles 1979:Figure IV-18). Two such vessels (ND12/M5, NE81) have tall, straight-sided necks; the third (Rho67) has a carafe neck. These shapes are mostly at home in the Central Mississippi Valley, especially in the region of Southeast Missouri.

Ten specimens are classified as high-shouldered bottles. These vessels have a relatively wide neck, and a more or less globular body in which the point of maximum diameter occurs higher than midway up the body's height (Figure 64b-d; Moore 1905:Figure 97). The likely source for most of them is the Central Mississippi Valley or the Tennessee-Cumberland area. However, the possibility cannot be ruled out that one or two are merely deviant local specimens.

Four examples of Bell Plain are hooded bottles, all with human effigy features (Moore 1907:Figure 28; Peebles 1979:Figure IV-20). It is worth noting for the sake of chronology that one of them (SG25) occurs in a Moundville II phase gravelot. All these vessels were presumably manufactured in the Lower Tennessee-Cumberland area or in the Cairo Lowland of southeast Missouri.

Two lobate bottles have a body consisting of four large lobes, surmounted by a narrow neck (Figure 65e). Both these specimens probably originated somewhere in the vicinity of southeast Missouri. The burial associations of one (SW26) date it to late Moundville II or early Moundville III.

Also in the sample is a lobate bowl, with four large lobes modeled into the wall, a short vertical neck and a notched lip. My best and rather unconfident guess is that it comes from the Lower Tennessee-Cumberland area or the Cairo Lowland.

The one stirrup-neck bottle in the sample has three separate necks that join together at a common orifice (Figure 47f). It undoubtedly was made in the Mississippi Valley, probably in the region of northeast Arkansas or southeast Missouri.

Of the remaining bottles, six (Rw246, Rw569, RW581,

ND3/M5, NE78, WR1) have a subglobular body with a wide neck (Moore 1905:Figure 68); four (Rho65, Rho265, NE15, SW46) have subglobular bodies with narrow necks; and one (WR1/M5) has a globular body with a short, narrow neck and three podal supports (Moore 1905:Figure 172). Many of these probably originated in the Central Mississippi Valley or the Tennessee-Cumberland area.

Three fish effigy bowls have been classified as Bell Plain, *variety unspecified*. One bowl (Rho149) has an everted lip and paired holes on either side of the rim, just like the specimens typical of the Nashville Basin (see, for example, Thruston 1890:Plate VIII). Another (WR15/M7) is unusually large for Moundville and has a flat head adorno with a serrated edge (Moore 1907:Figure 27); fish effigies of this kind are most commonly found in Tennessee (W. Autry, personal communication). The third specimen (EE109) is an outslanting bowl with flat lugs (attached to the vessel at the level of the lip) depicting the head and tail of a fish; this bowl contrasts sufficiently with local examples in both shape and placement of features to warrant a nonlocal classification, despite the fact that I cannot suggest a likely source.

Six frog effigies appear to be nonlocal, all of them resticted bowls. Two vessels (EE67, NG2) with relatively small, flat appliqué heads (Figure 65t; Peebles 1979:Figure V-4) are identical to illustrated specimens from the Nashville Basin (Thruston 1890:Plate VII), and probably were imported from somewhere in Tennessee. Four others (NE9, NE71, SE87, WN1/M7) belong to a group with large heads modeled directly in the vessel wall (e.g., Moore 1907:Figure 29; Peebles 1979:Figure IV-9); these vessels differ markedly from local specimens in various details of execution, but at the same time they are not similar enough to illustrated specimens from elsewhere to suggest a likely source.

Finally, the sample has in it several human effigy bowls, which are basically of two different kinds. The first kind has a horizontal lug on one side of the rim, and a human head adorno on the other (Figure 64l). In all three cases at Moundville (NE77, NE446, NG44), the head faces inward. The second kind of human effigy bowl has adornos representing the head and all four limbs added to its sides. The adornos are arranged in such a way that when the bowl is upright, the figure appears to be on its back (Figure 65k; Peebles 1979:Figures III-22, VII-8). Two such vessels at Moundville (SD847, WR66) fall into the type Bell Plain. All of these human effigy bowls are probably imports from the Central Mississippi Valley or the Lower Tennessee-Cumberland area.

Chronological Position. Taken over its entire geographical range, Bell Plain spans the Mississippi period from about A.D. 1000 to 1700.

D'OLIVE INCISED

This type includes shallow shell-tempered bowls, decorated on the rim interior with designs that are incised in a dry paste (Jenkins 1976:229-230; Coblentz 1978). The type seems to be indigenous to the Mobile-Pensacola region on the Gulf Coast.

D'Olive Incised, *variety unspecified*
(Figure 66d-e; Moore 1905:Figure 92)

Sample. 2 vessels, 2 sherds.

Description. One sherd (L.5/6N2W) and one vessel (F6/M5) exhibit a design consisting of line-filled festoons. The second vessel (W239) is decorated with zones of oblique parallel lines on the interior of its flaring rim. All rims are either scalloped or notched.

Chronological Position. The presence of one vessel in Mound F suggests that the type dates to about the Moundville II phase, a chronological assignment that is consistent with the stratigraphic position of the two sherds.

HOLLY FINE ENGRAVED

Vessels of this type have burnished surfaces and are decorated with engraved lines that tend to be closely spaced. The tempering material is usually grog or grit, sometimes with bone inclusions as well (Newell and Krieger 1949:81-90; Suhm *et al.* 1954:300-302). This type is native to the Caddoan area, particularly the region of east-central Texas.

Holly Fine Engraved, *variety unspecified*
(Figure 65d; Peebles 1979:Figure IV-26)

Sample. 2 vessels.

Description. One vessel is a cylindrical bottle (NE170) similar in design to certain illustrated examples from the George C. Davis site in Texas (Newell and Krieger 1949:Figures 291, 31f, 32a). The second is a crudely engraved rectanguloid bottle (SEH75), again with counterparts illustrated from the Davis site (1949:Figure 31b, b').

Chronological Position. Recent radiocarbon dates from the Davis site suggest that the type should date somewhere between A.D. 800 and 1250 (Story and Valastro 1977). The fact that one of the vessels at Moundville was associated with Moundville Incised, *variety Carrollton* (bu. 870/SEH) implies a Moundville I phase date that is not inconsistent with that range.

LAKE JACKSON DECORATED

This type, recently proposed by Schnell *et al.* (1981:171-173) for the Lower Chattahoochee area, includes jars decorated either with arches on the shoulder (as in Moundville Incised) or with a horizontal band of parallel lines on the neck. The tempering materials may include grit, shell, grog, or just about any combination of the three. With its rather broad definition, this type pertains to material from large portions of northwest Florida, and adjacent parts of Georgia and Alabama.

Lake Jackson Decorated, *variety unspecified*
(Figure 66f)

Sample. 1 sherd.

Description. The one sherd is from a shell-tempered standard jar, decorated with a band of broad, wet-paste incisions encircling the neck.

Chronological Position. Schnell *et al.* (1981:173) assign the type a date of A.D. 900-1400. The one specimen in the sample comes from the early Moundville III levels in the excavation north of Mound R, which levels probably overlap with the latest portion of the type's range.

LELAND INCISED

Leland Incised vessels are decorated with curvilinear scrolls made up of relatively broad incised lines. These vessels have burnished surfaces and are tempered with grog, sometimes mixed with shell (Phillips 1970:104-107; Williams and Brain 1982; Steponaitis 1981). The type is indigenous to the Lower Mississippi Valley and adjacent areas.

Leland Incised, *variety unspecified*
(McKenzie 1966:Figure 8d)

Sample. 1 vessel.

Description. The one vessel in the sample is a bottle, tempered with a mixture of shell and grog, and decorated with a three-line scroll.

Chronological Position. Although the vessel does not conform exactly to any of the established varieties of the type, its design resembles that of Fatherland Incised (Phillips's Leland Incised, *variety Fatherland*). The vessel therefore almost certainly postdates A.D. 1400.

MATTHEWS INCISED

This type, as most recently defined by Phillips (1970:127-128), is characterized by the presence of incised scrolls, guilloches, or arches running horizontally on the shoulders or necks of jars. Vessels of this type are shell tempered and unburnished. They are commonly found over an area stretching from southeast Missouri to central Tennessee, including regions of southern Illinois and western Kentucky. Two varieties occur in the Moundville sample.

Matthews Incised, *variety Beckwith*
(Figure 64j; Peebles 1979:Figure III-23)

Sample. 5 vessels.

Description. This variety includes jars with rectilinear designs, either a rectilinear guilloche (Rho213) or intertwined rectilinear bands (SD848, SM29, NN'12, <M>MAI-17/337). Three of the jars exhibit stylized frog effigy features, consisting of six nodes arranged around the shoulder: a triangular node representing the head, a dimpled node the rear, and four comma-shaped nodes the legs.

Chronological Position. Two of the vessels at Moundville occur in gravelots that can be independently dated to late Moundville II or early Moundville III (ca. A.D. 1350-1500). This makes Clay's (1979) assignment of *Beckwith* to the period after A.D. 1550 seem rather dubious.

References. Phillips 1970:128.

Matthews Incised, *variety Manly*

Sample. 1 vessel.

Description. The one vessel is a standard jar with two handles and a notched lip. The design consists of a series of arches (made with one line), placed on the shoulder. The arches are bordered along the top with a single row of punctations, and the V-shaped areas between adjacent arches are entirely filled in with punctations. All in all, the vessel is very similar to examples illustated from northeast Arkansas (e.g., Perino 1966:Figure 38 [bottom]).

Chronological Position. The gravelot (bu. 1979/Rho) containing the specimen dates to late Moundville II or Moundville III (ca. A.D. 1350-1550).

References. Phillips 1970:128.

MCKEE ISLAND CORD MARKED

This was a name first used by Heimlich (1952:27-28) to describe shell-tempered cord-marked wares on the Tennessee River. The type has since been expanded to cover similar material in the Lower Tennessee-Cumberland area as well (Clay 1963:247).

McKee Island Cord Marked, *variety unspecified*
(Figure 66g)

Sample. 1 sherd.

Description. The sherd exhibits fine, closely spaced cord impressions, each about 1 mm wide.

Chronological Position. On the Tennessee River, shell-tempered cord-marked ceramics occur perhaps as early as A.D. 1000 (Lewis and Kneberg 1946:90), and are found in protohistoric contexts as well. (Heimlich 1952:27-28). The one sherd from Moundville was found in the Moundville II phase levels, but given the degree of mixture in these levels it could well be from an earlier component.

MISSISSIPPI PLAIN

This name for unburnished shell-tempered plainware was first used in the Mississippi Valley (Phillips 1970:130-135, and references therein), and is now starting to be adopted in many other parts of the Southeast (e.g., Coblentz 1978). I have taken the liberty to speed this poliferation somewhat by referring to all unburnished shell-tempered plainwares at Moundville as Mississippi Plain, regardless of their precise geographical origin. Local vessels of this type are classified as *variety Warrior*, and nonlocal vessels are grouped together below under the rubric *variety unspecified*.

Mississippi Plain, *variety unspecified*
(Figure 64g-h, r; 65g; Moore 1907:Figure 33;
Peebles 1979:Figure III-4)

Sample. 28 vessels.

Description. Most of the vessels in this category are jars having attributes of shape that suggest a nonlocal origin. Especially distinctive are a series of jars with two strap handles that also exhibit at least one of the following features: (*a*) a pair of small horizontal lugs at the lip, spaced equidistantly from the handles; (*b*) stylized frog effigy features on the shoulder (Figure 64r). The small horizontal lugs are usually double pointed, and the effigy features typically consist of six adornos: a three-pronged ridge in front representing the head, a node in back (often with a craterlike dimple) representing the tail, and four

small nodes (usually comma shaped) on the sides suggesting
the legs. Four jars exhibit the lugs only (NE124, EE278,
EE131, SE4); three jars exhibit the effigy features only
(NE443, NE454, EE89); and seven jars exhibit both the lugs
and effigy features (SD731, SWG40, SM28, WR56, Mi397,
<I>SD15, <I>WP1). Most of these vessels were probably
imported from the Lower Tennessee-Cumberland area, where
such features appear to be rather common (see, for example,
Myer 1928:Plates 116, 117a, Figures 176-179, 182, 188-189;
Clay 1963:Figure 18 [upper left]). A number of these
vessels occur in gravelots that date to late Moundville II
or early Moundville III.

     Also in the sample are two jars that are probably
imports from the Central Mississippi Valley. One (NN'40) is
a standard jar with four "eared" handles (Figure 64g), very
similar to certain examples from northeast Arkansas (e.g.,
Moselage 1962:Figures 9-10). Its burial context dates it to
Moundville I or Moundville II. The other (SD21/M7) is a jar
with claw-shaped handles (Moore 1907:Figure 33), again
having counterparts in northeast Arkansas and adjacent
regions (Perino 1966:Figure 48; Phillips *et al.* 1951:Figures
84o, 92p). Its associated vessels date it to early
Moundville III.

     Several highly distinctive bottle forms also appear in
this category. One vessel (ND6) is a hooded bottle (Figure
65g; Peebles 1979:Figure III-4), probably from the
Tennessee-Cumberland area. Another (NE460) is a high-
shouldered bottle exhibiting on its shoulder crude human
head medallions, not unlike those typically found in
northeast Arkansas and southeast Missouri (Moore
1910:Figures 32, 33; Holmes 1903:Plate 14a; Potter and Evers
1880:Plate VII (121); Hathcock 1976:Plates 152, 154, 155).
Yet another is a crude globular bottle (Rho252), found in a
Moundville I phase context, that is virtually identical in
shape to specimens illustrated from Hobbs Island on the
Middle Tennessee River (Webb 1939:Plate 91b [right]).

MOUND PLACE INCISED

     This type name is applied to shell-tempered bowls
decorated with a horizontal band of parallel lines placed on
the exterior, just below the lip. The band is often
elaborated with loops or folds. This has traditionally been
a Mississippi Valley type (Phillips *et al.* 1951:147-148;
Phillips 1970:135), but recently it has come into use in the
Gulf Coast area as well (Coblentz 1978). All of the Mound
Place Incised vessels in the present sample come from the
latter area. It should be noted that the local stylistic
equivalents of Mound Place Incised are Carthage Incised,
variety Akron and Moundville Engraved, *variety Havana.*

          Mound Place Incised, *variety Mobile*
               (Figures 64p, 66a-b)

Sample. 3 vessels, 13 sherds (all from one vessel).

Description. This variety is characterized by a band in which the lowest line is widely separated from the lines above it. Two vessels (SEH8, SL2) in the sample are cylindrical bowls, and one (RW145) is a "potbellied" bowl with a notched lip (similar in shape to the vessel in Figure 65q). All the sherds come from a single vessel—a bowl with a rim that is thickened to the exterior. *Variety Mobile* seems to be indigenous to the Mobile-Pensacola region on the Gulf Coast.

Chronological Position. The vessel pictured in Figure 64p came from a gravelot that is dated to late Moundville II or early Moundville III. Similarly, the sherds from the stratigraphic sample were mostly found in levels pertaining to early Moundville III. Thus *Mobile* would seem to fit within the period of about A.D. 1300-1500.

References. Coblentz 1978.

<h2 style="text-align:center">Mound Place Incised, variety unspecified</h2>
(Figures 65j; 66c)

Sample. 1 vessel, 1 sherd.

Description. The vessel is a lug-and-rim-effigy bowl. Its rim adorno is a massive, inward-facing head of a bird. The tip of the lug has a circular, hollowed-out indentation in the center, and two hollowed-out triangular areas, one on either side of the central indentation. The design consists of four widely spaced incisions that encircle the rim. The one sherd in the sample comes from a cylindrical bowl with a thickened rim and a flat lip. The design appears to be similar to that of the vessel. Both of these specimens are probably indigenous to the Mobile-Pensacola region on the Gulf Coast.

Chronological Position. The flat, inward-facing bird effigy is stylistically most similar to local specimens that were made during Moundville I and II. The sherd was found in the late Moundville III deposits north of Mound R, but given the degree of mixture in these deposits the sherd itself could well be earlier.

NASHVILLE NEGATIVE PAINTED

This is a shell-tempered ware decorated with black negative painting, often on a ground that is red painted and/or white slipped (Phillips 1970:139-141). The type seems to be indigenous to an area stretching from the Nashville Basin in Tennessee to the Cairo Lowland in Missouri, and reaching as far north as the Lower Ohio Valley in southern Indiana.

Nashville Negative Painted, *variety unspecified*
(Figures 64a, 66j; Moore 1905:Figure 15, 1907:
Figure 20; Peebles 1979:Figure IV-15)

Sample.   6 vessels, 1 sherd.

Description.   All the vessels are bottles with a narrow, "carafe" neck.   The distinctive features of each are described below.

Two vessels (WR18/M7, <I>NR25), almost identical, are black on white.   The design consists of negative painted skull and hand motifs (Moore 1907:Figure 20; Peebles 1979:Figure IV-15).

Three other bottles are black-and-red on white.   One (Rho135) exhibits a rayed circle, or "sunburst," design. Another (Rho182) is decorated with a series of oval "heart" motifs (Figure 64a).   And the third (SL27) has a design consisting of rayed semicircles, alternating with rayed hanging scrolls (very similar to the one illustrated in Moore 1905:Figure 16).

Finally, there are two marginal specimens that do not exhibit negative painting but have been assigned to Nashville Negative Painted anyway because of their close similarity to other vessels of this type.   One (C1/M5) is a white-on-red bottle, illustrated by Moore (1905:Figure 15), that exhibits the same distinctive design—rayed semicircle and hanging scroll—as the vessel (SL27) just described. The other specimen is a sherd (Figure 66j) bearing the rayed circle motif, which was painted in black on a red background by means of a positive technique.

Chronological Position.   One sherd and one vessel (Rho182) were found in good Moundville I context, and probably date to the later part of the phase.   Two other vessels (Rho135, C1/M5) are associated with gravelots that date to late Moundville II or Moundville III.

NODENA RED AND WHITE

This is a red-and-white painted shell-tempered type that mainly occurs in the Central Mississippi Valley, between Southeast Missouri and the mouth of the Arkansas River (Phillips 1970:141-144).

Nodena Red and White, *variety unspecified*
(Figures 64m, 65b-c; Peebles 1979:Figure III-1)

Sample.   3 vessels.

Description.   The sample includes a simple bowl with reclining human effigy features (Rho307), a collared bottle (NED1), and a carinated bottle (EE84).   The latter two specimens are highly distinctive in shape and decoration, and undoubtely originated in the area of the Mississippi Valley just south of Memphis where numerous similar vessels have been found (e.g., Brown 1978a:32; 1978b:22, 25; Hathcock 1976:Plates 267, 269).

Chronological Position. In the Central Mississippi Valley, the type postdates A.D. 1400. It is therefore consistent that one of the vessels occurs in a gravelot associated with diagnostics of the late Moundville III phase (bu. 2068/Rho).

PARKIN PUNCTATED

This type includes shell-tempered vessels on which punctation is the sole decorative treatment (Phillips 1970:150-152). The range of this type as presently defined includes portions of the Central and Lower Mississippi Valley.

Parkin Punctated, *variety unspecified*
(Figure 64i)

Sample. 1 vessel.

Description. The vessel in the sample is a standard jar with two handles. The fingernail(?) punctations are confined to the upper portions of the vessel's exterior, covering the shoulder and the neck.

Chronological Position. The specimen was found in gravelot association with local ceramics dating to late Moundville II or early Moundville III (bu. 817/EI).

PENSACOLA INCISED

This type name refers to a burnished shell-tempered ware with incised decoration, commonly found in the Mobile-Pensacola region of the Gulf Coast (Willey 1949:464-466; Jenkins 1976:226; Coblentz 1978). Designs may consist of curvilinear scrolls or representational motifs, sometimes elaborated by hatching or punctation.

Pensacola Incised, *variety Little Lagoon*
(Figures 64k, s; 65p)

Sample. 4 vessels.

Description. This variety includes vessels decorated with representational "Southern Cult" designs. Three of the specimens from Moundville are bowls that exhibit highly conventionalized hand and eye motifs (SEH86, SL24, NN'3). The fourth vessel, a cylindrical bowl, is decorated with skulls and forearm bones (SEH9). Ironically, the latter is perhaps the single most famous vessel from Moundville; it has been illustrated far more often than any other (e.g.,

DeJarnette 1952:Figure 152; Fundaburk and Foreman 1957:Plate
35; Peebles 1978b:Figure 6), and was even adopted as the
logo for Mound State Monument. Yet there can be no doubt
that this vessel is an import: its shape and style are
alien to the local ceramic tradition and perfectly at home
on the Gulf Coast. In fact, sherds from virtually identical
vessels occur at Bottle Creek (B. Coblentz, personal
communication).

Chronological Position. Two of the vessels at Moundville
(SL24, NN'3) are from burial contexts that date to the
Moundville III phase.

References. Coblentz 1978.

Pensacola Incised, *variety Strongs Bayou*
(Figure 651; DeJarnette 1952:Figure 152 [left])

Sample. 1 vessel.

Description. The design in this variety consists of a
curvilinear scroll on a crosshatched background. The scroll
is carried out with a broad "trailed" incision, whereas the
cross-hatching is executed with a relatively fine line. The
one vessel in the sample is a cylindrical bottle.

Chronological Position. One would suspect, judging from the
stylistic similarities, that this variety is roughly
contemporary with Moundville Engraved, *variety Taylorville*,
and thus would date to Moundville II and/or Moundville III.
Unfortunately, the vessel at Moundville was not found in a
context that can be independently dated.

References. Coblentz 1978.

Pensacola Incised, *variety unspecified*
(Figure 65q; Peebles 1979:Figure IV-7)

Sample. 2 vessels.

Description. Two vessels in the sample have curvilinear
designs that do not fit any of the named varieties
established by Coblentz (1978). One is a subglobular bottle
(NW2), and the other is a "potbellied" bowl (NE53).

Chronological Position. The subglobular bottle occurs in a
burial that dates to Moundville I or Moundville II (bu.
1854/NW). The chronological position of the bowl is
unknown.

PLAQUEMINE BRUSHED

This is a Lower Mississippi Valley type, vessels of
which exhibit the surface treatment of brushing (Phillips

1970:152-153;   Williams   and   Brain   1982).   The   ware   is
tempered with grog, sometimes mixed with shell.

Plaquemine Brushed, *variety unspecified*
(Figure 65r)

Sample. 1 vessel.

Description.   The   vessel   is   a   beakerlike   jar   without
handles,   and   is tempered with a   mixture of grog and shell.
The brushing   is confined to the   upper half of   the vessel,
and is carried out in a herringbone pattern.

Chronological Position.   Plaquemine Brushed   appears in the
Lower Mississippi Valley at about A.D. 1200, and is known to
have been produced   in some regions perhaps as   late as A.D.
1500.   The   herringbone design in particular   is associated
with the   later end   of this range,   after about   A.D. 1350
(Steponaitis 1981).   It is gratifying to note,   therefore,
that the   gravelot containing the   vessel at   Moundville was
independently   dated   to late   Moundville II   or   early
Moundville III (bu. 1109/NR).

POUNCEY RIDGE PINCHED

As defined by Phillips (1970:154-155), this name refers
to a   shell-tempered ware that   is decorated by   pinching up
linear ridges of clay.   Geographically,   the   type's range
encompasses an area of the Mississippi Valley from the lower
St. Francis Basin south to the Lower Yazoo Basin.

Pouncey Ridge Pinched, *variety unspecified*
(Figure 66i)

Sample. 1 sherd.

Description.   The   one   sherd comes   from   an   unburnished
vessel, and is too small to make out either the shape of the
vessel or the design.

Chronological Position.   Pouncey as a type dates from about
A.D. 1350 to about A.D.   1500 (Williams   and Brain   1982).
Stratigraphically,   the   one sherd in our   sample was
associated with the   Moundville III phase levels,   which is
not out of line with these dates.

WALLS ENGRAVED

This is a burnished, shell-tempered ware decorated with
engraving or fine-line incision (Phillips 1970:169-171).
The type as currently conceived is restricted to material
from the Central Mississippi Valley,   where it is the

stylistic counterpart of Moundville Engraved.

Walls Engraved, *variety unspecified*
(Figure 64q)

Sample. 1 vessel.

Description. This is a rather unusual example of the type: a human effigy bottle on which the back of the figure is crosshatched. Judging from the vessel's shape and features, it probably comes from the general area of the Cairo Lowland.

Chronological Position. The vessel is associated with a gravelot (bu. 1045/NR) that is assigned to early Moundville III.

UNCLASSIFIED DECORATED (SHELL TEMPERED)

This category includes 22 (apparently) nonlocal vessels that are decorated, but cannot reliably be placed in any of the established southeastern types. A number of these vessels (or their designs) are illustrated (Figure 64e, f; 65i; Moore 1905:Figures 52, 81, 128, 136, 159), and each is briefly described in Appendix A.

UNCLASSIFIED DECORATED (SAND TEMPERED)

Four vessels fall into this category, all very similar in color, surface texture, and paste composition. Two of these vessels, a pedestaled bowl (SD350) and a simple bowl (SD351), have a notched lip and are decorated with a multilinear band at the rim (Figure 65m, o). Two others, both cylindrical bowls (SD749, WR11), are decorated with engraved festoons that are positioned just below a somewhat thickened area at the lip (Figure 65n). Their place of origin is unknown, but is probably somewhere to the east or southeast of Moundville, in the Fort Walton or South Appalachian culture area.

UNCLASSIFIED PLAIN (SAND TEMPERED)

The one vessel in this category (Rho127) is a pedestaled bowl with a notched everted lip. It is very similar in ware characteristics to the other sand-tempered vessels described here, and probably has the same general place of origin, wherever that may be.

G

Vessels Indexed by Type and Variety

The index below is divided into two sections, the first referring to local types, and the second referring to nonlocal types. Within each section, the named types are arranged alphabetically, with the "unclassified" categories last. Similarly, under each type heading, the named varieties are arranged alphabetically with *variety unspecified* last. More complete descriptions of all the vessels indexed below can be found in Appendix A.

LOCAL TYPES

Alabama River Incised

Variety Unspecified: NR7

Bell Plain

Variety Hale: AdB44,   Rho100,   Rho134,   Rho136,   Rho142,
   Rho148, Rho156, Rho157, Rho158, Rho172, Rho173, Rho174,
   Rho184, Rho220, Rho227, Rho255, Rho275, Rho302, Rho306,
   Rho337, Rho366, Rho167, Rho368,   Rho371,   Rw36,   Rw132,
   Rw133, Rw135, Rw138, Rw140, Rw142, Rw177, Rw226, Rw471,
   Rw473, B2, WB1/M5, WB3/M5, C6/M5, NC1, NC2,   NC3,   NC5,
   D1, ND6/M5, ND7, ND13, ND20/M5, ND34,   ED2,   ED4,   ED6,
   ED8, ED50, SED1, SED2, SED3, SED4, SED10, SED14, SED17,
   SED18, SED19, SED30, SED32, SED33, SED43, SD1,   SD2/M5,
   SD3, SD5/M7, SD10, SD20/M7, SD61/M7, SD77/M7, SD106/M7,
   SD109/M7, SD110/M7, SD169, SD251, SD364, SD482,   SD583,
   SD594, SD596, SD600, SD684, SD687, SD689 SD734,   SD736,
   SD743, SD747, SD806, SD811, SD815, SD816, SD818, SD821,

SD822, SD825, SD827, SD832, SD844, SD855, NE4, NE5,
NE11, NE17, NE19, NE26, NE30, NE31, NE33, NE36, NE39,
NE42, NE44, NE54, NE56, NE58, NE64, NE68, NE85, NE86,
NE89, NE92, NE93, NE95, NE129, NE134, NE140, NE148,
NE160, NE166, NE174, NE445, NE450, NE451, NE453, NE568,
NE570, NE571, NE575, NE581, NE583, NE600, NE603, EE2,
EE8, EE11, EE13, EE17, EE18, EE22, EE61, EE64, EE71,
EE72, EE74, EE76, EE77, EE80, EE82, EE87, EE110, EE111,
EE112, EE125, EE129, EE135, EE179, EE181, EE186, EE187,
EE202, EE203, EE237, EE238, EE242, EE260, EE277, EE281,
EE302, EE303, EE304, EE305, EE377, EE380, EE384, EE392,
EE394, EE395, EE396, EE430, EE431, EE444, EE447, EE475,
EE492, EE495, SE2, SE11, SE14, SE19, SE37, F13/M5,
F15/M5, EF3, NG1, NG9, NG13, NG23, NG24, NG31, NG39,
NG56, NG76, SG23, H3/M5, SWG46, SWG47, SWG49, SWG58,
SWG66, SWG67, SEH5, SEH7, SEH10, SEH18, SEH20, SEH82,
SEH87, SEH88, EI25, EI26, EI95, SL3, SL33, SL49, SWM41,
SWM42, SWM87, SWM93, SWM94, SWM141, SWM167, SWM175,
SWM178, SWM181, SWM186, SWM189, SWM222, SWM223, SWM226,
SWM252, SWM260, NN'2, O27/M5, O28/M5, O37/M5, WP16,
WP22, WP23, WP27, WP28, WP67, WP72, WP73, WP94, WP149,
WP152, WP156, WP158, WP159, WP161, WP171, WP186, WP213,
WP214, WP216, WP260, WP264, WP269, WP'29, WP'32, WP'34,
NR4/M5, NR5, NR15A/M5, NR20, NR21, NR23, NR23/M5, NR47,
NR102, NR112, NR118, NR119, NR121, NR124, NR160, NR161,
WR3, WR12, WR21, WR58, WR74, WR80, WR82, W81, W176,
W186, NW7, NW17, NW18, NW31, NW36, NW43, NW46, SW4,
SW20, SW21, SW25, SW41, SW52, Mi434, Mi435, Mi438,
<M>4, <M>6, <M>7, <M>8, <M>9, <M>10, <M>12, <M>13,
<M>-17/1429, <M>MAI-17/1431, <M>MAI-17/3367, <M>MAI-
17/3369, <M>MAI-17/3637, <M>MAI-17/4362, <M>MAI-
17/4376, <M>MAI-17/4394, <M>MAI-17/4397

Carthage Incised

Variety Akron: RPB(3), Rw26, Rw176, ED3, ED14, SED9, SD853,
    NE135, EE390, EE446, F12/M5, EI42, NN'19, WP160, WP165,
    WP212, WP217, NR43, NR44, NR46, NR97, NR101, WR50,
    WR65, NW25, NWW7

Variety Carthage: Rho226, B1, NE461, EE5, EE12, EE78, NG5,
    SEH15, EI41, SWM6/M7, WP29, WP83, WP85, WP121, WP259,
    WR85, WR3/M7, <M>19, <M>MAI-17/3642

Variety Fosters: Rw195, SED28, SD682, SWM190, SP122

Variety Moon Lake: Rho251, Rho257, SD267, SD745, NE185,
    SWG8, <I>SWG2

Variety Poole: SWG9, EI39

Variety Summerville: Rho190, Rw480, SEH85, EI43

Variety Unspecified: SD266, SWM95, WP153, <M>5, <M>MAI-
    17/4379

Mississippi Plain

Variety Warrior: Rho36, Rho39, Rho46, Rho84, Rho90, Rho107, Rho122, Rho154, Rho171, Rho212, Rho253, Rho312, Rho328, Rho329, Rho351, Rho369, Rho374, Rw128, Rw129, Rw139, Rw159, Rw165, Rw168, Rw228, Rw229, Rw245, NB2, NEC1/M5, NEC3/M5, NEC10/M5, ND5, ND10, ND11, NED3, NED7, SED5, SED11, SED15, SD6, SD29, SD31, SD32, SD171, SD262, SD365, SD473, SD579, SD595, SD599, SD679, SD680, SD681, SD683, SD688, SD741, SD744, SD746, SD748, SD837, SD838, SD842, NE2, NE14, NE18, NE25, NE27, NE55, NE65, NE74, NE88, NE136, NE138, NE192, NE444, NE452, NE464, NE576, NE585, NE587, NE591, NE593, EE88, EE108, EE124, EE132, EE156, EE157, EE159, EE381, EE382, EE387, EE389, SE9, SE12, EF1, NG4, NG32, SG4, SG5, SG14, SG15, SG24, SWG1, SWG4, SWG5, SWG7, SWG17, SWG25, SWG26, SWG29, SWG41, SWG44, SEH11, SEH22, EI27, EI30, EI40, SL47, SL56, SWM14, SWM180, SWM219, SWM230, NN'4, NN'13, NN'39, O3/M5, WP19, WP20, W/104, WP135, WP170, WP173, WP207, WP221, WP223, WP228, WP258, NR20/M5, NR27, NR28, NR41, NR42, NR96, NR106, NR115, NR116 NR117, N128, NR153, NR189, WR46, WR69, WR72, WR2/M7, W192, W220, NW5, NW8, NW11, NW12, NW14, NW15, NW19, NW21, NW22, NW23, NW24, NW30, NW33, NW35, NW39, NW42, SW2, SW5, SW9, SW13, SW14, SW15, SW17, SW18, SW40, SW45, SW50, SW53, SW55, SW57, SW61, SW63, SW64, Mi430, <I>NR25, <I>NW13, <M>3, <M>11, <M>11, <M>14, <M>15, <M>MAI-17/4374

Moundville Engraved

Variety Cypress: SED27, NR592, NR6/M5, SW62

Variety Elliots Creek: Rw43, SEH73, SEH83, WP61

Variety Englewood: Rw25, SD4/M5, SD585, EE10, <M>MAI-17/4354, <M>MAI-18/0414

Variety Havana: Rho48, Rho57, Rho161, B6, C7/M5, C21/M5, NEC6/M5, ND13/M5, NED4, SED13, SD248, SD826, SD834, NE37, NE38, NE50, NE165, EE210, EE322, NG11, EI2, SWM142, SWM170, O15/M5, O33/M5, WP32, WP47, WP52, WP71, WP187, NR9, NW16, SW31, NWW1, Mi456, MP12363

Variety Hemphill: Rho1, Rho110, Rho141, Rho164, Rho214, Rho219, RPB(1), RPB(4), Rw878, C2/M5, C4/M5, C8/M5, C12/M5, NEC9/M5, NEC11/M5, D4/M5, D5/M5, ND3, ND4, ND14/M5, NED10, SD1/M7, SD6/M7, SD7/M7, SD9/M5, SD13/M7, SD15/M7, SD18/M7, SD27/M7, SD28/M7, SD32/M7, SD33/M7, SD34/M7, SD42/M7, SD44/M7, SD48/M7, SD54/M7, SD59/M7, SD71/M7, SD86/M7, SD87/M7, SD88/M7, SD93/M7, SD154, SD362, SD472, SD586, SD733, SD742, SD805, SD814, SD836, SD849, NE59, NE60, NE61, NE63, NE79, NE80, NE90, NE127, NE128, NE145, NE458, NE582, NE596, NE599, EE1, EE3, EE4, EE7, EE25, EE75, EE126, EE155, EE166, EE182, EE234, EE343, EE391, EE416, SE8, F3/M5, F4/M5, F10/M5, NG3, NG10, NG25, NG30, SWG2, SWG3, SWG24, SWG52, SWG62, SWG63, SEH73, SEH74, SL1, SL21, SL31, SM30, SWM5/M7,

SWM15A/M7, SWM185, SWM188, NN'18, NN'38, O6/M5, O9/M5,
O10/M5, O16/M5, O18/M5, O20/M5, WP208, WP'19, WP'30,
WP'39, NR1/M5, NR9/M5, NR11/M5, NR17/M5, NR19/M5,
NR24/M5, NR25, NR30/M5, NR38, NR99, NR114, WR10, WR13,
WR59, WR81, WR2/M5, WR8/M7, WR28/M7, SW34, Mi62, Mi431

Variety Maxwells Crossing: Rho38, Rw439, SD95/M7, SD732,
NE602, O5/M5, SW10, SW23

Variety Northport: Rho170, Rho373, C17/M5, ND11/M5, NE7,
EE340, EF2, SWM1/M7, SWM131, SWM140, WP119, WP215,
NR100, NR127, <M>MAI-17/3348, <M>MAI-17/4368

Variety Prince Plantation: WP65, NR129

Variety Taylorville: Rho66,   Rho364,   C3/M5,   SD10/M5,
SD11/M7, SD82/M7, SD584, NE8, NE133, EE81, EE104,
EE133, EE180, EE188, EE385, EE429, SE3, SG16, EI15,
SWM2/M7, SWM132, SWM183, O31/M5, WP230, WR9, WR60

Variety Tuscaloosa: Rho104, Rho159, Rw440, Rw580, C13/M5,
ND16/M5, SED35, SD841, NE12, NE572, SE13, NG8, SWG23,
SL25, O14/M5, NR98, NR162, WR51, SW39, <M>MAI-17/4619,
<M>MAI-17/4620

Variety Wiggins: Rho102, Rho192, Rho304, Rho308, Rw126,
Rw227, Rw572, C9/M5, ND17/M5, SED6, SED8, SED34,
SD8/M7, SD14/M7, SD30, SD96/M7, SD840, NE6, NE147,
NE574, NE6, NE147, NE574, EE6, EE9, EE19, EE85, EE86,
EE94, EE130, EE136, EE137, EE160, EE204, EE445, NG6,
SWG6, SWG55, EI78, SWM220, NN'41, O19/M5, NR24,
NR31/M5, NR40 WR2, W219, <I>W50, <M>2, <M>MAI-18/O4367

Variety Unspecified: Rho109, NB6, ND28, SED7, SD103/M7,
NE1, NE67, NE132, EE383, SEH19, SWM2A/M7, WN1, WP218,
NR26/M5, Mi37, <I>SW353, <M>MAI-18/O434

Moundville Incised

Variety Carrollton: Rho132, Rw260, Rw442, ED54, ED71,
SD155, SEH45, SEH76, NQ1/M5, Mi1015

Variety Moundville: Rho163, Rw64, Rw182, SD265, NE597,
WP21, W310, NW26, <I>W50, <M>MAI-17/4381

Variety Snows Bend: WP30, NW9

Variety Unspecified: SD27

Unclassified Plain

Untempered: SD3/M5, EE307, SEH72, WP96

NONLOCAL TYPES

Andrews Decorated

Variety Unspecified: Rho101, Rho 177, SD45/M7, SWM166, SW19

Barton Incised

Variety Unspecified: Rho276, B3, WR53, W70, SW11, <M>MAI-17/4616

Bell Plain

Variety Unspecified: Rho65, Rho67, Rho149, Rho178, Rho189, Rho256, RPB(2), Rw246, Rw569, Rw581, ND1/M5, ND3/M5, ND12/M5, SD55/M7, SD247, SD810, SD847, NE9, NE15, NE71, NE77, NE78, NE81, NE82, NE122, NE130, NE169, NE446, NE448, EE67, EE109, EE236, F14/M5, SE18, NG2, NG44, SG25, SWG21, SWG45, SEH6, SEH14, NN'14, WN1/M7, WP229, WR1, WR52, WR66, WR83, WR1/M4, WR15/M7, SW26, SW46, Mi462

D'Olive Incised

Variety Unspecified: F6/M5, W239

Holly Fine Engraved

Variety Unspecified: NE170, SEH75

Leland Incised

Variety Unspecified: SWG16

Matthews Incised

Variety Beckwith: Rho213, SD848, SM29, NN'12, <M>MAI-17/3379

Mississippi Plain

Variety Unspecified: AdB34, Rho18, Rho252, Rw470, ND6, ND4, SD21/M7, SD731, NE124, NE125, NE443, NE454, NE460, EE89, EE131, EE278, SE4, SE10, SWG40, SM28, NN'40, NR152, WR56, Mi397, Mi440, <I>SD15, <I>WP1, <M>MAI-17/3646

Mound Place Incised

Variety Mobile: Rw145, SEH8, SL2

Variety Unspecified: ND33

Nashville Negative Painted

Variety Unspecified: Rho135, Rho182, C1/M5, SL27, WR18/M7,
    <I>NR25

Nodena Red and White

Variety Unspecified: Rho307, NED1, EE84

Parkin Punctated

Variety Unspecified: EI16

Pensacola Incised

Variety Little Lagoon: SEH9, SEH86, SL24, NN'3

Variety Strongs Bayou: EE201

Variety Unspecified: NE53, NW32

Plaquemine Brushed

Variety Unspecified: NR107

Walls Engraved

Variety Unspecified: WR57

Unclassified Decorated

Shell Tempered: Rho138, Rho153, Rho160, Rho228, Rw308,
    NEC8/M5, SD6/M5, SD813, NE131, EE206, SE16, EH76,
    SWM92, O26/M5, EO1/M5, NR27/M5, WR24, WR68, WR70, SW60,
    Mi61, <M>MAI-17/3375A

Sand Tempered: SD350, SD351, SD749, WR11

Unclassified Plain

Sand Tempered: Rho127

Vessels Indexed by Dimensions Other
Than by Type and Variety

More complete descriptions of the vessels indexed below can be found in Appendix A. Classificatory terms relevant to local vessels are defined in Chapter 3. Special terms that apply to nonlocal vessels only are treated briefly in the appropriate sections of Appendix F. An asterisk indicates that the vessel is nonlocal.

REPRESENTATIONAL MOTIFS

Bilobed Arrow: SWM5/M7, NR11/M5, SD48/M7, F3/M5

Bird Tail: F4/M5

Bird with Serpent Head: SD805

Crested Bird: SD86/M7, SD472, SD814, SEH73

Feather: SD849, NE599

Feathered Arrow: SWM5/M7

Forearm Bones: Rw195, SD88/M7, SD682, SEH9*, SWM15A/M7, SWM190, WP122, NR9/M5, NR25

Forked Eye Surround: ND14/M5

Greek Cross: SD154, SWM5/M7

Hand and Eye: Rho1,   Rw195,   C4/M5,   D4/M5,   ND3,   SED28,
SD27/M7, SD32/M7, SD71/M7, SD88/M7, SD682, NE61, EE126,
EE182, EE234, SWG52, SEH86*, SL24*, SWM15A/M7, SEM190,
NN'3*, O18/M5, WP122, WP208, WP'39, NR9/M5, NR19/M5,
NR27/M5*, NR38, WR1O, WR2/M5, WR8/M7

Human Head: F1O/M5

Insect: NG1O

Ogee: SD13/M7, O16/M5, WR28/M7

Paired Tails: Rho219, RPB1, RPB4, NEC11/M5, SD9/M5, SD93/M7,
SD742, NE6O, NE145, EE3, EE155, EE166, SE16*, NG3,
SWG24, SWG62, SEH74, SL1, SL21, SM30, OG/M5, O1O/M5,
WR13

Paired Wings: SD59/M7, NR24/M5

Radial Fingers: C2/M5, D5M5, SD7/M7, SD28/M7, NE128, EE7,
SWG2, O2O/M5, NR1/M5

Raptor: SD18/M7, SD54/M7, SD71/M7, SD362, SD586, NE8O,
EE416, SE8, SWG63, O9/M5, WP'30, SW34

Rayed Circle: SD733, SWM5/M7

Scalp: SD154, ND4, EE343, SWG3, NR9/M5, NR38

Skull: D4/M5, ND3, SEH9*, NR9/M5, NR25

Turtle: EE4

Windmill: C8/M5,   C12/M5,   NC9/M5,   SD15/M7,   NE79,   NE458,
EE391, NG25, SWM188, NR114

Winged Serpent: Rho110,   Rho141,   Rho164,   Rho214,   Rw878,
NED1O, SD1/M7, SD6/M7, SD33/M7, SD34/M7, SD42/M7,
SD44/M7, SD87/M7, SD836, NE59, NE9O, NE127, NE596, EE1,
EE25, EE75, NG30, SL31, SWM185, NN'18, NN'38, WP'19,
NR17/M5, NR3O/M5, WR59, WR81, Mi62, Mi431

Serpent (Miscellaneous): NR99

PAINTED DECORATION

Black Film: (commonly present in sample, but not systematically recorded)

Red Film (Interior Only): Rho132, SWG7, SWG29, WR2/M7, NW23

Red Film (Interior and Exterior): EE281

White Film: Rho302

Red and Black: SD20/M7

Red and White: Rho142, Rho306, Rw195, D1, EE87, EE125,
    EE203, SWG9, SWM87, WP122

Black on White: (no local vessels; see Nashville Negative
    Painted)

Red and Black on White: SD3 (also see Nashville Negative
    Painted)

Red Engraved: SEH71, SEH83

White Engraved: (no vessels in sample)

BASIC SHAPES

Carinated Bottle: EE84*, WR70*

Collared Bottle: AdB34*, NED1*, O26/M5*

Cylindrical Bottle: NEC8/M5*, ND14/M5, SD813*, NE127,
    NE170*, EE201*, F13/M5 SWG16*, SWM2/M7, NR25

High-Shouldered Bottle: Rho178*, Rw470*, SD247*, SD810*,
    NE169*, NE448*, NE460*, EE236*, F14/M5*, SE18*, SEH14*,
    WR83*

Hooded Bottle: ND6*, SD55/M7*, NE82*, SG25*, WR57*, Rho189*

Lobate Bottle: NE122*, SW26*

Narrow-Neck Bottle (Subglobular): Rho65*, Rho135*, Rho182*,
    Rho256*, C1/M5*, NE15*, EE12, SL27*, NR27/M5*, WR3/M7,
    WR18/M7*, SW46*, Mi431, <I>NR25*

Rectanguloid Bottle: Rho228*, SEH75*

Slender Ovoid Bottle: Rho172, Rho173, Rho174, Rw43,
    SD109/M7, NE58, O27/M5, O28/M5, WP61, WP149, WP152,
    WP161, WP213, WP214, WP216, W81, <M>MAI-17/3369

Stirrup-Neck Bottle: NN'14*

Subglobular Bottle, Pedestal Base: Rho1, Rho157, Rho170,
    Rw36, Rw227, Rw439, C3/M5, C4/M5, C12/M5, C13/M5,
    C17/M5, NEC9/M5, ND11/M5, ED50, SD13/M7, SD20/M7,
    SD103/M7, NE12, NE63, EE304, EE340, F3/M5, F4/M5,
    F10/M5, EF2, NG8, H3/M5, SWG23, SWM1/M7, SWM131,
    SWM141, SWM189, O16/M5, WP119, WP158, WP171, WP186,
    WP215, WP269, NR1/M5, NR4/M5, NR11/M5, NR26/M5, NR100,
    NR129, NR162, WR51, WR8/M7, W219, NW18, NW31, SW23,
    SW34, SW39, <I>W50, <M>MAI17/3348, <M>MAI-17/3367,
    <M>MAI-17/4620, <M>MAI-18/434.

Subglobular Bottle, Slab Base: Rho38, Rho66, Rho104, Rho159, Rw126, Rw133, Rw440, Rw572, Rw580, Rw581*, C8/M5, C9/M5, ND4, ND16/M5, SED38, SD8/M7, SD54/M7, SD71/M7, SD93/M7, SD95/M7, SD684, SD732, SD805, SD841, SD849, NE7, NE61, NE78*, NE133, NE568, NE570, NE572, NE599, EE133, EE204, EE242, EE343, EE385, SE13, SL1, SWM93, SWM188, WN1, O5/M5, O6/M5, O9/M5, O10/M5, O14/M5, O18/M5, O20/M5, WP65, WP67, WP'30, NR98, NR127, NW7, SW10, SW62, Mi431, <M>MAI-17/4368, <M>MAI-17/4619

Subglobular Bottle, Simple Base: AdB44, Rho102, Rho141, Rho164, Rho214, Rho219, Rho304, Rho308, Rho337, Rho364, Rho373, RPB1, RPB4, Rw25, Rw135, Rw569*, Rw878, B1, NC2, NEC11/M5, D5/M5, ND7, NED10, SED6 SED8, SED17, SED27, SED34, SED35, SD1/M7, SD4/M5, SD6/M5*, SD6/M7, SD9/M5, SD10/M5, SD15/M7, SD18/M7, SD30, SD32/M7, SD33/M7, SD34/M7, SD42/M7 SD44/M7, SD59/M7, SD77/M7, SD87/M7, SD88/M7, SD96/M7, SD110/M7, SD362, SD472, SD583, SD585, SD742, SD814, SD825, SD836, SD840, NE6, NE8, NE56, NE59, NE60, NE79, NE80, NE90, NE125*, EE140, NE147, EE160, NE166, NE574, NE576, NE582, NE592, NE596, NE600, NE602 EE1, EE4, EE6, EE7, EE9, EE10, EE13, EE17, EE19, EE22, EE25, EE74, EE75, EE78, EE80, EE81, EE85, EE86, EE94, EE129, EE130, EE136, EE137, EE166, EE180, EE188, EE303, EE305, EE383, EE391, EE429, EE431, EE445, EE492, SE3, SE8, F15/M5, NG5, NG6, NG9, NG10, NG25, NG30, NG56, SWG6, SWG24, SWG49, SWG55, SWG62, SWG63, SEH15, SEH19, SEH20, SEH73, SEH74, EI15, EI25, EI26, EI41, EI78, SL21, SL25, SL31, SWM6/M7, SEM15A/M7, SWM183, SEM185, SWM220, NN'18, NN'38, NN'41, WP27, WP83, WP85, WP159, WP208, WP230, WP'19, WP'39, NR9/M5, NR17/M5, NR19/M5, NR20, NR21, NR23, NR30/M5, NR31/M5, NR38, NR40, NR47, NR99, NR119, WR10, WR13, WR59, WR81, WR85, WR28/M7, SW45, Mi62, <M>2, <M>10, <M>MAI-17/1429, <M>MAI-17/4354, <M>MAI-17/4362, <M>MAI-18/437

Subglobular Bottle (Miscellaneous): ND3/M5*, SD7/M7, SD594, SD748, NE132, EE155, SEH87, WP156, NR24/M5, NR152*, WR2, NW32*

Bottle (Miscellaneous): Rho107, Rho109, Rho110, Rho153*, Rho158, Rho184, Rho192, Rho252*, Rw228, Rw229, Rw246*, ND28, SD169, SD741, SD811, NE92, NE131*, NE148, NE458, SG23, SWM140, SEM260, NR112, WR1*, WR52*, WR1/M5*, WR2/M5, NW36, SW5, SW13, SW50, SW60*, Mi61*, <M>4

Cylindrical Bowl: Rho101*, Rho161, Rho177*, RPB3, Rw26, B6, C2/M5, C7/M5, D4/M5, ND13/M5, ND17/M5, ED3, SED13, SD14/M7, SD27/M7, SD28/M7, SD45/M7*, SD82/M7, SD86/M7, SD584, SD586, SD596, SD749*, SD826, NE37, NE50, NE128, NE583, EE3, EE104, EE110, EE182, EE210, EE234, EE281, EE322, EE416, SE16*, NG3, SG16, SWG3, SWG58, SEH8*, SEH9*, SEH86*, S12*, SM30, SWM95, SWM132, SWM142, SWM166*, SWM170, O15/M5, O19/M5, O31/M5, WP259, NR9, NR24, NR153, WR3, WR11*, WR74, SW18, SW19*, SW31

Flaring-Rim Bowl (Deep): NB6, NC5, SD806, NE68, NE89, EE72, EE77, EE156, NG31, SEM190, NN'40, WP121, WP264, WR12,

WR82, <M>5

Flaring-Rim Bowl (Shallow):   Rho251, Rho257, Rho275,   Rw195,
    SD267, SD743, SD745, EE237, SWG46, EI30, SWM42, WP135,
    WP258, NR124, W239, W17, SW9

Flaring-Rim Bowl (Miscellaneous): Rho18*, ND1/M5*, F6/M5*

Lobate Bowl: NE130*

Outslanting Bowl: Rw473, SD1, SD154,   SG24,   SWM178,   NW25,
    <M>6

Pedestaled Bowl: Rho127*, ND20/M5, SD11/M7,   SD350*, NE129,
    EE160, EE380, SWG45*, O37/M5, WP73, WR60, W176

Restricted Bowl: Rho48,   Rho149*,   Rho226,   Rho302,   Rw226,
    ND13, ED14, SED9, SED33, NE4, NE9*, NE17, NE31,   NE36,
    NE39, NE71*, NE145, NE165,   EE8,   EE11,   EE67*,   EE126,
    EE181, EE187, EE377, EE394, EE444, EE475,   NG2*,
    NG11, SWG2, SWG21*, SWG52, EH76*, SEH83, SEH85,   SEH88,
    EI2, EI43,   SWM92*, SWM167, SEM175, SEM181,   SWM222,
    SWM223,   NN'3*,   WN1/M7*,   WP23,   WP52,   WP94,   NR6/M5,
    NR15A/M5, NW16, SW20, SW25, SW57, Mi438, Mi456,   <M>13,
    <M>MAI-17/4397

Short-Neck Bowl: D1, NE185, EE5, EE125, SWG8,   SWG9,   EI39,
    SWM252, WP29, WP122, WR21, <I>SWG2, <M>19

Simple Bowl: Rho39, Rho57, Rho134, Rho142, Rho171, Rho227,
    Rho255, Rho306, Rho307*, Rho367, Rho374, Rw142,   Rw165
    Rw176, Rw177, Rw308*, B2,   B3*,   WB1/M5,   C21/M5,   NC1,
    NC3, NE6/M5, ND3, ND33*, ND34, NED3,   NED4,   ED4,   ED8,
    SED2, SED7, SED11, SED14, SED15, SED19, SED30,   SED43,
    SD5/M7, SD10, SD48/M7, SD248,   SD266,   SD351*,   SD364,
    SD600, SD679, SD687, SD689, SD733, SD736, SD747, SD815,
    SD816, SD818, SD821, SD822,   SD827,   SD832,   SD834,
    SD847*, SD853, SD855, NE19,   NE26,   NE30,   NE38,   NE42,
    NE44, NE54, NE64, NE77*, NE85, NE86, NE93, NE95, NE134,
    NE135,   NE138,   NE174,   NE192,   NE446*,   NE451,   NE453,
    NE571, NE575, NE581, NE593,   NE603,   EE2,   EE18,   EE61,
    EE71, EE76, EE87, EE108, EE109,   EE111,   EE112,   EE135,
    EE179, EE203, EE206*,   EE238, EE260, EE277,   EE302,
    EE381, EE384, EE387, EE390, EE392, EE395, EE430, EE446,
    EE447, EE495, SE2, SE11, F12/M5, SE14, SE19, EF3, NG13,
    NG39, NG44*, NG76, SWG47,   SWG66,   SEH5,   SEH6*,   SEH7,
    SEH18, SEH71, SEH82, EI42,   EI95,   SL24*,   SL33,   SL49,
    SWM41, SWM94,   SWM180,   SWM186,   SWM226,   NN'2,   NN'19,
    O/M5, O33/M5, WP16, WP28, WP32,   WP153,   WP160,   WP165,
    WP187, WP212, WP217, WP218, WP'32, WP'34, NR43,   NR44,
    NR46, NR97, NR101, NR102, NR106, NR117,   NR118,   NR121,
    NR128, NR160, NR189,   WR9,   WR50, WR65,   WR66*,   WR80,
    WR15/M7*, W186, NW43, NW46, NW4,   SW14,   SW41,   SW55,
    SW61, SW63, NWW1, NWW7, Mi430, Mi435,   Mi440*,   Mi462*,
    <I>SW353,   <M>7,   <M>8,   <M>9,   <M>MAI-17/3637,   <M>MAI-
    17/3642,   <M>MAI-17/4374,   <M>MAI-17/4376,   <M>MAI-
    17/4394, <M>MAI-18/414, <M>MAI-17/3375A

Terraced Rectanguloid Bowl: SD3,   SD106/M7,   NEI,   NE67,
     SWM2A/M7, Mi37

Bowl (Miscellaneous):   Rho136, Rho156, Rw145*, SED3, SED18,
     SED32, SD3/M5, SD61/M7, SD682, NE27, NE53*, NE461,
     EE202, EE307, EE396, NG1, SWM5/M7 EO1/M5*, WP22, WP47,
     WP229, WP260, NR114, NR161, SW11*, Mi434, <I>NW13

Burnished Jar: Rho100, Rho220, Rho368, Rw132, Rw138, Rw140,
     Rw471, Rw480, ND6/M5, ED2, ED6, SED1, SED4, SED10,
     SD2/M5, SD482, SD844, NE5, NE450, SEH10, SWM87, WP72,
     WP'29, NR23/M5, WR58, SW52, <M>12, <M>MAI-17/1431,
     <M>MAI-17/4379

Neckless Jar (Unburnished):   (no whole vessels in sample)

Standard Jar (Unburnished, No Handles): ND14*, WP96, NR107*,
     WR24*

Standard Jar (Unburnished, 2 Handles):   Rho46,   Rho138*,
     Rho163, Rho193*, Rho253, Rho328, Rho329, Rw168, Rw260,
     NEC3/M5, NED7, ED54, SED5, SD21/M7*, SD27, SD32, SD171,
     SD262, SD265, SD731, SD744, SD837, SD848*, NE25, NE65,
     NE124*, NE443*, NE454*, NE597, EE88, EE89*, EE131*,
     EE132, EE278*, EE389, SE4*, NG4, SWG40*, SEH76, EI16*,
     EI27, SL56, SM28*, SM29*, NN'12*, NN'13, WP19, WP20,
     WP221, WP223, WP228, NQ1/M5, NR41, NR115, WR53*, WR56*,
     WR68*, WR69, WR72, WR70*, WR192, W220, W310, NW11,
     NW12, NW15, NW23, NW24, NW42, SW15, SW17, SW40, Mi397*,
     Mi1015, <I>NR25, <I>SD15*, <I>W50, <I>WP1*, <M>3,
     <M>11, <M>14, <M>MAI-17/3379*, <M>MAI-17/3646*, <M>MAI-
     17/4381, <M>MAI-17/4616*

Standard Jar (Unburnished, 4 Handles):   Rho160*, Rho212,
     Rho312, Rw64, Rw128, Rw245, Rw442, NEC10/M5, ND5, ND10,
     ND11, SD29, SD31, SD155, SD365, SD473, SD579, SD599,
     SD680, SD688, SD746, SD838, SD842, NE18, NE55, NE444,
     NE452, NE464, NE585, NE587, NE591, EE124, SE9, SE10*,
     SE12, NG32, SG15, SWG1, SWG4, SWG25, SWG26, SWG44,
     SEH11, SEH22, SL47, NN'39, NN'40*, WP21, WP30, WP104,
     WP207, NR20/M5, NR27, NR28, NR116, WR46, NW9, SW2,
     <M>15

Standard Jar (Unburnished, 5 Handles):   SD595

Standard Jar (Unburnished, 8 Handles):   Rw139, NEC1/M5, SD6,
     SD681, NE2, NE88, NE136, SEG5, SEM230, NR96, WR2/M7,
     NW14

Standard Jar (Unburnished, 10+ Handles):   NE14, SWG7, EI40,
     SWM14

Standard Jar (Unburnished,   Handle Number Indeterminate):
     Rho84, Rho90, Rho132, Rho213*, Rho276*, Rho351, Rho369,
     Rw129, Rw159, Rw182, ED71, SD683, NE74, EE382, SG14,
     SWG17, SEH45, SWM219, WP173, NR42, NW26, NW39

Composite Bottle: Rho67*, ND12/M5*, NE81*

Composite Bowl: Rho366, WB3/M5, NE445

Composite Bowl-Jar: Rho371

Composite Jar-Bowl: NE11

Double Bowl: EE82, SWG67, SL3, WP71, SW21

Miscellaneous Unusual Shapes: Rho148, CG/M5, NR5

Undiagnostic Fragments: Rho36,   Rho122,   Rho154,   Rho190,
     SD251, SD734, NE33, EE64, EE157, EE159, EE186, EF1,
     NG23, NG24, SG4, SG5, SWG41, SEH72, WP170, NW5, NW8,
     NW19, NW21, NW22, NW33, NW35, SW53, SW64

SECONDARY SHAPE FEATURES

Appliqué Neck Fillets: NB2, SWG29, NR7

Band of Nodes: Rho48, Rho220, ND13, EI2, SWM175, NW43

Beaded Rim: Rho227, Rho255, Rho306, Rho366, Rho371, Rw471,
     B2, WP3/M5, NC3, ND6/M5, SED10, SED14, SED43, SD2/M5,
     SD5/M7, SD10, SD364, SD600, SD687, SD689, SD736, SD815,
     SD818, SD821, SD822, NE5, NE11, NE42, NE85, NE86, NE95,
     NE174, NE445, NE450, NE453, NE571, NE581, EE2, EE18,
     EE61, EE76, EE87, EE135, EE277, EE395, EE430, EE447,
     SE11, SE14, SE19, EF3, SWG66, SEH5, SEH7, SEH10, SEH18,
     EI95, SL3, SL33, SWM186, NN'2, WP'32, NR23/M5, NR118,
     WR80, W186, SW4, SW41, Mi440*, <M>MAI-17/1431, <M>MAI-
     17/3637

Beaded Shoulder: NG24, <M>4, <M>13

Cutout Rim: ND20/M5, W176

Downturned Lugs: SD680, SD837, NN'39, <I>NR25

Folded Rim: SD265, NW26

Folded-Flattened Rim: (no whole vessels in sample)

Gadrooning: SW34

Grouped Nodes: Rw176, Rw480, NE39, NE134, SWG21*, WP16,
     NR106, <M>MAI-17/4374

Horizontal Lugs (Small, on Unburnished Jar):   SD731*,
     NE124*, EE131*, EE278*, SE4*, SWG40*, SM28*, WR53*,
     WR56*, Mi397*, <I>SD15*, <I>WP1*

Indentations: Rho104, Rho159, Rho170, Rw440, Rw572, C13/M5,
     C17/M5, NEC8/M5*, ND11/M5, ND16/M5, SED8, SD4/M5,
     SD841, NE7, NE12, NE38, NE570, NE572, EE94, SE13, NG3,
     NG8, SWG23, EI26, SL25, SWM140, SWM188, NN'41, O14/M5,

NR1/M5, NR11/M5, NR40, NR98, NR100, NR162, WR51, <M>2,
<M>MAI-17/4619, <M>MAI-17/4620

Lobate Protrusions: F14/M5*, SEH14*, NQ1/M5*

Lowered Lip: ND20/M5, SD3, SD350*, NE1, NE67, SWM2A/M7,
037/M5, WP73, W176

Notched Everted Lip: Rho127*, SD11/M7, NE129, EE160, EE380,
EE394, SEH6*, SWM167, WP73, WR60, SW18, <M>8

Notched Lip: Rho193*, Rw145*, ND1/M5*, ND14*, SED11,
SD350*, SD351*, SD745, NE130*, EE206*, EE390, FG/M5*,
SE16*, W239*, <M>5, <M>MAI-17/4394, <M>MAI-17/3375A*

Opposing Lugs: NE54, SWM178, <M>MAI-17/3375A*

Podal Supports: WR1/M5*

Scalloped Rim: NE89

Single Lug: Rho57, Rho161, Rho165, Rw177, C7/M5, C21/M5,
SD14/M7, SD27/M7, SD28/M7, SD584, SD586, SD596, SD826,
NE37, NE38, NE583, EE3, EE71, EE104, EE111, EE182,
EE210, EE234, EE302, EE416, NG39, SG16, SWG3, SM30,
SWM132, SWM142, SWM170, SWM180, SWM226, 015/M5, 019/M5,
031/M5, WR9, WR74, SW31, Mi435

Spouts: SED30, SD689, SD821, EE395

Vertical Lugs: NE461

Widely Spaced Nodes (on Bowl or Burnished Jar): Rho368,
SED10, SD48/M7, SD827, NE5, NE19, NE453, EE112, EE328,
EE392, EE395, SWG45*, SEH10, SWM87, 033/M5, NR15A/M5,
NR23/M5, <M>MAI-17/4379

Widely Spaced Nodes (on Unburnished Jar):   SD27, NE597,
EE131*, WP30

EFFIGY FEATURES

Alligator: NC1, ND6/M5, Mi438

Beaver: SD816, EE475

Bird (Miniature): SED3

Bird (Flat Head, Inward Facing): NEC6/M5, ND33*, SD248,
NE44, NG13, EI42, SWM94, WP212, WR65, NWW1, NWW7

Bird (Flat Head, Outward Facing): SED13, SEH82, NR43

Bird (Gracile Head, Outward Facing): Rho255, RPB3, SD834,
NR44, NR97, NW16

Bird (Head Missing): WP153, WP218

Conch Shell: EE384,   SE2,   F12/M5,   WP217,   <M>7,
     <M>MAAI-17/4376

Feline: EE203

Fish: Rho149*, Rho366, Rw142, ND28, ND34, SED19, SD110/M7,
     SD832, SD844, NE4, NE31, NE575, EE109*, EE179, EE187,
     EE260, EE377, SWG47, SL49, WP52, WP'34, WR15/M7*, SW20,
     SW57

Frog: Rho100, Rw138, Rw140, ED2, SED4, SD2/M5, SD61/M7,
     SD77/M7, SD482, NE9*, NE71*, EE67*, EE186, SE37, NG2*,
     WN1/M7*, WP72, WP'29, NR20, WR58 SW61, <M>10, <M>MAI-
     17/1431

Frog Heads: SED32, EE495

Frog, Stylized (on Unburnished Jar):   SD731*,   SD848*,
     NE443*, NE454*, EE89*, SWG40*, SM28*, NN'12*, WR56*,
     Mi397*, <I>SD15*, <I>WP1*, <M>MAI-17/3379*, <M>MAI-
     17/4616*

Human Figure (Reclining): Rho307*, SD847*, WR66*

Human Figure (Upright): Rho189*, SD55/M7*, NE82, SG25*

Human Head (Rim Effigy): NE77*, NE446*, NG44*

Human Head Medallions (on Bottle): NE448*, NE460*

Human Head Medallions (on Bowl):   Rho306,   SED14,   SED43,
     SD5/M7, NE86, NR118

Mammal, Unidentified: SED7, SWM95, WP160

Mussel Shell: Rho136, Rho156, SED18, EE82, NG1, SWG67,
     WP22, Mi434

Shell Spoon: EE396

Turtle: ED14, SED9, SD855, NE165, SW25

Turtle, Inverted: NE451

Miscellaneous Lug and Rim Effigy (Head Missing):   Rho142,
     Rw26, NED4, SD266, NE26, NG76, SWG58, WP165, NR46,
     NR101, NR102, NR121, WR50, NW25, NW46, Mi430, Mi456

Miscellaneous Unidentified: RPB2*, WB1/M5, SD3/M5, SEH88,
     O3/M5

References

Arnold, Dean E.
  1971 Ethnomineralogy of Ticul, Yucatán potters: etics and emics. *American Antiquity* 36(1):20–40.
Bareis, Charles J., and J. W. Porter
  1965 Megascopic and petrographic analyses of a foreign pottery vessel from the Cahokia site. *American Antiquity* 31(1):95–101.
Blakeman, Crawford H.
  1975 Archaeological investigations in the upper central Tombigbee Valley: 1974 season. Report to the U.S. Department of Interior, National Park Service, submitted by the Department of Anthropology, Mississippi State University, Starkville.
Bloch, Maurice
  1978 The disconnection between power and rank as a process: an outline of the development of kingdoms in central Madagascar. In *The evolution of social systems,* edited by J. Friedman and M. J. Rowlands. University of Pittsburgh Press, Pittsburgh.
Bohannon, Charles F.
  1972 *Excavations at the Bear Creek site, Tishomingo County, Mississippi.* Office of Archaeology and Historic Preservation, National Park Service, Washington, D.C.
Bozeman, Tandy K.
  1981 Moundville phase sites in the Black Warrior Valley, Alabama: preliminary results of the U.M.M.A. survey. *Southeastern Archaeological Conference Bulletin* 24:84–86.
Brewer, Willis
  1872 *Alabama: her history, resources, war record and public men, from 1540 to 1872.* Barrett and Brown, Montgomery, Alabama.
Brown, Ian W.
  1978a An archaeological survey of Mississippi period sites in Coahoma County, Mississippi. Report on file at the Lower Mississippi Survey, Peabody Museum, Harvard University, Cambridge.

1978b The J. O. Wheeler Collection, West Helena, Arkansas: pottery of the Kent and Old Town phases of the Mississippi period. Report on file at the Lower Mississippi Survey, Peabody Museum, Harvard University, Cambridge.

Brown, James A.
   1976   The Southern Cult reconsidered. *Midcontinental Journal of Archaeology* 1(2):115–135.

Chisolm, Michael
   1968   *Rural settlement and land use,* second ed. Hutchinson, London.

Clarke, Otis M.
   1964   Clay deposits in the Tuscaloosa Group in Alabama. *National Conference on Clays and Clay Minerals, Proceedings* 12:495–507.
   1966   Clay and shale of northwestern Alabama. *Geological Survey of Alabama, Division of Economic Geology, Circular* 20-B.
   1970   Clays of southwestern Alabama. *Geological Survey of Alabama, Division of Economic Geology, Circular* 20-E.

Clay, R. Berle
   1963   Ceramic Complexes of the Tennessee-Cumberland Region in Western Kentucky. Unpublished M.A. thesis, Department of Anthropology, University of Kentucky, Lexington.
   1979   A Mississippian ceramic sequence from western Kentucky. *Tennessee Anthropologist* 4(2):111–128.

Coble, R. L.
   1958   Effect of microstructure on the mechanical properties of ceramic materials. In *Ceramic fabrication processes,* edited by W. D. Kingery, pp. 213–228. Wiley, New York.

Coblentz, Benjamin
   1978   Depression era excavations at the Strongs Bayou site, 1Ba81, Baldwin County, Alabama. Manuscript in preparation.

Cotter, John L., and J. M. Corbett
   1951   Archaeology of the Bynum Mounds, Mississippi. *National Park Service, Archaeological Research Series* 1.

Cottier, John W.
   1970   The Alabama River phase: a brief description of a late phase in the prehistory of south central Alabama. In archaeological salvage investigations in the Miller's Ferry Lock and Dam Reservoir. Report to the National Park Service, on file at Mound State Monument, Moundville.

Cowgill, George L.
   1972   Models, methods and techniques for seriation. In *Models in Archaeology,* edited by David L. Clarke, pp. 381–424. Methuen, London.

Curren, Cailup B., Jr.
   1975   Preliminary analysis of the faunal remains. In Archaeological investigations in the Gainesville Lock and Dam Reservoir: 1974, by Ned J. Jenkins, pp. 207–248. Report to the U.S. Department of Interior, National Park Service, submitted by the Department of Anthropology, University of Alabama, Tuscaloosa.

Curren, Cailup B., Jr., and Keith J. Little
   n.d.   Archaeological investigations (1933–1980) of the protohistoric period of central Alabama. Manuscript on file, Department of Anthropology, University of Alabama, Tuscaloosa.

DeBoer, Warren R., and D. W. Lathrap
   1979   The making and breaking of Shipibo–Conibo ceramics. In *Ethnoarchaeology: implications of ethnography for archaeology,* edited by Carol Kramer. Columbia University Press, New York.

Deer, William A., R. A. Howie, and J. Zussman
  1962   *Rock-forming minerals, vol. 5: non-silicates.* Wiley, New York.
DeJarnette, David L.
  1952   Alabama archaeology: a summary. In *Archaeology of Eastern United States,* edited by James B. Griffin, pp. 272–284. University of Chicago Press, Chicago.
DeJarnette, David L., and Christopher S. Peebles
  1970   The development of Alabama archaeology: the Snow's Bend site. *Journal of Alabama Archaeology* 16(2):77–119.
DeJarnette, David L., and S. B. Wimberly
  1941   The Bessemer site. *Geological Survey of Alabama, Museum Paper* 17.
Drennan, Robert D.
  1976a   A refinement of chronological seriation using nonmetric multidimensional scaling. *American Antiquity* 41(3):290–302.
  1976b   Fabrica San Jose and Middle Formative society in the Valley of Oaxaca. *University of Michigan Museum of Anthropology, Memoirs* 8.
Ensor, H. Blaine
  1979   Archaeological investigations in the upper Cahaba River Drainage, north central Alabama. *Journal of Alabama Archaeology* 25(1):1–60.
Fewkes, Vladimir J.
  1944   Catawba pottery making. *Proceedings of the American Philosophical Society* 88(2).
Ford, James A.
  1936   Analysis of Indian village site collections from Louisiana and Mississippi. *Department of Conservation, Louisiana Geological Survey, Anthropological Study* 2.
Ford, Richard I.
  1974   Northeastern archaeology: past and future directions. *Annual Review of Anthropology* 3:385–413.
Friedman, Jonathan
  1975   Tribes, states, and transformations. In *Marxist Analyses and Social Anthropology,* edited by Maurice Bloch, pp. 161–202. Wiley, New York.
Fundaburk, Emma L., and M. D. Foreman
  1957   *Sun circles and human hands: the southeastern Indians—art and industry.* Fundaburk Publisher, Luverne, Alabama.
Griffin, James B.
  1946   Cultural change and continuity in eastern United States archaeology. In *Man in northeastern North America,* edited by Frederick Johnson. *Papers of the Robert S. Peabody Foundation for Archaeology* 3:3–95.
  1952   Prehistoric cultures of the central Mississippi Valley. In *Archeology of eastern United States,* edited by James B. Griffin, pp. 226–238. University of Chicago Press, Chicago.
Grim, Ralph E.
  1968   *Clay mineralogy,* second edition. McGraw Hill, New York.
Gupta, T. K.
  1972   Strength degradation and crack propagation in thermally shocked Al_2O_3. *Journal of the American Ceramic Society* 55(5):249–253.
Guttman, Louis
  1968   A general nonmetric technique for finding the smallest coordinate space for a configuration of points. *Psychometrika* 33(4):469–506.
Haag, William G.
  1939   Pottery type descriptions. *Southeastern Archaeological Conference Newsletter* 1(1).
Hall, Robert L.
  1977   An anthropocentric perspective for eastern United States prehistory. *American Antiquity* 42(4):499–518.

Hardin, Margaret Ann
  1979   Recommendations for a comparative stylistic analysis of Lubbub and Moundville ceramics: implications of the evidence of distinct complex-traditions and craft standardization at Moundville. Manuscript on file, Museum of Anthropology, University of Michigan, Ann Arbor.
  1981   The identification of individual style on Moundville Engraved vessels: a preliminary note. *Southeastern Archaeological Conference Bulletin* 24:108–110.

Hasselman, D. P. H.
  1969   Unified theory of thermal shock fracture initiation and crack propagation in brittle ceramics. *Journal of the American Ceramic Society* 52(11):600–604.
  1970   Thermal stress resistance parameters for brittle refractory ceramics: a compendium. *Bulletin of the American Ceramic Society* 49(12):1033–1037.

Hathcock, Roy
  1976   *Ancient Indian pottery of the Mississippi River Valley.* Hurley Press, Camden, Arkansas.

Heimlich, Marion D.
  1952   Guntersville Basin pottery. *Geological Survey of Alabama, Museum Paper* 32.

Holmes, William H.
  1883   Art in shell of the ancient Americans. *Bureau of American Ethnology, Annual Report* 2:185–305.
  1903   Aboriginal pottery of the eastern United States. *Bureau of American Ethnology, Annual Report* 20.

Hudson, Charles
  1976   *The southeastern Indians.* University of Tennessee Press, Knoxville.

Hulthén, Birgitta
  1977   On ceramic technology during the Scanian Neolithic and Bronze Age. *Theses and Papers in North-European Archaeology* 6. Institute of Archaeology, University of Stockholm Stockholm.

Hutchinson, Charles S.
  1974   *Laboratory handbook of petrographic techniques.* Wiley and Sons, New York.

Isphording, Wayne C.
  1974   Combined thermal and x-ray diffraction techniques for identification of ceramicware temper and paste minerals. *American Antiquity* 39(3):477–483.

Jenkins, Ned J.
  1975   Archaeological investigations in the Gainesville Lock and Dam Reservoir: 1974. Report to the U.S. Department of Interior, National Park Service, submitted by the Department of Anthropology, University of Alabama, Tuscaloosa.
  1976a   Terminal Woodland–Mississippian interaction in northern Alabama: the West Jefferson phase. *Southeastern Archaeological Conference Bulletin* 20, in press.
  1976b   Ceramic type descriptions. In Highway salvage excavations at two French Colonial period sites on Mobile Bay, Alabama, edited by D. L. DeJarnette. Report to the Alabama Highway Department, submitted by the Department of Anthropology, University of Alabama, Tuscaloosa.
  1981   Gainesville Lake Area ceramic description and chronology. *Archaeological investigations in the Gainesville Reservoir of the Tennessee–Tombigbee Waterway, volume II. University of Alabama Office of Archaeological Research, Reports of Investigations* 12.

Jenkins, Ned J., C. Curren, and M. DeLeon
  1975   Archaeological site survey of the Demopolis and Gainesville Lake navigation channels and additional construction areas. Report to the U.S. Army Corps of Engineers (Mobile), submitted by the Department of Anthropology, University of Alabama, Tuscaloosa.

Jenkins, Ned J., and J. J. Nielsen
  1974 Archaeological salvage investigations at the West Jefferson Steam Plant site, Jefferson County, Alabama. Report on file, Mound State Monument, Moundville.
Jennings, Jesse D.
  1941 Chickasaw and earlier Indian cultures of northeast Mississippi. *Journal of Mississippi History* 3(3):155–226.
Jones, Walter B.
  1932 Remarks given at the Conference on Southern Prehistory. National Research Council, Washington, D.C.
Jones, Walter B., and David L. DeJarnette
  n.d. Moundville culture and burial museum. *Geological Survey of Alabama, Museum Paper* 13.
Kendall, David G.
  1971 Seriation from abundance matrices. In *Mathematics in the archaeological and historical sciences,* edited by F. R. Hodson, D. G. Kendall, and P. Tautu, pp. 215–252. Edinburgh University Press, Edinburgh.
Kennedy, C. R.
  1977 Microstructural aspects controlling the thermal stress resistance of graphite. In *Workshop on thermal shock of ceramics: summary of proceedings,* edited by P. F. Becker, S. W. Freiman, and A. M. Diness. Office of Naval Research, Arlington, Virginia.
Kruskal, Joseph B.
  1964a Multidimensional scaling by optimizing goodness of fit to a nonmetric hypothesis. *Psychometrika* 29(1):1–27.
  1964b Nonmetric multidimensional scaling: a numerical method. *Psychometrika* 29(2):115–129.
  1971 Multi-dimensional scaling in archaeology: time is not the only dimension. In *Mathematics in the archaeological and historical sciences,* edited by F. R. Hodson, D. G. Kendall, and P. Tautu, pp. 119–132. Edinburgh University Press, Edinburgh.
LeBlanc, Stephen A.
  1975 Micro-seriation: a method for fine chronologic differentiation. *American Antiquity* 40(1):22–38.
Lewis, Thomas M. N., and M. Kneberg
  1946 *Hiwassee Island: an archaeological account of four Tennessee Indian peoples.* University of Tennessee Press, Knoxville.
Lingoes, James C.
  1973 *The Guttman–Lingoes nonmetric program series.* Mathesis Press, Ann Arbor.
Lingoes, James C., and E. Roskam
  1971 A mathematical and empirical study of two multidimensional scaling algorithms. *Michigan mathematical psychology program,* MMPP 71-1. Department of Psychology, University of Michigan, Ann Arbor.
Lupton, Nathaniel T.
  1869 Letter to Joseph Henry dated October 9, 1869. Records of accession number 1786, National Museum of Natural History, Washington, D.C.
Marshall, Richard
  1977 Lyon's Bluff site (22Ok1) radiocarbon dated. *Journal of Alabama Archaeology* 23(1):53–57.
Matson, Frederick R., Jr.
  1939 Further technological notes on the pottery of the Younge site, Lapeer County, Michigan. *Papers of the Michigan Academy of Science, Arts and Letters* 24(4):11–23.
Mauss, Marcel
  1967 *The gift: forms and functions of exchange in archaic societies,* translated by Ian Cunnison. Norton, New York.

McKenzie, Douglas H.

    1964   The Moundville phase and its position in southeastern prehistory. Unpublished Ph.D. dissertation, Department of Anthropology, Harvard University, Cambridge.

    1965   Pottery types of the Moundville phase. *Southeastern Archaeological Conference Bulletin* 2:55–64.

    1966   A summary of the Moundville phase. *Journal of Alabama Archaeology* 12(1):1–58.

Michals, Lauren

    1981   The exploitation of fauna during the Moundville I phase at Moundville. *Southeastern Archaeological Conference Bulletin* 24.

Middleton, James D.

    1882   Mounds on the Prince Plantation. Manuscript, catalog number 2400-Box l, National Anthropological Archives, Washington, D.C.

Million, Michael G.

    1975a   Research design for the aboriginal ceramic industries of the Cache River Basin. In *The Cache River archaeological project,* edited by M. B. Schiffer and J. H. House, pp. 217–222. *Arkansas Archaeological Survey, Research Series* 8.

    1975b   Ceramic technology of the Nodena phase peoples (ca. A.D. 1400–1700). *Southeastern Archaeological Conference Bulletin* 18:201–208.

    1976   Preliminary report on Zebree site ceramics. In *A preliminary report of the Zebree project: new approaches in contract archaeology in Arkansas, 1975,* edited by Dan F. Morse and Phyllis A. Morse, pp. 44–49. *Arkansas Archaeological Survey Research Report* 8.

    1978   The Big Lake phase pottery industry. In Excavation, data interpretation, and report on the Zebree Homestead site, Mississippi County, Arkansas, edited by Dan F. Morse and Phyllis A. Morse. Report submitted to the U.S. Army Corps of Engineers, Memphis, by the Arkansas Archaeological Survey, Fayetteville.

Moore, Clarence B.

    1899   Certain aboriginal remains of the Alabama River. *Journal of the Academy of Natural Sciences of Philadelphia* 11:289–348.

    1905   Certain aboriginal remains of the Black Warrior River. *Journal of the Academy of Natural Sciences of Philadelphia* 13:125–244.

    1907   Moundville revisited. *Journal of the Academy of Natural Sciences of Philadelphia* 13:337–405.

    1910   Antiquities of the St. Francis, White, and Black Rivers, Arkansas. *Journal of the Academy of Natural Sciences of Philadelphia* 14:254–364.

    1915   Aboriginal sites on the Tennessee River. *Journal of the Academy of Natural Sciences of Philadelphia* 16:170–428.

Moselage, John

    1962   The Lawhorn site. *Missouri Archaeologist* 24.

Myer, William E.

    1928   Two prehistoric villages in middle Tennessee. *Bureau of American Ethnology, Annual Report* 41:485–614.

Nance, C. Roger

    1976   The archaeological sequence at Durant Bend, Dallas County, Alabama. *Alabama Archaeological Society, Special Publication* 2.

Nash, William A.

    1972   *Schaum's outline of theory and problems of strength of materials,* second ed. McGraw-Hill, New York.

Newell, H. D., and A. D. Krieger

    1949   The George C. Davis site, Cherokee County, Texas. *Society for American Archaeology, Memoirs* 5.

Nielsen, Jerry J., and N. J. Jenkins

    1973   Archaeological investigations in the Gainesville Lock and Dam Reservoir. Report to the U.S. Department of Interior, National Park Service, submitted by the Department of Anthropology, University of Alabama, Tuscaloosa.

Nielsen, Jerry J., J. W. O'Hear, and C. W. Moorehead
  1973   An archaeological survey of Hale and Greene Counties, Alabama. Report to the Alabama Historical Commission, submitted by the University Museums, University of Alabama, Tuscaloosa.

O'Hear, John W.
  1975   Site 1Je32: community organization in the West Jefferson phase. Unpublished M.A. thesis, Department of Anthropology, University of Alabama, Tuscaloosa.

Owen, Thomas M. (compiler)
  1910   *Handbook of the Alabama Anthropological Society.* Alabama Anthropological Society, Montgomery.

Peebles, Christopher S.
  1971   Moundville and surrounding sites: some structural considerations of mortuary practices II. *Society for American Archaeology, Memoirs* 25:68–91.
  1974   Moundville: the organization of a prehistoric community and culture. Unpublished Ph.D. dissertation, Department of Anthropology, University of California, Santa Barbara.
  1978a Determinants of settlement size and location in the Moundville phase. In *Mississippian Settlement Patterns,* edited by Bruce D. Smith, pp. 369–416. Academic Press, New York.
  1978b Moundville: the form and content of a Mississippian society. In *Reviewing Mississippian development,* edited by Stephen Williams. University of New Mexico Press, Albuquerque, in press.
  1979   *Excavations at Moundville, 1905–1951.* University of Michigan Press, Ann Arbor.

Peebles, Christopher S., and Susan Kus
  1977   Some archaeological correlates of ranked societies. *American Antiquity* 42(3):421–448.

Peebles, Christopher S., C. M. Scarry, M. Schoeninger, and V. P. Steponaitis
  1979   A brief summary of research at Moundville by the University of Michigan Museum of Anthropology, May 1978 to May 1979. Report submitted to the National Science Foundation.

Perino, Gregory
  1966   The Banks Village site, Crittenden County, Arkansas. *Missouri Archaeological Society, Memoir* 4.

Phillips, Philip
  1970   Archaeological survey in the lower Yazoo Basin, Mississippi, 1949–1955. *Peabody Museum of Archaeology and Ethnology, Papers* 60.

Phillips, Philip, and Jame A. Brown
  1978   *Pre-Columbian shell engravings from the Craig mound at Spiro, Oklahoma,* paperback edition, part 1. Peabody Museum Press, Cambridge.

Phillips, Philip, James A. Ford, and James B. Griffin
  1951   Archaeological survey in the lower Mississippi alluvial valley, 1940–1947. *Peabody Museum of American Archaeology and Ethnology, Papers* 25.

Pickett, Albert J.
  1900   *History of Alabama, and incidentally of Georgia and Mississippi, from the earliest period,* Owen edition (first edition, 1851). Webb Book Company, Birmingham.

Porter, James Warren
  1964a Thin-section description of some shell tempered prehistoric ceramics from the American Bottoms. *Southern Illinois University Museum, Lithic Laboratory, Research Report* 7.
  1964b Comment on Weaver's "Technological analysis of lower Mississippi ceramic materials". *American Antiquity* 29(4):520–521.

1966   Thin-section analysis of ten Aztalan sherds. *Wisconsin Archaeologist* 47:12–27.

1971   Thin-section identifications of Spiro sherds. In *Spiro studies, vol. 3, pottery vessels,* by James A. Brown. *First Part of the Third Annual Report of Caddoan Archaeology—Spiro Focus Research,* pp. 244–246. University of Oklahoma Research Institute, Norman.

1974   Cahokia archaeology as viewed from the Mitchell site: a satellite community at A.D. 1150–1200. Unpublished Ph.D. dissertation, Department of Anthropology, University of Wisconsin, Madison.

Porter, James W., and Christine R. Szuter

1978   Thin-section analysis of Schlemmer site ceramics. *Midcontinental Journal of Archaeology* 3(10):3–14.

Potter, W. B., and Edward Evers

1880   *Contributions to the archaeology of Missouri by the archaeological section of the St. Louis Academy of Science, part I: Pottery.* George A. Bates, Salem.

Rappaport, Roy A.

1968   *Pigs for the ancestors: ritual in the ecology of a New Guinea people.* Yale University Press, New Haven.

1971   Ritual, sanctity, and cybernetics. *American Anthropologist* 73:59–76.

Rau, Charles

1876   The archaeological collections of the United States National Museum. *Smithsonian Contributions to Knowledge* 287.

Rye, Owen S.

1976   Keeping your temper under control: materials and the manufacture of Papuan pottery. *Archaeology and Physical Anthropology in Oceania* 11(2):106–137.

Rye, Owen S., and Clifford Evans

1976   Traditional pottery techniques of Pakistan: field and laboratory studies. *Smithsonian Contributions to Anthropology* 21.

Sahlins, Marshall

1972   *Stone Age economics.* Aldine, Chicago.

Scarry, C. Margaret Mosenfelder

1980   Excavations at Moundville 1978–1979: the University of Michigan Museum of Anthropology Moundville Archaeological Project. Manuscript on file, Museum of Anthropology, University of Michigan, Ann Arbor.

1981a   The University of Michigan Moundville excavations: 1978–1979. *Southeastern Archaeological Conference Bulletin* 24:87–90.

1981b   Plant procurement strategies in the West Jefferson and Moundville I phases. *Southeastern Archaeological Conference Bulletin* 24:94–96.

Schnell, Frank T., Vernon J. Knight, Jr., and Gail S. Schnell

1981   *Cemochechobee: archaeology of a Mississipian ceremonial center on the Chattahoochee River.* University Presses of Florida, Gainesville.

Schoeninger, Margaret J., and Christopher S. Peebles

1981   Notes on the relationship between social status and diet at Moundville. *Southeastern Archaeological Conference Bulletin* 24:96–97.

Searle, A. B., and R. W. Grimshaw

1959   *The chemistry and physics of clays and other ceramic materials,* third ed. Interscience, New York.

Sheldon, Craig T.

1974   The Mississippian-Historic transition in central Alabama. Unpublished Ph.D. dissertation, Department of Anthropology, University of Oregon, Eugene.

Shepard, Anna O.

1956   Ceramics for the archaeologist. *Carnegie Institution of Washington, Publication* 609.

Shepard, Roger N.
  1962   The analysis of proximities: multidimensional scaling with an unknown distance func-
         tion. *Psychometrika* 27:125–140, 219–246.
Shepard, Roger N., A. K. Romney, and S. B. Nerlove (editors)
  1972   *Multidimensional scaling: theory and applications in the behavioral sciences.* Seminar
         Press, New York.
Smith, Bruce D.
  1978   Variation in Mississippian settlement patterns. In *Mississippian settlement patterns,*
         edited by Bruce D. Smith, pp. 480–503. Academic Press, New York.
Steponaitis, Vincas P.
  1978   Location theory and complex chiefdoms: a Mississippian example. In *Mississippian
         settlement patterns,* edited by Bruce D. Smith, pp. 417–453. Academic Press, New
         York.
  1980   Some preliminary chronological and technological notes on Moundville pottery. *South-
         eastern Archaeological Conference Bulletin* 22:46–51.
  1981   Plaquemine ceramic chronology in the Natchez region. *Mississippi Archaeology*
         16(2):6–19.
Story, Dee Ann, and S. Valastro
  1977   Radiocarbon dating and the George C. Davis site, Texas. *Journal of Field Archaeology*
         4:63–89.
Suhm, Dee Ann, A. D. Krieger, and E. B. Jelks
  1954   An introductory handbook of Texas archaeology. *Bulletin of the Texas Archaeologi-
         cal Society* 25.
Swanton, John R.
  1911   Indian tribes of the lower Mississippi Valley and adjacent coast of the Gulf of Mexico.
         Bureau of American Ethnology, Bulletin 43.
Taylor, J. D., W. J. Kennedy, and A. Hall
  1969   The shell structure and mineralogy of the Bivalvia. Introduction: Nuculacea–
         Trigonacea. *Bulletin of the British Museum (Natural History), Zoology, Supplement* 3.
Thomas, Cyrus
  1891   Catalogue of prehistoric works east of the Rocky Mountains. *Bureau of American
         Ethnology, Bulletin* 12.
Thompson, Raymond H.
  1958   Modern Yucatecan Maya pottery making. *Society for American Archaeology,
         Memoirs* 15.
Thruston, Gates P.
  1890   *The antiquities of Tennessee.* Robert Clarke, Cincinnati.
van der Leeuw, Sander E.
  1977   Pottery, anthropology, and archaeology in the Andes, part II: Where to go? Paper
         presented at the 42nd annual meeting of the Society for American Archaeology, New
         Orleans.
  1979   Analysis of Moundville phase ceramic technology. Manuscript on file, Museum of
         Anthropology, University of Michigan, Ann Arbor.
  1981   Preliminary report on the analysis of Moundville phase ceramic technology. *South-
         eastern Archaeological Conference Bulletin* 24:105–108.
Walthall, John, and B. Coblentz
  1977   An archaeological survey of the Big Sandy Bottoms in the Black Warrior Valley.
         Report on file, Department of Anthropology, University of Alabama, Tuscaloosa.
Walthall, John A., and S. B. Wimberly
  1978   Mississippian chronology in the Black Warrior Valley: radiocarbon dates from Bes-
         semer and Moundville. *Journal of Alabama Archaeology* 24(2):118–124.

Waring, Antonio J., and Preston Holder
    1945   A prehistoric ceremonial complex in the southeastern United States. *American Anthropologist* 47(1):1–34.
Webb, William S.
    1939   An archaeological survey of the Wheeler Basin on the Tennessee River in northern Alabama. *Bureau of American Ethnology, Bulletin* 122.
Webb, William S., and D. L. DeJarnette
    1942   An archaeological survey of the Pickwick Basin in the adjacent portions of the States of Alabama, Mississippi, and Tennessee. *Bureau of American Ethnology, Bulletin* 129.
Welch, Paul
    1979   A synthesis of the West Jefferson phase: the Terminal Woodland of north-central Alabama. Manuscript on file, Museum of Anthropology, University of Michigan, Ann Arbor.
    1981   The West Jefferson phase: Terminal Woodland tribal society in west central Alabama. *Southeastern Archaeological Conference Bulletin* 24:81–83.
Whallon, Robert
    1972   A new approach to pottery typology. *American Antiquity* 37(1):13–33.
Willey, Gordon R.
    1949   Archaeology of the Florida gulf coast. *Smithsonian Miscellaneous Collections* 113.
Williams, Stephen, and J. P. Brain
    1982   Excavations at Lake George, Yazoo County, Mississippi. *Peabody Museum of Archaeology and Ethnology, Papers* 74, in press.
Wimberly, Stephen
    1956   A review of Moundville pottery. *Southeastern Archaeological Conference Newsletter* 5(1):17–20.
Wright, Henry T.
    1977   Recent research on the origin of the state. *Annual Review of Anthropology* 6:379–397.

Index

STUDIES IN ARCHAEOLOGY

Consulting Editor: Stuart Struever

Department of Anthropology
Northwestern University
Evanston, Illinois